Clinical Research in Pharmaceutical Development

DRUGS AND THE PHARMACEUTICAL SCIENCES

DRUGS AND THE PHARMACEUTICAL SCIENCES

A Series of Textbooks and Monographs

edited by

James Swarbrick
AAI, Inc.
Wilmington, North Carolina

1. Pharmacokinetics, *Milo Gibaldi and Donald Perrier*
2. Good Manufacturing Practices for Pharmaceuticals: A Plan for Total Quality Control, *Sidney H. Willig, Murray M. Tuckerman, and William S. Hitchings IV*
3. Microencapsulation, *edited by J. R. Nixon*
4. Drug Metabolism: Chemical and Biochemical Aspects, *Bernard Testa and Peter Jenner*
5. New Drugs: Discovery and Development, *edited by Alan A. Rubin*
6. Sustained and Controlled Release Drug Delivery Systems, *edited by Joseph R. Robinson*
7. Modern Pharmaceutics, *edited by Gilbert S. Banker and Christopher T. Rhodes*
8. Prescription Drugs in Short Supply: Case Histories, *Michael A. Schwartz*
9. Activated Charcoal: Antidotal and Other Medical Uses, *David O. Cooney*
10. Concepts in Drug Metabolism (in two parts), *edited by Peter Jenner and Bernard Testa*
11. Pharmaceutical Analysis: Modern Methods (in two parts), *edited by James W. Munson*
12. Techniques of Solubilization of Drugs, *edited by Samuel H. Yalkowsky*
13. Orphan Drugs, *edited by Fred E. Karch*
14. Novel Drug Delivery Systems: Fundamentals, Developmental Concepts, Biomedical Assessments, *Yie W. Chien*
15. Pharmacokinetics: Second Edition, Revised and Expanded, *Milo Gibaldi and Donald Perrier*
16. Good Manufacturing Practices for Pharmaceuticals: A Plan for Total Quality Control, Second Edition, Revised and Expanded, *Sidney H. Willig, Murray M. Tuckerman, and William S. Hitchings IV*
17. Formulation of Veterinary Dosage Forms, *edited by Jack Blodinger*

18. Dermatological Formulations: Percutaneous Absorption, *Brian W. Barry*
19. The Clinical Research Process in the Pharmaceutical Industry, *edited by Gary M. Matoren*
20. Microencapsulation and Related Drug Processes, *Patrick B. Deasy*
21. Drugs and Nutrients: The Interactive Effects, *edited by Daphne A. Roe and T. Colin Campbell*
22. Biotechnology of Industrial Antibiotics, *Erick J. Vandamme*
23. Pharmaceutical Process Validation, *edited by Bernard T. Loftus and Robert A. Nash*
24. Anticancer and Interferon Agents: Synthesis and Properties, *edited by Raphael M. Ottenbrite and George B. Butler*
25. Pharmaceutical Statistics: Practical and Clinical Applications, *Sanford Bolton*
26. Drug Dynamics for Analytical, Clinical, and Biological Chemists, *Benjamin J. Gudzinowicz, Burrows T. Younkin, Jr., and Michael J. Gudzinowicz*
27. Modern Analysis of Antibiotics, *edited by Adjoran Aszalos*
28. Solubility and Related Properties, *Kenneth C. James*
29. Controlled Drug Delivery: Fundamentals and Applications, Second Edition, Revised and Expanded, *edited by Joseph R. Robinson and Vincent H. Lee*
30. New Drug Approval Process: Clinical and Regulatory Management, *edited by Richard A. Guarino*
31. Transdermal Controlled Systemic Medications, *edited by Yie W. Chien*
32. Drug Delivery Devices: Fundamentals and Applications, *edited by Praveen Tyle*
33. Pharmacokinetics: Regulatory • Industrial • Academic Perspectives, *edited by Peter G. Welling and Francis L. S. Tse*
34. Clinical Drug Trials and Tribulations, *edited by Allen E. Cato*
35. Transdermal Drug Delivery: Developmental Issues and Research Initiatives, *edited by Jonathan Hadgraft and Richard H. Guy*
36. Aqueous Polymeric Coatings for Pharmaceutical Dosage Forms, *edited by James W. McGinity*
37. Pharmaceutical Pelletization Technology, *edited by Isaac Ghebre-Sellassie*
38. Good Laboratory Practice Regulations, *edited by Allen F. Hirsch*
39. Nasal Systemic Drug Delivery, *Yie W. Chien, Kenneth S. E. Su, and Shyi-Feu Chang*
40. Modern Pharmaceutics: Second Edition, Revised and Expanded, *edited by Gilbert S. Banker and Christopher T. Rhodes*
41. Specialized Drug Delivery Systems: Manufacturing and Production Technology, *edited by Praveen Tyle*
42. Topical Drug Delivery Formulations, *edited by David W. Osborne and Anton H. Amann*
43. Drug Stability: Principles and Practices, *Jens T. Carstensen*

44. Pharmaceutical Statistics: Practical and Clinical Applications, Second Edition, Revised and Expanded, *Sanford Bolton*
45. Biodegradable Polymers as Drug Delivery Systems, *edited by Mark Chasin and Robert Langer*
46. Preclinical Drug Disposition: A Laboratory Handbook, *Francis L. S. Tse and James J. Jaffe*
47. HPLC in the Pharmaceutical Industry, *edited by Godwin W. Fong and Stanley K. Lam*
48. Pharmaceutical Bioequivalence, *edited by Peter G. Welling, Francis L. S. Tse, and Shrikant V. Dinghe*
49. Pharmaceutical Dissolution Testing, *Umesh V. Banakar*
50. Novel Drug Delivery Systems: Second Edition, Revised and Expanded, *Yie W. Chien*
51. Managing the Clinical Drug Development Process, *David M. Cocchetto and Ronald V. Nardi*
52. Good Manufacturing Practices for Pharmaceuticals: A Plan for Total Quality Control, Third Edition, *edited by Sidney H. Willig and James R. Stoker*
53. Prodrugs: Topical and Ocular Drug Delivery, *edited by Kenneth B. Sloan*
54. Pharmaceutical Inhalation Aerosol Technology, *edited by Anthony J. Hickey*
55. Radiopharmaceuticals: Chemistry and Pharmacology, *edited by Adrian D. Nunn*
56. New Drug Approval Process: Second Edition, Revised and Expanded, *edited by Richard A. Guarino*
57. Pharmaceutical Process Validation: Second Edition, Revised and Expanded, *edited by Ira R. Berry and Robert A. Nash*
58. Ophthalmic Drug Delivery Systems, *edited by Ashim K. Mitra*
59. Pharmaceutical Skin Penetration Enhancement, *edited by Kenneth A. Walters and Jonathan Hadgraft*
60. Colonic Drug Absorption and Metabolism, *edited by Peter R. Bieck*
61. Pharmaceutical Particulate Carriers: Therapeutic Applications, *edited by Alain Rolland*
62. Drug Permeation Enhancement: Theory and Applications, *edited by Dean S. Hsieh*
63. Glycopeptide Antibiotics, *edited by Ramakrishnan Nagarajan*
64. Achieving Sterility in Medical and Pharmaceutical Products, *Nigel A. Halls*
65. Multiparticulate Oral Drug Delivery, *edited by Isaac Ghebre-Sellassie*
66. Colloidal Drug Delivery Systems, *edited by Jörg Kreuter*
67. Pharmacokinetics: Regulatory • Industrial • Academic Perspectives, Second Edition, *edited by Peter G. Welling and Francis L. S. Tse*
68. Drug Stability: Principles and Practices, Second Edition, Revised and Expanded, *Jens T. Carstensen*

69. Good Laboratory Practice Regulations: Second Edition, Revised and Expanded, *edited by Sandy Weinberg*
70. Physical Characterization of Pharmaceutical Solids, *edited by Harry G. Brittain*
71. Pharmaceutical Powder Compaction Technology, *edited by Göran Alderborn and Christer Nyström*
72. Modern Pharmaceutics: Third Edition, Revised and Expanded, *edited by Gilbert S. Banker and Christopher T. Rhodes*
73. Microencapsulation: Methods and Industrial Applications, *edited by Simon Benita*
74. Oral Mucosal Drug Delivery, *edited by Michael J. Rathbone*
75. Clinical Research in Pharmaceutical Development, *edited by Barry Bleidt and Michael Montagne*
76. The Drug Development Process: Increasing Efficiency and Cost-Effectiveness, *edited by Peter G. Welling, Louis Lasagna, and Umesh V. Banakar*
77. Microparticulate Systems for the Delivery of Proteins and Vaccines, *edited by Smadar Cohen and Howard Bernstein*
78. Good Manufacturing Practices for Pharmaceuticals: A Plan for Total Quality Control, Fourth Edition, Revised and Expanded, *Sidney H. Willig and James R. Stoker*

ADDITIONAL VOLUMES IN PREPARATION

Pharmaceutical Statistics: Practical and Clinical Applications, Third Edition, *Sanford Bolton*

Aqueous Polymeric Coatings for Pharmaceutical Dosage Forms: Second Edition, Revised and Expanded, *edited by James W. McGinity*

Clinical Research in Pharmaceutical Development

edited by
Barry Bleidt
Health Resources Consulting
South Charleston, West Virginia

Michael Montagne
Massachusetts College of Pharmacy
and Allied Health Sciences
Boston, Massachusetts

CRC Press
Taylor & Francis Group
an **informa** business
www.taylorandfrancisgroup.com

6000 Broken Sound Parkway, NW
Suite 300, Boca Raton, FL 33487
711 Third Avenue
New York, NY 10017
2 Park Square, Milton Park
Abingdon, Oxon OX14 4RN, UK

FIRST INDIAN REPRINT, 2015

Library of Congress Cataloging-in-Publication Data

Clinical research in pharmaceutical development / edited by Barry Bleidt, Michael Montagne.
p. cm. — (Drugs and the pharmaceutical sciences ; v. 75)
Includes index.
ISBN 0-8247-9745-0 (hardcover : alk. paper)
1. Drugs—Testing. 2. Clinical pharmacology. I. Bleidt, Barry. II. Montagne, Michael. III. Series.
[DNLM: 1. Chemistry, Pharmaceutical. 2. Clinical Trials. 3. Drug Industry—United States. 4. Socioeconomic Factors. W1 DR893B v. 75 1996 / QV 744 C641 1996]
RM301.27C576 1996
615'.1901—dc20
DNLM/DLC
for Library of Congress 96-26648
CIP

The publisher offers discounts on this book when ordered in bulk quantities. For more information, write to Special Sales/Professional Marketing at the address below.

Marcel Dekker, Inc.
270 Madison Avenue, New York, New York 10016

Printed and bound in India by Bhavish Graphics.

FOR SALE IN SOUTH ASIA ONLY

To

My daughter, Brittany Alice,
who is the inspiration and love of my life

My mother, Mary Frances,
without whose support this book
would never have been completed

Debe, my friend,
whose strength and caring were instrumental
during the early stages of my career

and to

Mike, my coeditor, colleague, and most of all, friend,
whose friendship was the key factor
in motivating me to complete this work

—*Barry Bleidt*

To my parents, Roland and Margaret Montagne

—*Mike Montagne*

Preface

This book draws on our more than 40 combined years of experience in pharmacy: We have been involved with medications and their development as researchers, educators, practitioners, and information scientists within the pharmaceutical industry. We have examined the drug development process from many vantage points over the years and have engaged in clinical research as academicians, pharmacists, monitors, and even as subjects.

We have brought together a group of knowledgeable individuals from various backgrounds, including the pharmaceutical industry, academia, governmental agencies, and clinical medicine, to present this new volume. During the initial stages of putting this book together, we invited physicians, researchers, academicians, and other clinicians considered to be experts in the field.

The purpose of this book is twofold. First, it is designed to highlight the changes in clinical research and drug development that have occurred since the early 1980s. Second, it is intended to serve as a reference text for those interested in learning about, pursuing careers in, or initiating clinical research.

One of the changes that has occurred on the clinical trial scene is that clinical pharmacists can now be primary investigators. The editors applaud the pharmacy profession for its growth in this area, enabling medicine and pharmacy to work together in this important field.

The clinical research process has evolved significantly over the past decade. In 1984, *The Clinical Research Process in the Pharmaceutical Industry*, edited by Gary M. Matoren (Marcel Dekker, Inc.), was considered a publishing milestone. It was the first comprehensive work devoted to such an important aspect of American science, business, and health care: *clinical research.* This new book incorporates some of the groundbreaking work of Mr. Matoren; in addition, it chronicles many of the advances that have been made in drug development and clinical research processes since Matoren's volume.

The current book examines the logistics and methodologies of the clinical research process. It explores these dynamic processes as they relate to the origin of drug products (pharmageny); the history of drug discovery and developmental research; governmental agencies' roles; clinical project coordination and administration; monitoring of clinical trials; research protocols and document preparation; pharmacoeconomics and cost–benefit research; outcomes and quality-of-life research; marketing and drug promotion; legal aspects of drug development; and ethical considerations in drug research and development.

The clinical research process has seen many improvements in recent years. Pharmacoeconomic and medical outcomes analyses of data have emerged as essential considerations in bringing new products to market. These fields are now ranked almost equally with therapeutic efficacy and product safety in evaluating whether a product will be considered an addition to an institution's formulary or designated as an essential drug product. Additionally, pharmacoeconomics and outcomes research have become recognized as scientific disciplines and are contributing to our increased understanding of the overall impact that medicinal therapies have on the patient and society. It is no longer a question of whether a drug product performs safely and efficaciously; it has become a matter of how well the new therapy compares, both economically and in terms of patient satisfaction, to other available medical options.

Computer modeling as a drug-design tool has become commonplace. Today, new products are "planned" much more than they were in the past, when serendipity and detective work (testing thousands of compounds) were the order of the day. A chemical structure now can be envisioned before it is synthesized and subsequently tested. This process saves time and money for companies developing new products.

There have been many other recent developments, including changes in federal laws and FDA regulations, as well as concerns about the impact of a patient's ethnicity, gender, and/or age on the pharmacokinetic properties of a drug. In our opinion, however, the advancement that has had the most significant impact on clinical trials is in the way in which they are now planned and coordinated. Rapid communications technology and project management techniques have resulted in a more efficient and effective research process, producing more reliable data and more useful information, with fewer resources, in less time.

This book is intended to serve as a multidisciplinary reference manual for those involved in clinical research, and as a textbook for courses on this topic. It is also designed as a guide on how to start or improve clinical research protocols. We hope that it will stimulate greater interest in this important subject and serve as a catalyst to those who may consider clinical research as a career or a business endeavor. Our experts were brought together to present practical information rather than strictly theoretical discussions. We believe that a wide variety of readers will find this book informative, useful, and interesting.

We would like to acknowledge the following key people, without whose assistance or motivation this work would never have been completed:

Lisa Ruby Basara—for keeping to the original timetable, for making sure her section followed the guidelines, and for being patient with the many delays in producing this book. We are grateful for her valuable contributions.

Gary Matoren—for writing the *first* book on the clinical research process, for initiating our involvement within this important discipline, and for his inspiration in overcoming adversity in order to complete a task.

We also wish to acknowledge our contributors, who dedicated some of their limited time resources toward producing this work.

This book would not have been possible without the kindness, patience, support, and guidance of the staff of Marcel Dekker, Inc. We especially wish to express our sincere gratitude to Sandra Beberman, Ted Allen, and Pam Sobotka.

Barry Bleidt
Michael Montagne

Contents

Contributors

Lisa Ruby Basara, Ph.D. Senior Market Research Analyst, Advanced Therapeutics and Oncology Division, Rhône-Poulenc Rorer, Collegeville, Pennsylvania

Barry Bleidt, Ph.D., Pharm.D. Medical Information Scientist, Health Resources Consulting, South Charleston, West Virginia

Albert Hofmann, Ph.D.* Burg i.L., Switzerland

Gamal Hussein, Pharm.D. Associate Professor of Clinical Pharmacy, Northeast Louisiana University, New Orleans, Louisiana

Robert L. McCarthy, Ph.D. Associate Professor of Pharmacy Administration, Massachusetts College of Pharmacy and Allied Health Sciences, Boston, Massachusetts

William F. McGhan, Ph.D., Pharm.D. Professor, School of Pharmacy, Philadelphia College of Pharmacy and Science, Philadelphia, Pennsylvania

*Formerly Director of Research, Sandoz Pharmaceuticals, Basel, Switzerland

Loren Miller, Ph.D. Quintiles, Inc., Research Triangle Park, North Carolina

Lloyd G. Millstein, Ph.D. Consultant, Regulatory Affairs, Raleigh, North Carolina

Michael Montagne, Ph.D. Massachusetts College of Pharmacy and Allied Health Sciences, Boston, Massachusetts

Horace D. Nalle, J.D. Counsel, Merck AgVet Legal Dept., Merck & Co., Inc., Rahway, New Jersey

Mickey C. Smith, Ph.D. Professor, Pharmacy Administration, School of Pharmacy, The University of Mississippi, University, Mississippi

Donald D. Vogt, Ph.D.* Pharmaceutical Historian, Limestone, Tennessee

---

*Retired

Clinical Research in Pharmaceutical Development

1

Clinical Research in Pharmaceutical Development: An Overview

Barry Bleidt

Health Resources Consulting
South Charleston, West Virginia

Michael Montagne

Massachusetts College of Pharmacy and Allied Health Sciences
Boston, Massachusetts

Welcome to the exciting world of clinical research and drug development! This book was designed to present a discussion of the many advancements that have occurred in these two complementary processes over the past two decades, as well as to serve as a practical guide for understanding these improvements. Some of the progressive items covered are:

- The team approach to drug development
- The integration of marketing personnel into these development teams
- The utilization of large project management techniques for clinical trials
- Understanding the compliance components involved in clinical research
- The concept of premature drug product removal from the marketplace
- The consideration of social and cultural aspects in drug development

Several unique chapters are presented in this work, about subjects that have yet to be described in published texts on drug development and clinical research. For example, the chapter by Mickey Smith and Lisa Basara on the synergistic relationship between pharmaceutical marketing and drug development should prove useful to both novices and experienced clinical research people. Another unequaled work is Dr. Montagne's discussion of the social aspects of drug development. Here, he presents a framework for a more-profitable and less-bothersome future to pharmaceutical companies who are willing to pay attention to the social and cultural considerations of drug development. Finally, we are most pleased to have the keynote contribution from Dr. Albert Hofmann, a former senior director of research at Sandoz Pharmaceuticals in Switzerland. In his chapter, he relates his own personal experience in the development of several very successful pharmaceutical products as well as his chance discovery of LSD (lysergic acid diethylamide).

The book is divided into five sections: first, an introduction and a keynote section; these are followed by drug development process, clinical drug research, and social and legal aspects sections. A brief description of the chapters within each section is presented. These discussions are followed by a regulatory supplement that contains a listing of pertinent federal clinical research regulations and a guide on how to obtain needed regulatory materials.

I. INTRODUCTION SECTION

Following this brief overview of the book is the chapter that introduces the drug development process. In "Pharmageny" (the genesis of drug products), a conspectus on the past, current, and future methods of discovering new drugs is presented by Dr. Bleidt. Here, the concepts of drug screening and molecular modeling are also introduced. More in-depth presentations of these topics are covered later in the text.

The next section is the keynote section. This position was saved for a very special chapter, an excellent reading adventure for almost anyone, even those with little or no interest in clinical trials or pharmaceuticals. We highly recommend this compelling commentary on chance, discovery, and society.

II. KEYNOTE SECTION

This section was reserved for a key figure in drug discovery, Albert Hofmann. In this contribution, he discusses the roles of "Planned Research and Chance Discovery in Pharmaceutical Development." Dr. Hofmann was an instrumental figure in the early years of pharmaceutical development. His research findings from experiments on ergot alkaloids led to several important drugs that made his employer (Sandoz) billions of dollars over the years. This rare first-hand account of his laboratory experiences has been presented only in one of the company's internal publications. Our readers are seeing this first-person account of the discovery of LSD—and some important pharmaceuticals developed from alkaloids—for the first time.

Dr. Hofmann discusses why it is important to have an open mind to the possibility of a chance discovery. His remarks are directed at showing "that pharmaceutical research does not, and indeed could not, always proceed as rigidly along planned lines as might appear from the publications in technical journals (which are mostly highly stylized from the scientific point of view)—but that chance, or rather what Walpole called 'serendipity,' has very often contributed much more to success and will probably continue to do so in the future." It is a real treat to read this chapter.

The next section is devoted to discussing the actual process of drug development. It discusses the evolution and roles of the clinical research process in drug development and the regulatory oversight of both endeavors.

III. DRUG DEVELOPMENT PROCESS SECTION

In "A Brief History of Clinical Research in Pharmaceutical Development," Drs. Vogt and Montagne describe the evolution of the pharmaceutical industry from the early 1900s to the present. Next, the authors write about the genesis of the clinical research process, its maturing into the technology of today, and the formalization of clinical trials as a science. Finally, an overview of the history of the drug regulatory process is discussed. They conclude that "the process of drug discovery, development, and clinical testing have become highly institutionalized and politicized during the twentieth century. This process has been affected by changes in political economics; the elaboration of basic research methodologies; the emergence of pharmacology, immunology and other specialized disciplines; the proliferation of educated scientific specialists; new methods of research management; and persistent elements of social control. The interplay of these factors have been strong determinants in the structure, direction, and performance of the pharmaceutical industry."

Next, "The Role of Clinical Research in the Drug Development Process" is presented by Dr. Montagne. First, there is an in-depth discussion of how a drug product comes onto the U.S. marketplace. The different types of studies that must be performed prior to human experimentation (preclinical research) is next presented along with an explanation of the four phases of clinical research. Then Dr. Montagne discusses the drug approval and regulation process.

This is followed by a look at the clinical drug trial process. The chapter ends with writings on the future of clinical research in drug development. "The process of clinical drug research in pharmaceutical development still is evolving. While this process is not perfect, changes are proposed constantly to improve it for the benefit of patients, health professionals, and the pharmaceutical industry."

In the third chapter of this section, "The FDA and the Regulatory Oversight of the Clinical Research Process in Drug Development," two pharmaceutical industry executives write about the FDA's oversight of the clinical research process. Drs. Miller and Millstein describe the protection of human subjects and the evolution of federal regulations, through which the FDA oversees clinical research.

They provide an excellent treatise on regulatory guidance and facilitation of the drug development process. Finally, a brief presentation on the internationalization of pharmaceutical development is included.

In the next section, the basic elements of what constitutes clinical research is detailed. A discussion of the types of research methodologies that must be employed and the procedures for performing them are presented.

IV. CLINICAL DRUG RESEARCH SECTION

This section presents the fundamental principles of clinical research. It contains guidelines for planning, implementing, supervising, and completing a full-scale research project. It also touches on the important concept of informed patient consent, discusses advancements in project management techniques, and explains the significance of two new scientific disciplines: pharmacoeconomics and health outcomes.

In "Pharmacokinetics: Interactions of New Drugs and the Human Body," Drs. Hussein and Bleidt discuss the significance of Phase 1 trials and the importance of the value of the parameters that are generated from these studies. Dr. Hussein is a rising star in the field of pharmacokinetics. He already has developed some of the most advanced, interactive, multimedia kinetic software available.

In this chapter, the basics of interpatient variability in a drug's effect are presented according to pharmacological theories (receptor hypothesis). Next, the pharmacokinetic concepts of adsorption, distribution, metabolism, and excretion are explained. In each part, the key population variables and methodologies utilized to determine their value are discussed. These numbers provide an information starting point to enable a practitioner to use the new drug. Once a patient has used the product, individualization of the parameters is possible and the population values determined from the Phase 1 studies may not be applicable anymore.

The next chapter, "Planning, Coordinating, and Monitoring Clinical Trials," is a handbook on the preparation for and management of human research studies. Dr. Bleidt's experience as a monitor for the Hypertension Optimal Therapy (HOT) Study is beneficial to the readers. The HOT Study is the largest intervention trial for investigating the treatment of high blood pressure ever undertaken, enrolling over 18,000 patients in over 30 countries. His wisdom helps in the presentation of much practical information throughout the chapter.

First of all, there is a discussion of the planning process that is necessary before beginning a clinical trial project, then information on selecting members of the Monitoring Team is presented along with a description of the various players that participate in a research investigation. The team approach is one of the project management techniques now utilized to make the process more efficient.

The essence of this chapter is that it was written as a guide for the successful execution of a clinical research project. It includes details of what should be contained in an Investigator's Notebook, how to account for and maintain the supply of investigational drugs, and the basics on monitoring the trials themselves. Finally, a dozen practical suggestions on how to administer a successful trial are given. Overall, for those interested in implementing or understanding clinical trials, this chapter is must reading.

One of the discussions inadvertently omitted from this chapter is on the creditializing of Clinical Research Coordinators (CCRC). The Associates of Clinical Pharmacology (ACP) grants certification to select individuals based on recognition of documented and verified work experience and after successful performance on an examination [1]. In 1995, a similar procedure was also initiated for Clinical Research Associates (CCRA). This process was implemented in order to set professional standards on education, knowledge, and experience for these associates [2].

This certification process is becoming more widely recognized by the pharmaceutical industry and may soon be required in order to perform in the two capacities. The Clinical Research Coordinators who have already achieved certification rank increased knowledge and professional recognition, along with personal satisfaction, highest among the goals achieved by their accomplishment [3].

The certification exam is given in multiple locations, including several sites in Canada and at least one other international spot. More information on the qualifications, testing sites, and costs of this certification process can be obtained from the Associates of Clinical Pharmacology, 1012 Fourteenth Street, NW, Washington, DC 20005 [phone: (202) 737-8100 or telefax: (202) 737-8101]. As clinical trials evolve, becoming more scientific and efficient, the idea of certifying the professionals associated with performing key tasks involved in the research will gain wider acceptance.

In the third chapter of this section, "The Protocol, Case Report Forms, and Patient Consent," the basics of how to plan, prepare, and implement a clinical research protocol are given. A page-by-page guide is presented of what should be contained in a protocol document. "The hallmarks of successful research efforts are careful planning and paying attention to fine details. The protocol is the blueprint for the entire project. It sets the stage for the production of sound results."

There is also a detailed discussion on the design and use of the patient case report forms and an introduction to one of the key concepts presented in this book, patient consent. In this latter part, the foundation is laid for how this notion of the informed patient came into existence and why it is so important. A copy of the Declaration of Helsinki (international recommendations guiding physicians in biomedical research involving human subjects) and the pertinent parts of the U.S. Code concerning informed consent of human subjects and institutional review boards are included in the appendices. Also contained in this chapter are sample case report forms for a hypothetical study intended to serve as a template for persons considering developing such documents for their own research.

In the penultimate chapter of the section, "Patient Outcomes and Drug Usefulness," an introduction to and implications of health outcomes and pharmacoeconomic research are presented. Here, Dr. Bleidt characterizes drug usefulness as "a product that is safe and efficacious to use, and that has a positive impact on the outcomes of the patient and/or medical facility."

The components that a well-designed outcomes research study should contain are presented in this chapter, including a superb discussion of study perspectives. The questions that should be answered by the research endeavor are detailed, as well. Though not specifically stated in the chapter, in the long run, it is best for a researcher to keep in mind the overall societal perspective when performing a clinical economic analysis. It is usually more difficult to find fault in a project that presents its findings from this viewpoint.

In the last chapter of the section, "Pharmacoeconomics and Quality of Life: Evaluating the Economic and Social Impact of Pharmaceuticals," Dr. William McGhan discusses the roles of quality-of-life and pharmacoeconomic research in the development of new products. These two newly developed scientific disciplines have become very important tools in marketing, as well as in the planning for new pharmaceutical products.

Dr. McGhan begins with an overview of the various types of analysis that are utilized in this kind of research and follows with an important discussion on economic perspectives. Next, he presents the concepts of quality-of-life outcomes and patient decisions. Specific examples of the different research methodologies, as they relate to a proposed drug therapy, are given at the end of the chapter. "A key impact to which pharmaceutical research needs to give continuing attention is the idea that the greatest benefit we can generate for society as a whole is to target and take more responsibility toward decreasing mortality, not just decreasing morbidity."

In the final section, the social and legal aspects of drug development are presented. Here, we identify some of the nonscientific issues that must be taken into account when bringing a new drug to the market and how to handle them.

V. SOCIAL AND LEGAL ASPECTS SECTION

This section is one of the hallmarks of our work. It contains two chapters on topics that are generally not associated with traditional clinical research and pharmaceutical development texts, though, as the reader will see after inspecting them, these subjects definitely should have been included. Both the marketing chapter and social aspects chapter are unmatched in this regard. We encourage you to explore their uniqueness and understand the significance of their content.

In the first chapter, the synergistic relationship between the Marketing Department and Research and Development (R&D) Department is described as complex, dynamic, and mostly differing in perspectives. Drs. Smith and Basara discuss the need for these two sometimes antagonistic groups to be involved in continuous, two-way communication throughout the new drug development process in order to have a more efficient and profitable outcome. They begin by stating that "the thread of marketing is woven throughout the fabric of the pharmaceutical industry."

In order to blunt some of the massive volume of criticism often associated with the "marketing" activities of the pharmaceutical industry, Drs. Smith and Basara first present a basic lesson on marketing. This was done to facilitate a better understanding of marketing as a useful business function and also to emphasize its importance to the health care delivery system of the nation. Next, they discuss the overall corporate perspective on the marketing and R&D interaction and the conceptual differences between the two departments and their perspectives.

Finally, the authors devote a substantial portion of their work to describing the integral role, via a time line, that marketing personnel should play during each of the critical phases of drug discovery and development and how they should be integrated into the development teams. Additionally, the details and the goals of the interchange between marketing and R&D during each phase of a new compound's life cycle are presented, as well as a clarification of the value of these interactions in terms of product success.

In the next chapter, Dr. Robert McCarthy presents an in-depth discussion on patient consent, following up on Dr. Bleidt's aforementioned foundation. His chapter, "Ethics in Clinical Drug Research," describes the basic concepts of ethical principles, moral rules, and various codes as they relate to providing an ethical framework for clinical drug studies. Next is a discussion on the roles and functions of an Institutional Review Board. Then, Dr. McCarthy poses, answers, and discusses at length relevant research questions and ethical dilemmas, covering such diverse topics as drug testing in various vulnerable populations (children, prisoners, women, and the mentally incompetent), the funding of clinical studies, and the use of placebos. Finally, he writes about the circumstances that may give rise to abandoning clinical studies and how this predicament should be handled.

The third contribution in this section comes from a senior drug industry attorney. It is the chapter "Legal Aspects of Prescription Drug Development in the United States." Here, Horace Nalle focuses on the critical points in the developmental process that generally raise issues that require legal advice, most of which is due to the heavy regulation of drug development by the Food and Drug Administration. Drug discovery and development, as well as clinical trials, are law-intensive processes. This chapter was written to serve as a guide as to where this input is needed and discusses the necessity of involving lawyers throughout the entire process.

In the final chapter of the book, Dr. Montagne discusses "Social Aspects of Pharmaceutical Development." Here he presents the importance of considering factors other than profit and regulatory hurdles during the drug development process. This part is another unique addition to our body of work. There has been little, if any, published debate on the impact of nonpharmaceutical factors on the use of drugs as it relates to development product. "In many instances, social factors can have a major influence on the drug discovery and developmental process," primarily through the beliefs and perceptions of those who use drugs. There is also a detailed discussion on the compliance component of clinical trials and how to minimize the impact of patient nonadherence.

Another interesting presentation contained in this chapter is that on pharmacomythologies, cultural perceptions about drugs that are without bases in fact. These illusory principles have become so widely accepted that they are considered fundamental principles. Also, there is an excellent treatise on two differing viewpoints on how a drug's effect is educed. One theory, from the sociological realm, states that drug action is primarily a function of the user's belief and perceptions added to social expectations and definitions for that drug. Another explanation, based on the more widely accepted pharmacological hypothesis, is that drug action is the direct result of the interaction, through a physiochemical bond, of a drug molecule with a cell or constituent part of a cell in the human body. A discussion of the significance of both theorems follows.

The chapter concludes by suggesting that as the end of the chemical era of drug discovery makes way for the biotechnological age, companies may find it more necessary than ever to attend to social and cultural considerations during the initial planning stages of drug development. If the beliefs and perceptions of those who are to use or prescribe the products is not considered, giving them appropriate weight within an apropos time frame, then the drugs may be approved in a negative social environment, thereby decreasing acceptance and lessening profits.

The next section of this chapter is provided as a regulatory supplement. Its primary purposes are to serve as a guide for finding the citations of pertinent federal regulations, with a list of clinical guidelines that are available, and also as a manual on how and where to obtain these items.

VI. REGULATORY SUPPLEMENT

As previously mentioned, there are two chapters devoted to discussing the federal regulation of clinical research and drug development, two that present the various aspects of informed patient consent from an ethical point of view, and one that takes a legal perspective of these topics. We felt that a handy guide to the huge volume of federal regulations was needed in order to remain true to the practical design of this book. Readers are reminded that there may be other jurisdictions which also have some legal authority over clinical investigations, such as state laws or local public health codes. We remind all interested parties to seek out, read, and understand all pertinent regulations before the planning stage begins.

It is essential that clinical investigators keep a copy of the most current federal regulations pertaining to their research because they are updated on an annual basis. Once a new volume is received, it should be reviewed for changes against the previous edition. Then, all current practices should be verified against any modifications in order to ensure continued compliance with the regulations. Of course, all major changes require institutional review board (IRB) approval and possibly the obtaining of new patient consent. The *Federal Register* is generally available in most libraries, especially legal and medical ones.

An alphabetical reference to pertinent federal clinical research regulation is provided in Table 1, which has been modified from a table that appeared in an article written by Deborah Rosenbaum, CRCC (4). In this listing under the heading "Guidelines Available," the title of apropos FDA summary information sheets is provided. These documents are intended to serve as guidelines to the regulations issued by the Department of Health and Human Services and the Food and Drug Administration. Table 2 presents the clinical guidelines that have been developed by FDA Advisory Committees and their consultants grouped according to therapeutic category. These digests contain a large volume of specific information on conducting clinical trials.

A. How to Obtain Federal Regulations and Guidelines

The *Code of Federal Regulations* and the *Federal Register* can be ordered directly by mail, with accompanying payment, from:

Table 1 Alphabetical Guide to Pertinent Federal Clinical Research Regulations [4, 5]

Subject	Citation	Contents/Guidelines Available (Date)
Abbreviated NDA	21CFR314.55	Organization of an Abbreviated New Drug Application and Abbreviated Antibiotic Application
Advertising	21CFR50.20 21CFR50.21 21CFR56.111	Advertising for Human Subjects for a Study
Adverse Events	21CFR310.305	Determining and Reporting
Compassionate Use IND	21CFR312.34	Treatment Use of Investigational Drugs (5/89)
Contract Research Organizations	21CFR312.52	(CROs)
Cooperative Research Review	45CFR45.114 21CFR56.114	Cooperative Research, Non-local IRB Review (2/89)
Data Management	21CFR312.62	see also Record Keeping
Emergency Drug Use	21CFR312.36	Emergency Use of an Investigational Drug (2/89) Guidance for the Emergency Use of Unapproved Medical Devices (10/22/85)
and Informed Consent	21CFR50.23	
Expedited Review	21CFR56.110	see *Federal Register*{*Fed. Reg.*} (V. 48:17, 1/27/91)
	46CFR8980	List of Research Activities Which May Be Reviewed Through the Expedited Review Procedure
Foreign Clinical Studies		(not under a US IND) see *Fed. Reg.* (V. 56:93, 1991)
Good Clinical Practices	Parts 50, 56, 312, 314, 812, & 8132 of 21CFR	see *Fed. Reg.* (V. 52:53, 3/19/87) Preamble and original review of regulations in Part VII, page 8790
Good Laboratory Practices for Nonclinical Laboratory Studies	21CFR58⇒	Good Laboratory Practice Regulations: Q & A (6/81) Additional specific guidelines available (contact FDA)
Good Manufacturing Practices	21CFR211⇒	Specific guidelines also available (contact FDA)
Information Amendment to IND	21CFR312.31	

(continued)

Table 1 Continued

Subject	Citation	Contents/Guidelines Available (Date)
Informed Consent	Parts 45, 50, & 56 of 21CFR	Informed Consent Regulations**
	21CFR312.60	Informed Consent and the Clinical Investigator (5/89)
and Emergency Drug Use	21CFR50.23	
Inspections	21CFR312.68	Compliance Program Guidance Manual (for Clinical Investigators)
	21CFR312.58	Compliance Program Guidance Manual (for Sponsors, CROs, Monitors)
		Compliance Program Guidance Manual (IRBs)
		Guide for Detecting Fraud in Bioresearch Monitoring Inspections (4/93)
Institutional Review Board (IRB)	21CFR56⇒	IRB Regulations**
Investigational Agent Management	21CFR312.57 21CFR312.59 21CFR312.6 21CFR312.62	Preparation of Investigational New Drug Products (draft) (2/88)
Investigational Devices	21CFR812⇒ 21CFR813⇒	(see also Medical Devices)
Investigational New Drug Application	21CFR312⇒	Clinical Development Guidelines (from FDA)
Investigator's Brochure	21CFR312.23(a.5)	
IND Annual Progress Report	21CFR312.33	
IND Safety Report (Report of Serious Adverse Event)	21CFR312.32 21CFR312.54	MEDWatch Form (FDA form 3500)**
Labeling	21CFR201.57 21CFR314.5(c.2.1)	see package inserts
Laboratory Certification	42CFR493	
Marketed Drugs		Investigation Use of Marketed Products (2/89)
MEDWatch form		(see also Serious Adverse Experience, IND Safety Report)
		FDA form 3500 **

Table 1 Continued

Subject	Citation	Contents/Guidelines Available (Date)
Medical Devices	21CFR812⇒	Guidance for Emergency Use of Medical Devices (10/85)
	21CFR813⇒	Guidance on Significant and Nonsignificant Risk Device Studies (2/89), IRBs and Medical Devices (2/89)
Monitoring	21CFR312.53 21CFR312.56	FDA Guideline for Monitoring Clinical Investigations (1/88)
New Drug Application	21CFR314⇒	specific guidelines for format and content also available
Obligations of Investigators	subpart D of 21CFR312	Regulatory Information for Investigators (9/92) Obligations of Investigators
	21CFR312.60	Required Recordkeeping in Clinical Investigations (5/89)
	21CFR312.70	Informed Consent and the Clinical Investigator (5/90) FDA Inspections of Clinical Investigators (5/89) Clinical Investigator Regulatory Sanctions (5/89) Treatment Use of Investigational Drugs Placebo-controlled and Active-controlled Drug Study Designs
Obligations of Sponsors	subpart D of 21CFR312 21CFR312.50 to 21CFR312.58	Obligation of Sponsors
Package Insert	21CFR201.57 21CFR314.5(c.2.1)	
Parallel Track		*Federal Register* (V. 57:73, 1992)
Post-Marketing Activities	21CFR314.80	
Product License Application		(refer to NDA)
Protocol	21CFR312.23(a.6)	
Protocol Amendment	21CFR312.30	
Record Keeping	21CFR312.62	Required Recordkeeping in Clinical Investigations (5/89)

(continued)

Table 1 Continued

Subject	Citation	Contents/Guidelines Available (Date)
Serious Adverse Experience	21CFR312.32 21CFR312.64	(see also IND Safety Report) MEDWatch Form (FDA form 3500)**
Statement of Investigator	21CFR312.53	FDA form 1572 **
Subjects	21CFR part 50	Payment to Research Subjects (2/89) **
Treatment IND	21CFR312.54	Treatment Use of Investigational Drugs (5/89)

Fed. Reg. = *Federal Register*; CROs = Contract Research Organization(s); V. = Volume; CFR = Code of Federal Regulations; IND = Investigational New Drug; NDA = New Drug Application; FDA = Food and Drug Administration; IRBs = Institutional Review Board(s); ⇒ = *et sequentia* (including all following parts); ** = items that are included in this book.

The Superintendent of Documents
Attention: New Orders
PO Box 371954
Pittsburgh, PA 15240–7954.

Credit card charge orders can be telephoned to the Government Purchasing Office Order Desk at (202) 512–1800 or telefaxed to (202) 512–2233.

Title 21 of the *Code of Federal Regulations* (*CFR*) is divided into the following parts:

Parts 1 to 99: General Regulations
- Part 50: Protection of Human Subjects
- Part 56: Institutional Review Boards

Parts 300 to 499: Drugs for Human Use, New Drugs, NDAs, Interpretive Statements and Antibiotics
- Part 312, Subparts A–F: Investigational New Drugs
- Part 314, Subpart D: Approval to Market a New Drug

Parts 600 to 799: Biologics, Diagnostic Substances, and Cosmetics

The Guidelines for the Monitoring of Clinical Investigators information sheet can be obtained through:

Bioresearch Program Coordinator (HFC–230)
5600 Fisher's Lane
Rockville, MD 20857

Table 2 Clinical Evaluation of Available Drug Guidelines [4,5]

General considerations for the Clinical Evaluation of Drugs
General considerations for the Clinical Evaluation of Drugs in Infants and Children
General considerations for the Clinical Evaluation of Analgesic Drugs
General considerations for the Clinical Evaluation of Antacid Drugs
General considerations for the Clinical Evaluation of Anti-Anginal Drugs
General considerations for the Clinical Evaluation of Anti-Anxiety Drugs
General considerations for the Clinical Evaluation of Anti-Inflammatory and Anti-Arthritic Drugs
General considerations for the Clinical Evaluation of Anti-Arrhythmic Drugs
General considerations for the Clinical Evaluation of Anticonvulsant Drugs
General considerations for the Clinical Evaluation of Antidepressant Drugs
General considerations for the Clinical Evaluation of Antidiarrheal Drugs
General considerations for the Clinical Evaluation of Anti-Epileptic Drugs
General considerations for the Clinical Evaluation of Antihypertensive Drugs (proposed)
General considerations for the Clinical Evaluation of Anti-Infective Drugs
General considerations for the Clinical Evaluation of Antineoplastic Drugs
General considerations for the Clinical Evaluation of Anti-Ulcer Drugs
General considerations for the Clinical Evaluation of Bronchodilator Drugs
General considerations for the Clinical Evaluation of Drugs for the Treatment of Congestive Heart Failure
General considerations for the Clinical Evaluation of Drugs to Prevent, Control and/or Treat Periodontal Disease
General considerations for the Clinical Evaluation of Drugs to Prevent Dental Caries
General considerations for the Clinical Evaluation of Drugs used in the Treatment of Osteoporosis
General considerations for the Clinical Evaluation of Gastric Secretory Depressant Drugs
General considerations for the Clinical Evaluation of General Anesthetics
General considerations for the Clinical Evaluation of G.I. Motility-Modifying Drugs
General considerations for the Clinical Evaluation of Hypnotic Drugs
General considerations for the Clinical Evaluation of Laxative Drugs
General considerations for the Clinical Evaluation of Lipid-Altering Agents
General considerations for the Clinical Evaluation of Local Anesthetics
General considerations for the Clinical Evaluation of Nonsteroidal Anti-Inflammatory and Anti-Rheumatic Drugs
General considerations for the Clinical Evaluation of Psychoactive Drugs in Children

(*continued*)

Table 2 Continued

General considerations for the Clinical Evaluation of Radio-Pharmaceutical Drugs
Guidelines for Abuse Liability Assessment
Guidelines for the Evaluation of Controlled-Released Drug Products
Guidelines for the Study and Evaluation of Gender Differences in the Clinical Evaluation of Drugs
Guidelines for the Study of Drugs Likely to be used in the Elderly

There are also audit/inspection resource guides available, such as the FDA Compliance Program Guidance Manual, Drugs and Biologics (#PB92–9206) from:

National Technical Information Service
5285 Port Royal Road
Springfield, VA 22161
[phone (703) 487-4650]

The specific manuals are:

7348.810 for Sponsors, CROs and Monitors
7348.811 for Clinical Investigators
7348.809 for Institutional Review Boards

It is highly recommended that the participants have a current copy of the pertinent manual as a reference. These books are relatively expensive (over $100).

The Center for Drug Evaluation and Research (CDER) has the following resources available:

Investigational New Drug Application Packet
Good Clinical Practices Packet
Federal Food, Drug, and Cosmetic Act (as amended)
IRB Information Sheet
Clinical Investigator Information Sheet
MEDWatch Packet
General Considerations for the Clinical Evaluation of Drugs (FDA 77–30–10)

Draft documents on GCPs, Guidelines for Investigators Brochure, Guidelines for Essential Documents for the Conduct of Study (*Federal Register*, 8/9/94).

These materials can be obtained by contacting:

CDER
Executive Secretariat Staff (HFD–8)
5600 Fisher's Lane
Rockville, MD 20857
[phone: (301) 594–1012 or fax: (301) 594–3302]

The rest of the Guidelines and summaries of information sheets noted in Tables 1 and 2 are available through the Freedom of Information Act. These documents were created to complement the regulations. They can be obtained from:

Food and Drug Administration
FOI Staff, HFI-35, Room 12A–16
5600 Fisher's Lane
Rockville, MD 20857
[phone (301) 443–6310]

There is also a CD-ROM, FDA reference disk available from the FDA Office of Information Resources Management that contains a large number of FDA manuals and documents. For more information about this resource, call (301) 443–6770. Additionally, the *Washington Post* offers an on-line service, Legis-Slate®, that contains the complete, updated *Federal Register* and *Code of Federal Regulations*. You can subscribe to part or all of this service, as needed. More information about this service can be obtained from (800) 877–6999.

VII. SUMMARY

This book was developed to provide information for those who are involved with or are interested in learning about clinical research and pharmaceutical development. The authors in this book are all experienced and trained in clinical research and drug development areas. They are experts in their field and offer much information and advice for the readers.

Several novel concepts, at least in terms of their application in clinical research, have been introduced. The team approach to drug development is included as part of several chapters. There is a growing need for an interaction between marketers and researchers in pharmaceutical firms and for lawyers and outside consultants to be a part of key decision-making steps. Although initially this might create some tension, the rewards are substantial in terms of higher profits, greater customer satisfaction, and less hassle in the drug development process. There is also a discussion of the social and cultural aspects of pharmaceutical discovery presented in the context of assisting those who act as sponsors to view important, less prevalent perspectives when planning and initiating the drug development process.

Another important component of this book is its practical nature. The chapters on protocol development, coordinating clinical trials, and regulatory overview are basic and easily understandable. These down-to-earth "how-to-get-it-done" presentations will enable most readers to initiate the planning process and permit them to implement a clinical study with little difficulty. The regulatory supplement to this particular chapter also assists with the start-up activities.

Finally, the notions of informed patient consent and the protection of human subjects are presented from an ethical standpoint by two authors and from the regulatory perspective by another. These discussions tie in very well with various chapters delivering information on the evolution of the clinical research and drug development processes.

It is our hope—and our design—that the contents of this book will be of substantial assistance to those professionals who encounter some of the cumbersome problems associated with clinical research and who must answer the questions and make the critical decisions affecting lives and profits. We also want to stimulate a discussion on key issues, such as the premature removal of drug products from the marketplace. It is our desire to direct a full-scale investigation or symposium into these phenomena and about other social impacts so that a more thorough understanding can be gleaned concerning these powerful forces and how to anticipate and account for them.

REFERENCES

1. Associates of Clinical Pharmacology, Certification Exams Candidate Handbook, *The Monitor 9*:4 (December 1995).
2. A. M. Valakas, Development of the CRA Certification Program, *The Monitor 9*: 4 (December 1995).
3. Stephens and Papke, Survey of Experienced Clinical Research Coordinators, *Appl. Clin. Trials* (September 1995).
4. D. Rosenbaum, Reference Guide to FDA Regulations, *The Monitor 9*:4 (December 1995).
5. 21 Code of Federal Regulations, *et seq.*

2

Pharmageny: The New Product Development Process

Barry Bleidt

Health Resources Consulting
South Charleston, West Virginia

Before a new drug product can be marketed in the United States, it must first be approved by an agency of the federal government, the Food and Drug Administration. The first step on the way through this long and arduous approval procedure is the actual discovery of a new, pharmacologically active, therapeutically useful compound, a process known as "pharmagenesis."

In the following sections, there will be a brief overview of the evolution of drug development. This subject is presented in greater detail in Chapter 4, "A Brief History of Clinical Research in Pharmaceutical Development," by Donald Vogt and Michael Montagne.

I. PHARMAGENOLOGY

The pharmaceutical development process has undergone exponential and rapid changes over the past two decades. Technological advancements in data handling, research communications, and molecular modeling have changed the way in which new drugs are derived and tested. This chapter will first briefly describe the way pharmacologically active drug molecules were discovered in the past and then it will detail the current pharmageny.

In the book *The Clinical Research Process in the Pharmaceutical Industry*, edited by Gary Matoren, two new words were coined in the first chapter to describe the origin of new drug products: "pharmogeny" (the genesis of drug products) and "pharmogenology" (the study of the process involved in the origin of new drug products) [1]. The spelling of these words has been updated to *pharmageny* and *pharmagenology*, respectively, for this work. This correction was made to remain true to the Greek origin of both words, *pharmakos*.

The public usually takes for granted the discovery process involved in producing the wide array of drugs currently available to treat diseases and to mitigate symptoms. These products and, of course, their development are the raison d'etre for the pharmaceutical industry [2].

The prescription drug business is similar to other commercial endeavors in that its products must meet demands and satisfy needs. Competition for these medicines occurs in many forms, including:

- Other drugs within the same therapeutic class
- Generic products (after patent expiration)
- Alternative treatments and therapeutic agents (nonprescription products, herbal remedies, etc.) used to treat the same disease or condition
- The refusal of third-party payers to reimburse for the use of the drug

The product's life cycle can be very short if the drug does not satisfy the needs of the patient or prescriber, or it can be quite long and very prosperous for the sponsor.

New drugs are the lifeblood of the research-intensive pharmaceutical manufacturers. Without these new products or potential agents in the developmental pipeline, a drug company will become less profitable and its stock will begin to lose value. When this situation occurs, the company is either absorbed by another, a merger is contemplated, or the company goes out of business. It is vitally important for these companies to focus on research and development of new products in order to remain competitive and to avoid a corporate downfall.

II. DRUG SCREENING—"THE WAY WERE WERE"

It used to be that serendipitous or chance discoveries were the rule in finding new drugs. Most of the substances had been used for centuries, surviving the challenge of modern scientific scrutiny for safety and efficacy from their basis in use in ancient medicine. The origin of these remedies was the haphazard or accidental finding that certain plants relieved pain or improved healing without also killing the patient. This is the process of detection that led to the widespread use of leeches and other forms of bleeding; it is also the same procedure that gave us some of our current products, such as digitalis, the opiate derivatives, and salicylates. Then the process of routine chemical compound screening was discovered.

At one time, even compound screening was a new technology. Paul Ehrlich, in his quest for an antimicrobial agent, is credited with being the first person to use a systematic approach to the discovery of new chemical moieties with the potential of becoming drug products [3]. Dr. Ehrlich, in utilizing the selective toxicity principle, synthesized an organoarsenical arsphenamine, called salvarsan, after screening a large number of stains and other chemicals for antiprotozoal and antispirochete activity. This breakthrough established a new paradigm for drug discovery— "wherein a biological model is used to facilitate the study of the biological effect of large numbers of chemicals" [4].

In Fig. 1, a depiction of the screening process is presented. This figure is not intended to show an exact representation of any specific company's research endeavors, but rather to provide a visual image of how drug screening works. A large number of chemical compounds must be tested using biological models in order to search for pharmacological activity. Only a few of the analyzed entities show potential usefulness as a therapeutic agent. Then these pharmacologically active molecules are subjected to safety evaluations and later, if all goes well, to human testing and possibly to regulatory approval as a new drug. The illustration also points out the inefficiency of this technique, requiring as it does thousands of compounds and hundreds of person-hours to develop a single useful product.

```
10,000 - compounds screened for activity
                      ↓
   100 - are found pharmacologically useful
                      ↓
    10 - pass animal safety tests
                      ↓
     1 - makes it to market
```

Fig. 1 Representative depiction of the screening process.

The discovery of this methodology led to a global search for new and different compounds and molecular moieties. Soil and plant samples from all over the world were sent to the screening centers of various companies looking for unique entities that could lead to new products. This seemingly chaotic procedure became a very successful approach in the cultivation of new drugs; nearly all of our post-penicillin antimicrobial agents were derived in this way, as well as many other useful therapeutic agents.

Through this discovery process, the comprehension of biological systems and pharmacological activity grew. From this type of research, the receptor site theory was brought forth, along with its chemical affinity and intrinsic activity notions. Once a useful compound was discovered, alterations could be made in its basic structure that could add to its utility, change its biological functioning altogether, or even make it less useful.

This molecular modification technique is called biologically directed chemical synthesis. A prime example of how this process can succeed occurred in the laboratories of Hoffmann-La Roche, where an alteration of a substituted quinazoline-3-oxide resulted in a pharmacological screening test that yielded positive results, despite the fact that all the other chemically related compounds examined showed no useful biological activity. From this new moiety, further molecular rearrangements were made that enhanced the biological activity of the compound, eventually leading to the synthesis of two benzodiazepines, chlordiazepoxide (Librium®) and diazepam (Valium®) [5].

This useful practice was very successful for many other manufacturers as well. Diverse pharmacological effects were uncovered via this process; acetazolamide (a carbonic anhydrase inhibitor) and several oral hypoglycemic agents (the sulfonylureas) were derived from sulfonamides, a class of antibacterial drugs.

The next evolutionary advance in drug development came in the search for specific enzyme inhibitors. Many of the earlier discovered enzyme inhibitors (found prior to 1980) were gleaned via the aforementioned methods. However, one pharmaceutical company, E. R. Squibb, through the Squibb Institute for Medical Research, set upon a different course of drug development. Their procedure was specifically directed toward finding an angiotensin-converting enzyme (ACE) inhibitor, armed with the knowledge that if they succeeded, the most likely result would be the discovery of a new class of antihypertensive agents. Captopril (Capoten®), the first ACE inhibitor, was the successful result of this search [6].

III. RATIONAL DRUG DESIGN—"THE WAY WE ARE"

Systematic approaches and sophisticated technologies are now available that enable us to design and discover new drugs more efficiently, replacing the older, more serendipitous methods. These changes in the drug discovery process are being driven by the need to improve the rate of return on research and development investments and the desire to obtain the immense profits derived by staying ahead of other companies. Much effort is now being directed toward a more logical approach, using chemical structure–based methods that coordinate computer modeling, x-ray crystallography, and other image-enhancement techniques.

This strategy of drug design and development involves selecting a specific target for the proposed drug's action, such as: Which enzyme's activity is to be modified? What biological function is to be altered? Which receptor is to be blocked or stimulated? Significant advances over the previous approach to drug design in the understanding of structure-activity relationships (SAR) and drug-mitigated biological functioning have made this more logical process possible. This new procedure is based on the supposition that if the structure of the active site of a receptor or enzyme is known, then a custom-made compound can be developed to elicit the desired response, either by blocking or stimulating at this specific point.

This rational approach to drug design begins with elucidating the structure of the receptor and its active site or learning which parts of an enzyme alter key biological functions by using computer modeling techniques. Once such a prototype target has been determined, medicinal chemists can then endeavor to synthesize a series of chemical molecules that best fit the receptor or that most alter enzymatic functioning. This interplay among structure-activity relationships, computer modeling, and chemical synthesis can lead to better products for specially chosen needs. The challenge, of course, is to produce a highly specific compound for the targeted receptor with minimal activity at alternate sites and few, if any, interactions with other biological functions.

The computer has become a powerful instrument in the drug design process. Three-dimensional visualization of molecular structures and receptor sites has provided a tremendous technological tool for scientists to use.

IV. BIOTECHNOLOGY

Biotechnology products have gone from being just a glimpse into the future to becoming a commonplace means of drug production and discovery. Products derived from biotechnological research have been available now for over a decade. The first wave of these products replaced endogenous proteins and were used in natural quantities to restore what was lacking in the body's current state either because of a congenital condition or as the result of disease (such as insulin deficiencies in a patient with diabetes mellitus). The second wave consisted of products that are administered in greater-than-normal doses in order to elicit their pharmacological effect(s) on intrinsic functions. Some of the currently marketed biotechnology products are listed in Table 1.

These products will account for an increasingly growing proportion of the new drugs introduced for many years to come. However, major changes are already occurring in the discovery process for these medicinals. Because of the stomach's acidity, proteinaceous materials cannot be orally administered without being destroyed. Efforts are now being channeled toward a new process called small-molecule-structure–based drug design. This entails the

Table 1 Examples of Currently Marketed Biotechnology Drugs

Used to Replace Endogenous Proteins
Insulin (human)
Epoetin alfa (erythropoietin)
Somatropin (growth hormone)
Used in Greater-than-Normal Concentrations
Interferon (alfa and gamma)
Alteplase
Granulocyte colony-stimulating factor
Granulocyte-macrophage colony-stimulating factor

development and synthesis of smaller versions of these proteins, called "peptide mimetics" [7]. These products will be able to be taken by mouth and will be even more useful to a larger percentage of the patient population because they could be self-administered on an outpatient basis.

Substantial advancements in the discovery process and, hence, tremendous therapeutic breakthroughs will, more than likely, come from companies involved in biotechnological research. The larger, traditional pharmaceutical companies already have recognized this fact and are buying up these companies, are entering into partnerships with them, or are supplying research (venture) capital to them in order to remain competitive in the drug marketplace.

V. THE FUTURE—NANOTECHNOLOGY—DESIGNER MOLECULES

Technologies are now being created and evolving that will enable us to design and modify individual molecules for specific purposes. In the future (over the next couple of decades), methodologies will be discovered that will enable scientists to grasp, maneuver, and alter single molecules. *Nanotechnology* is the science of molecular synthesis, manipulation, and manufacturing [8]. It is derived from the word nanometer, one billionth of a meter, referring to the size of atoms and molecules.

With current manufacturing techniques, the pharmaceutical industry produces yields of their products in substantially higher proportions than those that would occur in reactions under natural conditions (i.e., the current state-of-the-art synthetic processes are much more efficient than nature). With nanotechnology, however, yields will approach 100 percent. Drug purity standards may no longer be necessary, at least from the standpoint of limiting the presence of impurities.

In addition to applying this technology to the products themselves, new delivery methods will also be developed. These systems will simply take the desired products directly to the target site or enzyme. This will reduce adverse consequences and increase positive therapeutic results.

VI. SUMMARY

New drug products help advance medical practice and improve the lives of the patients they are used to treat. Being the first company to develop a class of needed medicines is also very profitable. This helps drive the pharmaceutical industry to improve continuously its discovery processes and research methodologies.

In the past, serendipity and systemic, yet random, drug screenings were the major pathways to new drug products. Now, a more rational system is being utilized. In the future, individual molecular manipulation will be the way new drugs are "created."

An excellent, more detailed presentation of the evolution of the drug discovery process is presented by Drs. Vogt and Montagne in Chapter 4.

REFERENCES

1. G. M. Matoren (ed.), *The Clinical Research Process in the Pharmaceutical Industry*. Marcel Dekker, New York, 1984.
2. M. Montagne and B. Bleidt, Social forces impacting on the premature removal of drug products from the marketplace, *Clin. Res. Prac. Drug Reg. Aff.* *5*:83–127 (1987).
3. P. Ehrlich, Pro and contra Salvarsan, *Wien Med. Wochenschr.* *61*:14–19 (1910).
4. E. S. Neiss and T. A. Boyd, Pharmogenology: The industrial new drug development process, *The Clinical Research Process in the Pharmaceutical Industry* (G. M. Matoren, ed.), Marcel Dekker, New York, 1984.
5. L. H. Sternbach, The benzodiazepine story, *Prog. Drug Res.* *22*:229–266 (1978).
6. D. W. Cushman et al., Development and design of specific inhibitors of angiotensin-converting enzyme, *Am. J. Cardiol.* *49*:1390–1394 (1982).
7. M. L. Kleiberg and L. A. Wanke, New approaches and technologies in drug design and development, *Am. J. Health Syst. Pharm.* *52*:1323–1336 (1995).
8. G. M. Fahy, Molecular nanotechnology and its possible pharmaceutical implications, *2020 Visions: Health Care Information Standards and Technologies* (C. Bezold, J. A. Halperin, and J. L. Eng, eds.), United States Pharmacopeial Convention, Rockville, Maryland, 1993.

3

Planned Research and Chance Discovery in Pharmaceutical Development

Albert Hofmann*

Burg i.L., Switzerland

*Formerly Director of Research, Sandoz Pharmaceuticals, Basel, Switzerland.

These observations on the various ways in which new drugs are developed, on the opportunities thereby presented for planning and for research directed at a specific objective, and on the part that chance plays throughout this process are intended for a wider category of readers. The questions that these readers often put to the chemist engaged in pharmaceutical research, when they are confronted with the complicated formula of a new drug, are:

How was the compound with this chemical constitution discovered?
How was it possible to foresee that this particular compound would produce the specified therapeutic effect?

The answer, of course, is that it was *not* foreseen: the effect was first observed in the patient after the results of pharmacological tests in animals had indicated that a trial in humans would be reasonable.

We do not know *why* a particular pharmacological effect is associated with a particular chemical structure.

All over the world, enormous sums have been devoted to research, employing more and more costly methods and technology, to discover *how* known drugs produce their effects, what biochemical and electrophysiological mechanisms are involved, and which structures of the organism are targeted. A formidable mass of information about such mechanisms of action has already been accumulated. Today we can say of many drugs that we know *how* they act and in what way, but we are still quite unable to say *why* they act as they do. There are no known laws defining the relation between chemical constitution and pharmacological effects. *All knowledge of the relations between chemical structure and pharmacological action is ultimately based on empirical data.*

I. SOURCES OF EMPIRICAL KNOWLEDGE ABOUT DRUGS

What is the source of this empirical knowledge and how has it been acquired?

It springs from four separate sources:

1. From the ancient sources of folk medicine and from the study of the active principles of medicinal plants
2. From modern biological research, from the investigation of substances with physiological activity
3. From the pharmacological screening of a very large number of synthetic compounds and natural materials
4. From the observed effects of drugs in patients

A. The Investigation of Folk Medicine and Ancient Medicinal Plants

First, some observations on the sources of active compounds from plant materials. Until about 100 years ago, nearly all medicines were of vegetable origin; few were prepared from animal organs, or were of a mineral nature. The famous physicians of antiquity, of the Middle Ages, and of the Renaissance were all great botanists. Aesculapius, the mythical father of medicine, was instructed in the virtues of medicinal plants by the centaur Chiron on the slopes of Mount Pelion, where herbs grew in abundance.

Until the rise of pharmaceutical chemistry, this wealth of drugs was recorded in comprehensive herbals and pharmacopoeias; these in turn were based on the herbals of antiquity, especially that of Dioscorides, dating from the first century A.D., and that of Galen, from the second century A.D. To whom are we indebted for the information about the effects of particular plants that they contain? They are unknown, nameless discoverers. It may well be that this knowledge was acquired empirically, in the course of searching for food in the vegetable kingdom, or, as is often supposed, the first human beings were already endowed with instincts that enabled them to recognize the curative properties of plants and to make use of them. At the beginning of scientific chemical pharmacy, it was possible to refer back to this reservoir of information; research projects were based on it and continue to be based on it to this day.

It was the knowledge of the narcotic, pain-relieving properties of poppy juice that induced the pharmacist Serturner to look for the active principle, and this led to the discovery of morphine. In consequence of this, many other medicinal plants were examined for the specific purpose of extracting the active principle, with the result that many alkaloids and non-nitrogenous substances were isolated in a pure form. In this way valuable medicines were discovered that have gained access to the pharmacopeia, either as the original natural substance, or in a chemically modified form. As examples of this one may cite morphine, atropine, quinine, digitoxin, ergotamine, and reserpine.

The most important of the old-established medicinal plants have been investigated, so that this once prolific source of new and valuable drugs is now almost exhausted.

Naturally, the development of drugs could not have proceeded without the collaboration of pharmacologists who tested the active principles isolated or chemically modified by the chemist and determined the activity and the toxicity by means of trials in animals; nor without the clinical research of physicians who tested the drugs picked out by the pharmacologists and established the proper indications and dosages by means of clinical trials in humans.

B. Physiologically Active Principles

Let us now turn to the second source of medicaments, the physiologically active principles. In this case, also, the chemist's work must begin with a starting material of known activity. In contrast with what we know about medicinal plants, this knowledge of particular pharmacological activities is not derived from old sources but is the product of modern biological research.

In this field, physiologists and pharmacologists have provided the basis for chemical research by investigating the functions of cells, tissues, and organ systems and also those of microorganisms. By way of example, one may mention the researchers whose work led to the isolation of insulin, adrenaline, the sex hormones, and the hormones of the adrenal cortex and the pituitary gland and so on, from which valuable medicaments have been developed.

Similarly, the discovery and isolation of the vitamins, and likewise of penicillin, are the products of this branch of pharmaceutical research.

Continuous refinement of the techniques and improvements in the instruments employed have yielded a wider and deeper understanding of the biochemistry of the cells, organs, and parts of organs. As soon as discrete activities have been localized, the chemist can begin the rewarding task of isolating the physiologically active principle, of elucidating its structure and, if possible, of synthesizing it and producing chemical modifications. At present, this is probably the most important and the most promising kind of research for obtaining new active substances that might possibly find medicinal applications. As a practical example, one might mention the discovery of new brain factors—peptides similar to endorphin—with analgesic properties. The medicaments resulting from this line of research have the further advantage that they are physiologically active principles that are natural to the body.

These first two routes for arriving at new medicaments have in common that both began with a known type of activity and proceed to the corresponding chemical structure by isolation of the active principle and elucidation of its constitution.

C. Pharmacological Screening

Another kind of approach, which involves proceeding from a known structure and looking for a corresponding activity, is employed for the investigation of synthetic compounds, and this is the third possibility for arriving at the relation between structure and activity.

The two possible lines of action open to a chemist engaged in research into synthetic compounds are governed by the screening program employed. If he is working within the scope of a general screening program, comprising all possible pharmacological, biological, and microbiological tests, no limits are imposed on his imagination in the synthesis of new compounds. He will synthesize as many new compounds as possible, or, at least, compounds that have not yet been submitted to pharmacological examination. He has no inkling of what sort of activity his substances may have—if, indeed, they have any activity whatsoever. Whether or not something useful is picked up in his pharmacological screening program is purely a matter of chance. A direct hit in the form of the establishment of a new relation between structure and activity (e.g., the 1,4-benzodiazepines, of which Librium was the first representative), although rare, is nevertheless always possible.

A screening program of a general type is much less frequently employed than is one directed at particular objectives (i.e., one restricted to tests for certain specified types of activity, such as the circulation, psychotropic activity, and blood glucose–reducing activity). A chemist who is engaged in such a directed project is no longer free to synthesize at random. He must restrict himself to substances that might be expected to exhibit the type of activity at which the particular project is directed, or to structures that he considers likely to have such activity in the light of knowledge acquired from the technical literature or from his own experience. He will then attempt to produce modifications of these that have not yet been pharmacologically tested. Original correlations between structure and activity rarely emerge from this kind of research, which is more likely to produce improvements on existing drugs.

D. Clinical Observation

We come now to the fourth source enumerated above, empirical knowledge of the activity of drugs derived from the effects actually observed in the patient.

Before any new drug with pharmacological activity—discovered by one of the three methods previously described—can gain admittance to the pharmacopeia, it must be judged and approved by the effects that it actually produces in the patient. However, because the pharmacological activity of a given substance usually shows considerable variation from one species to another, the type of action exhibited in humans very often differs from that in laboratory animals.

Not only is it impossible to predict the biological activity of a substance from its chemical structure, it is also impossible to predict its activity in human beings from the pattern of activity demonstrated in laboratory animals.

In consequence, only a very small percentage of the experimental products that come to clinical trial prove to be therapeutically useful in humans.

In recent years, the standards with which an experimental product must comply before the administrative authorities will permit it to be submitted to a clinical trial have been raised to an enormous extent. The reasons for this were the cases of toxicity, the worst being the thalidomide affair; most of the drug's damage (malformed infants were born to mothers who used it during pregnancy) did not result from any criminal negligence, but rather from the limited transferability of pharmacological data, such as toxicity, from laboratory animals to humans. The extensive data—on activity in various species of animal, on metabolism, and on toxicity—that must be submitted before a product is passed for clinical trial increase the cost of preclinical research to a level where it becomes almost intolerable, and thus it reduces the number of active substances that can be tested in humans and consequently the chance of finding new medicaments. But all preliminary trials in animals, however comprehensive they may be, cannot preclude the possibility of harmful side effects in humans with certainty.

The surprises that arise in the course of the clinical trial of an experimental product are, however, not necessarily of a disagreeable nature. Many useful activities of drugs have first come to light by being observed in the patient. The therapeutic effects shown in the trial were no less valuable, but they were not the ones that would have been expected from the type of pharmacological activity observed in animals. Alternatively, another case that has arisen many times is that medicaments that already had been introduced into therapy for particular indications were found in practice to have other valuable therapeutic effects, and there are many examples.

Isonicotinoyl-isopropylhydrazine (iproniazid), a bacteriostatic substance originally introduced into therapy for the treatment of tuberculosis, was found in practice to be also an antidepressant drug. A doctor observed that all the patients with tuberculosis that had been treated with this drug were strikingly cheerful.

The antidepressant properties of impramine—given as a tranquilizing agent—were similarly discovered by the effects produced in the patient.

Hydergine, a medicament belonging to the ergot group, was first introduced into therapy as an antihypertensive agent and for the promotion of peripheral perfusion, in the light of the pattern of pharmacological effects that it produced. In practice, what was particularly noticeable about this product was its alleviating influence on geriatric complaints; today, its principal application is in geriatrics.

A further example is the hypoglycemic activity of the aryl-sulfonyl-alkyl-urease of the type of tolbutamide, which was observed when a member of this class of compounds was undergoing clinical trial as a chemotherapeutic agent.

It is this unpredictability, the impossibility of designing rational chemical structures with specific pharmacological—let alone therapeutic—activity, the impossibility of this so-called "drug design" that sets bounds to planning in pharmaceutical research.

However, in proportion as planning is restricted, chance is unrestricted. Nevertheless, if those events that have been classed as accidental discoveries in pharmaceutical research are examined more closely, it turns out that what is involved is not mere luck, but rather *serendipity.* This word, which is ultimately derived from "Serendip" (the ancient name of Ceylon), was coined in 1754 by the writer Horace Walpole, from the title of the fairy tale "The Three Princes of Serendip"; the heroes of this tale "were always making discoveries, by accidents and sagacity, of things that they were not in quest of."

Thus, the discovery of the antidepressant activity of imipramine while it was being tested as a major tranquilizer, and of iproniazid while it was being tested as a tuberculostatic agent, is not a matter of blind chance, but rather serendipity, which always implies some degree of intelligent observation. At this point, one may well quote Pasteur's words: "In the field of observation, chance favors only the prepared mind."

In the next section, I propose to illustrate this theme by means of various experiences drawn from my own career.

II. EXAMPLES FROM SANDOZ RESEARCH

An example of a program of research corresponding precisely to the procedure of investigating folk medicines and plant materials is provided by the working plan that Prof. Arthur Stoll drew up for the Pharmaceutical Division of Sandoz, when he founded it in 1917: the isolation in pure and undamaged form of the active principles of tried and tested medicinal plants, in order to make them available to the physician as a stable form of the pure substance suitable for accurate dispensing by weight. For this purpose, Stoll and his colleagues developed new and delicate methods of isolation and purification.

Two drugs that were included in the program from the very beginning were ergot and squill (scilla maritima). Squill had already been used by the ancient Egyptians for the treatment of dropsy. There is evidence that midwives had been using ergot to stimulate labor contractions since the Middle Ages. The information available about the character of the components of these drugs included contradictory data.

A. A Natural Ergot Alkaloid, Ergotamine (Gynergen)

Stoll soon succeeded in isolating a crystalline alkaloid from ergot, and he named it "ergotamine." Ergotamine was the first chemically homogeneous alkaloid obtained from ergot. As early as 1906, an amorphous alkaloid preparation had been isolated by the Englishmen Barger and Carr, and they designated it "ergotoxine" because its pharmacological properties were predominantly of a toxic nature. Ergotamine, on the other hand, showed the kinds of activity attributed to the whole drug: a contracting action of the uterus and a sedative action on the sympathetic nervous system. Ergotamine was accepted into gynecology under the proprietary name Gynergen as a medicament for staunching postpartum hemorrhage, and into internal medicine as a sympatholytic and a central sedative agent. It seemed that the problem of ergot had been solved.

In 1932, however, an English gynecologist, Dr. Chassar Moir, demonstrated that aqueous extracts of ergot exerted a strong uterotonic effect that could not be attributed to the presence of ergotamine, this alkaloid being practically insoluble in water. Three years later, this water-soluble alkaloid with a specific action on the uterus was isolated independently in four different laboratories, one of them the Sandoz laboratory. This new ergot alkaloid was called "ergometrine" in England, while Stoll and Burckhardt in Basle called it "ergobasine," and it was subsequently named "ergonovine" by the international pharmacopeial commission. A year earlier, Jacob and Craig at the Rockefeller Institute in New York had discovered the moiety that is common to all ergot alkaloids, which they named "lysergic acid," and they were then able to show that the alkaline hydrolysis of ergobasine yields lysergic acid and the amino-alcohol L-2 aminopropanol. The constitution of ergotamine and ergotoxine was shown to be more complex: the lysergic acid in these compounds is attached to a residue of a tripeptide nature.

At that moment I had just concluded my first major piece of research in Stoll's laboratory: the elucidation of the structure of the basic framework of scilla-glycosides. As I had a free hand to undertake a new project, I suggested to Prof. Stoll that I might attempt a partial synthesis of ergobasine (i.e., a synthesis starting with lysergic acid). This was not merely of scientific but also of practical interest, because ergobasine, which was of medicinal value, was present in ergot only in very small amounts in comparison with alkaloids like ergotamine and ergotoxine.

Prof. Stoll warned me of the difficulties that were likely to rise, in view of the great instability of the ergot alkaloids, but he consented to the proposed experiments.

I could not use ergotamine as a source of the lysergic acid required for the synthesis but was obliged to use ergotoxine, which was cheaper and which was also being extracted on a considerable scale at the time during the Sandoz production of ergot alkaloids.

Certain observations that I made while purifying ergotoxine for the hydrolytic experiments first aroused my suspicions that ergotoxine was not a homogeneous alkaloid. Thus, in experiments directed toward the synthesis of ergobasine, I encountered the ergotoxine problem, the solution of which at a later date led to an important pharmaceutical product.

After the initial difficulties caused by the great instability of lysergic acid, I found that Curtius's method afforded the means of coupling lysergic acid with amines through an acid-amide type of linkage. In the first stage of the synthesis, during the production of the hydrazide, the lysergic acid is racemized and isomerized. The resolution of the racemic isolysergic acid hydrazide into its optical antipodes was achieved by the use of di-*p*-toluyl-L-tartaric acid, one of the substituted tartaric acids specially produced for this purpose. When the azide of *d*-lysergic acid reacted with L-2-aminopropanol, a compound was obtained that was identical with ergobasine. Thus, for the first time, the partial synthesis of a naturally occurring ergot alkaloid was achieved (see Fig. 1).

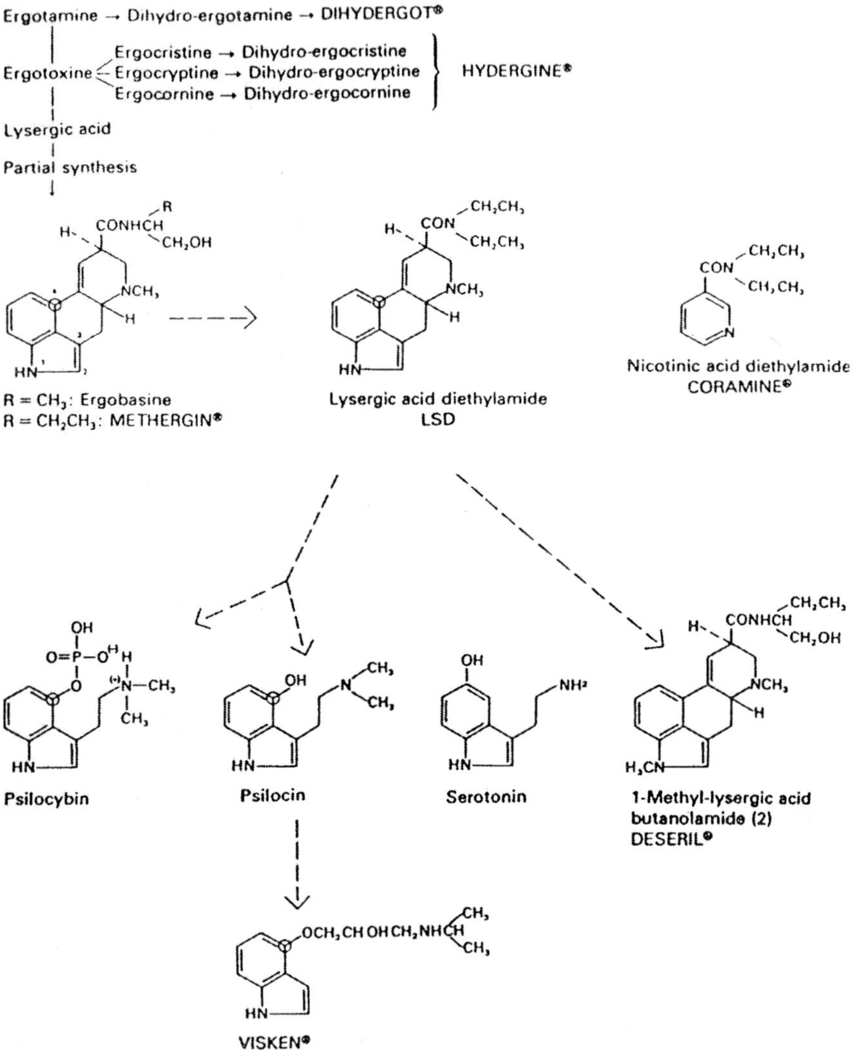

Ergotamine → Dihydro-ergotamine → DIHYDERGOT®

Ergotoxine:
- Ergocristine → Dihydro-ergocristine
- Ergocryptine → Dihydro-ergocryptine
- Ergocornine → Dihydro-ergocornine

} HYDERGINE®

Lysergic acid

Partial synthesis

R = CH_3: Ergobasine
R = CH_2CH_3: METHERGIN®

Lysergic acid diethylamide
LSD

Nicotinic acid diethylamide
CORAMINE®

Psilocybin

Psilocin

Serotonin

1-Methyl-lysergic acid butanolamide (2)
DESERIL®

VISKEN®

Fig. 1 Partial synthesis of a naturally occurring ergot alkaloid.

B. A Semisynthetic Ergot Derivative (Methergin)

Taking ergobasine as the prototype and employing this method of synthesis, it was now possible to plan a project with the objective of producing oxytocic compounds (compounds stimulating contraction of the uterus). In the course of this project, my colleague, Dr. J. Peyer, developed a rational method for the production of homologous amino-alcohols (i.e., amino-alcohols with carbon chains of various lengths), which I coupled with the lysergic acid by means of an amide link. The resultant chemical modifications of ergobasine were then tested in Prof. Ernst Rothlin's pharmacological department in a special screening procedure designed for the detection of oxytocic activity. The next higher homologue of ergobasine, the modification with one more carbon atom in the side chain, *d*-lysergic acid-L-butanolamide, showed optimum pharmacological properties. This compound was introduced into obstetrics in the form of the salt with maleic acid under the proprietary name Methergin, and it is now the leading product for staunching postpartum hemorrhage.

The development of Methergin from ergobasine is an example of the transformation of a prototype with no more than a trifling modification of the molecule. In such a case it may be expected that the general pattern of activity will be retained and that merely quantitative changes will occur. If, on the other hand, considerable variations are introduced into the structure of the prototype, changes of a qualitative nature in the pharmacological activity must be expected accordingly, although these can hardly be predicted. Nevertheless, in this case also, the chemist does not usually introduce modifications at random, but rather according to speculations based on structural models with a known activity. It is in the selection of these models that the chemist can bring into play what may be termed feeling or intuition.

C. A Further Semisynthetic Ergot Derivative—LSD

Lysergic acid diethylamide, which I produced by the method of synthesis developed for ergobasine, was a speculative modification of this kind. The model for this compound was nicotinic acid diethylamide, which is an established analeptic (circulatory and respiratory stimulant), available under the proprietary name Coramine. As the D-ring of lysergic acid is a modified nicotinic acid ring, I hoped that the new compound, lysergic acid diethylamide, would also have analeptic properties.

In Professor Rothlin's report on the pharmacological activity of lysergic acid diethylamide, the oxytocic activity was estimated to be 70% that of ergobasine. It was also noted that the animals were restless under the anesthetic. This new compound with the laboratory designation LSD 25 (the 25th compound synthesized in the series of lysergic acid amides) did not arouse any further pharmacological interest, however.

I had expected something more from the pharmacological examination, although this was no more than my feeling at the time. Five years after this first synthesis, I prepared a further small quantity of LSD 25, in order to submit it to a more extensive examination. As in the first production, it was no more than a few hundredths of a gram. It was necessary to separate the product of the synthesis from isolysergic acid isomers by chromatography on an alox column and I used dichloroethylene as a solvent. The lysergic acid diethylamide was then crystallized from methanol as the tartrate. That afternoon, while engaged in this, I drifted into an eerie, dreamlike state. I went home early and was impelled to lie down and close my eyes. In this condition I had a vision of fantastic shapes and colors. Whatever thought I entertained was instantly present to my mind's eye as a plastic image, which seemed to be part of the real world. This extraordinary state of consciousness was not unpleasant and it passed after a few hours.

I suspected that these hallucinations were the result of some sort of laboratory intoxication, and I immediately thought of the dichloroethylene that I had been using for the chromatography. The next day in the laboratory, I cautiously inhaled the vapors of this solvent. Nothing happened. Then I tested the lysergic acid diethylamide, which I had also been handling on the day of the incident. However, because I was in the habit of taking precautions when dealing with ergot alkaloids, I did not really believe that I could conceivably have absorbed enough of this substance to produce any effect. If the LSD 25 was the actual cause of the disturbance, then it must be an extraordinarily powerful substance. Being a cautious fellow, I therefore began to experiment on myself with the smallest amount of the suspected substance that could be expected to produce any effect, 0.25 milligrams of lysergic acid diethylamide tartrate, intending to increase the dose gradually. There was, however, no occasion for this. Even the first minimum dose of one quarter of a milligram induced a state of intoxication with very severe psychic disturbances, and this persisted for about 12 hours. These profound and revolutionary changes in the experience of the external world and in the sense of identity have already been sufficiently described, so that there is no need for me to add my account. This first planned experiment with LSD was a particularly terrifying experience because at the time, I had no means of knowing if I should ever return to everyday reality and be restored to a normal state of consciousness. It was only when I became aware of the gradual reinstatement of the old familiar world of reality that I was able to enjoy this greatly enhanced visionary experience.

In LSD, a psychotropic substance of unprecedented potency had been discovered. I had been looking for a circulatory stimulant and I had found a psychic stimulant. Serendipity was the way. Despite all my precautions, the dose that I had selected for this first planned LSD experiment was five times as much as the mean effective dose, which is only about 0.05 mg. To form some conception of the potency of LSD, it is only necessary to consider that 1 g would be enough to keep 20,000 human beings in a state of hallucinogenic intoxication for 12 hours.

The highly specific psychotropic activity of LSD made it a valuable tool for psychiatric and neurophysiological research. LSD has also found applications as a medicinal adjunct in psychoanalysis and in psychotherapy. However, LSD research suffered a severe setback, from which it has not yet recovered, when LSD was first caught up in the wave of drug-taking in the United States and figured in the headlines as "Drug No. 1" for a time during the sixties. This diversion to the "drug scene" is an abuse of LSD that is altogether at variance with its real character; it led to numerous incidents, some of which were of a serious nature, and it has undoubtedly done a great disservice to LSD research. In my opinion, the last word has not yet been said about the possible medical applications of this drug.

We come now to a characteristic of pharmaceutical research that finds little expression in scientific publications. This consists in the fact that the byways of research often lead to more significant results than the high road selected as the basis for the plan. One can sometimes reach such a fruitful side road by following up so-called chance observations, always assuming that this is permissible and is not precluded by the constraints that a strictly directed program imposes on the chemist.

I found myself on just such a fruitful byroad when I followed up the observations that I had made during the purification of ergotoxine that was to be used as the starting material for the synthesis of ergobasine. As I already mentioned, I had the impression that ergotoxine was not a homogeneous alkaloid.

Lysergic acid derivatives do not form salts readily, but I found that they would combine with the di-para-toluyl-tartaric acid that I had developed for the resolution of racemic isolysergic acid hydrazide to yield salts that crystallized very well. With this acid, ergotoxine likewise formed a magnificently crystalline salt, or rather a mixture of salts, for the fractional crystallization of the di-para-toluyltartrate of ergotoxine actually yielded three distinct crystalline products that differed in solubility. The alkaloids isolated from them crystallized spontaneously. One of these was identical with an alkaloid that Stoll and Burckhardt had recently isolated in the course of Sandoz ergot production and which they had name ergocristine. Both of the others were new. I named one ergocornine and the other ergocryptine, because it had remained hidden in the mother liquor for such a long time. It was demonstrated many years later that ergocryptine occurs in the form of two structural isomers, which we designated α-ergocryptine and β-ergocryptine.

D. Hydrogenated Ergot Alkaloids (Hydergine and Dihydergot)

The resolution of ergotoxine, which had been regarded as a homogeneous alkaloid for more than 30 years, into three or four homogeneous alkaloids provided a new and confirmed basis for further pharmacological investigations. The literature contained contradictory data on the pharmacological activity of ergotoxine; these had obviously arisen because various investigators had been working with different ergotoxine preparations, and the relative proportions of components of ergotoxine preparations from different sources varied considerably. I supplied to Professor Rothlin for pharmacological investigation not only the homogeneous components of ergotoxine, but also their dihydro-derivatives. Jacobs and Craig of the Rockefeller Institute had shown that the exocyclic double bond of lysergic acid can be selectively hydrogenated and that dihydrolysergic acid is stable, whereas lysergic acid and its derivatives exist in solution as an equilibrium mixture of the lysergic acid form and the isolysergic acid form. The pharmacological activity of the isolysergic acid derivatives is much weaker than that of the corresponding lysergic acid derivatives. Prof. Rothlin and his colleagues in the pharmacological department found that the ergotoxine alkaloids stabilized by hydrogenation exhibited an interesting pattern of activity that differed considerably from that of the natural nonhydrogenated alkaloids. There was dilatation of the blood vessels instead of contraction and reduction in blood pressure, stronger sympatholytic properties, and greatly reduced toxicity. In view of this pattern of activity, the dihydro-derivatives of the three ergotoxine alkaloids—in the ratio 1:1:1—in the form of their water-soluble methane-sulfonates were introduced into therapy under the proprietary name Hydergine. As mentioned above, Hydergine did not become established as an antihypertensive, but in practice it proved to be an effective geriatric agent; in terms of sales it now stands well at the head of the Sandoz list of pharmaceutical products.

At that time I also hydrogenated ergotamine and submitted dihydroergotamine for pharmacological testing. The principal purpose was to produce not a pharmacologically different derivative, but rather a stabilized ergotamine. Ergotamine solutions that were available in the form of ergotamine tartrate under the proprietary name Gynergen had the disadvantage that a high proportion of the ergotamine they contained was transformed into the corresponding isolysergic acid alkaloid ergotaminine, which is pharmacologically inactive. We hoped that the stabilizing influence of hydrogenation would prevent this. The hydrogenation, however, had not merely a stabilizing effect, but, as with the alkaloids of the ergotoxine group, caused profound changes in the pattern of pharmacological activity. Dihydroergotamine, in contrast with ergotamine, instead of causing contraction of the blood vessels, exerted a stabilizing effect on the blood vessels and on the blood pressure; it exhibited increased sympatholytic properties and reduced toxicity. This pattern of pharmacological activity proved to be therapeutically useful. Under the proprietary name Dihydergot, dihydroergotamine has found a place in therapy for the treatment of postural hypotension and vascular headache. What was planned was the stabilization of ergotamine; what was found was a new medicament.

Let me now go back once more to LSD. Although LSD itself could not be developed into a therapeutically useful pharmaceutical product, nevertheless, as indicated below, it provided the stimulus for the development of a new drug; in addition, it has led indirectly to the production of a further pharmaceutical product. This is an example of a not uncommon way in which new drugs are found.

E. LSD as a Serotonin Antagonist Leads to Deseril

The English physiologist J. H. Gaddum showed that LSD is an extremely active antagonist of serotonin. Serotonin is an endogenous active substance that is widespread in warm-blooded animals. It is a neurotransmitter that also plays a part in the biochemistry of psychic functions. As serotonin is involved in inflammatory processes and in certain forms of migraine, a serotonin inhibitor might possibly exhibit therapeutic properties. LSD itself could not be used as a therapeutic serotonin inhibitor, because of its psychic hallucinogenic properties. Our pharmacologists therefore suggested that we look for a chemical modification of LSD that retained the serotonin antagonism, but not the hallucinogenic properties of LSD. Out of the many

LSD derivatives prepared by Dr. Franz Troxler, who was my coworker at the time, bromo-LSD proved to be the first serotonin antagonist without the hallucinogenic components of the activity. When the search was extended to other derivatives of lysergic acid, the optimum serotonin-antagonist was found to be l-methyl-lysergic acid butanolamide. Under the proprietary name of Sansert (Deseril), this product was introduced into therapy for the prophylactic treatment of migraine.

Finally, I should like to refer briefly to a further investigation that LSD has brought into our company.

F. From LSD to the Mexican Magic Mushroom

In spring 1957, through the mediation of Dr. Dunant, the director of Sandoz Paris at the time, Professor Roger Heim, the director of the Laboratory of Cryptogamy in Paris, approached the Chemical Research Department of the Pharmaceutical Division of Sandoz Basel and asked if we would like to collaborate in the chemical investigation of the Mexican magic mushroom. I accepted his proposal with pleasure. Professor Heim had made a botanical identification of the fungus used by certain Mexican Indians in their religious rituals and for various healing practices of a magical nature; he had also succeeded in cultivating some of the new species of fungus, which were predominantly strains belonging to the genus *Psilocybe*, in the laboratory. The age-old secret cult of the Mexican Indians had been rediscovered in 1954–1956 by two American investigators, Mr. and Mrs. Wasson. After attempts to isolate the active principle of the mushrooms in Paris and in two laboratories in the United States had proved fruitless, Prof. Heim turned to us; he thought that, thanks to our experience with LSD, which had properties that were qualitatively the same as those of the magic mushroom, we might be better placed to solve this problem. In this way, LSD introduced the magic mushroom into our laboratory.

As none of my colleagues showed any enthusiasm for the examination of the mushroom (at that time anything that was in some way connected with LSD was unpopular with the senior management), I undertook the isolation experiments myself together with my trusty assistant, Mr. Hans Tscherter, who had worked with me for many years.

Drs. Arthur Brack and Hans Kobel, my colleagues in the microbiological laboratory at the time, succeeded in making a considerable improvement in the cultivation of *Psilocybe mexicana* in the laboratory. With this material, and thanks to the testing of the extract on myself and several of my colleagues and assistants, who volunteered to serve as guinea pigs—tests in animals having yielded no clear results—we succeeded in isolating the active principles and in crystallizing them in a pure form. We named these substances psilocin and psilocybin.

When the pure active substances became available, it was possible—by joining forces with my coworkers Dr. A. Frey, Dr. H. Ott, Dr. Th. Petrzilka and Dr. F. Troxler—to elucidate the structure and to carry out the synthesis.

The structure of the active principle of the mushrooms is remarkable, among other reasons, because—like lysergic acid and, hence, like LSD—it is an indole derivative with a substituent in the number 4 position, and because it is closely related to serotonin. In my opinion, psilocybin and psilocin deserve further study in experimental psychiatry in themselves as as prototypes for chemical modifications.

The psilocybian research, however, had further practical consequences and, like LSD, it led indirectly to an important new medicament.

G. From the Mexican Mushroom to Visken

Dr. Troxler, who had developed a rational synthesis for 4-hydroxyindole, the starting material for psilocybin, was in consequence engaged in a project designed to develop new substances with an inhibiting effect on beta-adrenergic receptors. Beta-adrenergic receptor inhibitors are employed therapeutically to regulate cardiac function. Propranolol (Inderal) was a known prototype with this kind of activity. It had been found that substances with this type of activity are obtained if the isopropylamino-2-hydroxypropyl side chain that is characteristic of propranolol is connected with an aromatic system with a phenol hydroxyl group through an ether-like linkage. Among the many phenols used by Dr. Troxler for the synthesis of his substances that were to be tested as beta-adrenergic receptor inhibitors was 4-hydroxyindole, which was available only in his laboratory. This was the very combination that turned out to be a direct hit. Under the proprietary name Visken, this new drug has acquired a leading position among the beta-adrenergic receptor inhibitors, especially for the treatment of hypertension.

Without LSD, the magic mushroom would never have entered our laboratory; without the work on the magic mushroom, 4-hydroxyindole would not have been available, and consequently Visken would not have been discovered. In conclusion, I hope that my remarks have served to show that pharmaceutical research does not, and indeed could not, always proceed as rigidly along the planned lines as might appear from the publications in the technical journals (which are mostly highly stylized from the scientific point of view)—but that chance, or rather what Walpole called "serendipity," has very often contributed much more to success and will probably continue to do so in the future.

REFERENCES

B. Berde and H. O. Schild, *Ergot Alkaloids and Related Compounds*, Springer, New York, 1978.

A. Hofmann, *Die Mutterkornalkaloide*, Ferdinand Enke, Stuttgart, 1964.

A. Hofmann, LSD—My Problem Child, Tarcher, Los Angeles, 1983.

A. Hofmann, R. Heim, A. Brack, H. Kobel, A. Frey, H. Ott, T. Petrzilka, and F. Troxler. Psilocybin und Psilocin, zwei psychotrope Wirkstoffe aus mexikanischen Zauberpilzen, *Helv. Chim. Acta 42*:1557 (1959).

R. E. Schultes and A. Hofmann, *The Botany and Chemistry of Hallucinogens*, 2nd Ed., Charles C. Thomas, Springfield, IL, 1980.

4

A Brief History of Clinical Research in Pharmaceutical Development

Donald D. Vogt

Limestone, Tennessee

Michael Montagne

Massachusetts College of Pharmacy and Allied Health Sciences
Boston, Massachusetts

> Substances able to exert their final action exclusively on the parasite harbored within the organism would represent, so to speak, *magic bullets* which seek their target of their own accord.
>
> —P. Ehrlich, 1906 [1]

> The newest strategies for drug development and evaluation are biotechnology and computer-assisted molecular modeling and genetic engineering. [These] techniques allow testing and refining of potentially beneficial substances *before* laboratory testing occurs.
>
> —L. Basara and M. Montagne, 1994 [2]

I. INTRODUCTION

Within this century, there have been several paradigmatic shifts in the approach to the discovery and development of drugs: the testing of natural (plant) substances for useful biological properties; the clinically empirical analysis (i.e., screening) of large numbers of substances for desirable physiological activity in model organisms; and the systematic molecular manipulation of original or parent compounds to optimize their pharmacological properties. More recently, computer-assisted molecular modeling has permitted the testing and refining of ideas before laboratory work is undertaken. The contemporary paradigm of drug development evolved from the concept of drug-receptor interactions. The drug-receptor theory is epitomized by the elucidation of structure-activity relationships between chemical substances and physiological receptors, and it has been useful in explaining the activity of known drugs and more recently in designing new drug molecules [2].

During the first decades of the present century, a paradigmatic shift in therapeutics is also discernible. The traditional centuries-old drug armamentarium had been largely superseded in practice in the nineteenth century by such drug entities as the alkaloids, endocrines, and the antisera of Emil von Behring. After 1906, Paul Ehrlich's concept of chemotherapy was seminal to a new era in therapeutics; the search for "magic bullets" had begun. Through much of the nineteenth century, the pharmaceutical industry prepared dosage forms of the traditional material medica in response to a demand by practitioners. The development of totally new drug entities reversed the relationship between medical practice and industry in which the latter would increasingly lead innovations in practice. Particularly after 1930, determination of the rational medical uses of drugs through informal experience in practice with different patients was no longer considered adequate or safe. At the same time, the drug industry was called upon to provide something more than assurance of quality; the innovators were now also creating the knowledge of drug use and transferring this knowledge to the practitioner.

One of the principal problems of the industry has been to formalize and to ensure the integrity of the clinical research process. Idiosyncratic empirical studies by independent practitioners have largely been replaced by a more tractable process of controlled clinical experimentation to provide assurances of safety and efficacy within acceptable limits. Instead of a methodic study and observation of the effects of an unknown chemical, contemporary therapeutics hypothesizes the main effects a priori and places the drug on "trial" to prove pharmacological activity (i.e., efficacy) and to determine the significance of side effects (i.e., safety).

II. DEVELOPMENT OF THE PHARMACEUTICAL INDUSTRY

By the end of the nineteenth century, pharmaceutical technology had become largely industrialized. Medicinal products that formerly had been prepared secundum artum were being manufactured for large-scale wholesale distribution. Many of the manufactured ethical drug dosage forms were, in contemporary terms, inactive or useless. The industry had not been called upon to determine safety and efficacy. The more responsible companies employed botanists to detect adulterated or inferior crude drugs. In some companies, such as Parke-Davis and Eli Lilly, chemists were assaying fluid extracts and other products for purity and uniformity. Research was limited essentially to problems of production.

Until World War I, German hegemony in fine chemicals, including pharmaceuticals, was virtually uncontested [3]. Expansion of this science-based industry had been an important facet of Germany's rapid industrialization and economic growth, especially after the Franco-Prussian War. German universities had developed highly competent chemists capable of translating scientific advances into technological progress. Even more important, there was a highly trained core of professional chemists capable of carrying out systematic research in close association with German industry.

In general, most of the important pharmaceuticals that were produced in this country were controlled by German-owned interests and patents. With the onset of World War I, the halt of German imports necessitated a complete restructuring of the American chemical industry, and more particularly pharmaceuticals. The American Council of National Defense, during the summer of 1917, authorized the Federal Trade Commission to issue nonexclusive licenses to domestic manufacturers for the production of pharmaceuticals formerly protected by German patents.

American fine chemical manufacturers, including the drug makers, entered the 1920s with the proceeds from the highly profitable war years, newer plants and equipment, improved methods of production with special regard for the basic principles of chemical engineering, an awareness of economic and technical efficiency in production, low federal taxes and interest rates, a growing domestic market, and a new tariff law. The economic stage was set for the coming research revolution.

By the mid-1930s, American pharmaceuticals were within the realm of "big business." Extensive plant and equipment had been devoted to the commercial production of biological products, particularly antisera and vaccines. Almost overnight, these investments were threatened by the rapid advent of the sulfonamides. In most industries, cost-cutting innovations, process improvements, new applications, and similar changes do not ordinarily exert undue pressure upon an entire industry. In the pharmaceutical industry, the impact of the sulfonamides was profound. Over 6000 derivatives of sulfanilamide were prepared and tested for antibacterial and toxicological activities.

The drug industry had felt the first blasts of J. A. Schumpeter's "perennial gale of creative destruction." Henceforth, innovation would be the key to industrial growth in drugs and institutionalized research and development (R&D) would be the instrument by which a continuous process of innovation would be accomplished. There remained the ever-present possibility that a new development might occur at any time, the discovery of a new and more effective sulfonamide or an entirely new antibacterial entity. This focused attention on the problems of investment in plant and processes that might become obsolete overnight, and on recovering costs and a reasonable profit as quickly as possible.

In the period after World War II, the 1950s were again years of active growth in the pharmaceutical industry. The general prosperity resulted in the rapid amortization of plant and equipment. Rapid growth, characterized by a stream of new products, enabled pharmaceutical manufacturers to increase production, raise wages, maintain prices at a remarkably even level, pay attractive dividends, provide internal funds for modernization and expansion, and more significantly, finance R&D. One of the dominant economic strengths was the accumulation of liquid capital. Tax reductions built faster and stayed higher in those instances where new equipment and processes were rapidly introduced. The flow of new products was essential to keep pace with the rapid increase in capital stock and vice versa. The rate of capital investment increased with innovational change and the rate of profit also increased. Internally funded R&D became institutionalized.

III. GENESIS OF THE CLINICAL RESEARCH PROCESS

The development of the research process probably had its genesis in Renaissance Europe, becoming fully evolved as a self-conscious process in the seventeenth century [3]. Early Greek philosophers constructed a system of explaining natural phenomena on the basis of speculative reflection. Hippocratic medicine was based both on a knowledge of the natural sciences of the time and, more important, on clear and rational reasoning of cause-and-effect relationships. Emphasis was placed on the value of practical observation of the process of disease rather than on theory.

Galen was the principal authority in anatomy and physiology until the seventeenth century. It was not until the dogma was challenged by Renaissance scholars that modern medical science could begin to take shape. The authority of Galen was tested by Andreas Vesalius, who demonstrated in his *De Humani Corporis Fabrica* (1543) serious discrepancies in Galen's anatomic teachings. William Harvey's *De Motu Cordis* (1628) integrated known but ineffective facts into a new comprehensive generalization. His theory was fully supported by experimentation. Harvey was but one participant among many in a "scientific revolution," demonstrating by experiment and accessory evidence a conclusion that was diametrically opposed to traditional assumptions [4,5].

In the eighteenth century, William Withering introduced the rational clinical use of digitalis through controlled clinical experimentation. His 10-year study of digitalis and his clinical findings, based on 163 case histories, was published in 1785 [6]. Francois Magendie, a nineteenth-century French clinician, was the acknowledged founder of experimental physiology. The chemical isolation of the alkaloids and the halogens afforded clinicians and physiologists a number of chemically pure substances of known composition, which allowed for true quantitative experiments. This had not been possible with the old extracts and raw substances with their uncertain concentrations of active principles. Working with the various recently isolated alkaloids, Magendie proceeded in a rational order: preparation of the substance from raw materials; determination of the physical and chemical properties; effects on animals; effects on healthy and diseased human subjects; indications; and application in various dosage forms [7].

Magendie's pharmacological research was continued by his pupil Claude Bernard. His *Introduction to Experimental Medicine*, published in 1865, synthesized the basic philosophic ideas of the nineteenth-century physiologists. He insisted on proof and counterproof in confirming experiential data as expressions of philosophic doubt carried as far as possible [8]. It was in the Paris School of clinicians that systematic clinical studies became routine through the influence of Pierre Louis, who introduced his numerical (i.e., statistical) method in the 1820s. Although not the first clinician to use statistics, Louis was the founder of medical, as opposed to vital, statistics [9].

The concept of clinical study in a patient population and the use of control groups in the design of experiments may have began with James Lind. His epochal *Treatise on the Scurvy* was published in 1753:

> [I] took twelve patients . . . with scurvy. . . . Their cases were as similar as I could have them. . . . They lay together in one place and had one diet common to all. Two of these were ordered each a quart of cyder a day. Two others took twenty-five drops of elixir of vitriol three times a day upon an empty stomach. Two others took two spoonfuls of vinegar three times a day. . . . Two of the worst patients were put upon a course of seawater. Of this they drank half a pint every day. The two remaining patients took an electuary recommended by a hospital surgeon made of garlic, the most sudden and visible good effects were perceived from the use of oranges and lemons, one of those who had taken them being at the end of six days fit for duty. The other was the best recovered of any in his condition [10].

Almost half a century later, in 1798, Edward Jenner performed controlled experiments in humans to assess the value of vaccination against smallpox [6]. However, the use of a control group for comparative purposes was not realized until the twentieth century.

A. The Scientific Method

The scientific method evolved from Rene Descartes' work in geometry and was given its first description in his *Discourse on Method* (1637). Descartes suggested the application of specific mathematical methods to all types of scientific inquiry, outlining a method for analysis that still dominates medical research today. The major tenets of this method are a priori reasoning and a physicalistic approach, epitomized today by quantitative, experimental designs in studying phenomena. John Graunt undertook the first attempt to interpret mass biological phenomena and social behavior from numerical data (births and deaths in London) in his treatise *Natural and Political Observations Made Upon the Bills of Mortality* (1662).

Jacob Bernoulli's *Ars Conjectandi* (1713), the first attempt at deducing statistical measures from individual probabilities, resulted in what is referred to today as the Law of Large Numbers. These first attempts at analyzing phenomena through the use of numbers, forerunners of modern statistical methods, were refined and standardized in the nineteenth century in the surge of activity and development in mathematics, philosophy, and all the sciences in general. Both Carl Friedrich Gauss's *Disquisitions Arithmetical* (1801) and Pierre de Laplace's *Theorie Analytique des Probabilities* (1812) were instrumental in refining current knowledge and in developing statistics as a mathematical discipline with potential application to social issues and industrial problems. These works formulated a framework for number theory, presented theories of probability, and set forth a calculus for determining the occurrence of chance events and the significance of error in scientific measurement.

The real breakthrough came at the turn of this century when a number of scientists began employing statistical measures in experiments and other research studies. They saw the process of interpreting research results as a statistical exercise, with the primary purpose of attempting to determine or explain the amount of error present in their measurement techniques. The development of the theory and practice of experimental designs, led by R. A. Fisher's *Statistical Methods for Research Workers* (1925) and *The Design of Experiments* (1935), signaled a shift to planning and performing experiments with the intent of controlling for errors or chance events. The basic work on experimental designs was undertaken in agricultural research, where a variety of alternative treatments were applied to plots of land, sometimes arranged in blocks, on which a particular crop was grown. Specific measurements were made at various points in time and analyzed comparatively to arrive at a set of results concerning the impact of the treatment given. Consequently, the contemporary experimental method is described as a comparative study of specific intervention or treatment (i.e., a drug entity) with alternative treatments or no treatment (i.e., the control group) involving the randomized selection and placement of cases (i.e., patients) into each of the various treatment groups.

The early use of experimental designs and statistical techniques were in agriculture and industry, where application to problems of product development, manufacturing efficiency and refinement, and quality assurance had a significant impact. The advantages of experimental designs (replication, randomization, and economy of arrangement) were well suited to industrial research. What resulted was a shift in emphasis concerning observational errors and other irregularities in our ability to scientifically examine and measure phenomena. Prior to this century, scientists, through theories of probability and random errors, attempted to fix statistical limits within which experimental results were acceptable despite variations. The change in emphasis to the design of experiments was an attempt to make certain that the structure of the research study is logical, that it is broad enough to serve as a foundation for inference, and that every recognizable and avoidable source of error has been eliminated. Of course, the theory of experimental designs has its own flaws and inherent problems, some of which are very complex—requiring solutions through additional strategies and techniques. As Fisher states, "Experimental observations are only experience carefully planned in advance" [11].

B. Clinical Drug Research: The Clinical Trial

The nature of clinical drug studies has also changed from auto-experimentation and direct screening in patients for potentially useful drugs to the multiphase testing of specific compounds, first in healthy subjects and then in those patients with the medical condition or symptomatology for which the compound was designed.

Auto-experimentation, wherein a researcher serves as a subject in his experiment, has been referred to as one of the strongest and yet unappreciated traditions in medical and drug research. Although some auto-experimental studies have resulted in tragic ends, many have led to important discoveries and breakthroughs, and a few have been seminal in opening and defining important categories of substances for extensive clinical research [12]. Additionally, such auto-experimentation probably had a profound influence on the individual researcher and practitioner in terms of the ethics of giving the drug to patients, the actual nature and extent of the effects present in the drug experience, and the therapeutic potential and indications of the drug in clinical therapy. Just as the individual clinical researcher has become part of a larger group of scientific specialists, so the intensely personal spirit of auto-experimentation has become a more detached and depersonalized statistical view with an emphasis on the process of research itself.

The pharmaceutical industry quickly adopted experimental designs to develop and screen new compounds, improve production, and test the drugs for therapeutic value. The full potential of experimental designs and controlled studies was realized in the 1940s and 1950s when, as part of the immense growth in knowledge and technology and the war effort, controlled clinical trials were adopted as a standard way of assessing the value of drug entities. Finally, in the 1960s, the controlled clinical trial became the norm of pharmaceutical research, when the double-blind strategy of testing (i.e., keeping both patient and observer unaware of the nature of the medication being given) was adopted for supposedly eliminating problems of the placebo phenomenon and other spurious factors. Regulations in the 1960s requiring the proof of efficacy for drug entities reinforced the importance of controlled clinical experiments and made them the standard method of pharmaceutical research.

Experimental studies, however, are not a perfected method, and clinical drug trials are not the only source of truly reliable medical evidence.

The objective of a clinical trial is to ensure a high probability that the better treatment is identified. Integral to this approach is the use of controls, a collection of patients who provide responses to which the effects of a specific therapy can be compared. The term "control" does not necessarily involve randomization, and a controlled clinical trial is not necessarily a randomized clinical trial. Controls may consist of patients receiving no treatment, different treatment, or the same treatment with a different dose or administered according to a different dosing schedule. When a control group is chosen by a method other than randomization, the researcher must assume either that the control and treatment groups are identical with respect to all important variables except the treatment under study or that all relevant differences can be corrected. The randomized trial is most useful and appropriate when the value of a new therapy is uncertain [13].

Many authors have pointed out the less than humanistic nature of medical experimentation and the problems of statistical and conceptual design of experiments, much of which are exacerbated by ethical issues and regulations on human experimentation. In considering the failure of the basic principles of biometric science to adequately evaluate the complex response of a human subject to a treatment, Feinstein [14] has noted that the therapeutic sciences are based on hard, precise, easily measured information (e.g., laboratory values, demographic data, financial costs) from which most of the uniquely human distinctions of people have been systematically excluded. For instance, the double-blind technique masks iatrotherapeutic and placebo effects, and the controlled clinical trial does not answer completely the questions of what happens to a patient when given a treatment and which of the many things that do happen are important in evaluating the worth of the treatment.

Tukey [15] has pointed out that demonstrated effectiveness, either quantitative or qualitative, is far from being perfected in clinical trials. He notes that even the term "clinical trial" has a wide variety of meanings from clinical inquiry, where some treatment is hoped to be of help to some class of patients not specified in advance and massive amounts of data are collected and analyzed, to the other extreme of focused clinical trial, where both the class of patients and the end point of therapy are specified in the initial protocol. He states that possible consequences of this confusion about what a clinical trial is include unbalanced boundaries of efficacy, the use of historical controls, and not very sequential designs in experimental studies.

C. Clinical Drug Research: Formalization of a Science

Many factors have shaped the scientific content of this highly specialized area of inquiry, both in the development of the preclinical sciences and the formalization of the controlled clinical research process.

One indication of the dynamic development of the preclinical sciences is exemplified by the dramatic restructuring of pharmacology. In 1926, pharmacology was considered to be that part of physiology that was concerned with the actions of substances other than foods upon the living organism. Pharmacology was modestly defined by some as "all scientific knowledge concerning drugs" [16]. Toxicology was described as the detection of the effects of poisons and the diagnosis and treatment of poisoning. Almost 30 years later, the mainstream of academic pharmacology and toxicology still retained much of this global scope [17].

On the other hand, there was evidence of a new approach. In 1931, James C. Munch published a classic study entitled *Bioassays: A Handbook of Quantitative Pharmacology*. This work demonstrated, among other things, that pharmacometrics had become detached from classical pharmacology. Further, the book contained much data relating to drug evaluation. At the same time, no effort was devoted to the problem of reliability. While such works were important, at that time problems were still being considered by the statistics of small numbers, up to the probability units. Later studies showed an increasing interest in statistical analysis of the biological evaluation of drugs that contributed to the control of the reliability of results. The concept of drug toxicity became much broader in scope to include, by the 1960s, drug allergies, blood dyscrasias, and teratogenic effects, as well as behavioral toxicity.

In the 1970s, social pharmacology began to describe a number of social factors that are important in drug-taking behaviors and experiences, many of which had been ignored to that time [18]. Prior to the experimentalistic approach developed in the twentieth century, all that physicians and scientists knew about the action of drugs was obtained from direct observation of their patients and subjects who had taken them for some purpose. It has been noted that what medical science knew of most psychoactive drugs, such as opium, cannabis, cocaine, ether, and chloroform, resulted from addicts' and other users' accounts of their addictions and drug-taking experiences [19]. However, with the advent of the currently favored sociotechnological approach, scientists and clinicians moved away from such observational data and began to perform experiments on subjects in laboratory settings.

What has resulted, in descriptions of effects for many drugs, is a dichotomy between drug taker and researcher. This difference in approach may be one reason why pharmacology has been unable to explain many types of drug-taking experiences and the placebo phenomenon. In many instances, especially with regard to social and nonmedical drug taking, users' descriptions vary with the normative pharmacological textbook account.

The development of the contemporary formalized clinical research process also was dependent on the emergence of a corps of highly skilled scientific research personnel, the organization of research, the favorable economic growth of the pharmaceutical industry, and by social forces exemplified by legislatively mandated objectives. Barber [20] has noted that the education and communication processes inherent in the training of research personnel and clinicians socializes these individuals into a specific and standard way of thinking and doing things, based on the normative mind-set (paradigm) of the status quo research establishment. The education and training that a future research chemist, pharmacologist, physician, or pharmacist receives will dictate, in most instances, how that individual will assume his or her role in an industrial or clinical setting.

Through much of the nineteenth century, American scientific education lagged behind that of Europe. The reform of medical education, neglected during the Civil War, was resumed in the 1870s. In the 1890s, the University of Pennsylvania set up a laboratory for clinical research and an associated institute of biology. In the Midwest, the University of Wisconsin and Northwestern University began regular courses in the newer preclinical sciences [3]. The first American Ph.D. in pharmacy was awarded at Wisconsin in 1902. Thirty years later, only 11 doctorates were awarded in the pharmaceutical sciences within the 1932/33 academic year in American institutions [21].

Until about 1900, American research had been generally associated with the university, with teaching and the advancement of knowledge. By 1950, foundations constituted the major source of private funds for research in the biomedical sciences. After 1913, Rockefeller boards contributed about $4 million to research in mental health, and the Rockefeller Foundation, in 1929, concentrated its medical research support in this field. This concentration of support by this and other foundations determined recruitment of research and teaching personnel and, more importantly, defined research areas. Other major foundations such as the Commonwealth, Macy, and Carnegie concentrated research funds in specific program areas as well as channeling interest at the expense of neglecting the broader spectrum of basic research [22].

IV. EVOLUTION OF THE DRUG REGULATORY PROCESS

Social expectations were considerably heightened by the advent of the "miracle drugs," sulfonamides, penicillin, and succeeding antibiotics. The dramatic quantum leaps in all areas of scientific endeavor during and after World War II appeared to many to signal the beginning of an age when all things were possible for science to accomplish, given sufficient support and the right focus. At the same time, serious doubts were being raised about the social responsibilities of the drug industry [23].

In general terms, before the 1930s, patients looked to their physicians for assurances of safe and efficacious therapy. The major pharmaceutical companies had largely assumed the responsibility for providing assurances of the quality of the raw material in their finished products, uniformity of potency, efficacy in terms of traditional therapeutic standards, stability, and elegance in appearance. The introduction of new chemical entities into therapeutics, particularly after midcentury, forced the industry to assume much of the ultimate responsibility for therapy. At the same time, the highly visible Congressional hearings of the 1950s and early 1960s led to a rather widely held social impression that the pharmaceutical industry was not acting in the public interest. The media were quick to capitalize on the problems that must inevitably arise in drug therapy. The profitability that had triggered and financed dramatic R&D programs was condemned as public exploitation. Many of these doubts influenced efforts toward governmental intervention, some of which were based on revisions of legislation passed in the early years of this century.

The Pure Food and Drugs Act of 1906 was primarily aimed toward the elimination of unclean and adulterated foods from the market. The legislation, secondarily, was directed toward patent medicine abuses. Prescription drugs were subject to control but received less attention. In 1923, there was an increased intensity in drug control work; attention was focused on the bioassay of important drugs and their preparations, with an emphasis on adherence to standards of purity.

The Food, Drug, and Cosmetic Act of 1938 was intended to protect the public against quackery and the sale of dangerous drugs. The Elixir of Sulfanilamide tragedy triggered an administrative procedure for premarketing clearance of new drugs of uncertain safety. Section 505 of the new act forbade the introduction of new drugs into interstate commerce without U.S. Food and Drug Administration (FDA) determination that the new drug application satisfied regulatory specifications.

The passage of the Harris-Kefauver Amendment of 1962 added a new dimension requiring the evaluation of a new drug's safety and efficacy. This legislation made the government an active participant in the search process, because FDA approval was required for testing procedures of investigational new drugs before testing could proceed for the filling of a new drug application. The FDA was administratively empowered to withdraw approval of a new drug application for a number of causes, including questions of the drug's safety or lack of substantial evidence of effectiveness. This substantial evidence was to consist of adequate and well-controlled investigations by scientific experts to evaluate the effectiveness of the drug involved so that the drug would elicit the effect it was purported to have under the conditions of use for which it would be prescribed.

In 1970, "substantial evidence" was defined in greater detail. Now, adequate and well-controlled investigations had to include a formal test with explicit objectives, defined selection procedures for subject and control groups, methods for observation and recording, and statistical analysis. The test drug could be compared with a placebo, another drug known to be active from past studies, or with no treatment. Clinical experience was relegated to the final stage (i.e., Phase 4, also called postmarketing surveillance) of drug testing well after the commitment to manufacture and promote the drug had been made. Consequently, the trend in the 1990s is toward the conceptualization and implementation of postmarketing surveillance systems to detect the occurrence of problems with a drug's safety and efficacy.

V. CONCLUSION

The processes of drug discovery, development, and clinical testing became highly institutionalized and politicized during the twentieth century. Each has been affected by changes in political economics; the elaboration of basic research methodologies; the emergence of pharmacology, immunology, and other specialized disciplines; the proliferation of educated scientific specialists; new systems of research management; and persistent elements of social control. The interplay of these factors have been strong determinants in the structure, direction, and performance of the pharmaceutical industry.

The clinical research process, which is probably in an evolving stage, attempts to meet this social demand in a simple and defensible manner. The influence of societal demand on research is no different in our own time than in former years: The call in the early 1970s to wage a "war on cancer" resulted again in an explosion of basic science and industrial and clinical research efforts aimed to finding a cure. This ongoing effort has resulted in the massive screening of new compounds for chemotherapeutic activity and has spawned a whole research focus and industry with the study of interferon and other contemporary magic bullets.

Finally, the recent focus on human experimentation and the ethics of drug taking will have a profound impact on the future development of new drug entities and clinical research. Informed consent, patient rights, and institutional review boards have already affected clinical research in many settings. Additionally, the use of placebos in controlled clinical trials are also being reevaluated by some in an ethical context [13]. These changes in societal concerns, governmental interventions and regulations, and individual patient rights may well alter many aspects of pharmaceutical development, including the focus of research efforts, the nature of clinical experimentation, the costs and feasibility of drug development, and perhaps the purpose of drug taking and the functions of drugs in society.

REFERENCES

1. P. Ehrlich, Address delivered September 1906, *The Collected Papers of Paul Ehrlich* (F. Himmelwert, ed.), Pergamon Press, Elmsford, NY, 1973.
2. L. R. Basara and M. Montagne, *Searching for Magic Bullets: Orphan Drugs, Consumer Activism & Pharmaceutical Development*, Haworth Press, Binghamton, NY, 1994.
3. R. H. Shryock, *American Medical Research*, Commonwealth Fund, New York, 1947.
4. E. H. Ackerknecht, *A Short History of Medicine*, rev. ed., Roland Press, New York, 1968.
5. A. C. Crombie, *Medieval and Early Modern Science*, rev. ed., Vol. 2, Doubleday (Anchor Books), Garden City, NY, 1959.

6. C. D. Leake, *An Historical Account of Pharmacology to the Twentieth Century*, Thomas, Springfield, Ill., 1975.
7. E. H. Ackerknecht, *Medicine at the Paris Hospital, 1794–1848*, John Hopkins University Press, Baltimore, 1967.
8. C. Bernard, *An Introduction to the Study of Experimental Medicine*, Macmillan, New York, 1927.
9. F. H. Garrison, *An Introduction to the History of Medicine*, 4th ed., Saunders, Philadelphia, 1929.
10. J. H. Gaddum, *Proc. R. Soc. Med. 47*:195 (1954).
11. R. A. Fisher, *The Design of Experiments*, Oliver & Boyd, Edinburgh and London, 1935.
12. L. K. Altman, *N. Engl. J. Med. 286*:346–352 (1972).
13. D. P. Byar, R. M. Simon, W. T. Friedewald, J. J. Schlesselman, D. L. DeMets, J. H. Ellenberg, M. H. Gail, and J. H. Ware, *N. Engl. J. Med. 295*:74–80 (1976).
14. A. R. Feinstein, *Lancet 2*:421–423 (1972).
15. J. W. Tukey, *Science 198*:679–684 (1972).
16. G. Bachmann and A. R. Bliss, *The Essentials of Physiology and Pharmacodynamics*, 2nd rev. ed., Blakiston, Philadelphia, 1926.
17. J. C. Krantz and C. J. Carr, *The Pharmacologic Principles of Medical Practice*, 3rd ed., Williams & Wilkins, Baltimore, 1954.
18. B. L. Svarstad, Sociology of drugs in health care, *Pharmacy Practice: Social and Behavioral Aspects* (A. I. Wertheimer and M. C. Smith, eds.), 3rd ed., Williams and Wilkins, Baltimore, 1989.
19. H. W. Morgan (ed.), *Yesterday's Addicts: American Society and Drug Abuse, 1865–1920*, Univ. of Oklahoma Press, Norman, 1974.
20. B. Barber, *Drugs and Society*, Russell Sage, New York, 1967.
21. D. D. Vogt, M. Montagne, and H. A. Smith, *Am. J. Pharm. Educ. 45*:232–237 (1981).
22. The American Foundation, *Medical Research: A Midcentury Survey* (E. E. Lape, ed.), Little Brown, Boston, 1955.
23. P. Temin, *Taking Your Medicines: Drug Regulation in the United States*, Harvard University Press, Cambridge, MA, 1980.

5

The Role of Clinical Research in the Drug Development Process

Michael Montagne

Massachusetts College of Pharmacy and Allied Health Sciences
Boston, Massachusetts

Modern drug development has evolved into a complex process that involves a number of components. The act of drug discovery starts with basic scientific characterization of a newly identified or synthesized molecule; it then charts a course through safety evaluation in animals, formulation development, clinical pharmacology studies, evaluation of safety and efficacy in humans, the regulatory process, marketing, manufacture and supply, postmarketing surveillance, and international development [1,2]. While basic pharmaceutical research may create useful compounds, their beneficial applications are brought to light through clinical research [3].

I. THE AMERICAN DRUG DEVELOPMENT PROCESS

There are four major steps in the drug development process (see Fig. 1) [4, 5]. Drug development begins with identification of potentially useful compounds through preclinical research. Compounds showing promise that a pharmaceutical company wishes to explore are approved for further study, clinical testing, by the U.S. Food and Drug Administration (FDA). Clinical testing occurs in four phases, three of which take place before the drug is approved for the market. The final step of drug development involves review and approval of the drug and marketing it to the public.

A. Step 1: Preclinical Research

Initial discovery and synthesis of a new chemical compound are the beginning of preclinical research toward the marketing of a prescription drug. Discovery of an effective and safe drug may involve the consideration of hundreds of chemical structures and molecular formulas initially before one becomes a truly useful prescription drug. According to the Pharmaceutical Manufacturers Association (PMA), a drug requires 12 years and over $270 million to undergo study, testing, and evaluation before it can be marketed to the public [1]. Drug discovery and synthesis are unique processes, and there is no standard mechanism for finding a safe and effective pharmaceutical agent.

Evaluation of a potential new drug begins in the laboratories of pharmaceutical manufacturers and involves testing in animals. Both short-term (1 to 3 years) and long-term (2 to 10 years) research is conducted to determine safety and efficacy of a new compound. Until it is believed that the compound might be both safe and effective in humans, it remains in a researcher's laboratory. Hundreds of compounds are synthesized, developed, and researched in this manner each year, compared with the 20 to 30 new drugs that are approved annually by the FDA.

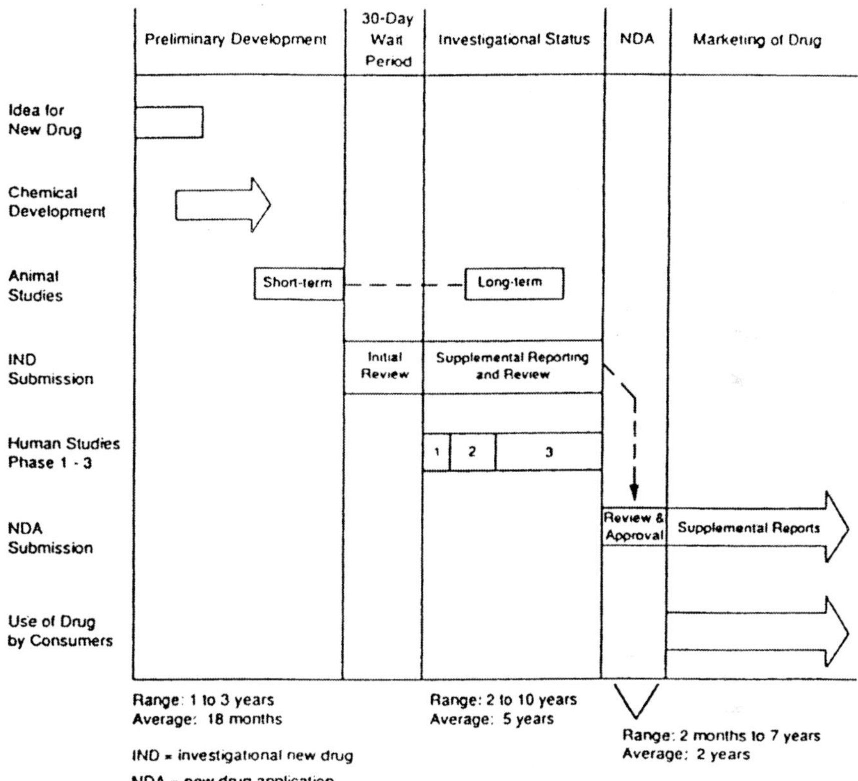

Fig. 1 Basic drug development process. Source: Food and Drug Administration.

B. Step 2: Filing an Investigational New Drug Application or a New Drug Application

After successful laboratory and animal tests with a new compound, the second step toward achieving marketing approval is submission of an investigational new drug (IND) application to the FDA. An investigational new drug is a new pharmaceutical product that has not been shown to be safe and effective in humans, but that does seem to be safe and effective in the management of a disease or condition on the basis of animal tests.

An IND is submitted by a pharmaceutical manufacturer or sponsor to the FDA to request permission to conduct clinical trials of the drug in humans. After a 30-day IND-review period, the sponsor is allowed to investigate the clinical value of the drug. If there are any concerns about the drug's safety, the FDA places the IND on clinical hold, and the sponsor may not begin testing until changes are made to eliminate safety concerns. Because the Food, Drug, and Cosmetic Act allows investigational new drugs to be shipped from state to state within the United States, researchers around the country can evaluate the drug in a variety of patients. Specific components of an IND are listed in Table 1.

C. Step 3: Clinical Testing of the New Drug

Unless the FDA puts an IND on clinical hold during the review period, clinical testing of the drug can begin. The overall goal is to collect and review data to determine whether the possibility of dangerous adverse events outweighs the expected usefulness of the drug. Clinical trials, before marketing, are conducted in three phases.

1. Phase 1: Clinical Pharmacology and Toxicology

The first phase of clinical testing is directed at determining the drug's safe dosage range, the preferred administration route, the mechanisms of absorption and distribution in the body, and possible toxicities. These tests usually are conducted in a small number (20–80) of normal healthy volunteers and

Table 1 Components of an Investigational New Drug Application

Descriptive name of the drug
Drug's route of administration
Complete list of both active and inactive ingredients
Quantitative composition of the drug
Source of the new drug
Chemical and manufacturing information
Preclinical test results (any clinical studies or experience)
Clinical study protocol
Scientific training and experience of investigators
Statements that the sponsor will notify the FDA when and why studies have been discontinued
A notice that an institutional review board will be responsible for continuing review of the proposed study
A description of plans to ensure that procedures are followed to protect human subjects

require less than 12 months to complete. A majority (50%–70%) of compounds tested in Phase 1 are abandoned because of problems with safety or efficacy.

2. *Phase 2: Initial Clinical Efficacy and Tolerability*

The purpose of this clinical testing phase is to learn more about the drug's safety and efficacy in treating a certain disease or symptom. These studies still use a small number (50–200) of volunteers who have the disease or symptom for which the drug seems to be effective. Additional animal testing also can occur during Phase 2 to gain further information about the drug's long-term safety. Phase 2 trials usually require up to 2 years. If the studies show that the drug is useful in a particular disease and animal data show no unwarranted harm, the sponsor can proceed to Phase 3. To facilitate the transition in the scope of the clinical trials, a meeting is usually held between the sponsor and the reviewing division of the FDA to discuss the sponsor's plans for Phase 3 study. According to the FDA, approximately one-third of new drugs will continue on to Phase 3 (see Fig. 2) [1].

3. *Phase 3: Treatment Efficacy*

This phase of clinical trials involves the most extensive drug testing. Phase 3 studies assess safety, efficacy, and appropriate dosage range for the drug

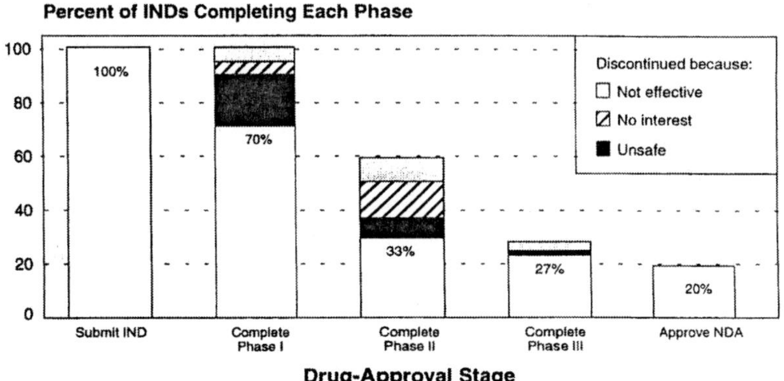

Fig. 2 Percentage of INDs completing each phase of clinical testing.

in treating a specific disease in a large group of patients. The number of patients involved can range from several hundred to several thousand, depending on the drug. During Phase 3 studies, the drug is used by practicing physicians in the manner similar to the way in which it would be used when marketed. Additional testing to characterize more specifically the adverse effects of the drug are also conducted in Phase 3. On average, only about 25% of new drugs successfully complete Phase 3 testing.

D. Step 4: Review and Approval of the New Drug Application

After clinical testing of the new drug, the manufacturer is required to submit a new drug application (NDA) to the FDA. For biologics, the sponsor is required to submit a Product License Application (PLA). NDA submission marks the beginning of the final step in the drug approval process. The NDA is divided into six sections: chemistry, pharmacology, pharmacokinetics, microbiology, clinical, and statistics.

Upon receipt at the FDA, each NDA is assigned an application number and checked for completeness, and the application is assigned and distributed to one of six drug-reviewing divisions. The six divisions are responsible for specific classes of drugs and consist of clinical reviewers, pharmacologists, and chemists. Consultants with expertise in biochemistry and statistics also are involved. Outside reviewers, known as FDA Advisory Committees, are identified and recruited to complement the FDA staff. The FDA review staff is required to process the NDA within 180 days, called the regulatory review period. During the review process, the FDA can request additional information of the sponsor, which can extend the time period necessary for approval. The NDA review and approval process usually requires 2 to 3 years.

The NDA review and approval process nears completion when the FDA sends the drug's sponsor an approvable letter. This letter is sent when the FDA believes that the NDA will be approved, but only if specific additional information or material is submitted or specific conditions (changes in labeling) are agreed to by the sponsor. The sponsor has 10 days to respond to the FDA, and the response may consist of:

Filing an amendment to the NDA or notifying the FDA that the company intends to file an amendment

Withdrawing the NDA from consideration

Requesting the FDA to provide an opportunity for a hearing to question the existence of grounds for denial of the NDA

Notifying the FDA that the company agrees to an extension of the review period

Most sponsors respond by amending the NDA to include requested information. Upon review of all components of the NDA, a review package consisting of a draft action letter, the reviews, and possibly a summary basis of approval is prepared by the FDA. The summary basis of approval reiterates the key findings and characteristics of the new drug, including safety and efficacy data, pharmacokinetic parameters, and product labeling.

A supplemental new drug application (supplemental NDA) is submitted when a drug's sponsor requests approval to promote an existing drug with either a new indication or new labeling, or when manufacturing procedures have changed. Because the same regulations and requirements do not apply for review and approval of a supplemental NDA as for a standard NDA, the request does not undergo the same scope of review and is approved more quickly.

Phase 4: Postmarketing Surveillance

After a drug is approved for marketing, the sponsor must continue to submit information to the FDA on a regular basis. Such data requirements are considered Phase 4 clinical trials, and are a part of postmarketing surveillance of the drug product. Since the early 1970s, the FDA has been responsible for monitoring the safety and quality of drugs. Physicians, pharmacists, nurses, and other health care professionals are asked to report adverse drug reactions to the FDA using a standard form, or a telephone call if the reaction is life-threatening or dangerous. Another part of Phase 4 studies involves clinical trials of the drug in various subgroups of patients, such as children or women.

II. DRUG APPROVAL AND REGULATION IN THE UNITED STATES

A. The U.S. Food and Drug Administration and Drug Regulation

The federal government is the primary regulator of drug products in the United States [6,7]. The U.S. Food and Drug Administration is the agency of the federal government that is responsible for

Premarketing clearance of all new drug products
Regulation of all drug labeling
Regulation of manufacturing

Regulation of bioequivalence standards
Postmarketing surveillance

The FDA's Center for Drug Evaluation and Research (CDER) is responsible for the review and approval of new drug products, including both prescription and nonprescription drugs. There are eight offices of the CDER: The Director, Management, Epidemiology and Biostatistics, Compliance, Drug Standards, Pharmaceutical Research Resources, and two offices dealing with drug evaluation (the first dealing with cardio-renal, neuro-pharmacological, chemotherapeutic and radiopharmaceutical, surgical-dental, coagulation, and gastrointestinal drug products; the second dealing with anti-infective, endocrine, and antiviral drug products). Biologics are reviewed and approved by the FDA's Center for Biologics Evaluation and Research (CBER).

Drugs are defined as natural or synthetic substances that are effective in the prevention, treatment, or cure of disease. Biologics are any virus, therapeutic serum, toxin, antitoxin, vaccine, blood, blood component or derivative, allergenic product, or similar product applicable to the prevention, treatment, or cure of diseases or injuries of humans.

All meetings with the FDA are held at the pleasure of the agency, and requests for meetings must be judicious [8]. Meetings during the pre-IND phase are possible depending on the history of the chemical compound and certain other exceptions, but, for the most part, they are not necessary. The first key meeting between the sponsor and the FDA occurs after the end of Phase 2 studies. End of Phase 2 conferences are especially important for new molecular entities constituting important therapeutic gains, drugs with important toxicity problems, compounds representing a moderate therapeutic gain, or a marketed drug with an important new indication. End of Phase 3, or pre-NDA, conferences are held with sponsors of INDs that represent new molecular entities (NME), and these meetings can help accelerate the approval process [8].

In addition to monitoring the drug development process and ensuring timely approval of safe and effective medicines, the FDA also is responsible for regulation of prescription drug advertising [1]. Advertising is an unofficial term in the regulatory literature that is generally applied to all forms of drug marketing, including printed matter, promotional advertisements, all forms of labeling (which encompasses audio and visual information, exhibits, and communications through all forms of media), and verbal statements. Responsibility for regulating nonprescription drug marketing, especially advertising in media intended for viewing by consumers, rests with the U.S. Federal Trade Commission (FTC).

Early in the drug-approval process, the FDA classifies a new drug by chemical type and therapeutic potential. This system of classification provides a rating for each drug on the basis of its comparability to currently marketed products, as well as a priority rating for review (see Tables 2–4). Until January 1992, therapeutic potential ratings described the importance of the therapeutic gain provided by the new product (Table 3). In 1992, however, the system was changed to the current rating system based on review status (Table 4).

B. Productivity of the U.S. Drug Approval Process

Although 20 to 30 NMEs are approved each year, many new chemical entities are not. Estimates indicate that, in general, only one in 2000 new chemicals is found sufficiently safe and effective by the FDA [1,9,10]. In addition, only one-quarter of new chemical entities that are given IND status

Table 2 Food and Drug Administration Chemical Rating System

1. New Molecular Entity. The active portion or moiety has not been marketed (either as a parent compound, salt, ester, or derivative) in the United States for use as a single or combination drug product.
2. New Salt. The active moiety is marketed in the United States by the same or another manufacturer, but the particular salt, ester, or derivative is not yet marketed in the United States either as a single or combination product.
3. New Formulation. The compound is marketed in the United States by the same or another manufacturer, but the particular dosage form or formulation is not.
4. New Combination. The product contains two or more compounds that have not previously been marketed together in a drug product in the United States by any manufacturer.
5. Already Marketed Product. The product duplicates a drug product (same active moiety, same salt, same formulation, or same combination) already marketed in the United States by another firm.
6. New Indication. The product adds a new indication for a drug product already marketed in the United States by the same firm.
7. Marketed without an NDA. The drug is on the U.S. market, but does not have an approved NDA.

NOTE: these chemical types are not mutually exclusive; a new formulation (Type 3) or a new combination (Type 4) can contain a new molecular entity (Type 1) or a new salt (Type 2). In such cases, both numbers are used in the overall classification number of the drug.

Table 3 Food and Drug Administration Therapeutic Rating System (Pre-1992)

AA. AIDS Drug. Any drug that might be effective in treating acquired immunodeficiency syndrome (highest-priority review).

A. Important Therapeutic Gain. The drug might provide effective therapy or diagnosis for a disease that is not adequately treated or diagnosed by any marketed drug, or provide improved treatment of a disease through enhanced effectiveness or safety (including decreased abuse potential).

B. Modest Therapeutic Gain. The drug has a modest, but real, potential advantage over other marketed drugs (i.e., greater patient convenience, elimination of an annoying but not dangerous side effect, potential for large cost reduction, less frequent dosage schedule, or usefulness in specific subpopulations of those with the disease).

C. Little or No Therapeutic Gain. The drug essentially duplicates one or more already marketed drugs in medical importance and therapeutic usage (lowest-priority review).

H. Orphan Drug Candidate. The drug might meet criteria for orphan drug designation.

V. Designated Orphan Drug. The drug has received orphan drug designation, entitling the manufacturer to tax credits and exclusive marketing rights.

NOTE: These ratings are mutually exclusive. Only one of these letters is included in a drug's overall classification.

receive marketing approval (Fig. 2). In the 1970s, twice as many investigational new drugs were approved for the marketplace. It appears that legal and economic reasons have become more influential in preventing a new drug's approval than scientific or therapeutic ones. Additional reasons for chemical substance rejection include [1]:

Table 4 Food and Drug Administration Therapeutic Rating System (Post-1992)

P. Priority Review. A drug that might be valuable in the treatment of AIDS, cancer, or other life-threatening illnesses or conditions. These drugs receive high priority in order to facilitate testing and approval.

S. Standard Review. A product that is not an AIDS drug, a major breakthrough in treatment, or orphan drug. In other words, a drug that was rated "B" or "C" using the old system.

H. Orphan Drug Candidate. See Table 3.

V. Designated Orphan Drug. See Table 3.

Problems in the synthesis or production of the drug on a large-scale basis.
Problems with drug stability or general quality.
Drug is not effective.
Drug has too many adverse effects and is not safe.
Drug has too many side effects.
Drug is too expensive to manufacture.
Drug's patent status is unclear.

An additional rationale for the decrease in new drug approvals might be decreased productivity in pharmaceutical research and development. Possible reasons for this decline include deficiencies in knowledge of the causes of diseases; patent infringement from identical competitor products, especially in biotechnology; chemical research focuses too much on simple molecular manipulation; totally new therapeutic compounds and approaches are difficult to identify and develop [1].

C. Facilitating the Drug Approval Process

In 1987, the FDA issued Interim Regulatory Procedures for patients with AIDS and other serious diseases [11,12]. Among other provisions, these procedures codified and expanded the acceptance by the FDA of accelerated new drug applications (accelerated NDA). An accelerated NDA is submitted for drugs that might be effective in the treatment of life-threatening diseases and rare diseases. The major objective of the Interim Regulatory Procedures was to facilitate approval of drugs that have been shown to be safe and effective in such conditions.

This procedure allows the use of investigational drugs to treat patients with a serious or immediately life-threatening disease. It is important to realize that treatment IND regulations do not alter the stages of the drug approval process. They only allow the use of the drug in patients other than those enrolled in a clinical trial. The accelerated drug review process, which was proposed and adopted in 1988, permits the FDA to review and approve a new drug before all three phases of clinical trials are completed (see Fig. 3). If it is clear that a drug is effective and beneficial to patients, it can be approved before clinical trials are complete. As the first AIDS therapy to be approved by the FDA, zidovudine served as the model for this accelerated review system. The results of these treatment IND regulations included more freedom in clinical trial design, improved adverse reaction reporting systems, increased consultation between the FDA and drug sponsors, and streamlined procedures for proposing and conducting clinical studies.

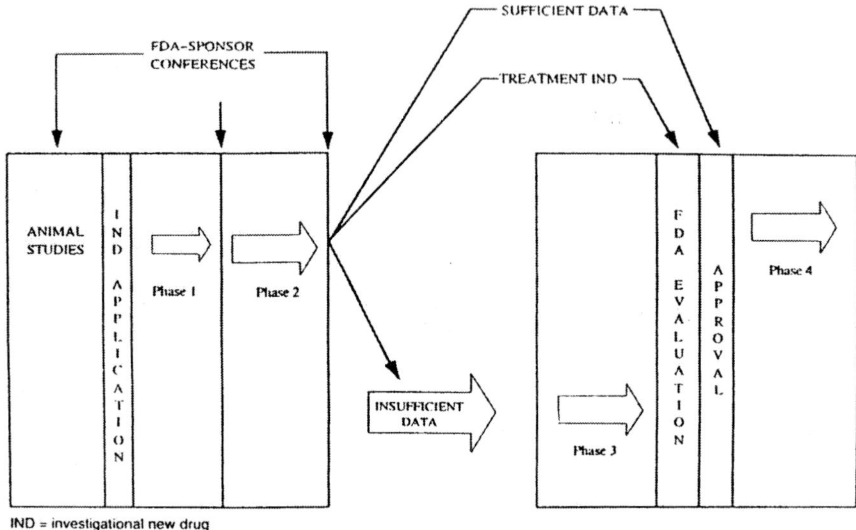

Fig. 3 The accelerated NDA process. Source: Food and Drug Administration.

Additional changes in the drug approval process include a continued focus on accelerated drug approval, along with the use of surrogate end points, external reviewers, approaches to international harmonization, and computerized databases. The average length of NDA review for drugs is 30 months, but it has been estimated that the time for NDA review process can be reduced further. Thus, the total time to bring a drug through preclinical and clinical research, as well as review and approval, could be compressed from 117 to 66 months, a 56% decrease (see Fig. 4).

Orphan drugs, or medications that treat diseases that affect less than 200,000 people in the United States, are almost always given treatment IND status because of the nature of the diseases for which they have been developed [13]. In 1983, the Orphan Drug Act was passed to minimize barriers associated with developing and marketing orphan drugs. The legislation, which amended the Federal Food, Drug, and Cosmetic Act, was designed to prompt research and advancement of drugs with little commercial value through the establishment of financial incentives for pharmaceutical manufacturers. If a drug is developed for a disease that affects more than 200,000 people, but its sponsor demonstrates that there is no reasonable expectation

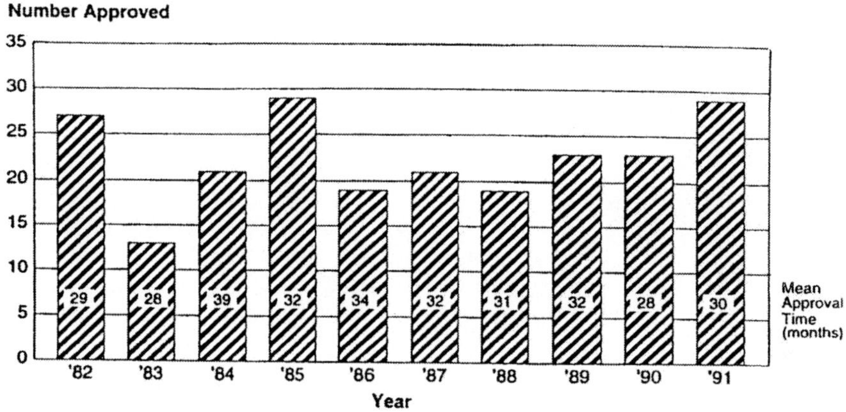

Fig. 4 Mean approval time for new drugs. Source: Food and Drug Administration.

that the costs of its research will be recovered from sales in the United States, the drug can receive orphan drug status.

After defining the restrictions of the terms "rare disease" and "orphan drug," the Orphan Drug Act established four major provisions to help sponsors and researchers overcome the barriers associated with orphan drug development [14]:

Exclusive marketing rights for 7 years after approval
Tax credits (up to 50%) for clinical testing
Grants and contracts to support clinical and preclinical orphan drug research
Flexibility and assistance in regulatory processes

III. THE CLINICAL DRUG TRIAL PROCESS

A. Contemporary Clinical Drug Trials

There are many different types of contemporary drug trials that use a variety of methods [15]. The goals of Phase 3 and Phase 4 clinical drug trials are to determine the therapeutic benefits and identify adverse reactions of the new drug, after it has passed safety testing in animals and safety, dosage range, and efficacy studies in humans. The design of clinical trials varies by certain components: what specific treatments are being evaluated and compared, how patients are selected for the different study groups, and who of the parties involved know which patients are receiving the experimental treatment and which ones are receiving other treatments or no treatment.

Clinical drug trials have been found to range considerably. There is clinical inquiry, a simple, nonexperimental method in which only one group of patients receives a new drug, and massive amounts of data are collected and analyzed to see whether the drug had any effect. No control or comparison group is used. There also is the controlled clinical trial, in which the control group consists of participants not from the original pool of potential study patients. In other words, a controlled trial may not include the process of random assignment of all patients at the beginning into the different treatment groups. The best method for determining the true therapeutic benefit of a new unknown drug therapy is the randomized and controlled clinical trial. A clinical trial today is often performed at more than one facility. These multisite studies may link together a number of hospitals, clinics, and research centers, in order to increase the number and diversity of the subjects who choose to participate.

B. The Randomized Controlled Clinical Trial

Few people would argue today that the most scientific and ethical method for investigation of new drug therapies is the randomized clinical trial [16, 17]. The main objective of this method is to make certain that after the trial is over the better (or best) treatment of all those studied is identified. The key component in a randomized clinical trial is the use of a control group and randomization of subjects into the study groups.

There are some circumstances where the randomization process may not be justified. This issue has arisen in the recent research on drugs for treatment of AIDS. Study subjects with AIDS feel that they all should be in the clinical trial: No one should be denied an experimental treatment because he or she was randomly selected to be in the control or placebo group. Regardless of whether a randomization process is justified or not in a particular drug study, patients always should be informed of any randomization process that is affecting their treatment choices.

Most clinical trials are based at universities, usually at the medical school's teaching hospitals, at large research-based hospitals, or at pharmaceutical company laboratories. Potential clinical trial subjects usually are notified of and recruited through private practitioners, newspaper advertisements and other announcements of planned or ongoing research studies, or through private medical and health care clinics that engage in contracted research projects.

Even though there has been much progress in the design and conduct of clinical trials, they still are far from a perfect method of study. The clinical drug trial may be thought of as a large-scale, standardized alternative to the process whereby individual clinicians gradually accumulate knowledge through direct clinical experience with a particular therapy. Clinical trials answer only those questions that have been asked specifically. One criticism concerning the usefulness of clinical trials is that the experimental conditions of the trial often differ so much from the conditions encountered in clinical practice that the trial's results may not be applicable to real-life situations. The quality of clinical trials has been another concern expressed over the past 10 years. In a review of previous clinical trials, it was found that the majority of them were judged to be uncontrolled or poorly controlled, or otherwise poorly designed [18]. The proportion of adequately controlled trials to all research studies actually declined over the past three decades.

A recent development has been the multicenter clinical trial, which is an experiment that involves two or more clinical facilities, each of which is responsible for recruitment, treatment, and follow-up of patients under a commonly agreed plan. Data and information from all of the centers is combined in the research analysis stage. Multicenter trials have a number of advantages. The majority of single trials that are performed have too few patients, so a multicenter approach can greatly increase the number of participants in the study. Such trials, however, can be more complex to organize and operate, and more costly to run. Such trials not only have the potential for recruiting adequate numbers of patients, but the range of different people involved usually leads to a better research design and more careful execution of the study. The larger number of clinics and the different patient populations also may provide a more realistic test of the treatment in question.

An important technical aspect of clinical drug development is the area or project team [4]. Early in the development process the important technical expertise includes the disciplines of chemistry, biology, pharmacology, and law (for determining patent rights); later in the process, the key disciplines include pharmacology and toxicology, pharmacy, medicine, epidemiology and biostatistics, law, and marketing.

Clinical drug development has so many diverse inputs that a multidisciplinary project team is necessary to drive the development process [19]. The most effective actions of project teams are to recommend termination of the development process as soon as sufficient negative evidence is available. Management of clinical drug development involves primarily maintenance of continuity in the whole process [19]. This is especially important because the clinical research process is more sensitive to breaks in continuity than the basic preclinical research process, due to such factors as the multidisciplinary aspects of this research and the various departments and groups involved in generating data (from clinical management to regulatory concerns to marketing activities, all centered on the clinical application of the new drug).

Future trends in clinical drug development include industrial consolidation, international uses of clinical trial data, the use of contract research organizations, operating trends at the FDA, the impact of generic drug products, shifting nature of patient populations, and the need to demonstrate improved quality of life as a component of the drug approval process [19]. From a regulatory perspective, the interest is in discerning drugs that are potentially approvable and applying the clinical drug development data to post-approval patient populations. From the corporate perspective, however, drug development is viewed as a series of regulatory hurdles. In the end, the objective of research and development should not be to create new products that compete with older ones, but to develop products that are unique and innovative and thus have no competition.

IV. THE FUTURE OF CLINICAL RESEARCH IN DRUG DEVELOPMENT

The general public's attitudes toward clinical drug trials are quite positive. In a 1982 survey, only 6% of the respondents felt medical research in the United States was *not* ethical [20]. Participation in clinical trials was seen, by the respondents, as benefiting patients and society by helping to improve medical knowledge. The current drug development and approval process, however, is viewed by other people as (a) relying heavily on the standard of "sound science," (b) assuming that being a research subject was a burden that should be distributed as equitably as possible among all patients with the disease who might possibly participate in a clinical trial, (c) preparing to make a trade-off of slower medical advances in return for discoveries that are better monitored and controlled, and (d) taking an adversarial posture by the regulators toward the pharmaceutical companies, instead of a collaborative one.

Many problems and issues still exist, such as choosing whether the gains in knowledge from a slight alteration in the experimental design of the trial justify increased risks to patients, or determining when it is permissible to withhold standard treatment. Some of these issues have become more important recently, with an increased incidence of certain infectious (AIDS) and chronic diseases. The general public, though supportive of clinical drug trials, is beginning to question the ethics of placebo control groups in experiments and the lengthy period of time it usually takes to transfer experimental results to general medical practice. The public's strong support for clinical drug trials may have resulted from the development, over the 1960s and 1970s, of informed consent procedures. The importance of public opinion on the development of new drugs should not be underestimated [10].

Some critics feel that these challenges to the traditional drug development system will change it radically in the near future. The focus will shift to a patient or consumer rights orientation. FDA control over the flow of prescription drugs may be reduced, especially in the realm of importation of foreign products. Future changes in drug regulatory policies, even if directed at one category of drugs or diseases, will be expanded almost immediately to include many other drugs and diseases. There may be less concern, especially on the part of patients, for the risks of drug experimentation. The control and operation of clinical trials will shift from investigators at large research hospitals and clinics to include physicians from all types of backgrounds and institutions. The dominance of the randomized, controlled clinical trial may become weakened. More recently, drug development may be moving away from defining the research goal in terms of disease entity to defining it in more general biomedical terms [9]. Other people have called for less radical approaches, such as restructuring the present drug approval process.

The process of clinical drug research in pharmaceutical development still is evolving. While this process is not perfect, changes are proposed constantly to improve it for the benefit of patients, health professionals, and the pharmaceutical industry.

REFERENCES

1. L. R. Basara and M. Montagne, *Searching for Magic Bullets: Orphan Drugs, Consumer Activism and Pharmaceutical Development*, Haworth Press, Binghamton, NY, 1994.
2. R. B. Smith, *The Development of a Medicine*, Stockton, London, 1985.
3. G. M. Matoren (ed.), *The Clinical Research Process in the Pharmaceutical Industry*, Marcel Dekker, New York, 1984.
4. C. G. Smith, *The Process of New Drug Discovery and Development*, CRC Press, Boca Raton, FL, 1992.

5. A. Myers and S. R. Moore, *Drug Intel. Clin. Pharm. 21*:822 (1987).
6. Anonymous, FDA Backgrounder 91–1.0:1 (1991).
7. M. Mathieu, *New Drug Development: A Regulatory Overview*, Rev. ed., Parexel, Cambridge, MA, 1990.
8. R. A. Guarino (ed.), *New Drug Approval Process*, 2nd ed., Marcel Dekker, New York, 1993.
9. F. Gross (ed.), *Decision Making in Drug Research*, Raven Press, New York, 1983.
10. Y. C. Martin, E. Kutter, and V. Austel, *Modern Drug Research: Paths to Better and Safer Drugs*, Marcel Dekker, New York, 1989.
11. H. Edgar and D. J. Rothman, *Milbank Q. 68*:111 (1990).
12. B. Scoville, *Clin. Pharmacol. Ther. 49*:229 (1991).
13. C. V. Gordon and D. E. Wierenga, "The Drug Development and Approval Process," Orphan Drugs in Development, Pharmaceutical Manufacturers Association, Washington, DC, 1991.
14. L. C. Weaver, *Wellcome Trends in Pharmacy*, 4 (1991).
15. K. K. Uberla, *Control. Clin. Trials 1*:295 (1981).
16. D. H. Spodick, *Am. J. Med. 73*:420 (1982).
17. D. H. Spodick, *JAMA 247*:2258 (1982).
18. E. Hemminki, *Methods Inf. Med. 21*:81 (1982).
19. D. M. Cocchetto and R. V. Nardi, *Managing the Clinical Drug Development Process*, Marcel Dekker, New York, 1992.
20. R. B. Cassileth, E. J. Luck, D. S. Miller, and S. Hurwitz, *JAMA 248*:968 (1982).

6

The FDA and the Regulatory Oversight of the Clinical Research Process in Drug Development

Loren Miller

Quintiles, Inc.
Research Triangle Park, North Carolina

Lloyd G. Millstein

Consultant, Regulatory Affairs
Raleigh, North Carolina

I. INTRODUCTION

The fundamental mission of the Food and Drug Administration (FDA) is consumer protection, which is accomplished through the passage and enforcement of regulations for this purpose. The FDA was granted broad statutory authority through the Federal Food, Drug and Cosmetic Act of 1938 (the "Act") to regulate the interstate shipment of drugs by requiring sponsors to obtain premarketing clearance based on the demonstrated safety of a product. This regulatory authority, as well as amendments to the Act, was the result of perceived deficiencies on the part of the pharmaceutical industry to adequately protect the public health (e.g., sulfanilamide and thalidomide events). In 1962, the Kefauver-Harris amendments to the Act resulted in regulatory control over many aspects of the clinical research process. This included the requirement that sponsors demonstrate the effectiveness of their drugs in scientifically valid studies, the establishment of informed consent guidelines, defining preclinical safety data that justifies human drug testing, and the establishment of adverse reaction reporting requirements. In addition, the amendments provided the FDA with the authority to regulate the manner in which clinical research is conducted by requiring investigators and sponsors to maintain study records that must be open to inspection by regulatory authorities. The 1962 amendments and subsequent amendments to the Act have solidified the FDA's regulatory influence over every step in the clinical research process from the time an Investigational New Drug (IND) application is filed to review and approval of a New Drug Application (NDA) and prescription drug advertisements and other descriptive printed matter.

A key aspect of the 1962 amendments was the requirement that sponsors file a notice of "Claimed Investigational Drug Exemption" or IND to initiate clinical trials with experimental drugs. Clinical studies are not allowed to commence unless data provided in the IND (most INDs are evaluated on the basis of preclinical safety information because few clinical safety data are available at the time of IND submission) are judged to provide a margin of safety for testing in human subjects. The IND allows a sponsor to ship drug across state lines to clinical investigators for purposes of research.

In the 1970s, the IND regulations were modified to provide more details regarding the obligation of sponsors, investigators, and monitors. These amendments also defined the responsibilities of Institutional Review Boards (IRBs) and outlined the key elements of informed consent.

In 1987, the IND regulations were modified (IND Rewrite) to strengthen adverse reaction reporting requirements, establish criteria for "clinical holds," clarify communications between the FDA and sponsors, and eliminate the need for INDs for marketed drugs for which safety is not an issue and for studies being conducted that do not support new clinical indications.

Finally, in an effort to provide early treatments for life-threatening and severely debilitating illnesses, regulations for the treatment, use, and sale of investigational drugs were developed in 1989. These regulations allow for the expanded treatment of life-threatening illness prior to drug approval when reasonable evidence of safety and effectiveness has been demonstrated in controlled clinical trials and when no available marketed therapy exists. They were modified in 1992 to formally allow the use of surrogate end points in clinical trials that provide evidence for an indication for life-threatening or severely debilitating diseases. These regulations provide for both expedited development and review of innovative therapies. Finally, the FDA indirectly (without formal regulations) influences the clinical development of drugs through the issuance of clinical guidelines and in "talk papers" and publications that provide both regulatory and scientific insights into the drug development process.

In summary, the evolutionary history of federal regulations indicates that the FDA has sought to regulate clinical research by protecting the rights of human subjects, making sure sponsors provide valid scientific data to support marketing claims, and providing guidance for clinical research and formal regulatory initiatives designed to facilitate the development of drugs for life-threatening and severely debilitating diseases.

II. PROTECTION OF HUMAN SUBJECTS

A. Filing an IND

Federal regulations (21 CFR 312) require that sponsors justify—largely on the basis of preclinical safety testing—introducing drugs into human testing.

The FDA must make a judgment that humans are not exposed to unreasonable risks. The key elements in the IND are the following:

1. Short-term toxicity studies. These are usually of 2 weeks' to 3 months' duration. The investigational compound is usually administered to two species by the route of intended administration. Longer term and special studies should proceed concurrently with advanced clinical investigations.
2. Clinical development plan and initial study protocol. The initial study is usually a dose-tolerance and pharmacokinetic profile analysis.
3. Investigator information. Investigators must be medically qualified to administer test drug and conduct the study. The sponsor must obtain a signed agreement from investigators that they will perform the study and provide adequate supervision to other medical staff participating in the study and will maintain control over the investigational drug and not use it for purposes outside the protocol.
4. Pharmacology. Pharmacology studies consisting of modeling designs that demonstrate the purported actions of the drug and secondary pharmacology studies that further define the safety profile are included in the IND.
5. Chemistry, manufacturing and controls. The composition of the drug substance, method of manufacture, and profile of the product must be specified. A key aspect of the review of this information is whether the chemistry of the new drug resembles other known toxins.
6. Investigator's brochure. The investigator's brochure outlines for the investigator and Institutional Review Board a summary of all available safety data, a description of the pharmacological modeling studies that describe the proposed mechanism of action of the drug, and a description of the pharmacokinetic profile of the drug and its biological disposition. In addition, a summary of any available human testing data and a summary of risks and benefits must be included.

B. Clinical Investigations and Protocols

Section 505 of the Food, Drug, and Cosmetic Act and 21 CFR 314.126 states that proof of efficacy must be based on "adequate and well-controlled investigations, including clinical investigations, by experts qualified by scientific training and experience to evaluate the effectiveness of the drug involved."

Approval of a new drug application or supplemental clinical indication usually requires two well-controlled clinical trials that have a placebo control arm. Open trials do not meet the criteria of "well-controlled" and are insufficient to provide evidence of efficacy from a regulatory perspective (21 CFR 314.126).

The clinical protocol defines the context within which a study is performed. Included in the protocol are the objectives of the study, methodology, and statistical treatment. According to 21 CFR 312.23, an adequate and well-controlled study should contain the following elements:

Name, addresses, and resume(s) of investigator(s)
Name and address of the IRB
Assurance of compliance with informed consent
Purpose and objectives of study
Description of statistical methods
Inclusion/exclusion criteria
Description of study design
Dosing selection and justification
Clinical laboratory tests

It is important that protocols be well written and easily interpretable and have scientific validity because the results will determine approvability of the drug being evaluated.

C. Selection of Subjects for Clinical Research Studies

Federal regulations (21 CFR 312.3) define a study subject as "a human who participates in an investigation, either as a recipient of the investigational new drug or as a control. A subject may be a healthy human or a patient with a disease."

Only those subjects may be enrolled in research studies who are not considered vulnerable to exploitation. These include patients who have severe physical and mental illness, the educationally disadvantaged, institutionally dependent subjects, and the economically disadvantaged. In addition, prisoners may not be used in research because of informed consent issues [1].

Clinical investigators often advertise for research subjects to increase accrual rates. Information contained in advertisements must not be misleading; advertisers must not offer pronounced inducements to participate and must not claim that the drug being tested is safe or effective, or equivalent or superior to other treatments. Advertising for research subjects is governed by informed consent regulations and must be reviewed and approved by the Institutional Review Board (IRB). Information contained in advertising should contain the following:

Name and address of investigator(s)
Purpose of research and eligibility criteria
A description of study benefit
Location of the research facility and contact person

Payments may be made to subjects participating in research studies, but the amount and method of payment must be approved by the IRB to determine if the payment has unduly influenced study participation. Amount and method of payment should be outlined in the informed consent.

D. Institutional Review

Because most clinical research is conducted at medical centers or research institutions, an oversight committee governing the conduct of clinical research at the local institution, or IRB, assures that the rights and welfare of human subjects are protected (21 CFR 56.102). The IRB determines that the study being conducted is valid scientifically and that the benefits of the study outweigh the risks. In addition, the IRB must assure that study subjects are adequately informed about the nature of the study and potential risks of proposed treatment.

Part 56 of the CFR outlines IRB membership requirements, its functions, informed consent requirements, review procedures, criteria for approving protocols, and record keeping.

An IRB must be made up of at least five members appointed by the institution who have the professional competence to evaluate the proposed research from a scientific, legal, regulatory, and moral perspective. The protocol for a multisite clinical trial must be reviewed by an IRB for each site.

A key element of these regulations is that specific criteria for the approval of research proposals be met. These include that risks to subjects be minimized and are balanced against benefits; subject selection is equitable; informed consent is obtained and documented from the volunteer or legal representative; that the study be monitored for continuing safety; and that the privacy and confidentiality of patients be maintained. For foreign investigations, refer to the Tokyo revision of the Declaration of Helsinki and the laws of the country in which the research is to be conducted (see 21 CFR 312.120).

The goal of the IRB is to protect subjects, the institutions, the investigator, and sponsor. When all of these parties adequately understand the ramifications of the research being performed, the scientific research process is facilitated [1,2].

E. Informed Consent

Patients should not enter into clinical trials without an adequate understanding of the implications of study participation or against their will (21 CFR 50.20). The basic elements of informed consent include the following:

Purpose of research, duration of study participation, and a description of experimental procedures
A description of risks and benefits
A description of alternative courses of treatment
A statement that indicates that patient records remain confidential and that the FDA may inspect patient and investigator records
A statement as to whether compensation or alternative medical treatment is available and who to contact in the case of injury
A statement that study participation is voluntary

Additional elements that may be included in the consent form when appropriate are:

Potential risks of treatment in conjunction with pregnancy
The circumstances under which a volunteer participation may be terminated
Any financial costs the subject may accrue as a result of participation
The consequences of a subject's decision to withdraw from the study
A statement that any new findings from the study be provided to the patient
The number of subjects participating

The Institutional Review Branch of the FDA inspects IRBs for deficiencies in compliance with the above regulations and has the authority to issue corrective letters to IRBs that are not complying with the regulations. The first type of letter is issued for minor violations and requires no formal response by the IRB. If IRBs are found to be in serious violation of existing regulations, a letter titled "Notice of Adverse Findings" may be issued. The IRB is required to respond within 30 days. Subjects may not be enrolled in clinical trials until deficiencies are corrected. A follow-up inspection usually takes place within one year. Another type of letter titled "Notice of Opportunity for Informal Conference" requires a response within 10 days. A meeting is requested by the agency with representatives from the IRB to discuss potential disqualification and/or corrective actions [1,3].

F. Clinical Hold

The FDA can delay or terminate clinical trials if subjects are exposed to untoward risks, if investigators are judged to be unqualified, if the investigator's brochure is inaccurate or misleading, or if the IND contains insufficient data to evaluate the safety of the drug prior to human exposure (21 CFR 312.42). Clinical holds can be issued during any phase of clinical research but most are probably initiated prior to phase I testing. The IND Rewrite regulations allow the FDA to issue a clinical hold for scientific deficiencies in addition to safety concerns.

The clinical hold may be informal, with sponsors being verbally asked by the reviewing division to delay the start-up of a clinical trial for a 30-day period. This usually occurs because the medical reviewer has not completed his or her review. If safety concerns are considered serious by the FDA, a clinical hold may be issued by telephone or letter. Once this happens, all subject enrollment in clinical trials must cease. Agency approval is required prior to the re-initiation of clinical trials.

The agency has set up a formal oversight committee to resolve disputes surrounding clinical holds. FDA reviewers and supervisors involved in the clinical hold present their rationale for their decision to this committee. The committee members discuss the appropriateness of the clinical hold with the reviewers. The committee communicates directly with the reviewing division and not the sponsor. If a hold is reversed by the committee, this will be communicated through the reviewing division. History suggests that clinical holds are upheld by the clinical hold committee

G. Adverse Reaction Reporting

Federal regulations (21 CFR 312.32) require that the safety of volunteers participating in clinical trials be continually monitored throughout the course of the development program. During the IND stage of drug development, all adverse drug reactions (ADRs) that are considered serious and/or unexpected and thought to be associated with the use of the drug are subject to "alert" reporting. Serious means that there is a significant hazard; unexpected means that the serious event has not as yet been described in the investigator's brochure.

Depending on the nature and seriousness of the event, the time frame in which the event is reportable differs. A serious unexpected ADR must be reported to the FDA within 10 working days, in writing. If the ADR is fatal or life-threatening, the agency must be notified by telephone within 3 working days from the time of receipt of the information with a 10-day follow-up written report. In the written report, the sponsor must refer to all previously submitted safety reports previously filed concerning similar ADRs and evaluate the ADR relative to the previously reported similar events. Other ADRs that are nonserious; serious and expected; not related, deaths; and dropouts must be reported in an IND annual report [4,5].

In summary, federal regulations have been primarily designed to protect human subjects during all aspects of the clinical research process. These include:

1. Requiring sponsors to justify initial testing of drugs in humans by filing an IND, the basis of which is extensive preclinical safety testing
2. Establishing criteria for subject selection for human testing and/assuring the use of qualified investigators
3. Assuring local control over the research process through the use of IRBs
4. Assuring that volunteers in research studies are adequately informed as to the nature and risks of the research
5. Assuring that the safety data contained in IND are adequate to protect volunteers and that the proposed research can be delayed or terminated by the FDA if adequate safeguards are not present
6. Requiring that sponsors report promptly to the FDA untoward adverse reactions that occur during clinical testing

III. COMPLIANCE AND ENFORCEMENT: SPONSORS AND INVESTIGATORS

A second way in which the FDA regulates the clinical research process is by (a) defining the roles and responsibilities of both investigators and sponsors and (b) auditing the conduct of clinical studies by both investigators and sponsors.

Federal regulations covering sponsors and investigators outline their responsibilities and specify what processes and activities should be inspected based on Good Clinical Practices (GCP) guidelines.

A. Responsibilities of Sponsors

According to the regulations outlining the responsibilities of sponsors (21 CFR 312.50), sponsors are responsible for selecting qualified investigators, providing them with information needed to conduct a study, and assuring that the investigator follow procedures outlined in the protocol and assure that FDA and investigators are promptly informed of significant ADRs or other risks associated with the use of the drug [6].

1. Selecting Investigators and Monitoring Studies

a. Investigator Selection. The sponsor must have all participating investigators complete and sign a Statement of Investigator Form (Form-FDA

1572), which contains information about the investigator and any sub-investigators and site of the study. By signing this form, the investigator pledges that the study will be conducted according to the regulations governing clinical investigations.

b. Monitoring the Investigation. A study must be monitored to validate study data and assure that safety of human subjects participating in the trial is maintained. Studies should be monitored according to written procedures. Periodic site visits must be conducted by the sponsor in which subject records and case report forms are examined, and investigator activities are monitored to assess compliance with regulations.

2. Information for Investigators

Prior to study initiation, the investigator must be properly informed about the profile of a drug through the investigator's brochure and any other information pertinent to the safety of the drug. Investigators must also be updated periodically on any new developments such as ADRs or new toxicology information that bears on safety.

3. Drug Disposition

The sponsor must assure that the investigator accounts for the use of investigational drug and maintain records of drug shipments. These records must be maintained for at least 2 years following the marketing of a drug or study completion. The sponsors must ensure that all unused drug is returned or disposed of after study completion or discontinuation.

B. Responsibilities of Investigators

According to the regulations defining the responsibilities of investigators, an investigator is responsible for seeing that a study is conducted according to IND regulations, that research follows the protocol, and that the rights and welfare of participating subjects are maintained (21 CFR 312.53). Investigators have the following responsibilities [1].

1. Maintaining Control of the Drug

Drug can be administered only to subjects involved in the approved clinical protocol by the investigator or his designee. Drug may not be diverted for other uses. In addition, the investigator must prepare and maintain dispensation records.

2. Record Keeping

The investigator must keep data and case report forms for 2 years following marketing approval or discontinuation of an IND.

3. IRB Approval and Informed Consent

The investigator must obtain IRB approval for the study and obtain informed consent from all patients who enroll in the trial. Changes to the study protocol cannot be made without IRB approval. Changes to the protocol such as an extension of the study require another informed consent.

4. Information for Sponsors

The investigator must update the sponsor on the incidence of adverse reactions that are thought to be causally related to drug.

C. The Inspection Process

The FDA Bioresearch Monitoring Program was established in 1977 to conduct audits of clinical investigators, sponsors, IRBs, and animal testing facilities. The purpose of these audits is to protect the rights and welfare of human subjects and to evaluate the quality and integrity of the data used to support a clinical indication and whether that data can be validated through an inspection of both sponsor and investigator records. Audits are conducted by field investigators who are located at district offices throughout the United States and are employed by the Division of Scientific Investigations of the FDA.

There are two major classes of inspection, Routine and For Cause. *Routine* inspections are performed for pivotal clinical studies, the data from which are submitted in an NDA. Scientists from the FDA Office of Scientific Investigations are responsible for selecting the studies to be audited, and selecting patients from the studies for purposes of record examination. Following the inspection, the results are conveyed to the investigator, and a Form FDA-483 is completed that outlines the deficiencies that were found. These findings are also reported to the local headquarters in the form of an Establishment Inspection Report (EIR). An inspectional letter is then issued to the investigator. If only minor compliance problems are noted, a "No Action" letter is issued. If significant deficiencies are noted, a "Voluntary Action Indicated Level-2" letter is issued. The purpose of this letter is to provide remediation for the investigator. The last type of letter is the "Voluntary Action Indicated Level-3" or "Notice of Adverse Findings." The investigator must respond in writing to this letter.

For Cause inspections are triggered for very serious violations or for the following reasons:

The investigator has participated in a very large number of studies that appear to the naked eye to be unmanageable.

The clinical investigator has conducted studies outside his or her medical expertise.
Safety and efficacy findings at a particular site depart significantly from findings at other sites.
Sponsors find difficulty in obtaining case report forms from the investigator, or other serious deficiencies are noted.

The goal of the FDA inspection process is to determine whether the investigator is in compliance with the regulations governing the conduct of clinical trials. FDA inspectors will perform a general inspection examining the conduct and monitoring of a study and a data audit. The audit includes an examination of the following:

1. Study conduct
   a. Nature and extent of sponsor monitoring
   b. Drug disposition and accountability
   c. Protocol adherence
2. Informed consent
   Signed informed consent obtained from all test subjects?
3. IRB approval
   Protocol and amendments approved by IRB?
4. Patient records
   a. Patient records organized and is source data available to support case report forms?
   b. Has investigator kept study records for 2 years after termination of the study or approval of an NDA?

Selected case report forms are requested by the Office of Scientific Investigations to be sent by the sponsor. These are forwarded to the field investigator, who on arrival at the site will compare the case report forms with the investigators' records to determine if the patient existed, the diagnosis, and the response to treatment.

The FDA also monitors the sponsor mainly with respect to the adequacy of the sponsor's monitoring program for clinical trials. An effective monitoring program by the sponsor ensures both the protection of subject welfare and validity of the database. An FDA auditor will examine the following:

Training and qualifications of the clinical monitor
Standard Operating Procedures (SOPs) for monitors
Institutional Review Board (IRB) approval for the study

Clinical Trial Material (CTM) supply accountability
Compliance with ADR reporting
Evidence for a pre-study site visit and periodic site visits

Periodic site visits by monitors represent the key manner in which the sponsor determines whether an investigator has complied with study procedures. Monitors are responsible for determining the following:

Study protocol is being followed.
Study facilities were evaluated.
Amendments to the protocol have been reported to the IRB.
The investigator has reported ADRs to the sponsor in a timely fashion.

There are three major problem areas that can affect the validity of a study and for which an FDA inspector will give particular attention to during an audit. These are absent or incomplete informed consent forms, protocol deviations that are unaccounted for, and inadequate or unavailable patient records and/or case report forms.

Failed inspections can result in investigator disqualification, termination of the IND, and/or discontinuation of the study [3,7,8].

IV. REGULATORY GUIDANCE AND FACILITATION OF THE DRUG DEVELOPMENT PROCESS

The FDA has exerted considerable influence on the drug development activities of pharmaceutical sponsors in the past 10 years. This has occurred in two major ways. First, the FDA provides guidance to pharmaceutical sponsors by issuing guidelines for clinical research, providing both educational and regulatory information to sponsors through the FDA Advisory Committee system, encouraging meetings with sponsors, and providing informal guidance in "talk papers" or publications. A second way the FDA exerts influence on the drug development and clinical research process is to issue regulations that facilitate the development of drugs that have a clear and unequivocal benefit to patients with life-threatening or severely debilitating diseases. These regulations provide sponsors with incentives to develop drugs for which there is a strong perceived clinical need and for which few alternative therapies are available. The passage of these regulations has been largely spurred by the AIDS epidemic and the need for innovative approaches to the treatment of this disease.

A. Regulatory/Scientific Guidance

1. Clinical Guidelines

One manner in which the FDA helps sponsors conduct clinical research is to issue clinical guidelines (21 CFR 312.145) that are specific to a therapeutic area (e.g., clinical guidelines for the evaluation of anti-anginal drugs). In these guidelines, the design of clinical trials pertinent to proving clinical efficacy, defining clinical end points, safety parameters, dose response variables, and other issues germane to a particular therapeutic area are outlined. There are approximately 25 guidelines specific to clinical therapeutic areas as well as other general guidelines, manufacturing guidelines, bioequivalence guidelines, etc. Unfortunately, many of the clinical guidelines were issued in the 1970s, and most are undergoing revision in an effort to keep up with both changing science and regulations. Sponsors are advised not to overinterpret these guidelines, but to use the information they contain in conjunction with the most recent advances in scientific thinking to develop a clinical trial program that adequately demonstrates safety and efficacy of the product under development.

2. FDA–Sponsor Meetings

Sponsors often need to meet with the FDA reviewing division to discuss drug development plans, obtain advice on the studies needed to support an indication, and inform the agency about particular safety issues that might affect the development plan. The most common meetings are the pre-IND, End of Phase 1, End of Phase 2, pre-NDA meetings and End of the Review Conference (21 CFR 312.47). Divisional policies on the scheduling of meetings are highly divergent. For example, the Division of Anti-Viral Drugs may schedule more sponsor meetings than other divisions because of the nature of the drug applications submitted to that particular division. Many drug applications are for drugs to treat life-threatening diseases such as AIDS. Because these drugs are subject to expedited development and review (21 CFR 312 Subpart E), frequent meetings between the sponsor and FDA are necessary in order to resolve issues affecting approval.

The pre-IND meeting is usually scheduled to determine whether any additional pharmacology/toxicology studies are needed over and above those usually conducted to support an IND.

The End of Phase 1 meeting is granted for sponsors developing drugs for life-threatening diseases because development times are often abbreviated. Therefore, early agreement on the design of pivotal clinical trials and safety data collection is desirable.

The End of Phase 2 meeting is for the sponsor to demonstrate that based on testing in Phase 2 clinical trials, it is safe to conduct more large-scale Phase 3 trials. Most sponsors also attempt to show the agency some preliminary evidence of efficacy at this meeting. The sponsor may also wish to obtain an agreement with the FDA on any additional data that might be needed to support an NDA. Often agreements are made on formatting of medical reports and statistical treatment of the data.

The pre-NDA meeting is designed to provide a summary of the NDA, usually through a preliminary format that outlines the various reports contained in the NDA application. The sponsor will usually inform the agency that sufficient evidence for efficacy and safety exists to support the application.

The End of the Review Conference often takes place after an action letter on an application, usually a non-approval letter. The agency and the sponsor can determine what steps are necessary to remediate the deficiencies in the application.

Most of these meetings afford the FDA an opportunity to influence drug development during the IND stage so that applications submitted to the agency contain the necessary and sufficient data to support a clinical claim.

3. Advisory Committees

The FDA often seeks the opinion of outside experts to aid the agency in making decisions on the approvability of a drug. It is believed that qualified experts provide a balanced perspective in the deliberation process. Each reviewing division within the FDA has established one or more Advisory Committees (e.g., Cardio-Renal Advisory Committee, Anesthetic and Life Support Advisory Committee). These committees comprise scientific experts from academic medicine. In addition, a consumer representative, biostatistician, and other additional members deemed to be important by the agency may serve on these committees. Each committee has an executive secretary appointed by the FDA Advisory Committee office who handles the administrative functions of the committee.

These committees meet periodically and their deliberations are usually conducted in an open public forum. They often address a variety of issues, including the development and revision of clinical guidelines, whether a drug application contains sufficient safety and efficacy information for approval, and/or special labeling revisions such as class labeling statements.

The role of the Advisory Committee is to assess the risks and benefits of drugs to determine their adequacy in the treatment of various diseases. The Advisory Committee system is adept at helping the agency make critical decisions regarding risk/benefit evaluations. There are numerous examples of the effectiveness of this process. For example, the Gastrointestinal Drugs Advisory Committee failed to approve domperidone, a promotility drug developed for gastroparesis, because the sponsor failed to provide any comparative safety data with a standard treatment, metoclopramide, and because domperidone exhibited marginal efficacy in clinical trials [9]. In another example, The Advisory Committee failed to approve lidoflazine, a calcium channel blocker, for the treatment of angina. Although the sponsor was able to show that the drug was equal in effectiveness to other marketed anti-anginals, in one study, a 2% mortality rate was found among patients who experienced atrial fibrillation. Deaths were reportedly due to the induction of a proarrhythmia, torsade de pointes. The Advisory Committee concluded that the risks of the life-threatening arrhythmias outweighed the benefits and recommended that the sponsor perform a prospective trial in patients at risk for the development of arrhythmias and in addition perform an efficacy study in an intolerant refractory group before approval could be considered [10].

Although there is no requirement regarding the amount of safety data needed to support the approval of a drug, it is the responsibility of the Advisory Committee to perform a risk-benefit analysis based on the scientific expertise of its members and their knowledge of the current state of medical standards, practice, and ethics.

4. Publications/Talk Papers

In an effort to facilitate the development of drugs for life-threatening and severely debilitating diseases such as AIDS or cancer, the FDA collaborates with outside consultants and other governmental agencies such as the National Institutes of Health to expedite drug approvals. In 1991, the FDA and the National Cancer Institute published a paper outlining clinical end points that might be used to obtain approval for cancer drugs [11]. The rationale for using clinical end points other than survival to demonstrate efficacy was presented. In addition, comparative trials are necessary only if clinical benefit cannot be demonstrated without them. When the benefit of new cancer treatments is dramatic, these data need not necessarily be based on a randomized trial.

It is recognized that all cancer drugs will not produce a complete cure and many exhibit pronounced toxicities. Any drug approved for use in cancer must balance clinical benefit versus toxicity. For example, a drug with substantial toxicity but added benefit in refractory patients may be approved.

Or, a drug with less efficacy than standard treatment but a superior safety profile could be approved.

End points other than survival may be used to demonstrate clinical effectiveness. These include disease-free survival, complete response rate, response rate, and quality of life.

Disease-free survival is a valid end point when a disease is marked by symptomatic recurrences, such as breast cancer. An improvement in symptoms translates into an improved quality of life.

For a number of cancers, a complete treatment response can correlate with an increased rate of survival, or for solid tumors such as melanoma, with a response rate of 20% or above. Thus, both complete and partial response may be acceptable criteria for demonstrating benefits.

Quality of life measures may be acceptable in conjunction with some of the above measures and may include improvement in tumor-related symptoms, improved psychological functions, and decrease in hospital stay. These types of publications provide needed information to industry for the design of pivotal clinical trials.

FDA "talk papers" are prepared by the FDA Press Office to guide FDA personnel in responding with consistency and accuracy to questions from the public on subjects of current interest. Although talk papers are not intended for general distribution outside the FDA, the information they contain is public. Copies are available to the public at the FDA Press Office.

The FDA—through the development of clinical guidelines, use of Advisory Committees, allowing for formal contacts with the agency, and provision of scientific guidance through the issuance of publications and talk papers—guides and influences the clinical development process.

B. Regulatory Facilitation

In the interest of providing maximum public health benefit, the FDA has promulgated a variety of regulations that facilitate the development of needed drugs and provides for the broader use of experimental drugs in life-threatening and severely debilitating diseases.

1. Treatment Use and Sale of Investigational New Drugs

In 1987, regulations were passed that make promising new drugs available early in the drug development process and before a drug is approved to large numbers of patients (21 CFR 312.34). These regulations not only allow patients access to new drugs quickly but also make possible the collection of safety data in a large sample of patients over a brief period of time. This exposure is obtained through a Treatment IND. These regulations were spurred largely as a response to AIDS advocacy groups who sought a more concerted effort by the agency to review and approve drugs for this disorder. The approval of zidovudine (AZT) for AIDS provides an example of what these regulations intended. Drugs developed for any immediately life-threatening (e.g., advanced congestive heart failure) or serious (e.g., advanced multiple sclerosis) disease in which death is a likely consequence without quick access to treatment are candidates for Treatment INDs.

Treatment IND status is granted only when effective alternative treatment is unavailable, when the drug is undergoing evaluation in controlled clinical trials, and the sponsor is actively pursuing marketing approval.

The regulations governing the conduct of clinical studies under an IND apply to treatment INDs. Obtaining informed consent and IRB approval, and reporting adverse reactions in a timely fashion, are requirements that must be adhered to.

Patients may be charged for a drug under a Treatment IND. However, prior written approval must first be obtained from the FDA. Charges cannot exceed manufacturing, research, and development costs. Only a small number of sponsors of Treatment INDs have taken advantage of this aspect of the regulations. Also, the sponsor may not commercially distribute, promote or test market the investigational drug (21 CFR 312.7).

Approximately 20 drugs have been granted Treatment IND status for such diverse conditions as Parkinson's disease, AIDS, infant respiratory distress syndrome, obsessive-compulsive disorder, *Pneumocystis* infection in AIDS, and Gaucher's disease.

A major advantage of the Treatment IND to the sponsor is quick review and approval of drugs by the FDA. The average time to approval for these drugs is 8 months. These regulations are of prime benefit to patients needing unique therapies for otherwise untreatable, refractory, and degenerative diseases [12,13].

2. Subpart E Designation

The Subpart E regulations (21 CFR 312.80) were issued to expedite both development and review of drugs for life-threatening and severely debilitating disease. A key aspect of these regulations is sponsor-agency consultation very early in the drug development process in which preclinical and clinical studies necessary for the filing of an IND are agreed upon. Meetings between the agency and sponsor may be frequent, resulting in the submission of a Treatment IND and timely review of the application by the agency.

3. Subpart H Designation

The Subpart H rule (21 CFR 314.500–314.560) allows for the use of surrogate end points as primary measures in studies of drugs purported to affect the well-being of patients with life-threatening disease. A surrogate end point is a laboratory marker or physical sign that is used as a substitute for a clinically meaningful end point. For example, elevated cholesterol may be a risk factor for future cerebral vascular events. Therefore, a reduction in cholesterol levels may improve the probability of survival in patients at risk for coronary artery disease. The FDA has approved drugs on the basis of surrogate end point data, provided a link is established between the surrogate end point and clinical benefit. The approval of most antihypertensive drugs is a case in point. The Subpart H regulations provide for the approval of a drug even when the link is not well established, provided that the sponsor conducts well-controlled studies following approval to demonstrate clinical benefit. A drug may be withdrawn from the market if the surrogate marker does not predict clinical benefit.

These regulations also carry a number of postmarketing restrictions, including restricting distribution of drug supplies and requiring the submission of promotional materials prior to advertising or even prior to marketing approval.

According to Temple [14], the use of surrogate end points can be problematic for the following reasons.

1. The purported relationship between the surrogate and clinical benefit may prove to be inaccurate. For example, the use of surrogate end points in cardiovascular disease represents a case in which an improvement in end points—such as cardiac output and exercise tolerance with inotropic drugs—results in high mortality rates despite short-term benefits.
2. The benefits of a drug may be overestimated based on effect on the surrogate end point because overall clinical improvement may be minimal. For example, a reduction in tumor size produced by an anticancer drug may translate into minimal clinical benefit or survival.
3. The use of surrogates emphasizes only one effect of a drug. Most drugs have multiple properties, some of which may be detrimental to long-term clinical benefit. For example, diuretics lower blood pressure, which may prevent future cardiovascular events, but also lower potassium and increase glucose levels, which could exacerbate cardiovascular disease. For all of the above reasons, the link between the surrogate end point and associated clinical benefit must be eventually validated by the sponsor who attempts to hasten drug approval by obtaining Subpart H status.

4. Orphan Drugs

The Orphan Drug Act was implemented in 1983 to foster the development of drugs for rare diseases that otherwise might not be developed because of limited marketability and patent protection. The passage of the Act represents another way in which the agency influences the clinical development process of pharmaceutical sponsors by providing incentives for the development of these treatments. The applicable regulations implementing the Act are 21 CFR 316.1 to 316.52.

A rare disease is one in which less than 200,000 patients per year are affected or one in which more than 200,000 individuals are affected, but the costs of development and marketing are unlikely to be recouped. A major incentive for industry to develop such drugs is the exclusivity provision of the act, which allows 7 years' exclusivity after the approval date. Another application for the same orphan indication may be approved only if the original sponsor agrees to it or if the sponsor cannot guarantee sufficient marketing supplies. The act was amended in 1990 to allow for shared exclusivity between two sponsors developing a product for the same disease.

The act also guarantees that the sponsor receive written guidance from the agency as to the required clinical and preclinical studies needed for approval of an orphan drug. In addition, grants from the Orphan Drug Office and tax credits are additional incentives that a sponsor may take advantage of [12].

Thus, the FDA through the issuance of new regulations and through informal guidance exerts significant influences over the drug development process in the United States. New regulations facilitate the development of needed and unique drugs by reducing development times and speeding the review process. The agency is more collaborative and interactive with pharmaceutical sponsors who are developing breakthrough drugs in order to maximize benefits to public health than with sponsors who are developing drugs with little perceived therapeutic benefit beyond currently marketed therapies.

VI. INTERNATIONAL REGULATORY ISSUES

Because of the conflicting demands for new medical advances on the one hand and cost controls for pharmaceuticals and medical care in general on the other, both government and industry have realized that there is considerable potential savings in terms of governmental and regulatory resources and pharmaceutical spending by harmonizing regulatory requirements around the world. The competitiveness of global markets has placed pressures on regulatory agencies to eliminate duplicative regulatory burdens on industry and unnecessary burdens to foreign trade.

The FDA has concluded that international harmonization advances its public health mission by decreasing the spread of disease both within countries and across borders; improving the quality, safety, and efficacy of important products; increasing patient access to safe and effective products; increasing the flow of medical information between countries; and, in the long term, maximizing FDA resources.

Achieving harmonization is not likely to be a smooth process, especially in the areas of use of foreign data to support NDAs, safety assessment and safety data reporting, design of pivotal clinical trials, and agreements on clinical end points. Some of these issues are covered in current regulations while others are being discussed within the International Conference on Harmonization.

A. Foreign Data

Acceptance of foreign clinical data in support of an NDA is provided by the regulations (21 CFR 312.120) if foreign studies are well designed and ethically conducted using qualified investigators. These studies do not need to be conducted under a U.S. IND and may be used as the sole basis for marketing approval, provided that the data is verifiable and is applicable to the U.S. population.

However, the approval of many drugs in the United States based solely on foreign data is unlikely because of the following reasons:

1. Diagnostic criteria for certain disorders may differ across cultures.
2. Therapeutic practices and standards of medical care are widely different.
3. Concomitant therapies differ across countries.
4. Body size differs across cultures, which may affect dosing requirements.
5. Genetic differences in drug metabolism may differentially influence drug action and affect generalizability.
6. General health and diet can influence study results.

Therefore, some experience in a U.S. population may be important prior to marketing. In addition, conducting studies in the United States allows for medical opinion leaders to gain experience with the drug and to pass on this experience to other physicians. In addition, exposure in the U.S. population provides experience in special patient populations such as the elderly, children, and "at risk" populations [15].

If foreign data constitute the majority of exposure in an NDA, it is important to meet with the agency to determine what the necessary data requirements will be for registration.

To be acceptable in support of U.S. registration, foreign studies must be conducted according to Good Clinical Practices. A foreign study conducted under a U.S. IND must conform to U.S. regulations. If not conducted under a U.S. IND, foreign studies must meet the Helsinki guidelines or the laws and regulations of the country in which the study is conducted.

Foreign studies are likely to be audited by the Office of Scientific Investigations if they are pivotal to the approval of an application. Often, inspection of foreign study sites may be problematic. According to Barton [7], the most common deficiencies are poor record keeping, protocol violations, problems with informed consent, and inadequate drug accountability.

One source of problems for U.S. sponsors conducting trials overseas is that U.S. and European Community (EC) guidelines differ on a number of Good Clinical Practice issues, especially in the areas of adverse reaction reporting and records retention. Adverse reaction reporting is more stringent in the United States; requiring foreign investigators to report adverse reactions on the U.S. regulatory time line can be a potential problem for U.S. sponsors. On the other hand, EC guidelines require that investigators retain study records for up to 15 years, in contrast to the U.S. requirement of 2 years after study completion or drug approval. In addition, sponsors are required to keep study records for the lifetime of a product for studies conducted in EC countries [16].

Sponsors using foreign clinical trials as a major source of data for U.S. approval must remain cognizant of the above compliance factors.

B. International Harmonization of Regulatory Requirements

As the cost of drug development and support for regulatory oversight increases, a need for streamlining exists to maximize efficiency in the review and approval of drugs. This entails that drug development programs have a world-wide focus and an elimination of multiple registration requirements across different countries.

In an effort to achieve this goal, an International Conference on Harmonization (ICH) was established to develop a single set of requirements for drug testing that may be used for worldwide registration. The conference has been organized by the Commission of the European Communities, the FDA, and the Japanese Ministry of Health and Welfare along with professional pharmaceutical associations affiliated with various countries.

The International Conference on Harmonization has met three times, in Brussels in 1991, Orlando in 1992, and Japan in 1995. Preparation for these meetings is coordinated by a steering committee, which is chaired by one of the regulatory agencies and is rotated annually. The steering committee is advised by three expert working groups on safety, quality, and efficacy consisting of representatives from both industry and regulatory bodies. Topics for harmonization are selected by the steering committee on the basis of advice by the expert working groups.

The ICH committee has addressed issues critical to the development of both safe and effective medications worldwide. These include international standards for adverse reaction reporting, special populations, the extent of needed safety exposure, dose-response requirements needed for registration, and good clinical practices.

1. Safety Data Management

The ICH working group has concentrated on developing standard definitions for clinical safety reporting and the outlining of methods for expedited reporting. The following definitions that apply to adverse experiences were developed in cooperation with the World Health Organization.

a. Adverse Event (or Experience) "Any untoward medical occurrence in a patient or clinical investigation subject administered a pharmaceutical product which does not necessarily have a causal relationship with this treatment."

b. Adverse Drug Reaction (ADR) "All noxious and unintended responses to a medicinal product related to any dose should be considered adverse drug reactions."

c. Unexpected Adverse Drug Reaction "An adverse reaction, the nature or severity of which is not consistent with applicable product information."

d. Signal "Reported information on a possible causal relationship between an adverse event and a drug, the relationship being unknown or incompletely documented previously. Usually more than a single report is required to generate a signal, depending upon the seriousness of the event and the quality of the information."

e. Serious Adverse Event or Reaction "A serious adverse event (experience) or reaction is any untoward medical occurrence that at any dose:

Results in death
Requires inpatient hospitalization or prolongation of existing hospitalization
Results in persistent or significant disability/incapacity

Is life threatening
Is a congenital anomaly/birth defect

Cancers and congenital anomalies/birth defects should also be regarded as "serious" even if they do not result in one of the outcomes listed above.

Other important medical reports that may not be immediately life threatening or result in death or hospitalization are convulsions, blood dyscrasias, drug dependency or abuse, or emergency room treatment for allergic bronchospasm.

f. Unexpected Adverse Drug Reaction An unexpected ADR is one in which the nature and severity of the event is not consistent with that outlined in the Investigator's Brochure or other source documents. This includes expected ADRs that change in severity or specificity. The Working Group recommended that a Core Safety Data Sheet (CSDS) be included in the Investigators Brochure that periodically updates expected ADRs.

Adverse drug reactions should be subject to alert reporting if they are serious, unexpected, and bear a plausibly causal relationship to drug treatment. Any ADR information that influences the risk-benefit assessment of the drug, such as an increase in incidence or severity, lack of efficacy in a life-threatening disease, and data such as carcinogenicity findings from animal studies, is reportable.

Serious unexpected ADRs should be reported within 15 calendar days. If the ADR is life threatening, regulatory agencies must be notified within 5 days by telephone or writing of knowledge of the event with a complete written report submitted within 10 days. If the drug is already marketed and late-phase research is still being conducted, the 15-day clock applies unless the study involves a new population or indication [17].

2. Special Populations

The ICH has examined the design of clinical trials to ensure that special populations such as the elderly are represented, so that the results are generalizable to the population as a whole once a drug is approved. The recent ICH guideline for special populations addresses the elderly. The following recommendations are made in this guideline:

1. It is important to include patients aged 75 and above in clinical trials, and to avoid arbitrary upper age cutoffs and the exclusion of patients with concomitant diseases.
2. Geriatric patients should be included in sufficient numbers to permit comparisons with a younger population. In addition, the database

should be examined for the presence of age-related differences in adverse events and efficacy.

3. Pharmacokinetic differences between younger and older patients should be examined to determine if hepatic or renal differences in functioning influence the pharmacological effects of drugs. Age-related differences may be evaluated in late Phase 2/early Phase 3 testing through the use of a pharmacokinetic screen or formal pharmacokinetic studies. The pharmacokinetic screen involves obtaining blood samples for "trough" plasma level determinations under steady-state conditions. A few samples are collected from a large number of patients with the time of sample collection being recorded. With a large number of patients, the influence of a variety of demographic and disease variables as they relate to drug plasma levels can be assessed. In contrast, the more formal pharmacokinetic analysis requires specialized single- or multiple-dose pharmacokinetic analysis comparing young and old patients.

   Other types of pharmacokinetic/pharmacodynamic studies that should be considered are studies in the renally or hepatically impaired, dose-response trials, and drug interaction studies [18].

3. Dose-Response Studies

The ICH assessed the design of pivotal dose-response studies and the use of dose-ranging studies prior to the conduct of Phase 3 dose-response trials. Internationalizing requirements for these types of trials allows for more efficient global drug development by providing a common database that multiple regulatory agencies can evaluate.

A key feature of dose-response studies is to characterize dose-related effects for efficacy and adverse reactions. This allows for dosing recommendations based on perceived risk-benefit judgments.

Dose-response curves are more easy to obtain when the response variable is easily measured and characterized (e.g., blood pressure). Dose titration in individual patients allows for accurate estimates of dosing in larger scale trials. When a given response is delayed in onset (e.g., treatment of depression; survival in a variety of diseases), dose titration studies are not easily conducted. The early use of multiple-dose parallel studies may be needed. Parallel studies should contain three or more dosage levels, one of which should be placebo. This allows for a test of linearity.

The dose-response guidelines stress that dose-response characterization should be an integral part of drug development for all new drugs [19].

4. The Extent of Population Exposure to Assess Clinical Safety: Long-Term Treatment of Non–Life-Threatening Conditions

For a drug that is to be used for long-term treatment, it is necessary to characterize the nature and frequency of adverse events occurring over a period of time. The number of drug exposures needed to describe the adverse reaction profile will depend on the incidence and seriousness of the adverse events. The guideline suggests that for most drugs, the incidence and seriousness of most adverse events can be determined within 6 months, provided patients are treated at therapeutic doses. A cohort of 300 to 600 patients may be needed for this purpose. To assess whether common events increase or decrease over time and to determine the incidence of common events whose onset is delayed, up to 100 patients may need to be treated for up to 1 year.

NDAs for new chemical entities could contain up to 1500 patients. Larger databases may be needed if late-occurring ADRs or an increase in frequency or severity of ADRs is likely; if there is a need to be more specific about the incidence of rare ADRs; where the benefit of the therapy is small relative to the risk; or where the drug treatment may add to the existing level of morbidity [20].

5. Good Clinical Practices

The acceptance of clinical data from a variety of countries around the world is critical to the harmonization process. The ICH Expert Working Group has reached consensus on the format and content of the Investigator's Brochure and the essential documents required for the conduct of global clinical studies [21].

The documents required are classified according to the stage of a study they are generated; before, during and after study completion; and whether the said documents appear in the investigator and/or sponsor files.

Master files are established for both investigator and sponsor prior to the initiation of the study. It is the responsibility of the study monitor to determine that investigator and sponsor files are complete.

a. Before the Clinical Trial The following documents should be one file before the start of the trial in both investigator and sponsor files:

Investigator brochure
Signed protocol, amendments, case report form
Patient information sheet, informed consent, and advertisement for study
Information on compensation

Insurance statement, if applicable
Signed study agreement between institution, sponsor, and investigator
IRB approval
Instructions for handling investigational product and study materials
Details of drug shipment
Certificate of analysis
Treatment-decoding information for emergencies

In addition, the sponsor files should contain:

Sample of container label
Master randomization codes
Prestudy monitoring report
Study initiation monitoring report

b. During the Clinical Trial Both sponsor and investigator files should contain the following:

Investigator brochure update
Revisions to protocol, CRFs, informed consent, subject information sheet, and advertisement
IRB or ethics committee opinions on protocol, amendments, informed consent
Regulatory authorizations/notifications
CVs for additional investigators
Updates of medical laboratory values or technical procedures
Documentation of clinical trial material shipment
Completed case report forms
Documentation of case report form corrections
Notification to investigator of safety alert reports
Interim or annual reports to the IRB
Log of subjects screened for study entry and enrolled
Drug accountability

In addition, the files of the sponsor should contain:

Certificate of analysis of new batches of investigational products
Monitoring reports of site visits
Subject code list

Investigator files should also contain the following:

Signed informed consent forms
Source documents

c. After Completion or Termination of the Study The investigator and sponsor files should contain:

Documentation of product accountability and product destruction
Final report to IRB and final clinical report if needed
Records of retained body fluid/tissue samples
Completed subject code listing (investigator only)
Audit certificate and closeout monitoring report (sponsor only)

Harmonization is a continuing process that will eventually result in an elimination of redundance in regulatory requirements around the world and achieve agreement on the interpretation and application of regulations. The goal of the ICH is likely to be achieved because of the continuing dialogue between regulatory agencies and the pharmaceutical industry.

VI. SUMMARY

The FDA, by virtue of the Food, Drug, and Cosmetic Act of 1938 and amendments to the Act, exerts substantial control over all aspects of human clinical testing in the United States.

The primary goal of regulations governing human testing is the protection of human subjects. Sponsors conducting clinical testing are required to file an IND; prepare scientifically acceptable clinical protocols that are completed by qualified clinical investigators; select volunteers for inclusion in studies who meet eligibility requirements; assure the study undergoes institutional review; and assure that the investigator obtains informed consent from study volunteers and reports ADRs that occur in clinical testing to both the sponsor and FDA in a timely fashion. In addition, the FDA has the authority to delay or eliminate clinical testing if subject safety or the scientific validity of the study is in doubt.

To assure that the sponsor and clinical investigators comply with the regulations governing human testing, the FDA has the authority to audit investigators and sponsors to determine if each has complied with Good Clinical Practice requirements.

Finally, the FDA facilitates the development of drugs for life-threatening and severely debilitating diseases by promulgating regulations that provide incentives for sponsors to test, develop, and market drugs for these diseases. In addition, the FDA provides guidance in clinical development through the use of Advisory Committees, issuance of clinical guidelines and talk papers, and facilitating sponsor-agency interactions.

The FDA has joined with other regulatory agencies around the world and with professional pharmaceutical organizations to internationalize requirements for product registration and Good Clinical Practices. International harmonization of regulatory requirements is to the advantage of all regulatory authorities and the public they serve because the drug development process will be streamlined and, hence, expedited.

REFERENCES

1. A. M. Horowitz, Good clinical practices, *Multi-Company, Multi-Country Clinical Trials: Implementation, Monitoring and Regulations* (R. Simmons, ed.), Interpharm. Press, Buffalo Grove, IL, 1993, p. 123.
2. P. W. Goebel, The role of the institutional review board, *Drug Info. J. 22*:161 (1988).
3. G. Turner, A. B. Lisook, and D. P. Delman, FDA's conduct, review, and evaluation of inspections of clinical investigators, *Drug Info. J. 21*:117 (1987).
4. W. W. Vodra, A comparison of drug requirements for drug experience reports before and after FDA approval, Presentation at the Food, Law and Drug Institute, Washington, DC, 1987.
5. H. P. Shu, Regulatory aspects of the development of new chemical entities in the United States, *Multi-Company, Multi-Country Clinical Trials: Implementation, Monitoring and Regulations* (R. Simmons, ed.), Interpharm Press, Buffalo Grove, IL, 1993, p. 58.
6. J. R. Wilson, Sponsor responsibilities for the on site inspection of clinical trial data, *Reg. Affairs 4*:221 (1992).
7. B. L. Barton, FDA's inspections of US and non-US clinical studies, *Drug Info. J. 24*:463 (1990).
8. T. J. Kirsch, Sponsor education of clinical research investigators in the clinical research process, *Drug Info. J. 22*:181 (1988).
9. J. H. Lewis, Risk/benefit assessment of new drugs; perspective of a former FDA Advisory Committee Member, *Drug Info. J. 27*:1037 (1993).
10. L. L. Miller, Risk/benefit assessment of new drugs: the "greased pig" of drug development, *Drug Info. J. 27*:1011 (1993).
11. J. A. O'Shaughnessy, R. E. Wittes, G. Burke, M. A. Friedman, J. R. Johnson, J. E. Niederhuber, M. L. Rothenberg, J. Woodcock, B. A. Chabner, and R. Temple, Commentary concerning demonstration of safety and efficacy of investigational anticancer agents in clinical trials, *J. Clin. Oncol. 9*:2225 (1991).
12. M. E. Haffner, The Food and Drug Administration's interim rule for expedited development and approval of drugs for life threatening illnesses: orphan drug designations, *Reg. Affairs 1*:201 (1989).
13. S. R. Shulman and D. S. Raiford, FDA regulations provide broader access to unapproved drugs, *J. Clin. Pharmacol. 30*:585 (1990).

14. R. Temple, Trends in pharmaceutical development, *Drug Info. J.* *27*:355 (1993).
15. P. Botstein, Clinical data generated in other countries, Presentation at the Symposium of Pharmaceutical Development, Administration and Ethics, Tokyo, Japan, 1987.
16. D. Cocchetto, Comparison of good clinical practice guidelines in the United States versus the European Community, Presentation at the 27th Annual Meeting of the Drug Information Association, Washington, DC, 1991.
17. Expert Working Group Report, Clinical safety data management: definitions and standards for expedited reporting, draft consensus text, International Conference on Harmonization of Technical Requirements for the Registration of Pharmaceuticals for Human Use, June 24, 1993.
18. Expert Working Group Report, Studies in support of special populations: geriatrics, ICH harmonised tripartite guideline, International Conference on Harmonization of Technical Requirements for the Registration of Pharmaceuticals for Human Use, June 24, 1993.
19. Expert Working Group Report, Dose response information to support drug registration, draft tripartite guideline, International Conference on Harmonization of Technical Requirements for the Registration of Pharmaceuticals for Human Use, March 10, 1993.
20. Expert Working Group Report, The extent of population exposure to assess clinical safety for drugs intended for the long term treatment of non-life threatening conditions, draft tripartite guidelines, International Conference on Harmonization of Technical Requirements for the Registration of Pharmaceuticals for Human Use, October 27, 1993.
21. Expert Working Group Report, Good clinical practices: addenda on investigators brochure and essential documents, draft consensus text, International Conference on Harmonization of Technical Requirements for the Registration of Pharmaceuticals for Human Use, October 27, 1993.

7

Pharmacokinetics: Interactions of New Drugs and the Human Body

Gamal Hussein

Northeast Louisiana University
New Orleans, Louisiana

Barry Bleidt

Health Resources Consulting
South Charleston, West Virginia

A new drug is only as good as it proves itself to be once it is studied in humans. Theoretical calculations and animal models are used only as predictors of how a drug will act once it gets into the body. The extensive animal safety testing that is performed for a new product is designed to weed out drugs that may cause acute poisoning, lead to long-term toxicities, or present an undesirable number of adverse effects. By the time a drug is first used in people, there is a reasonable assurance that the product will be safe. There are, of course, no absolute guarantees. Many drug entities have made it to the Phase 1 trials, only to be pulled from further consideration because of information discovered during this phase.

I. INTRODUCTION

One determinant of how drugs act is interpatient variability (that is, the differences among patients—based on each's individual biological and/or genetic composition—that account for a very large portion of the variation in drug activity). Pharmacokinetic studies are the predominant part of the first phase of clinical trials. They are performed in order to establish the population parameters for important drug actions and to see how the drug, as a chemical entity, reacts with the biological functioning of the body.

These Phase 1 drug tests involve learning the key facts about how a drug will act or react in humans. There are many factors that can have an impact on a drug's effect. Table 1 presents some of the variables that can affect how a drug will act. Each factor will be discussed in subsequent sections.

Pharmacokinetic data extracted from animal research are used to estimate the initial doses that will be studied in humans. Clinical pharmacokinetic trials may include bioavailability/disposition studies (which are performed to investigate pharmacokinetic parameters such as rate of absorption, volume of distribution, metabolic pathways and elimination rate constants after single and multiple-dose administration), dose-response studies (Phase 1, 2, and 3), and drug-interaction studies (drug-drug, drug-nutrient and disease-drug interaction). Pharmacokinetic studies require the collection of various bodily fluids (e.g., blood, urine, semen) and the investigation of which is (are) the major organ(s) responsible for eliminating the drug from the body.

Pharmacokinetic studies are often associated with pharmacodynamic assessment. Pharmacodynamic studies are designed to measure the physiologic effects of a drug (e.g., reduction in blood pressure or decreased number of seizures). The drug's effect is correlated with different doses or concentrations in various body fluids and tissues. Severe adverse reactions discovered

Table 1 Intra-Patient Variables in Drug Actions

Race
Gender
Age
Pregnancy status
Kidney function
Liver function
Gastrointestinal status
Hydration level
Stomach pH
Food consumption
Concurrent drug therapy
Coexisting disease states
Nutritional state
Physical health status
Mental health status

during early phases of clinical trials may lead to the discontinuation of such studies.

Pharmacokinetic studies are also conducted in detail after the drug-approval process has been completed. Drug disposition studies in different patient populations are usually addressed after the drug has been prescribed many times and used by patients with various disorders (e.g., hepatic or renal dysfunction). While early phases of clinical trials may provide some data with regard to drug disposition in the elderly and women, data on drug disposition in other patient populations (such as the obese, those in critical care, children, oncology patients, or pregnant women) are actually assessed years later in studies utilizing larger numbers of patients than those 20 to 80 patients usually associated with Phase 1 trials.

Data extracted from clinical trials need to be assessed very carefully. Issues related to patient demographics and pertinent populations, the accuracy of doses given (time schedule that was followed), the data collection process, and the analytical techniques used for measuring drug concentrations as well as the methods used for statistical analyses need to be addressed with extreme caution [1,2].

For further details on the setting and the methodology required to conduct population pharmacokinetic research, the reader is referred to more specialized texts such as the *Guide to Clinical Trials* by Bert Spiker (New York, Raven Press, 1991). If the reader is interested in an interactive learning experience in basic and clinical pharmacokinetics, he or she is referred to an innovative, multimedia program, Practical Pharmacokinetics: Interactive Computer Program, developed by ClinPharm International (available at [504] 443-5243). The latter software is particularly useful for clinicians or others who want to learn about pharmacokinetics or for those who wish to update or expand their knowledge base in this subject area.

Pharmacokinetics is the study of how drugs act within the body. It involves the absorption, distribution, metabolism, and excretion of drugs. In this chapter, these parameters will be described relating to new compounds in clinical trials. The key data that should be extracted from these studies will also be discussed.

II. ABSORPTION

In order for a medicine to act, it must first enter the body. Injectable products are sent, via their various administration routes, directly into the body. Intravenous or intra-arterial drugs are generally considered 100 percent available, because they are placed directly into the systemic circulation. Intramuscular and subcutaneous injectable dosage forms are also considered highly available, as there is little to interfere with their entrance into the general circulation.

The scenario is much different, however, for orally administered medicinal products. In this case, the drugs must first pass through the gastrointestinal (GI) tract and then enter the portal circulation before reaching the body. The concept of drug absorption is a collective process. It is the sum of all mechanisms that influence the quantity of an orally administered dose that eventually reaches the systemic circulation. These complex mechanisms include passive absorption, active transport (which requires the expenditure of energy), pre-systemic metabolism, and GI drug degradation.

The two key components that contribute to the amount of a drug that ultimately gets into the systemic circulation are:

1. The fraction of the dose that gets absorbed from the GI tract
2. The extent to which it may undergo any pre-systemic metabolism [3]

A. Fraction of Dose Absorbed

The larger the fraction of drug absorbed from the stomach or intestines, the more bioavailable the product is considered. Some drugs vary greatly in their absorption fraction, depending on the existing circumstances at the time. For example, many antibiotics are readily absorbed in the absence of food, but if taken right after a meal, the percentage delivered to the systemic circulation is markedly decreased. The presence of antacids and certain other products (especially chelating agents) also can have a substantial impact on the amount of drug absorbed. It is important to discover these facts and quantify them before a product is put onto the market.

There are other variables that are known to influence drug absorption; some of them are listed in Table 2. For example, actively transported drugs become less available in the geriatric patient. This condition may be the result of a diminished blood flow to the area, fewer cofactors or transport proteins present, or changes within the GI cell's structure due to aging [4]. Some key vitamins and minerals, such as iron, thiamin, calcium, and B_{12}, also display reduced absorption in these individuals [5].

Another factor that affects drug absorption is gastric pH. Many products cannot be given orally because they are destroyed by the strongly acidic conditions of the stomach. Proteins, such as insulin, and other acid-labile molecules are available only as injectable dosage forms for this reason. Other drugs directly alter the pH, either by blocking the parietal cell's production of acid (such as proton pump inhibitors) or by acting as a buffer, thereby diminishing the effect of the produced acid.

There may be conditions present that alter the amount of stomach acid present. In some patients classified as acid hypersecretors (such as those

Table 2 Variables That Influence Drug Absorption

Quantity of drug ingested
Gastric or intestinal motility
pH
Gastric emptying rate
Gastric or intestinal musocal blood flow
Gastric or mucosal permeability
Composition of GI secretions
Volume of GI secretions
Coexistence of certain disease states
Availability of cofactors for active transport
Drug interactions
Presence or absence of food
Number of functioning absorbing cells
Energy available for active transport

with Zollinger-Ellison syndrome), the plethoric acid production keeps the pH at such a low number that excessive stress is placed on the stomach and the entire alimentary canal. Sometimes these conditions cause an erosion of the mucosal lining, thereby having a negative impact on drug absorption. In other patients, there may be a decline in parietal-cell function (due to age or disease), resulting in less acid secretion and an increase in gastric pH [6].

The acidity level of the GI tract can determine where and how much of a drug is absorbed. Weakly acidic drugs are usually best absorbed in an environment where the pH is lower than the pKa (negative log of the dissociation constant) of the chemical entity. In this case, the product remains more lipid soluble by staying un-ionized, thereby being more capable of passing through the lipid barriers that separate the GI tract from the systemic circulation. On the other hand, weakly basic drugs are absorbed best from a more alkaline condition, such as that found in the upper small intestine. Sometimes an acidic environment is necessary for a product to work. For example, acid hydrolysis is necessary to convert some "prodrugs" into their active form before absorption, by cleaving off a portion of the chemical moiety. In other situations, an acid-catalyzed reaction may reduce absorption.

However, the fact that most of the presently marketed drugs do not change their absorption characteristics in altered gastric pH means that they depend on passive diffusion in order to gain access to the body. In the future, drugs may depend even less on an acidic or basic environment in order to get into the systemic circulation. New dosage forms may be surrounded by a type of coating that shields them from the low pH of the stomach, to be released in a more hospitable environment. This is the basic strategy behind the time-release technology of today. The coating materials of the future envisioned by this author would be part of a delivery system that sends the drug directly to its site of action.

Two other significant factors that have an impact on drug absorption are gastric emptying rate and GI motility. Because most products depend on passive diffusion, the amount of time the drug is in contact with the mucosal wall is important. Delayed gastric emptying can alter significantly the time it takes a drug to reach its absorption sites. Increased GI motility can diminish the amount of time the drug remains in proximity with the surfaces it requires for absorption. Conversely, slowed GI motility can increase the amount absorbed and thereby cause more drug to enter the systemic circulation [7].

The clinical trials performed in Phase 1 determine the value of these pharmacokinetic parameters associated with a new drug. Drug absorption characteristics are important parameters to investigate and to quantify before a drug is brought to market.

B. Pre-Systemic Metabolism

The second factor involved in a new product's bioavailability is the amount of it remaining after the "first-pass effect." The body has evolved in such a manner that absorbed materials from the GI tract must pass through the portal circulation before gaining access to the systemic circulation. This situation exposes the substances to liver enzymes and to potential metabolism. Some products, such as the oral nitrates, are removed in substantial proportions by this hepatic first-pass metabolism, thereby necessitating that much larger doses be given orally in order to achieve a therapeutic concentration in the blood.

Another factor involved is the pre-systemic metabolism that takes place in the GI tract or that is caused by the GI flora. With some drugs, sufficient product is eliminated through these mechanisms before absorption that a larger dose must be given orally in order to compensate for this loss.

Thus, the results gathered from Phase 1 trials are used to quantify the new drug's bioavailability, represented by the symbol "F" in pharmacokinetic equations [8] where,

$$F = \text{Fraction absorbed} \times \text{fraction escaping first-pass metabolism}$$

III. DISTRIBUTION

Once a drug is absorbed, it must reach its active site in a concentration sufficient to produce a desirable effect. Drug distribution is the extent to which a drug is dispersed throughout the body. The intensity of the pharmacological effect of an agent is directly proportional, in most cases, to the amount of drug that reaches the active site, in a form recognizable by the receptor or enzyme. In other words, if an ingested agent is modified by the body prior to its arrival at the target, the effect it exerts could be greatly diminished.

Another key parameter that must be determined in these pharmacokinetic trials is how and to what extent the product is dispersed throughout the body. Does it even reach the active site? The concentration of the drug

Table 3 Factors That Affect Drug Distribution

Patient's age
Body hydration level
Fat percentage of tissues
Cardiac output
Vessel permeability
Plasma protein levels
Plasma pH
Lean body mass
Nutritional state
Physical health status

at the receptor is dependent on several key factors. Table 3 lists some of the factors that affect drug distribution.

The first factor involved in determining the concentration of the drug at the target site is how much of it is plasma protein bound. The amount of drug available as free concentration is determinant of the drug's activity, not the proportion that is protein bound. Some highly protein bound drugs may require greater doses in order to elicit a response because of this effect. Also, these agents are possibly more subject to other drugs displacing them from their carriers, thereby causing more to be available at the receptor site. This is an example of a drug–drug interaction.

Most acidic drugs are bound to serum albumin, whereas most basic ones bind to alpha-acid glycoprotein. However, some products bind to red blood cells or other tissues. Changes in the number or amount of these binding sites can alter the concentration at the receptor greatly. Variation among different patient populations may lead to altered drug disposition as well [9,10].

The patient's nutritional status or age impact on both the quantity and quality of the plasma proteins present. In geriatric or malnourished patients, the plasma albumin may have less affinity for the drug, there may be fewer binding sites available, or there may be a smaller volume of distribution [11].

These possible variations in effect are some of the reasons why healthy human volunteers are used in Phase 1 studies, rather than patients. The drug–protein binding relationship is an important parameter to quantify in these initial trials.

A. Volume of Distribution

Another parameter that is paramount to investigate and to quantify is a new drug's volume of distribution. This concept is used to describe the movement of a drug from the bloodstream into its surrounding tissues. It is the size of the compartment necessary to account for the total amount of drug within the body, if it were present throughout the body in the same concentration as that found in the plasma. This volume does NOT necessarily refer to any specific, identifiable compartment of the body. An appreciation of how a new drug is dispersed throughout the body is important to predict the clinical effect that a drug may exert at any given dose. It is also important to know whether or not the drug will reach its site of action in concentrations sufficient to elicit the desired effect.

The volume-of-distribution process is dynamic. Drug dispersion is a function of the physiological-chemical properties of the product that is being investigated, coupled with the interplay of the biological-physiological forces that drive tissue perfusion. The volume of distribution is defined as the ratio of the concentration of drug in the body to the amount found in plasma. This concept assumes that drug transfer between body compartments is proportional to the amount of drug in plasma. This relationship is expressed by the following equation [12]:

$$V_d = V_p + V_t \times \frac{(F_{up})}{(F_{ut})}$$

where V_d = calculated volume of distribution
V_p = actual plasma volume
V_t = physiological volume of extracellular tissues
F_{up} = free unbound fraction of drug in plasma
F_{ut} = free unbound fraction of drug in tissue

This equation also illustrates how changes in the relative amount of drug binding can alter the volume of distribution significantly. It also demonstrates how the quantity of water in any body compartment affects this parameter.

B. Receptor Sensitivity

Another factor that can influence a new drug's action is the receptor sensitivity of the individual [13,14]. This concept, though not directly related to the drug's distribution, is a key factor in the level of effect that is generated. Disease, age, and genetic defects are the most common factors that affect the sensitivity of the receptor, the minimal concentration of a drug that will elicit an action.

In a supersensitive patient, less drug will be necessary to stimulate the receptor. This may be the result of genetic modification, disease state, or other drug therapy. In a reduced-sensitivity state, receptors will need more agonist in order to trigger the desired response. On the other hand, less antagonist would be needed to block a physiological function.

The drug's volume of distribution (V_d) is one of the parameters that must be quantified during Phase 1 clinical trials. Information about receptor sensitivity is not readily gleaned from initial studies. However, it is an important variable for practitioners to consider who are determining the proper dosing schedule and dosage range for a patient. The data gathered from these studies are used to quantify the V_d and, once the product makes it to the market, the numerical values for V_d in different patient populations are usually printed in the package insert and later updated in the published literature.

IV. METABOLISM

Drug metabolism is a very complex process involving both hepatic and extrahepatic enzymatic systems. The liver is the primary metabolic site. However, the kidney, lungs, and other organs can be involved in metabolism. Some products have active metabolites. When this circumstance occurs, it means that the response elicited by the drug is also evoked by its metabolite. This situation can prolong the effect of the administered agent.

One of the primary results obtained from preliminary animal testing and Phase 1 trials for a new drug is the identification of its metabolites, active or inactive. Pharmacokinetic studies, using radioactive-labeled drugs, are used to determine the metabolic pathways and by-products.

Similar to the other aforementioned parameters, drug metabolism also can be influenced. Table 4 lists some of the factors that affect drug metabolism. It is critical to know what impact various conditions will have on a drug's degradation and its subsequent elimination.

One of the most influential factors is liver function. Certain conditions drastically reduce the activity of hepatic enzymes. When this occurs, it can be expected that the effect of the drug will be prolonged. The most significant of these circumstances affecting liver function are:

Decreased hepatic blood flow
Age

Table 4 Factors That Affect Drug Metabolism

Liver function
Cardiac output
Nutritional state
Physical health status
Concurrent drug therapy
Smoking
Recreational drug use
Alcohol intake

Hepatitis
Alcoholic liver disease
Concurrent therapy with a drug known to inhibit liver enzymes (such as cimetidine)
Drug abuse, especially cocaine or heroin
Malnutrition

Other situations may actually increase the activity of hepatic metabolism. When this occurs, an increase in the dose is generally needed to elicit the same effect. Two of the circumstances that may cause this response are:

Smoking (tobacco or marijuana)
Concurrent therapy with a drug known to induce liver enzymes (such as phenobarbital)

There are a variety of chemical-reaction pathways that the body uses to inactivate foreign and endogenous materials. Sometimes more than one method is utilized simultaneously. Generally, the end result is inactivation of the drug and a metabolite that is more easily excreted from the body. Understanding metabolic processes may explain the reason for certain adverse reaction that result from accumulation of the drug or its metabolites in certain tissues.

Understanding the interplay of these factors and metabolism is important in optimizing drug therapy with new agents. The more knowledge that clinicians receive from initial clinical trials, the fewer problems that might occur once the product is marketed.

Detailed knowledge and comprehension of these metabolic conduits and their by-products can also be used in the development process to create "prodrugs." These products are pharmacologically active compounds that have had their structure modified so that it is activated through metabolism and inactive until metabolized. These drugs are synthesized in order to bypass GI breakdown or the first-pass effect and for other reasons.

A. Clearance

The elimination rate of a new drug is one of the most critical variables in predicting its disposition. The clearance value refers to the volume of blood cleared of the drug per unit time. The major organs of clearance must be identified during these initial trials. The concept of clearance was developed as a tool to quantify these properties. Total clearance is the sum of all processes involved in drug elimination. The mathematical representation of this concept is [8]:

$$CL_t = CL_r + CL_h + CL_o$$

where CL_t = total body clearance
CL_r = renal clearance
CL_h = hepatic clearance (metabolism)
CL_o = other organ clearance

If other organs or systems are involved in drug metabolism or elimination to a significant degree, then the clearance rate from these sites would need to be included in the above equation (as shown); usually, however, this fraction is not included.

Three theoretical models have been proposed to articulate the relationship between hepatic blood flow and metabolic clearance: "flow-limited," "function-limited," and the middle ground between the other two concepts. Flow-limited clearance occurs when a drug is very efficiently removed by the body because of its high extraction ratio [15]. Minor changes in hepatic circulation have a more pronounced impact on the clearance of this type of agent as compared to those with a low extraction ratio. Lidocaine and propranolol are two examples that fit this hypothesis.

Function-limited clearance is on the opposite end of the scale. In this situation, a drug possessing a low extraction ratio is metabolized effectively, yet inefficiently [16]. Theophylline is believed to fit this model. The last model applies to most drugs and is located between the other two extremes. These products usually have intermediate extraction ratios, and changes in liver blood flow have minimal, if any, effect on their metabolism rates [17]. Understanding in what way and how rapidly a drug is eliminated, under varying conditions, is crucial.

Table 5 Factors That Affect Drug Elimination

Glomerular filtration rate
Kidney function
Liver function
Cardiac output
Renal blood flow

Another parameter that is usually discovered or confirmed during Phase 1 clinical trials is the metabolic pathway the body uses to inactivate the drug. The identity of any major metabolites is also ascertained, including those that are active or those that may cause other problems. It is also important to ascertain what impact decreased liver function, age, reduced organ blood flow, smoking, or concurrent drug therapy will have on the new drug's metabolism.

V. EXCRETION

Once a product has entered the body, it must then either leave the body or accumulate within it. The two major organs of elimination are the kidney and the liver. However, many other tissues in the body can be part of the removal process. For example, there are drugs that cross the placenta, enter the milk of lactating mothers, leave via perspiration, or are exhaled from the lungs, among other methods.

In Table 5, some of the factors that affect a drug's elimination from the body are presented. Most of these components are those that have an impact on the kidney, the major organ of elimination. Here drugs can be filtered out, secreted into the urine, and/or reabsorbed back into the systemic circulation.

Renal clearance is the sum of the filtration through the glomeruli, the process of secretion into the tubules plus the process of reabsorption from the tubules. Renal dysfunction may lead to reduced elimination and increased toxicities of some drugs. In a reduced-cardiac-output state (due to disease, age, or drug therapy), less blood reaches the kidney to be processed and drug product eliminated. There are also age-related and disease-related decreases in the glomerular filtration rate (GFR) and, possibly, in tubular secretion. These conditions may lead to higher serum concentrations of a drug than may normally be expected from a particular dose. This may be due to diminished clearance or to a reduction in the drug's apparent volume of distribution.

As opposed to the difficulty in estimating intrinsic hepatic drug metabolism, renal clearance can be very accurately measured by collecting a 24-hour urine sample and measuring the volume of creatinine present. Inuline clearance also provides a reasonable estimate of GFR; however, in clinical practice, the creatinine clearance (CL_{cr}) derived from the level of measured serum creatinine is commonly used, with an acceptable degree of accuracy, to assess kidney function. Several equations have been developed and used to estimate creatinine clearance by measuring the patient's serum creatinine and by using knowledge of the patient's age, weight, and body surface area [18–20]. The following equation is commonly used for adults [8]:

$$CL_{cr} = \frac{(140 - \text{age}) \times \text{body weight (in kg)}}{72 \times \text{serum creatinine}}$$

This calculation applies to males; in order to convert the figures so that they are applicable to females, multiply the answer (the calculated clearance) by 0.85. This computation takes into account the smaller muscle mass of women.

Tubular secretion and reabsorption processes may be quantified through the use of chemical markers or models. Benzylpenicillin and ceftizoxime are used to assess anionic tubular secretion; cimetidine and ranitidine are used to assess cationic tubular secretion.

A. Drug Half-Life

One of the most practical ways to express a new drug's elimination rate is to calculate its half-life, which is the amount of time required to remove 50% of the drug from the body. This figure is mathematically defined by the following equation [8]:

$$t_{1/2} = \frac{0.693 \times V_d}{CL_t}$$

where $t_{1/2}$ = Drug's calculated half-life
V_d = Drug's calculated volume of distribution
CL_t = Drug's total clearance

Alteration in the volume of distribution, the clearance, or both may lead to prolongation or shortening of the expected $t_{1/2}$. If you are able to measure a new drug's half-life through a time-series of blood drawings and know its total clearance, you can calculate its volume of distribution (V_d).

Another key parameter quantified during these pharmacokinetic studies is the drug elimination rate constant (K_E). Where:

$$CL_t/V_d = K_E = 0.693/\, t_{1/2}$$

The most practical parameter that can be utilized to help estimate appropriate drug dosing intervals is the drug's half life ($t_{1/2}$). Different K_E may be identified to describe a drug's elimination from different tissues as well.

VI. SUMMARY

It is important to know how drugs act in a healthy person. This is the primary reason why Phase 1 clinical trials enlist normal individuals, rather than patients who are suffering from the condition the drug is designed to treat. Pharmacokinetic studies are designed to furnish data on the baseline parameters for drug products in four key areas: absorption, distribution, metabolism, and excretion.

In the design of Phase 1 clinical trials, the ability to gather sufficient data in order to determine the value of these key pharmacokinetic parameters is crucial. The data gleaned from these human experiments help establish dosage ranges, dosing intervals, and efficacy/safety/toxicity profiles of the product and, if applicable, desirable blood/tissue concentrations.

The most important figures obtained from these initial studies of a drug are its half-life, absorption fraction, volume of distribution, and, in some cases, the protein-binding percentage. Although some degree of interpatient variability cannot be predicted, determining these pharmacokinetic parameters for new drugs is critical information. The population data gathered from these clinical studies provide an *information starting point* for the practitioner. The value of these population parameters is used in initial dosing calculations and as part of the decision-making process that will determine whether or not a particular patient can use a product and, if yes, what the dose and regimen will be.

REFERENCES

1. M. M. Reidenberg, The quality of clinical research, *Clin. Pharmacol. Ther. 47*: 669–70 (1990).
2. J. M. Scavone, *Essentials of Clinical Research*, 1st ed., Healthways Communications, Boston, MA, 1991.

3. J. T. Moss and B. Bleidt, Effects of aging on drug disposition, *US Pharmacist 14*:7 (1989).
4. J. L. Cohen, Pharmacokinetics in aging, *Am. J. Med. 80* (*Suppl. 5*):31 (1986).
5. P. P. Lamy, *Prescribing for the Elderly*, PSG Wright, Littleton, MA, 1980.
6. M. C. Geokas and B. J. Hasellback, The aging gastrointestinal tract, *Am. J. Surg. 117*:8 (1960).
7. D. J. Greenblatt, E. M. Sellers, R. I. Shader, Drug disposition in old age, *N. Engl. J. Med. 306*:11 (1982).
8. J. G. Wagner, *Fundamentals of Clinical Pharmacokinetics*, Drug Intelligence Publications, Hamilton, IL, 1975.
9. R. J. Cammarata, G. P. Rodman, R. H. Fennell, Serum anti-gamma-globulin and anti-nuclear factors in the aged, *JAMA 199*:1 (1967).
10. R. Dybkaer, M. Lauritzen, and R. Krakauer, Relative reference values for clinical chemical and hematological quantities in healthy elderly people, *Acta Med. Scand. 209*:1 (1981).
11. D. J. Greenblatt, Reduced serum albumin concentrations in the elderly: a report from the Boston Collaborative Drug Surveillance Program, *J. Am. Geriatr. Soc. 27*:1 (1972).
12. M. Rowland and T. N. Tozer, *Distribution and Clinical Pharmacokinetics: Concepts and Applications*, Lea & Fibiger, Philadelphia, PA, 1980.
13. S. Husted and F. Andreasan, The influence of age on the response to anticoagulants, *Br. J. Pharmacol. 4*:7 (1977).
14. A. M. M. Shepard, D. S. Herwick, T. A. Moreland, and I. H. Stevenson, Age as a determinant of sensitivity to warfarin, *Br. J. Pharmacol. 4*:4 (1977).
15. C. M. Castleden and C. F. George, The Effect of Aging On the Hepatic Clearance of Propranolol, *Br. J. Pharmacol. 7*:1 (1979).
16. W. L. Jusko, M. J. Gardner, A. Mangione, et al., Factors affecting theophylline clearances: age, tobacco, marijuana, cirrhosis, congestive heart failure, obesity, oral contraceptives, benzodiazepines and alcohol, *J. Pharm. Sci. 68*:12 (1979).
17. H. R. Ochs, D. A. Greenblatt, E. Woo, et al., Reduced quinidine clearance in elderly persons, *Am. J. Cardiol. 42*:5 (1978).
18. D. W. Cockcroft and M. H. Gault, Prediction of creatinine clearance from serum creatinine, *Nephron 16*:31 (1976).
19. R. W. Jelliffe, Creatinine clearance: bedside estimates, *Ann. Intern. Med. 79*:604 (1973).
20. T. D. Bjornsson, Use of serum creatinine concentration to determine renal function, *Clin. Pharmacokinet. 4*:200 (1979).

8

Planning, Coordinating, and Monitoring Clinical Trials

Barry Bleidt

Health Resources Consulting
South Charlestown, West Virginia

Medication use dates far back into ancient times, when superstition, serendipity, bias, and religious beliefs determined the modes of medical care delivery. More recent times, where scientific methodology interacts with the art of medicine, still exude overtones of this unusual history.

Evolution of the drug development process also brought with it a corresponding progression in human experimentation. The clinical trials sponsored between 1960 and 1980, while scientifically more advanced than previous efforts, were often sponsored in an indiscriminate fashion. Sometimes, sponsors supported clinical researchers and institutions that rarely delivered usable results. There was little direction and virtually no planning in many of these endeavors. The application of project management techniques is the parameter that has changed the most in clinical research.

Drug development is the purposeful pursuit of scientific data to characterize and quantify a new drug product and document its usefulness. The usual terms that are used to describe the result of drug development—safety and efficacy—have been omitted from the above definition intentionally. The term "usefulness" connotes both safety and efficacy, plus a positive effect on medical outcomes.

In the following sections, the planning, coordinating, and monitoring of clinical trials will be discussed.

I. INTRODUCTION

Planning and monitoring clinical trials are simply components of a much larger project management task, whose sole aim is to bring the product onto the market as quickly and with as much information as possible. The current monitoring process evolved from the deficient, poorly run practices of yesteryear. Now, the discipline employs detailed procedures and methodologies designed to manage the multiple activities performed and limited resources available to a research project in order to generate new drug information that is medically useful and scientifically sound.

The monitoring process actually begins prior to the initiation of clinical trials, during the drug's preclinical phase. It continues after the product is marketed, through Phase 4, postmarketing surveillance, for as long as the sponsor continues to gather drug information and experiences. In reality, clinical trial monitoring is a specialized management procedure, in which the project team oversees, modifies, and reigns over the sequence of studies, such that the result of these efforts is a scientifically valid, clinically functional database that soundly documents the product's usefulness.

II. PREPARING FOR THE CLINICAL TRIALS

The clinical trial monitoring team is primarily concerned with the interactions among the product sponsor, the clinical researchers, and the pertinent regulatory agencies (usually state and/or federal drug bureaus). The various roles assumed by these participants are—inherently—sometimes at odds with each other. Contrary points of view are a natural part of this process, as each group sees its respective part differently than do the others. Managing group dynamics, maintaining good relations, and establishing open, responsive communication channels among these groups may indeed be the most difficult task of the monitoring team.

It is important to realize that each of the players has his or her own agenda and objectives going into the research effort. The sponsor wants quality results in as short a time frame as is ethically and scientifically possible. The clinical researchers need to balance the demands of participating in multiple projects and, possibly, juggle their clinical and/or academic duties as well. The regulatory agencies generally want to protect the public health and prevent unsound data from being used in the medical decision-making process. However, the common objective among all players is to initiate and to complete quality research projects, yielding useful results consistent with currently accepted medical standards and ethical considerations. The monitoring team acts as the cohesive force that holds these groups together in order to accomplish their joint purpose.

One way to increase the chance for success in clinical trials is to make sure that each of the aforementioned groups has significant input into the various aspects of these procedures. By having the various parties involved throughout the process, there are benefits that accrue to the monitoring team and, subsequently, to the sponsor: problems are minimized, communication channels are established, resource utilization is optimized, and expectations are realized.

There are five steps in the clinical research process [1]:

1. Pre-planning
2. Planning
3. Implementation
4. Documentation
5. Interpretation

The pre-planning activities are important in that they focus attention on obtaining the desired results from each of the subsequent steps. It is at this point that crucial determinations are made by the sponsor. Who will head the monitoring team? Who or which institutions will be involved in the clinical and outcomes research? Who will act as the primary contact point at and liaison with the regulatory agencies? Who will analyze and interpret the generated data? Is the use of outside monitors warranted? Once these questions have been answered and the key personnel enlisted, the next step can begin. As each individual participant is identified, he or she should then be included in the subsequent steps and activities.

Strategic planning is the next step. Here, the specific objectives that are to be ascertained from the studies are defined. This phase involves forecasting or quantifying some very critical parameters. The actions that are to be performed here include the following: time frames must be projected; required resources must be estimated (including investigational drugs, money, personnel); specific procedures must be laid out; documentation needs must be anticipated; key contacts with all the groups must be identified; communication channels must be established; contingency plans must be drawn up; and Institutional Review Board (IRB) and other regulatory requirements must be studied. Each activity to be executed within the clinical trial must have a time and resource budget developed and expected results formulated for it, and all these actions must comply with all regulatory requirements.

In step three, implementation, the tactical phase begins. It is here that the actual monitoring begins, even though the team leaders have been involved with the preplanning and planning stages. First, the monitoring team must be organized and trained; then, the precise methodologies under which the research will be conducted are developed. This process comprises creating detailed protocols for the use of the new drug and developing the data collection documents, patient consent, and case report forms.

Once these items have been developed, the other primary participants and the backup groups are instructed in the protocol's procedures, research methods, data handling requirements, and patient care techniques and advised on time and budget constraints. It must be reemphasized that all steps executed during the drug development process must conform to current regulatory requirements or follow discussions held with regulatory personnel (in written form) within the prescribed time frame.

In step four, documentation, the research begins; data are generated; the monitors supervise the data collection process at timely intervals; information is submitted for preliminary analysis; and feedback is given to the researchers (and their respective IRB), sponsors, regulatory officials, and data interpreters. Preliminary results are important to collect. Information gathered here can be used to improve the protocol and its research methodologies, to revise patient consent forms, to improve patient care, and to prevent wasted resources.

Data interpretation is the final step. The collected information is organized, analyzed, interpreted, and packaged for presentation to the involved groups and for submission to the Food and Drug Administration. It is important for the monitoring team and the sponsor to prepare and deliver a final report to all the investigators (and their respective IRBs) involved with the study. This feedback is critical in maintaining a quality relationship that might be needed for other new drug studies; for Phase 4, post-marketing research; or for supplemental applications exploring new indications for the product.

A common component of successful clinical trials is good information flow and open communication channels among the participants. Each and every participant needs to be advised as to progress made and to problems incurred by the other parties. The better these processes are implemented,

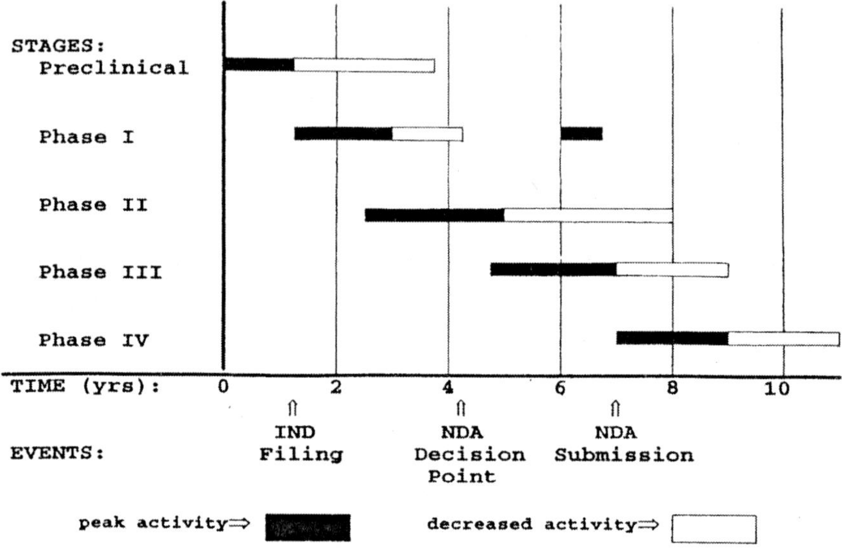

Fig. 1 Developmental continuum of a new drug.

the more timely and more sound will be the findings that are generated from the collected data. Feedback and follow-up are key techniques that can be used to accomplish the established goals.

While the ultimate goals of drug development remain constant, the specific objectives of the research vary depending on where in the developmental continuum you focus (see Fig. 1). It is the monitoring team's responsibility to see that these different targets are met. In general, the purposes of the research effort, by stage, are:

Preclinical—animal studies, initial marketing potential assessment, safety evaluation, indication determination, IND data

Phase 1—first-in-human studies on healthy volunteers, quantify pharmacokinetic parameters, sometimes early indication trials (in life-threatening conditions), placebo and gold-standard comparative trials, medical outcomes methodologies explored

Phase 2—first-in-patient studies, small number of subjects (except in life-threatening conditions), refine dosage parameters, efficacy and safety research, early medical outcomes data and comparative trials, NDA decision point

Phase 3—larger numbers of patients, expanded trials to prove efficacy, demonstrate safety, show benefit on patient outcomes

Phase 4—postmarketing studies, look for rare side effects, unofficially look for new uses (requires more Phase 3 studies to verify), continued gathering of pharmacoeconomic data

III. THE MONITORING TEAM

One of the most crucial steps in the drug development process is selecting individuals for the drug monitoring team. Its staffing must be a high priority of and performed by the top-level management of the new drug's sponsor(s). This commitment ensures that the team will make sure that the objectives of the company are met. The members of the team should come primarily from within the corporation. However, the use of outside experts or consultants can be most valuable in certain situations. The actual site monitors can also be nonemployee contractors. Once the members have been chosen and the primary corporate objectives established, the team can begin to function along the lines of the five steps mentioned above. The drug monitoring team is a dynamic one, with new members coming on during certain phases and others leaving, once their tasks have been completed. Figure 1 presents the developmental continuum of a new product.

In order for the team to succeed, it must operate in the following manner:

Each member must be completely committed to the project and to accomplishing its goals.

Individual team member achievements should be highly publicized (internally, at least) and made visible, while failures should be handled privately and any repercussions should be absorbed by upper-level persons.

Each member must have concise, clear instructions as to his or her expected role(s).

Prompt feedback to team members and project participants must be maintained, especially to upper-level management.

The team leader must be able to integrate the mixed talents of the members, building on and using their individual strengths. During critical phases of the study and time crunches, only a minimal amount of other duties should be requested of the team members. This is why outside monitors can be a valuable resource to the team. Drug development is such a complex process that the matrix organizational style of management should be utilized.

In this situation, each team member maintains ties with his or her respective departments or units and also works closely with the team leadership.

For the project to succeed in a timely, cost-conscious manner, the sponsor's leadership must carefully plan, prioritize, select, and supervise the project team. In this way, the corporate needs can be identified, articulated, and, finally, implemented by the members.

IV. THE PARTICIPANTS

The drug-monitoring team deals with the many participants involved with the clinical research process. Ultimately, they are responsible to the upper-level management of the sponsoring corporation(s) (and their stockholders, when applicable), for meeting the objectives of the studies. In a larger sense, they are also accountable to society as a whole, holding the public's trust that sound research and honest presentation of the data will occur.

Each of the participants has a role to play and is a key component in the development of new drugs. The drug monitoring team's position and responsibilities have been delineated in a previous section. The position of each of the other characters—the sponsors, the principal investigators, the site coordinators, the IRB, the FDA, and the monitors—is presented below.

A. Sponsor(s)

The sponsor is the corporation(s) or institution(s) that initiate(s) the filing of the IND, the Notice of Claimed Investigational Exemption for a New Drug. The investigational drug researchers are not generally considered sponsors, except in the rare case where some of the early human trials are completed in-house.

The sponsors are financially and legally liable, as well as responsible for the integrity of the project and the results. They perceive drug development as the key to future company growth through new products. Being the pioneer of a new class of therapeutic agents carries with it a tremendous financial incentive and reward.

B. Principal Investigators

Individuals are selected to serve as clinical researchers based on their expertise in studying investigational drugs or their reputation (or that of their institution) in the area of the drug's proposed therapeutic classification (e.g., cardiovascular or oncology). Generally, Phase 1 studies are performed by the former group and Phase 2 through 4 trials by the latter. Once the Phase 1 pharmacokinetic parameters have been established, it is important to bring in the recognized leaders (researchers and clinicians) within the therapeutic field to the clinical trials. By bringing in an outside panel early, the credibility of the overall research effort is increased [2]. It is also paramount to have outcomes experts and pharmacoeconomic specialists involved in the Phase 1 through 4 efforts.

These experts should be chosen so that others, especially the regulatory-review scientists and the key medical thought leaders, will be assured that the results garnered and published are representative of the product's actual clinical profile. If this is the case, other physicians will be more apt to use it for their patients. Physicians (MD or DO), clinical pharmacologists (PhD), or clinical pharmacists (PharmD) can act as the principal investigator (PI) of the project.

The PI should be picked based on prior, positive experiences with the company or with other drugs within the therapeutic class. The key qualifications should be the ability to deliver sound research data in a timely fashion within budget constraints, while maintaining open communications and interacting positively with the monitoring team. Any other criteria that are used for selection, such as politics or favoritism, invite problems. Each PI is required to fill out an FDA Form 1572, Investigators Statement. An example of this document is found in Appendix I. Once completed, one copy is to be sent to the trial coordinating center and one copy placed in the Investigator's Notebook.

The investigator's reputation is also very much on the line, so quality work and honest presentation of the data are important to the researcher.

C. Site Coordinators

Another key member of the clinical research team is the site coordinator. These individuals are usually health care professionals (such as nurses, pharmacists, or technologists), but they could be paramedical personnel. This group is responsible for recruiting patients for the study, scheduling their appointments, making sure the appropriate drugs are available, and entering the data from the patient's chart onto the case report form. In other words, they handle the day-to-day undertakings of the project. They also are able to help in the development of the site's budget for the project.

This group is made up of research professionals, who know how to make a project work and who can be good detectives when things go wrong. They want smooth-running protocols with little interference, minimal paperwork, and few problems. Be consistent and straightforward with them and respect their position and they will help to produce the consistent and quality results needed.

D. Institutional Review Boards

Investigators must have a home, an institution where the patients receive their medical care. Each such facility must have an Institutional Review Board (IRB) in place before experimental drug trials can be performed using human subjects. The IRB must approve the protocol, patient consent procedure, and forms prior to the acceptance of the facility as a research site.

A more in-depth discussion of IRB responsibilities and functions is presented by Robert McCarthy in Chapter 13, "Ethics in Clinical Drug Research." The investigators themselves cannot be members of such a review panel, nor be involved in the selection process or performance evaluation of any of its members.

The membership of these boards must have an adequate number of members with varying backgrounds (i.e., not all members can be research scientists). They are responsible to the institution and its patients for reviewing and approving the research protocol before it is implemented. These players want ethical research performed on informed patients with as few risks involved as possible.

E. Food and Drug Administration

The federal agency responsible for investigational drugs, their labeling, and their subsequent marketing is the Food and Drug Administration (FDA), part of the Department of Health and Human Services. There are regional branches located throughout the country, but the primary review-process site for New Drug Applications and Investigation New Drug exemptions is in Washington, DC. The monitoring team leader and other liaison personnel may have to make frequent trips to these offices in order to interact with the key people within the agency.

In some cases, a state agency with responsibilities similar to those of the FDA may also have jurisdiction. This is particularly true in California, where recently enacted state laws permit earlier human experimentation for lifesaving new products developed for terminal illness, such as AIDS or cancer. It is important to know which agency is primarily responsible and the corresponding regulations governing clinical research.

The regulatory agencies are responsible to the general citizenry as protectors of their health and welfare from unacceptably risky products, from fraudulent research, and from misleading promotion. These players want an open, honest, complete presentation of the data in a timely manner. As human beings, these individuals may have concerns and a certain level of distrust toward those whom they oversee. Historically, not all companies have acted ethically, and unsound or altered data have been submitted. Developing the trust of the regulatory personnel involves the personal integrity of the monitoring team members and sometimes the monitors.

F. Monitors

The monitors can be physicians, pharmacists, or other health professionals. They are either contracted out as consultants who specialize in such work or are employed directly by the sponsor. They review the protocols, make sure each site is in full compliance, minimize the number of patients lost to follow-up, and scrutinize the patient case report forms for errors. A person may monitor more than one site for a specific project.

Using outside monitors is an excellent way to utilize corporate resources. It frees up members of the monitoring team for other tasks. Impartial monitors (i.e., those who are on contract) are especially good to utilize during outcomes and pharmacoeconomic studies. They provide a unique perspective, minimizing potential pro-company or pro-institutional bias in the results. It is also critical to use them in Phase 1 "core" studies, where the pivotal data are being generated. The monitors are responsible for retrieving the information and sending it back to the central collection point. These players want well-defined protocols with easy-to-complete case report forms and simple data transmission procedures. They also keep in close contact with the drug monitoring team, the investigators, and the site coordinators.

G. The Subjects

One of the most overlooked participants in clinical trials is the subjects themselves. They are either healthy human volunteers (for Phase 1) or patients with specific condition(s) (for Phases 2–4). It is important they are capable of giving an informed consent to being treated (i.e., they understand the risks involved with the experimental therapy and the dangers associated with not receiving the currently accepted treatment). These players want minimal risk, as little inconvenience as possible, and, in the case of the patients, relief from their affliction.

V. THE STUDY: PLANNING AND IMPLEMENTATION

A. The Investigator's Notebook

In order to facilitate consistency among the different research centers, an Investigator's Notebook must be developed and assembled. This book is essentially the "instructor's manual" for the study. The guide should contain as much of the scientific and clinical data available on the investigational drug(s) as possible. Its purpose is to serve as a complete reference guide for all medical information available at the start of the clinical trials, and it must be updated regularly throughout the study in order to keep it current.

Other things that should be part of the Investigator's Notebook include:

The complete, detailed, easy-to-follow clinical protocol
Step-by-step study procedures
A copy of Investigator's Statement, FDA Form 1572
The site's copy of the IRB approval letter and approved patient consent form
Case Report Forms
Patient log books
Monitor visit log
Drug accountability procedures and master inventory form
A place to file all communications received and a copy of those sent

One of the key factors involved in the production of a quality research effort is an Investigator's Notebook containing clear, concise, and complete information. Utilizing a checklist for each procedure can assist in making communications flow better and maintaining the investigator's files. These forms are an easy-to-use, step-by-step list of everything that needs to be completed; they contain a space to check off the activity when it is performed. An example of this type of document is presented in Appendix II for a hypothetical cardiovascular clinical trial.

B. The Drug Supply

Another goal of the extensive planning process that precedes the initiation of human testing is to make sure ample supplies of the investigational drug(s) and other medications, if necessary, are available when needed. These items must be manufactured and packaged before the research can begin. This process should be coordinated by the team leader with the production and packaging departments.

In double-blind, comparative trials, the control drug(s) must be reformulated to have an identical appearance to that of the study drug(s). The containers must also be blinded, so that neither the patient nor the researcher knows which product is which. In nonblinded studies, sufficient quantities of the control drug(s) must also be made available in a formulation dictated by the protocol. The amount of time required to complete these manufacturing and labeling tasks should be factored into the time line during the planning process.

C. The Protocol

One of the major steps in preparing for a clinical trial is the development of the protocol for the study. This research procedural guide is one of the keys in assuring a well-run research effort and obtaining useful data. This process is covered in detail in the next chapter.

D. The Case Report and Patient Consent Forms

Two of the primary components of the protocol are the case report form and patient consent documents. It is sufficient to say here that the easier these materials are to use, the fewer the number of errors that will occur. These forms and their preparation are also discussed in subsequent chapters.

E. Data Reliability

When the clinical studies are performed at several different institutions, this is known as a multiclinic trial. In this case, it becomes necessary to test the interrater reliability of the key laboratory and clinical parameters that are to be measured. In other words, do the various researchers obtain the same value for a particular factor? If a large variation exists among the sites, the data may not be able to be pooled together for analysis, the results may be less sound and more subject to criticism, and resources may have been expended with few useful results.

Interrater reliability can be maintained within acceptable limits by thoroughly training the observers and measurers in the techniques and methods to be used throughout the study. The goal of this type of preparedness is to create consistent scoring by each center and thereby improve the quality of the data generated. The scoring of key variables in a control situation must be uniform among the different units.

F. Getting Started

Once the investigator's binder, the patient kits, case report forms, and the investigational and other protocol drugs have arrived at the site, it is time for an initial visit by select members of the drug monitoring team and/or the monitor(s). At this time, the site coordinator, principal investigator, and other pertinent study personnel will be fully briefed on the protocol and the data handling requirements; trained in completing the case report forms; told how, when, and where to report adverse events; and informed about the time and budget constraints of the project.

During this first visit, deadlines are established for recruiting a sufficient number of patients who meet the study's criteria, and arrangements are made for periodic follow-up site visitations and record inspections. This meeting is critical in setting the proper tone for the working relationship among the sponsor(s), the monitors, the investigators, and drug monitoring team members.

VI. THE STUDY: COORDINATION

Once subjects have been recruited, the clinical trial begins. The drug monitoring team, either through its members or via the outside monitors, must make sure that each site keeps on time, stays within budget, follows the protocol, completes the case report forms accurately, and reports adverse events in complete compliance with governing regulations. The monitor should also collect copies of the annual IRB renewals and patient consent form updates for the project.

A good monitor will know the protocols so well that she or he can spot any variation from it promptly and be able to investigate the departures thoroughly. A good monitor will provide sound, accurate reasons to the drug monitoring team and the sponsor for any deviations in the procedures and prompt feedback to the investigators on how to correct any problems. As with any study, some flexibility must be given to the practitioners. Sometimes, out of practical or medical necessity, protocol deviation occurs. If a protocol must be changed, then so must the IRB approval and patient consent forms. The FDA probably will have to be notified in these cases as well.

A. Quality Control

One of the primary purposes of a well-run, thoroughly planned monitoring effort by the team and the monitors is to ensure that quality data is generated. The more pivotal the study, the more intense the monitoring should be.

These quality assurance (QA) efforts of the monitor(s) provide feedback to the sponsors and investigators as well as certifying sound data collection from the source documents. Another important aspect of clinical trial QA is the proper training of the researchers and their associates on study responsibilities and methodologies. During the planning phase, the site selection process should make sure that each site has sufficient time to devote to the study as well as ample administrative support.

The Case Report Form (CRF) audit procedure is a necessary step and an efficient utilization of resources. Data must be checked against source documents for transposition errors, missing information, and inaccurate reporting. Such close supervision by the monitors has an additional benefit: it keeps the investigator's files in order for a potential FDA inspection.

For the pivotal studies, the monitoring team should establish a special data-audit committee. The purpose of this group is to check, on a random basis, the accuracy of the monitors. This double-check system is critical for these core trials. It helps to ensure reliable data entry onto the appropriate form, accurate transcription of information from the medical records, and complete compliance with protocol during the crucial early phases. The findings from these core studies are the basis of several important decisions, including whether or not to continue studying the potential product. The data and results obtained from them must be accurate and complete.

B. Adverse Events

Another aspect of good clinical research practices, as well as FDA regulations, is the mandate that serious adverse drug events occurring during the trial be reported promptly to the monitor or directly to the sponsor. It is the sponsor's responsibility to notify the FDA and other investigators involved with the same drug and their respective IRBs about these discoveries. These adverse events could be a side effect of the therapy, a serious drug interaction, or a drug product problem (trouble with its formulation). The patient's informed consent form must be regularly modified to reflect new adverse events, then re-approved by the IRB, and, finally, re-signed by the patient in order to ensure that he or she understands the consequences of these additional findings.

Some of the less-serious adverse events that may have been logged onto the CRF earlier in the trial could provide a forewarning of what might occur later. Close monitoring practices can detect these signs and allow the management to make decisions about the design of the protocol or even the fate of the drug at an earlier stage.

Even after a drug is marketed, adverse events must still be reported to the appropriate agencies. Each such occurrence should be submitted to the FDA MedWatch Program on Form 3500. A copy of this Medical Products Reporting Program Form is presented in Appendix III.

C. Drug Accountability

The responsibility for investigational drugs is divided between the sponsor and the research site, once the drugs have been shipped. It is important for both participants to understand this shared accountability and work together in maintaining good records and storing the drugs safely. The investigator should keep track of to whom, when, and where the drugs are dispensed and the monitor should regularly audit the records against the available inventory. The safe storage requirements imply both restricting the drug's availability to nonauthorized personnel and keeping the products in a proper environment (i.e., in conditions that do *not* promote product deterioration).

The drug accountability procedures should be developed during the planning stage. The best way to facilitate this activity is to consider using research sites that have pharmacy departments experienced with clinical trials and that employ a research pharmacist who is in charge of investigational drug distribution. This individual can also be of great assistance in monitoring protocol compliance. The site coordinator, as well as the pharmacy, should keep a master inventory form in the Investigator's Notebook along with copies of the shipment documents.

The monitor should also visit the pharmacy during the initial meeting and inform the appropriate personnel of the protocol's expected drug-keeping requirements. Periodic, follow-up visits to the pharmacy are also important.

VII. THE FINAL REPORT

Once a study has been completed, the monitor should make a final visit to each clinical trial site and formally terminate the project. At this time, unused drugs need to be sent back to the sponsor, final payment arrangements for the grant should be agreed on, and record-keeping requirements discussed (usually records are kept for 2 years after the drug is approved, *not* after the study is over).

Table 1 Terminal Report Information Needs of Participants

SPONSOR
Status report on the progress of trial(s)
Budget status
Data for monograph preparation, promotional claims, and answers to questions from health professionals
Information for legal department
INVESTIGATOR
Grant reimbursement schedule
Publication rights
Summary of data generated for presentations and publications
Reports from other centers
FDA
Package insert material
IND annual reports
NDA submission data

The final patient visit for the project is the last opportunity to observe the subject and to measure the appropriate parameters. These data are entered onto a special form. An example of a final-visit case report form is located in Appendix IV.

The final report of the monitor or monitoring team should satisfy the informational demands of the various participants. Some of these needs are presented in Table 1. The final tabulation of data and complete analyses should be sent to the sites as soon as possible. This promptness is important so that the investigator can begin writing a manuscript for publication or preparing a presentation on his or her findings. These articles are key information pathways to clinicians, other researchers, and competitors.

VIII. KEYS TO ADMINISTERING SUCCESSFUL TRIALS

There are several factors that are key to running a successful clinical trial. By following these suggestions, the chances for obtaining quality research and sound, useful data are greatly increased.

1. Plan, plan, plan—failing to plan is planning to fail.
2. Define clear, concise, and complete objectives in the protocol.

3. Communicate with investigators as to their expectations and responsibilities.
4. Train all participants thoroughly in their expected activities and record-keeping requirements.
5. Simplify protocols, research methods, and forms.
6. Focus attention on regulatory requirements and issues.
7. Use institutions with a clinical-trial-experienced pharmacy department employing a research pharmacist.
8. Employ the use of outside monitors.
9. Maintain a good information exchange among the participants.
10. Follow up, follow up, follow up.
11. Feedback, feedback, feedback.
12. Better planning yields better tools, resulting in better research.

IX. SUMMARY

The monitoring team essentially act as diplomats, going among the participants (sponsor, researcher, regulator) and keeping all focused upon their common objective—being part of a quality research effort yielding useful data within the prescribed time frame and under budget. The key to accomplishing this is the preplanning and planning steps.

During the five steps, outside advisors can be very useful, especially in the preplanning and planning phases. As mentioned above, the use of outside monitors is highly recommended as a means to conserve resources and prevent corporate time demands from interfering with critical phases of the studies.

APPENDIX I

FDA Form 1572: Investigator's Statement

DEPARTMENT OF HEALTH AND HUMAN SERVICES PUBLIC HEALTH SERVICE FOOD AND DRUG ADMINISTRATION STATEMENT OF INVESTIGATOR *(TITLE 21, CODE OF FEDERAL REGULATIONS (CFR) Part 312)* (See instructions on reverse side.)	Form Approved: OMB No. 0910-0014 Expiration Date: June 30, 1992 *See OMB Statement on Reverse.* NOTE: No investigator may participate in an investigation until he/she provides the sponsor with a completed, signed Statement of Investigator, Form FDA 1572 (21 CFR 312.53(c))
1. NAME AND ADDRESS OF INVESTIGATOR	
2. EDUCATION, TRAINING, AND EXPERIENCE THAT QUALIFIES THE INVESTIGATOR AS AN EXPERT IN THE CLINICAL INVESTIGATION OF THE DRUG FOR THE USE UNDER INVESTIGATION. ONE OF THE FOLLOWING IS ATTACHED: ☐ CURRICULUM VITAE ☐ OTHER STATEMENT OF QUALIFICATIONS	
3. NAME AND ADDRESS OF ANY MEDICAL SCHOOL, HOSPITAL, OR OTHER RESEARCH FACILITY WHERE THE CLINICAL INVESTIGATION(S) WILL BE CONDUCTED.	
4. NAME AND ADDRESS OF ANY CLINICAL LABORATORY FACILITIES TO BE USED IN THE STUDY.	
5. NAME AND ADDRESS OF THE INSTITUTIONAL REVIEW BOARD (IRB) THAT IS RESPONSIBLE FOR REVIEW AND APPROVAL OF THE STUDY(IES).	
6. NAMES OF THE SUBINVESTIGATORS (*e.g., research fellows, residents, associates*) WHO WILL BE ASSISTING THE INVESTIGATOR IN THE CONDUCT OF THE INVESTIGATION(S).	
7. NAME AND CODE NUMBER, IF ANY, OF THE PROTOCOL(S) IN THE IND FOR THE STUDY(IES) TO BE CONDUCTED BY THE INVESTIGATOR.	

FORM FDA 1572 (12/91) PREVIOUS EDITION IS OBSOLETE.

8 ATTACH THE FOLLOWING CLINICAL PROTOCOL INFORMATION:

☐ FOR PHASE 1 INVESTIGATIONS, A GENERAL OUTLINE OF THE PLANNED INVESTIGATION INCLUDING THE ESTIMATED DURATION OF THE STUDY AND THE MAXIMUM NUMBER OF SUBJECTS THAT WILL BE INVOLVED.

☐ FOR PHASE 2 OR 3 INVESTIGATIONS, AN OUTLINE OF THE STUDY PROTOCOL INCLUDING AN APPROXIMATION OF THE NUMBER OF SUBJECTS TO BE TREATED WITH THE DRUG AND THE NUMBER TO BE EMPLOYED AS CONTROLS, IF ANY; THE CLINICAL USES TO BE INVESTIGATED; CHARACTERISTICS OF SUBJECTS BY AGE, SEX, AND CONDITION; THE KIND OF CLINICAL OBSERVATIONS AND LABORATORY TESTS TO BE CONDUCTED; THE ESTIMATED DURATION OF THE STUDY; AND COPIES OR A DESCRIPTION OF CASE REPORT FORMS TO BE USED.

9. COMMITMENTS

I agree to conduct the study(ies) in accordance with the relevant, current protocol(s) and will only make changes in a protocol after notifying the sponsor, except when necessary to protect the safety, rights, or welfare of subjects.

I agree to personally conduct or supervise the described investigation(s).

I agree to inform any patients, or any persons used as controls, that the drugs are being used for investigational purposes and I will ensure that the requirements relating to obtaining informed consent in 21 CFR Part 50 and institutional review board (IRB) review and approval in 21 CFR Part 56 are met.

I agree to report to the sponsor adverse experiences that occur in the course of the investigation(s) in accordance with 21 CFR 312.64.

I have read and understand the information in the investigator's brochure, including the potential risks and side effects of the drug.

I agree to ensure that all associates, colleagues, and employees assisting in the conduct of the study(ies) are informed about their obligations in meeting the above commitments.

I agree to maintain adequate and accurate records in accordance with 21 CFR 312.62 and to make those records available for inspection in accordance with 21 CFR 312.68.

I will ensure that an IRB that complies with the requirements of 21 CFR Part 56 will be responsible for the initial and continuing review and approval of the clinical investigation. I also agree to promptly report to the IRB all changes in the research activity and all unanticipated problems involving risks to human subjects or others. Additionally, I will not make any changes in the research without IRB approval, except where necessary to eliminate apparent immediate hazards to human subjects.

I agree to comply with all other requirements regarding the obligations of clinical investigators and all other pertinent requirements in 21 CFR Part 312.

INSTRUCTIONS FOR COMPLETING FORM FDA 1572
STATEMENT OF INVESTIGATOR:

1. Complete all sections. Attach a separate page if additional space is needed.
2. Attach curriculum vitae or other statement of qualifications as described in Section 2.
3. Attach protocol outline as described in Section 8.
4. Sign and date below.
5. FORWARD THE COMPLETED FORM AND ATTACHMENTS TO THE SPONSOR. The sponsor will incorporate this information along with other technical data into an Investigational New Drug Application (IND). INVESTIGATORS SHOULD NOT SEND THIS FORM DIRECTLY TO THE FOOD AND DRUG ADMINISTRATION.

10. SIGNATURE OF INVESTIGATOR	11 DATE

Public reporting burden for this collection of information is estimated to average 1 hour per response, including the time for reviewing instructions, searching existing data sources, gathering and maintaining the data needed, and completing reviewing the collection of information. Send comments regarding this burden estimate or any other aspect of this collection of information, including suggestions for reducing this burden to:

Reports Clearance Officer, PHS Hubert H. Humphrey Building, Room 721-B 200 Independence Avenue, S.W. Washington, DC 20201 Attn: PRA	and to:	Office of Management and Budget Paperwork Reduction Project (0910-0014) Washington, DC 20503

Please DO NOT RETURN this application to either of these addresses.

APPENDIX II

Sample Checklist-Style Form

CHECKLIST FOR RESEARCH SITE ACTIVATION		
Activity	**Date**	**Initials**
Completed and signed Investigators Statement (FDA form 1572). - one mailed to Central - one in Investigator's Notebook		
Patient consent form to be submitted to IRB sent to Central Processing in special envelope.		
Protocol submitted to IRB for approval.		
Protocol approved and signed. - one copy of approval letter mailed to Central - one in Investigator's Notebook		
CVs of all investigators mailed to Central Processing in special envelope.		
Patient consent form submitted to IRB.		
Patient consent form approved by IRB. - one copy of letter mailed to Central - one in Investigator's Notebook		
List of IRB members placed in Investigator's Notebook.		

APPENDIX III

FDA Form 3500: Medical Products Reporting Program

MEDWATCH
THE FDA MEDICAL PRODUCTS REPORTING PROGRAM

For VOLUNTARY reporting by health professionals of adverse events and product problems

Form Approved: OMB No. 0910-0291 Expires: 12/31/94 See OMB statement on reverse

FDA Use Only (MB)

Triage unit sequence #

Page ___ of ___

A. Patient information

1. Patient identifier — In confidence
2. Age at time of event: or Date of birth:
3. Sex — female / male
4. Weight — lbs or kgs

B. Adverse event or product problem

1. Adverse event and/or Product problem (e.g., defects/malfunctions)
2. Outcomes attributed to adverse event (check all that apply)
   - death (mo/day/yr)
   - life-threatening
   - hospitalization – initial or prolonged
   - disability
   - congenital anomaly
   - required intervention to prevent permanent impairment/damage
   - other:
3. Date of event (mo/day/yr)
4. Date of this report (mo/day/yr)
5. Describe event or problem
6. Relevant tests/laboratory data, including dates
7. Other relevant history, including preexisting medical conditions (e.g., allergies, race, pregnancy, smoking and alcohol use, hepatic/renal dysfunction, etc.)

C. Suspect medication(s)

1. Name (give labeled strength & mfr/labeler, if known) #1 #2
2. Dose, frequency & route used #1 #2
3. Therapy dates (if unknown, give duration) from/to (or best estimate) #1 #2
4. Diagnosis for use (indication) #1 #2
5. Event abated after use stopped or dose reduced — #1 yes no doesn't apply; #2 yes no doesn't apply
6. Lot # (if known) #1 #2
7. Exp. date (if known) #1 #2
8. Event reappeared after reintroduction — #1 yes no doesn't apply; #2 yes no doesn't apply
9. NDC # (for product problems only)
10. Concomitant medical products and therapy dates (exclude treatment of event)

D. Suspect medical device

1. Brand name
2. Type of device
3. Manufacturer name & address
4. Operator of device — health professional / lay user/patient / other:
5. Expiration date (mo/day/yr)
6. model # / catalog # / serial # / lot # / other #
7. If implanted, give date (mo/day/yr)
8. If explanted, give date (mo/day/yr)
9. Device available for evaluation? (Do not send to FDA) — yes / no / returned to manufacturer on ___ (mo/day/yr)
10. Concomitant medical products and therapy dates (exclude treatment of event)

E. Reporter (see confidentiality section on back)

1. Name & address — phone #
2. Health professional? yes / no
3. Occupation
4. Also reported to — manufacturer / user facility / distributor
5. If you do NOT want your identity disclosed to the manufacturer, place an " X " in this box.

FDA — Mail to: MEDWATCH, 5600 Fishers Lane, Rockville, MD 20852-9787 or FAX to: 1-800-FDA-0178

FDA Form 3500 (6/93)

Submission of a report does not constitute an admission that medical personnel or the product caused or contributed to the event.

APPENDIX IV

Sample Final Visit Form: Antihypertensive Study

FINAL VISIT

Patient ID-number [ ]   Patient Initials [ ]

Date of visit: [day] [month] 19 [year]

BLOOD PRESSURE AND HEART RATE

SBP	DBP	HR	SBP	DBP	HR	SBP	DBP	HR
mmHg	mmHg	beats/min	mmHg	mmHg	beats/min	mmHg	mmHg	beats/min

ANTIHYPERTENSIVE MEDICATION

Medication taken up to this visit

TRADE NAME OF DRUG	STRENGTH	# DOSES	CHANGE?
1.			
2.			
3.			
4.			

OTHER VISITS

Has the patient been to any extra visits since the previously scheduled study visit? no [ ] yes [ ] ⇒⇒⇒ How many visits? [ ]

MAIN EVENTS SINCE PREVIOUS VISIT

Non-fatal events (if yes, complete NON-FATAL EVENT FORM)

MI	no [ ]	yes [ ]
Stroke	no [ ]	yes [ ]
Angina Episode	no [ ]	yes [ ]
Other cardiovascular event	no [ ]	yes [ ]

Investigator's signature

FINAL VISIT (CON'T)

MAIN EVENTS SINCE PREVIOUS VISIT (CON'T)

Fatal events no ☐ yes ☐ ⇒ (If yes, complete FATAL EVENT FORM)

Hospitalizations
Other hospitalizations? no ☐ yes ☐ ⇒ Days in hospital ☐

Cause

SIDE EFFECTS

Has the patient experienced any adverse events due to the treatment since the last visit? no ☐ yes ☐ ⇒ Specify

Was it considered a serious side effect? no ☐ yes ☐
⇓
(Complete SERIOUS SIDE EFFECT FORM)

12-LEAD EKG AND SERUM CREATININE AND CHOLESTEROL LEVELS

Has the final EKG recording been taken? yes ☐
(Please attach EKG to the following FINAL VISIT EKG FORM)

Have the final S-Creatinine and S-Cholesterol sample been taken? yes ☐
(Please enter the results below.)

CREATININE AND CHOLESTEROL SERUM LEVELS

Date of blood sample: day month 19 year

Serum Creatinine (mg/dl): Serum Cholesterol (mg/dl):

BODY MEASUREMENT

Weight kg

Investigator's signature

FINAL VISIT EKG

Patient ID-number [| | | |] **Patient Initials** [|]

Date of EKG [day |] [month |] **19** [year |]

The EKG recordings should be attached in this box. Each strip should be marked with the Patient Identification Number. Each strip must have a minimum of four QRS-complexes plus an amplitude test signal. Six standard precordial leads and the following leads are required: I. II. III. aVR. aVF. aVL. This form should be given to the Monitor or sent to the Central Data Center in the specially marked envelope.

Investigator's signature

REFERENCES

1. C. L. Bendush and F. J. Novello, The Monitoring Process, *The Clinical Research Process in the Pharmaceutical Industry* (G. Matoren, ed.), Marcel Dekker, New York, 1984.
2. Zitter Group, *The 1992 Insurance Company Outcomes Study*, Zitter Group, San Francisco, 1993.

9

The Protocol, Case Report Forms, and Patient Consent

Barry Bleidt

Health Resources Consulting
South Charleston, West Virginia

Clinical research involves examining the use of drugs, devices, or other treatments in humans. The purpose of these studies is to produce results either confirming or refuting the usefulness of a therapy for a specific condition or combination of diseases. During the drug development process, Phase 1 and 2 investigations generate the "core" data—the initial information and baseline findings that will be certified or contradicted by subsequent research efforts.

One of the primary keys to producing sound results from a quality research effort is the development of a valid and reliable protocol. The exploratory process must be controlled and well organized. In addition, the protocol must be easy to follow for multiple investigators at different sites on varied patients. Meaningless results and wasted resources will be the product in the absence of an excellent protocol. It is well worth the effort, time, and personnel to create a sound document. The specific objectives of individual protocols depend on what stage of development the drug is in (Phases 1–4), the urgency of society's need for the drug (new chemical entity or not), and the condition(s) it will be used to treat (life-threatening, acute, long-term, contagious, etc.).

The protocol, case report forms, and an introduction to patient consent are discussed in this chapter.

I. THE PROTOCOL

Prior to the initiation of Phase 1 studies, sufficient animal data have been gathered to support the use of the drug in humans [1]. From this information, the potential uses of the product should already be established. Now, it is the time in the drug development process to design studies that will affirm (or disprove) the safety, efficacy, and usefulness of the drug in people.

The protocol, once developed, is subject to review and modification by the Institutional Review Boards (IRB) of the respective research institutions and by the regulatory agencies. It is a complex instrument with multiple parts. Table 1 provides a listing of the key components of a clinical trial protocol. Each of the separate areas will be discussed in the following sections as they should be encountered in a well-put-together document.

A. Pre-Introduction Pages

Located prior to the text portions of the protocol are the title page, table of contents, and abstract. The title page identifies the name of the study and serves as the front cover for the document. The sponsor(s) may or may not be identified here. The table of contents is a very convenient and user-

Table 1 Key Sections of a Protocol

A. Title Page
B. Table of Contents
C. Abstract
D. Introduction
   1. General Statement of Purpose
   2. Animal Study Information
   3. Clinical Data (if available)
   4. Time Frame–Events Schematic Diagram
E. Research Goals
   1. Research Statement
   2. Primary Research Objectives (no more than three)
   3. Secondary Objectives (not required)
F. Study Design and Research Methodology
   1. Type of Study
   2. Recruitment of Subjects
   3. Inclusionary Criteria
   4. Exclusionary Criteria
   5. Control Group
   6. Randomization Procedure
   7. Sample Size
   8. Duration of Study
   9. Variables
G. Data Analysis
H. Incomplete Follow-up Procedures
I. Case Report Forms
J. IRB Approval Documents
K. Bibliography

friendly item to include. This page helps the investigators find the section for which they may be looking. The abstract is a short synopsis (under 200 words) of the general objectives of the study.

B. Introduction

This section provides the background information on both the drug(s) and the study. Protocols for research in the earlier phases contain much more animal study information in this part than for later phases, which contain more clinical (human) data. A general introduction, containing a statement of the study's purpose, is the first page. This is a general statement of why the study is being performed, not the specific objectives of the investigation.

Sometimes, a schematic of the events versus the time frame for the investigation is also included here. This diagram helps to visualize the overall process. An example of a time frame–events graph for a hypothetical high blood pressure clinical trial is presented in Fig. 1.

C. Study Aims

The primary objective of drug development and clinical research is the purposeful pursuit of scientific data characterizing and quantifying a new drug product and documenting its usefulness [2]. In this section of the protocol,

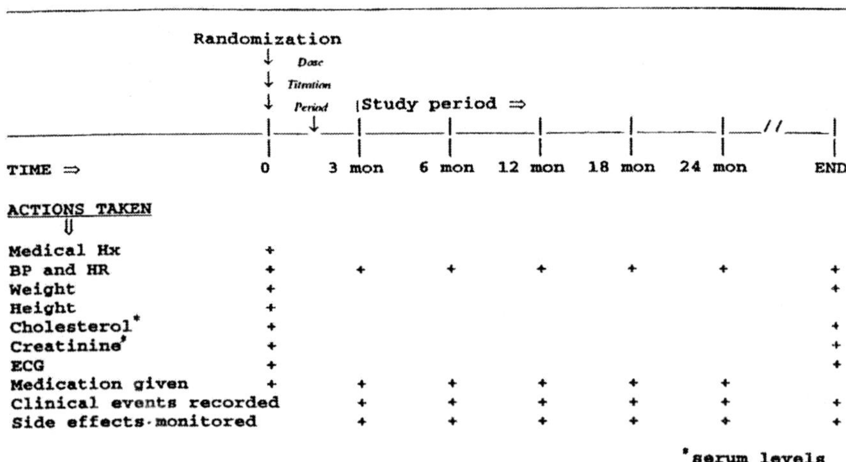

Fig. 1 Schematic representation of the time frame–events for a hypothetical hypertension clinical trial.

the specific objective(s) of the study is (are) detailed. This critical portion of the protocol should be a well-written, clear, concise statement elucidating exactly what is being investigated. Questions that are to be answered by the discovery process are posed in this part.

Well-designed studies rarely have more than two or three closely related, primary objectives. These statements must be written without prejudicial commentary that may forecast the result. The statement "to prove the efficacy of Drug Z5Q4A as an antihypertensive agent" is biased toward a positive-result expectation and, therefore, is poorly worded. A more properly worded objective would be stated as "to assess the effect of Drug Z5Q4A in hypertensive patients relative to its usefulness, if any." There may be several secondary aims of the project, obtained as a consequence of performing the research and not as its main mission. "Controversy arising from the results of many clinical trials emanates from confusion over the objectives, not from the results per se" [3].

For example, in Phase 1 trials, the objectives are usually related to the determination of the pharmacokinetic properties of the new product. In life-threatening conditions, such as AIDS or cancer, sometimes an early assessment of the drug's efficacy begins here. It is also common to compare the product's effectiveness to a placebo and/or to the drug-of-choice for the conditions to be treated (the "gold standard") here. Phase 2 trials generally assess the adverse event profile (type, frequency, intensity, etc.) of the new drug, as well as its degree of efficacy for a specific condition(s).

For a new drug, an assessment also should be made of its benefit to overall medical outcomes, as compared to other treatments. This research begins in late Phase 1 trials and is one of the primary objectives of Phase 3. Outcomes research is covered in subsequent chapters in greater detail.

D. The Study Design

This section of the protocol delineates the research methodology that is to be used in order to accomplish the previously established objectives. The study design is a key area where the scientific validity of the overall project is determined. A poor study design will yield poor results, whereas a sound undertaking will produce valid findings, as well as shield the subjects from potential harm or unnecessary exposure to the experimental agent. Statisticians are important consultants to employ during the development of the research design.

The protocol should include the following components and their respective methodologies and procedures:

1. What type of study is it? (open vs. closed, single- or double-blinded, crossover, etc.)
2. What are the controls? (placebo and/or "gold standard")
3. What are the patient eligibility requirements?
4. What is the sample size? (i.e., how many patients are needed?)
5. How will the patients be randomized into treatment groups?
6. If there is a crossover design or use of other agents, is there a washout period, and is it of sufficient length?
7. What is the duration of the study?

Another source of tremendous controversy is clinical trials in the sample size. A survey of 612 articles revealed that data were presented from studies having 10 or fewer subjects in 38% of them [4]. There should be a sufficient number of subjects in the study in order to accomplish its objectives. False-negative results are one of the potential problems when there are too few patients. Several statisticians should be consulted for this key determination.

A well-designed study also should include the procedures for the following components of using an investigational drug:

1. What are the drugs, investigational and control, that will be used in the study?
2. Is concomitant therapy permitted?
3. What dosage forms or route(s) of administration will be employed?
4. What strengths and dosing schedules will be used?
5. When will the drugs be administered?
6. What appearance will the drugs have and in what packaging will they come?
7. How will the drug(s) be blinded?
8. In a blinded study, what is the decoding procedure for an emergency medical situation?
9. How and when will unused drugs be disposed?

In order to be consistent, as many of the variables as possible should be kept constant, including the number of daily dosage forms administered and doses given during the titration phase. The number of daily doses given can be kept uniform by using a placebo when needed. Another important factor that should remain as identical as possible among the subjects is the stomach contents, especially during pivotal Phase 1 core studies. This parameter includes the total fluid intake volume, patient hydration level, what type of meal is ingested and how much, and when the dose will be administered relative to eating.

E. The Study Plan

The preferred variables in a clinical trial are a chronological sequence of objective measurements. The protocol should specify what, when, how, and where these measures are to be taken. Details of the laboratory and medical procedures and their associated calibrations and interpretations belong in an addendum to the protocol, located in the back of the Investigator's Notebook.

Next, the protocol lays out the procedures for recruiting patients, qualifying or enrolling subjects, titrating the dose(s) or response(s) to study specifications, and, finally, performing the study. Healthy volunteers (for Phase 1) and patients who suffer from the condition to be studied (for Phases 2, 3, and 4) are recruited via broadcast or print media, among other ways. Those people who seem to meet the eligibility requirements are asked to come in for an assessment visit. During this appointment, it is determined whether or not the patient meets the criteria for inclusion or exclusion for the study. If the guidelines are met, the patient qualifies as a subject and informed consent is obtained from him or her. At this point, the patient is officially enrolled in the study.

Once enrolled, the patient is randomized into a treatment group, and his or her baseline parameters that are germane to the study are measured. An example of a randomization visit form from an antihypertensive study appears in Appendix I. There are specific spaces on the form for each pertinent measurement. The style of the document is a modular format. This type of form helps to prevent mistakes and is much easier to use. There is a box for the investigator's signature at the bottom of each page to affirm completion of all tasks.

Once randomized, the subjects begin their respective therapy. A reasonable length of time (depending on the type of medication) is set aside as the titration phase. During this time, the patient is brought within the parameters specified in the protocol (e.g., blood pressure reduced to a set level). The dose of the drug is progressively increased or decreased (titrated) as needed to elicit the desired response. A patient who cannot be brought within the acceptable range may have to be dropped from the study.

Randomization of patients has usually been done by the principal investigator at the clinical site. Now, thanks to modern technology, this procedure can be performed by the monitoring team, with assistance of a statistician. The patient information form (see Appendix I), once completed, can be sent via facsimile transmission to a central location. Here, patients can be randomized for all sites using the same procedure (standardization). The research site is then notified, via fax, within a specified time frame (usually 3 to 5 days) which treatment group or target parameter group to place the patients. This procedure continues until the enrollment phase is over.

Once the titration phase has been completed, the treatment phase begins and each patient is studied during his or her scheduled, regularly occurring, follow-up visit. A follow-up visit form from a hypothetical high blood pressure study as before is presented in Appendix II. Note the similarity between the documents in Appendix I and Appendix II. The treatment phase continues until the study is completed. The time line is usually a predetermined number of months or it can entail a specific benchmark, such as a set number of events occurring during the study.

In some studies, especially Phase 1 trials, there may be a post-treatment phase. In this case, the patient is monitored after discontinuation of her or his therapy for delayed adverse events or post-drug effects for a preset period of time.

The study plan should also include a section on the training procedures that will be employed to instruct the investigator and all pertinent research personnel about the protocol.

F. Statistical Considerations

Most sponsors have in-house statisticians who are fundamental in the protocol design, trial implementation, and data analysis and interpretation. Additional outside help is sometimes employed, especially with outcomes data or pharmacoeconomic information. These specialists help in the determination of the sample size necessary to fulfill the requirements of each phase, assist in the matching or pairing of patients (if the methodology calls for this), and provide preliminary analysis for feedback early in the study.

The statistical tests that will be used are delineated in this section of the protocol. Sometimes, the expected accuracy of the measurements is also presented.

G. Incomplete Follow-up

Significant effort must be put forth to follow the patient according to the protocol (i.e., until the study is over). When it is not possible for a patient to complete the study, the reason for this early discontinuance should be determined. This section of the protocol should provide instructions for dealing with incomplete follow-up. Patients may leave a study as the result of circumstances involving the study or therapy (side effects, lack of efficacy, loss of interest, fatal event, etc.) or because of other conditions (moved from area, loss of transportation to center, family problems, etc.). A sample incomplete follow-up form for an antihypertensive study is found in Appendix III. At the conclusion of the study, the patient's status with respect to the events being investigated (i.e., did the patient leave because of an adverse event?) and the source of this information are entered onto the form.

The procedures for reporting serious or fatal adverse events should also be specified in the protocol. It is important to make the sample size of the study sufficiently large in order to compensate for the loss of patients during the research. This problem is usually more of a concern in long-term trials (over 12 months).

H. Other Sections

The patient case report forms are also part of the protocol, as well as the informed consent documents. Their development and utilization are presented in the next sections of this chapter. The standard clauses relating to IRB review and approval of the protocol are also included in the protocol, as well as patient consent provisions.

A list of all references cited in the introductory section and other places is usually presented here as a bibliography. In large, multicenter studies, the members of the grant steering and executive committees are sometimes listed, as well as each national coordinator for multinational trials. Addendums are also included as part of the protocol. Sometimes, these pages contain a detailed disclosure of laboratory or medical tests or procedures that must be utilized and the corresponding calibrations and calculations that must be performed during the study.

II. THE CASE REPORT FORMS

Once the above procedures have been planned and developed, the case report forms (CRF) can be designed. They become part of the protocol itself and integrated into its steps. A well-designed research plan can be destroyed by incomplete and inaccurate record keeping. The data management portion of a study is accomplished via the CRFs.

The patient's medical records and associated attachments are the primary data source documents; they are the origin of all pertinent information. Once the patient has been seen by the clinician and the entries made onto his or her chart, the data are then logged onto the CRF. It is important to have an easy-to-use, simple-to-follow, logically flowing form.

CRFs have evolved into a modular form. "A module is a group of related data elements, and a modular CRF is a series of modules used together in a clinical trial" [3]. Two examples of this type of document are presented in Appendixes I and II. The use of a modular CRF makes it easier to improve upon its own design. Information gathered from problems associated with employing the form in the field can be utilized to modify subsequent versions.

During the developmental process for CRFs, one of the key factors that should be considered is the form's ease of use by the researcher or data-entry person. A well-devised form will minimize errors, decrease the time spent on entries, improve data submission back to the monitoring team, enhance editing and monitoring activities, and optimize the overall use of resources.

In this information age, CRFs also serve as a basis for easily submitting the data to the central processing center. The monitors can utilize a portable computer with specially developed clinical-trial software. With these tools, they can enter data directly from the CRF into the computer and transmit it directly to the center. Near-instant data retrieval and feedback is now possible. This procedure conserves resources, allows for critical decisions to be made at earlier times (such as revision of the protocol, termination of the study, etc.), and detects deviations faster. The software should be designed so that entries that are nonsensical (letters for numbers, values too large or small, etc.) automatically send a visual and audible signal to the monitor. With this mechanism in place, he or she can double-check the entries on the spot. Additionally, some other critical parameters (such as subjects not within the acceptable range or deviations in dosing schedules) can be flagged, identified, and rechecked before leaving and maybe even corrected. During this data-entry process, the monitor also has the opportunity to verify the CRF against the medical record.

III. PATIENT CONSENT

The two primary ethical concerns in clinical trials are experimental versus accepted treatment and informed versus uninformed consent. Detailed information must be presented to the patient about the research project, explaining the risks versus the benefits of participation in the study. A patient consent document is developed from this information. This form is considered part of the protocol. Each institution must approve these documents, separate from and in addition to the protocol.

The consent forms are dynamic documents (i.e., they are subject to being changed). As new adverse events are uncovered at any site, all researchers are informed about them. Then, changes must be made in the patient consent form to reflect these discoveries, a new IRB approval is required, and new patient consent must be obtained in order to continue treatment with the experimental agent. In large trials, this procedure can be very frustrating and time consuming, but it is necessary to do it, both from an ethical and a regulatory point of view.

The basis of IRB approval and patient consent, from a regulatory standpoint, is found in federal regulations [5]. A copy of the two pertinent sections of these regulations, Informed Consent of Human Subjects and Institution Review Boards, is found in Appendix IV. Guidelines for clinical trials are also provided by the Declaration of Helsinki, recommendations guiding physicians in biomedical research involving human subjects [6]. A copy of this document is presented in Appendix V.

The general information for the patient consent form is provided by the sponsor (the protocol, all available drug information, etc.); however, each institution has its own requirements about specific contents. These nuances are why it is important for the monitoring team to review these documents prior to submission to the IRB. Consent must be documented by a dated signature of the subject on the consent form. Legally incompetent subjects must have the written consent of a parent, legal guardian, or legal representative. It is a good idea to have the consent-giving process witnessed for all participants.

The investigators are responsible for obtaining the initial approval of the study protocol and the patient consent document by their IRB. It is also their duty to ensure that the continuing review of these items takes place at an interval not to exceed 1 year. In order to ensure compliance with this vital section, a good procedure to follow is to withhold the initial shipment of investigational drugs until after the patient consent forms and protocol have been approved by the IRB and a copy of this approval has been received by the monitoring team. The monitor can also assist in enforcing this key provision, especially the renewal portion for long-term projects.

Another patient concern is the confidentiality of the medical data. Under the Freedom of Information Act, information furnished by clinical investigators and IRBs will be kept confidential by the FDA if, and only if this data is maintained in confidence by the investigator and the corresponding IRB. It is a good idea to have the investigator affirm that he or she will maintain all information gathered in the study or received from it in confidence and will divulge such data only to his or her own IRB under a similar understanding of confidentiality.

Dr. Robert McCarthy presents a further discussion of patient consent issues and Institutional Review Boards in Chapter 13, "Ethics in Clinical Drug Research."

IV. SUMMARY

There are many influences that come into play in developing and managing large clinical and outcomes studies. Many of these factors are controllable; some are not. The hallmarks of successful research efforts are careful planning and paying attention to the fine details. The protocol is the blueprint for the entire project. It sets the stage for the production of sound results. Considerable thought, effort, and resources should be put into the protocol's development. The stronger the foundation is for a study, the more valuable will be the data obtained from it.

The Case Report Forms (CRF) are an important component of the protocol. While the medical charts are the source documents, the CRFs serve as the final data record of the patient's responses. From these forms, the information is transmitted back to the sponsor for analysis. These documents should be designed so that they are easy to use and help prevent errors.

Through careful planning, many of the problems that could occur in running a large-scale clinical research project can be minimized or even avoided altogether. Developing a well-designed protocol and logical Case Report Forms are key components of this planning effort.

APPENDIX I

Sample Randomization Visit Form: Antihypertensive Study

RANDOMIZATION VISIT

Please ensure that all details are complete and correct. A patient can only be entered once.
PLEASE FAX THIS FORM IMMEDIATELY TO THE CENTRAL DATA CENTER
Target diastolic blood pressure group will be faxed back to you within five days.

PATIENT IDENTIFICATION

Date of Birth [day | month] 19 [year]

Patient ID-number [| | | |]

Patient Initials [|]

PATIENT DESCRIPTION

SEX male ☐ female ☐

RACE White ☐ Black ☐ Asian ☐ Other ☐

ANTIHYPERTENSIVE TREATMENT

Previous antihyper - tensive treatment? no ☐ yes ☐

SMOKING HABITS

Current smoker? no ☐ yes ☐

ENROLLMENT BLOOD PRESSURE

DATE [day | month] 19 [year]

SBP [mmHg] DBP [mmHg] HR [beats/min] (Copy values from patient chart)

MEDICAL HISTORY

Previous MI?	no ☐	yes ☐	------- last event	month	year
Other coronary heart disease (e.g., angina pectoris)	no ☐	yes ☐			
Previous stroke?	no ☐	yes ☐	--------last event	month	year
Diabetes mellitus?	no ☐	yes ☐			
Chronic obstructive lung disease .treated by drugs?	no ☐	yes ☐			

QUALIFYING BLOOD PRESSURE (100 ≥ DBP ≤ 115)

(Three BP measurements before randomization on two occasions, separated by at least one week)

[day | month] 19 [year]			[day | month] 19 [year]		
SBP	DBP	HR	SBP	DBP	HR
mmHg	mmHg	beats/min	mmHg	mmHg	beats/min
SBP	DBP	HR	SBP	DBP	HR
mmHg	mmHg	beats/min	mmHg	mmHg	beats/min
SBP	DBP	HR	SBP	DBP	HR
mmHg	mmHg	beats/min	mmHg	mmHg	beats/min

BODY MEASUREMENTS

Weight [kg]

Height [cm]

Date of Randomization visit : [day | month] 19 [year]

Investigator's signature

RANDOMIZATION VISIT (con't)

Patient Identification Number [ ] **Patient Initials** [ ]

PREVIOUS ANTIHYPERTENSIVE THERAPY

Calcium channel blocker	no ☐	yes ☐
Beta-blocker	no ☐	yes ☐
ACE-inhibitor	no ☐	yes ☐
Diuretic	no ☐	yes ☐
Other	no ☐	yes ☐

Specify

OTHER MEDICATIONS

Indicate other chronic medications that the patient is on this visit

Antiarrhythmic agents	no ☐	yes ☐
Digitalis glycosides	no ☐	yes ☐
NSAIDs	no ☐	yes ☐
Lipid lowering drugs	no ☐	yes ☐
Other analgesics	no ☐	yes ☐
Steroids	no ☐	yes ☐

CREATININE AND CHOLESTEROL SERUM LEVELS

Date of blood sample : day [ ] month [ ] 19 year [ ]

Serum Creatinine (mg/dl): [ ] Serum Cholesterol (mg/dl): [ ]

Investigator's signature

RANDOMIZATION VISIT EKG

Patient ID-number [| | | |] **Patient Initials** [|]

Date of EKG [day |] [month |] **19** [year |]

The EKG recordings should be attached in this box. Each strip should be marked with the Patient Identification Number. Each strip must have a minimum of four QRS-complexes plus an amplitude test signal. Six standard precordial leads and the following leads are required: I, II, III, aVR, aVF, aVL. This form should be given to the Monitor or sent to the Central Data Center in the specially marked envelope.

Investigator's signature

APPENDIX II

Sample Follow-Up Visit Form: Antihypertensive Study

FOLLOW-UP VISIT **X months**

Patient ID-number [ ] **Patient Initials** [ ]

Date of visit: day [ ] month [ ] 19 year [ ]

BLOOD PRESSURE AND HEART RATE

SBP	DBP	HR	SBP	DBP	HR	SBP	DBP	HR
mmHg	mmHg	beats/min	mmHg	mmHg	beats/min	mmHg	mmHg	beats/min

ANTIHYPERTENSIVE MEDICATION

Medication taken up to this visit				Medication prescribed at this visit			Discontinued due to side effects?	
TRADE NAME OF DRUG	STRENGTH	# DOSES	CHANGE?	Strength	Doses / Day	D/C ?	NO	YES
1.							☐	☐
2.							☐	☐
3.							☐	☐
4.							☐	☐

New drug(s), strength and daily dose.

OTHER VISITS

Has the patient been to any extra visits since the previously scheduled study visit? **no** ☐ **yes** ☐ ⇒⇒⇒ **How many visits?** [ ]

MAIN EVENTS SINCE PREVIOUS VISIT

Non-fatal events (if yes, complete NON-FATAL EVENT FORM)

MI	no ☐	yes ☐
Stroke	no ☐	yes ☐
Angina Episode	no ☐	yes ☐
Other cardiovascular event	no ☐	yes ☐

FOLLOW-UP VISIT (CON'T)

MAIN EVENTS SINCE PREVIOUS VISIT (CON'T)

Fatal events no ☐ yes ☐ ⇒ (If yes, complete FATAL EVENT FORM)

Other hospitizations? no ☐ yes ☐ ⇒ Days in hospital ☐

Cause

SIDE EFFECTS

Has the patient experienced any adverse events due to the treatment since the last visit? no ☐ yes ☐ ⇒ Specify

Was it considered a serious side effect? no ☐ yes ☐

⇓

(Complete serious side effect form)

Investigator's signature

APPENDIX III

Sample Incomplete Follow-Up Form: Antihypertensive Study

INCOMPLETE FOLLOW-UP

When the study is terminated, complete this form for patients who cannot or who refuse to keep their scheduled appointment(s).

Patient ID-number ☐ Patient Initials ☐

Date: day | month 19 year

REASON FOR INCOMPLETE FOLLOW-UP

Moved? no ☐ yes ☐

Unwilling to cooperate? no ☐ yes ☐

Other reason: no ☐ yes ☐ ⇒⇒ Specify

Date when last seen in clinic: day | month 19 year

MAIN EVENTS SINCE LAST ATTENDED VISIT

Have there been any main events since the last visit? no ☐ yes ☐ ⇒(complete NON-FATAL or FATAL EVENT FORM)

INFORMATION SOURCE

Patient seen in clinic?: no ☐ yes ☐ ⇒ day | month 19 year

Telephone contact? no ☐ yes ☐ ⇒ day | month 19 year

Personal visit? no ☐ yes ☐ ⇒ day | month 19 year

Contact with a relative? no ☐ yes ☐ ⇒ day | month 19 year

Other source: no ☐ yes ☐ ⇒ day | month 19 year

⇓

Specify

Investigator's signature

APPENDIX IV

Federal Regulations Pertaining to Institutional Review Boards and Informed Patient Consent

PART 56-INSTITUTIONAL REVIEW BOARDS

Subpart A-General Provisions

§56.101 Scope.

(a) This part contains the general standards for the composition, operation, and responsibility of an Institutional Review Board (IRB) that reviews clinical investigations regulated by the Food and Drug Administration under sections 505(i), 507(d), and 520(g) of the act, as well as clinical investigations that support applications for research or marketing permits for products regulated by the Food and Drug Administration, including food and color additives, drugs for human use, medical devices for human use, biological products for human use, and electronic products. Compliance with this part is intended to protect the rights and welfare of human subjects involved in such investigations.

(b) References in this part to regulatory sections of the Code of Federal Regulations are to chapter I of title 21, unless otherwise noted.

§56.102 Definitions.

As used in this part:

(a) *Act* means the Federal Food, Drug, and Cosmetic Act, as amended (secs. 201-902, 52 Stat. 1040 et seq., as amended (21 U.S.C. 321-392)).

(b) *Application for research or marketing permit* includes:

(1) A color additive petition, described in part 71.

(2) Data and information regarding a substance submitted as part of the procedures for establishing that a substance is generally recognized as safe for a use which results or may reasonably be expected to result, directly or indirectly, in its becoming a component or otherwise affecting the characteristics of any food, described in §170.35.

(3) A food additive petition, described in part 171.

(4) Data and information regarding a food additive submitted as part of the procedures regarding food additives permitted to be used on an interim basis pending additional study, described in §180.1.

(5) Data and information regarding a substance submitted as part of the procedures for establishing a tolerance for unavoidable contaminants in food and food-packaging materials, described in section 406 of the act.

(6) An investigational new drug application, described in part 312 of this chapter.

(7) A new drug application, described in part 314.

(8) Data and information regarding the bioavailability or bioequivalence of drugs for human use submitted as part of the procedures for issuing, amending, or repealing a bioequivalence requirement, described in part 320.

(9) Data and information regarding an over-the-counter drug for human use submitted as part of the procedures for classifying such drugs as generally recognized as safe and effective and not misbranded, described in part 330.

(10) Data and information regarding an antibiotic drug submitted as part of the procedures for issuing, amending, or repealing regulations for such drugs, described in §314.300 of this chapter.

(11) An application for a biological product license, described in part 601.

(12) Data and information regarding a biological product submitted as part of the procedures for determining that licensed biological products are as safe and effective and not misbranded, described in part 601.

(13) An *Application for an Investigational Device Exemption*, described in parts 812 and 813.

(14) Data and information regarding a medical device for human use submitted as part of the procedures for classifying such devices, described in part 860.

(15) Data and information regarding a medical device for human use submitted as part of the procedures for establishing, amending, or repealing regulations for such device, described in part 861.

(16) An application for premarket approval of a medical device for human use, described in section 515 of the act.

(17) A product development protocol for a medical device for human use, described in section 515 of the act.

(18) Data and information regarding an electronic product submitted as part of the procedures for establishing, amending, or repealing a standard for such products, described in section 358 of the Public Health Service Act.

(19) Data and information regarding an electronic product submitted as part of the procedures for obtaining a variance from any electronic product performance standard, as described in §1010.4.

(20) Data and information regarding an electronic product submitted as part of the procedures for granting, amending, or extending an exemption from a radiation safety performance standard, as described in §1010.4.

(21) Data and information regarding an electronic product submitted as part of the procedures for obtaining an exemption from notification of a radiation safety defect or failure of compliance with a radiation safety performance standard, as described in subpart D of part 1003.

(c) *Clinical investigation* means any experiment that involves a test article and one or more human subjects, and that either must meet the requirements for prior submission to the Food and Drug Administration under section 505(i), 507(d), or 520(g) of the act, or need not meet the requirements for prior submission to the Food and Drug Administration under these sections of the act, but the results of which are intended to be later submitted, or held for inspection by, the Food and Drug Administration as part of an application for a research or marketing permit. The term does not include experiments that must meet the provisions of part 58, regarding nonclinical laboratory studies. The terms *research, clinical research, clinical study, study,* and *clinical investigation* are deemed to be synonymous for purposes of this part.

(d) *Emergency use* means the use of a test article on a human subject in a life-threatening situation in which no standard acceptable treatment is available, and in which there is not sufficient time to obtain IRB approval.

(e) *Human subject* means an individual who is or becomes a participant in research, either as a recipient of the test article or as a control. A subject may be either a healthy individual or a patient.

(f) *Institution* means any public or private entity or agency (including Federal, State, and other agencies). The term *facility* as used in section 520(g) of the act is deemed to be synonymous with the term *institution* for purposes of this part.

(g) *Institutional Review Board (IRB)* means any board, committee, or other group formally designated by an institution to review, to approve the initiation of, and to conduct periodic review of, biomedical research involving human subjects. The primary purposes of such review is to assure the protection of the rights and welfare of the human subjects The term has the same meaning as the phrase *institutional review committee* as used in section 520(g) of the act.

(h) *Investigator* means an individual who actually conducts a clinical investigation (i.e., under whose immediate direction the test article is administered or dispensed to, or used involving, a subject) or, in the event of an investigation conducted by a team of individuals, is the responsible leader of that team.

(i) *Minimal risk* means that the probability and

magnitude of harm or discomfort anticipated in the research are not greater in and of themselves than those ordinarily encountered in daily life or during the performance of routine physical or psychological examinations or tests.

(j) *Sponsor* means a person or other entity that initiates a clinical investigation, but does not actually conduct the investigation, i.e., the test article is administered or dispensed to, or used involving, a subject under the immediate direction of another individual. A person other than an individual (e.g., a corporation or agency) that uses one or more of its own employees to conduct an investigation that it has initiated is considered to be a sponsor (not a sponsor-investigator), and the employees are considered to be investigators.

(k) *Sponsor-investigator* means an individual who both initiates and actually conducts, alone or with others, a clinical investigation, i.e., under whose immediate direction the test article is administered or dispensed to, or used involving, a subject. The term does not include any person other than an individual, e.g., it does not include a corporation or agency. The obligations of a sponsor-investigator under this part include both those of a sponsor and those of an investigator.

(l) *Test article* means any drug for human use, biological product for human use, medical device for human use, human food additive, color additive, electronic product, or any other article subject to regulation under the act or under sections 351 or 354-360F of the Public Health Service Act.

(m) *IRB approval* means the determination of the IRB that the clinical investigation has been reviewed and may be conducted at an institution within the constraints set forth by the IRB and by other institutional and Federal requirements.

[46 FR 8975, Jan. 27, 1981, as amended at 54 FR 9038, Mar. 3, 1989:56 FR 28028, June 18, 1991]

§56.103 Circumstances in which IRB review is required.

(a) Except as provided in §§56.104 and 56.105, any clinical investigation which must meet the requirements for prior submission (as required in parts 312, 812, and 813) to the Food and Drug Administration shall not be initiated unless that investigation has been reviewed and approved by, and remains subject to continuing review by, an IRB meeting the requirements of this part.

(b) Except as provided in §§56.104 and 56.105, the Food and Drug Administration may decide not to consider in support of an application for a research or marketing permit any data or information that has been derived from a clinical investigation that has not been approved by, and that was not subject to initial and continuing review by, an IRB meeting the requirements of this part. The determination that a clinical investigation may not be considered in support of an application for a research or marketing permit does not, however, relieve the applicant for such a permit of any obligation under any other applicable regulations to submit the results of the investigation to the Food and Drug Administration.

(c) Compliance with these regulations will in no way render inapplicable pertinent Federal, State, or local laws or regulations.

[46 FR 8975, Jan. 27, 1981: 46 FR 14340, Feb. 27, 1981]

§56.104 Exemptions from IRB requirement.

The following categories of clinical investigations are exempt from the requirements of this part for IRB review:

(a) Any investigation which commenced before July 27, 1981 and was subject to requirements for IRB review under FDA regulations before that date, provided that the investigation remains subject to review of an IRB which meets the FDA requirements in effect before July 27, 1981.

(b) Any investigation which commenced before July 27, 1981 and was not otherwise subject to requirements for IRB review under Food and Drug Administration regulations before that date.

(c) Emergency use of a test article, providing that such emergency use is reported to the IRB within 5 working days. Any subsequent use of the test article at the institution is subject to IRB review.

(d) Taste and food quality evaluations and consumer acceptance studies, if wholesome foods without additives are consumed or if a food is consumed that contains a food ingredient at or below the level and for a use found to be safe, or agricultural, chemical, or environmental contaminant at or below the level found to be safe, by the Food and Drug Administration or approved by the Environmental Protection Agency or the Food Safety and Inspection Service of the U.S. Department of Agriculture.

[46 FR 8975, Jan. 27, 1981, as amended at 54 FR 9038, Mar. 3, 1989: 56 FR 28028, June 18, 1991]

§56.105 Waiver of IRB requirement.

On the application of a sponsor or sponsor-investigator, the Food and Drug Administration may waive any of the requirements contained in these regulations, including the requirements for IRB review, for specific research activities or for classes of research activities, otherwise covered by these regulations.

Subpart B - Organization and Personnel

§56.107 IRB Membership.

(a) Each IRB shall have at least five members, with varying backgrounds to promote complete and adequate review of research activities commonly conducted by the institution. The IRB shall be sufficiently qualified through the experience and expertise of its members, and the diversity of the members, including consideration of race, gender, cultural backgrounds, and sensitivity to such issues as community attitudes, to promote respect for its advice and counsel in safeguarding the rights and welfare of human subjects. In addition to possessing the professional competence necessary to review the specific research activities, the IRB shall be able to ascertain the acceptability of proposed research in terms of institutional commitments and regulations, applicable law, and standards of professional conduct and practice. The IRB shall therefore include persons knowledgeable in these areas. If an IRB regularly reviews research that involves a vulnerable category of subjects, such as children, prisoners, pregnant women, or handicapped or mentally disabled persons, consideration shall be given to the inclusion of one or more individuals who are knowledgeable about and experienced in working with those subjects.

(b) Every nondiscriminatory effort will be made to ensure that no IRB consists entirely of men or entirely of women, including the institution's consideration of qualified persons of both sexes, so long as no selection is made to the IRB on the basis of gender. No IRB may consist entirely of members of one profession.

(c) Each IRB shall include at least one member whose primary concerns are in the scientific area and at least one member whose primary concerns are in nonscientific areas.

(d) Each IRB shall include at least member who is not otherwise affiliated with the institution and who is not part of the immediate family of a person who is affiliated with the institution.

(e) No IRB may have a member participate in the IRB's initial or continuing review of any project in which the member has a conflicting interest, except to provide information requested by the IRB.

(f) An IRB may, in its discretion, invite individuals with competence in special areas to assist in the review of complex issues which require expertise beyond or in addition to that available on the IRB. These may not vote with the IRB.

[46 FR 8975, Jan. 27, 1981, as amended at 56 FR 28028, June 18, 1991:56 FR 29756, June 28, 1991]

Subpart C - IRB Functions and Operations

§56.108 IRB Functions and Operations.

In order to fulfill the requirements of these regulations, each IRB shall:

(a) Follow written procedures: (1) For conducting its initial and continuing review of research and for reporting its findings and actions to the investigator and the institution: (2) for determining which projects require review more often than annually and which projects need verification from sources other than the investigator that no material changes have occurred since previous IRB review: (3) for ensuring prompt reporting to the IRB of changes in research activity: and (4) for ensuring that changes in approved research, during the period for which IRB approval has already been given, may not be initiated without IRB review and approval except where necessary to eliminate apparent immediate hazards to the human subjects.

(b) Follow written procedures for ensuring prompt reporting to the IRB, appropriate institutional officials, and the Food and Drug Administration of: (1) Any unanticipated problems involving risks to human subjects or others: (2) any instance of serious or continuing noncompliance with these regulations or the requirements or determinations of the IRB: or (3) any suspension or termination of IRB approval.

(c) Except when an expedited review procedure is used (see §56.110), review proposed research at convened meetings at which at least a majority of the members of the IRB are present, including at least one member whose primary concerns are in nonscientific areas. In order for the research to be approved it shall receive the approval of a majority of those members present at the meeting.

(Information collection requirements in this section were approved by the Office of Management and Budget (OMB) and assigned OMB control number 0910-0130)

[46 FR 8975, Jan. 27, 1981, as amended at 56 FR 28028 June 18, 1991]

§56.109 IRB Review of research.

(a) An IRB shall review and have authority to approved, require modifications in (to secure approval), or disapprove all research activities covered by these regulations.

(b) An IRB shall require that information given to subjects as part of informed consent is in accordance with §50.25. The IRB may require that information, in addition to that specifically mentioned in §50.25, be given to the subjects when in the IRB's judgment the information would meaningfully add to the protection of the rights and welfare of subjects.

(c) An IRB shall require documentation of informed consent in accordance with §50.27, except that the IRB may, for some or all subjects, waive the requirement that the subject or the subject's legally authorized representative sign a written consent form if it finds that the research presents no more than minimal risk of harm to subjects and involves no procedures for which written consent is normally required outside the research context. In cases where the documentation requirement is waived, the IRB may require the investigator to provide subjects with a written statement regarding the research.

(d) An IRB shall notify investigators and the institution in writing of its decision to approve or disapprove the proposed research activity, or of modifications required to secure IRB approval of the research activity. If the IRB decides to disapprove a research activity, it shall include in its written notification a statement of the reasons for its decision and give the investigator an opportunity to respond in person or in writing.

(e) An IRB shall conduct continuing review of research covered by these regulations at intervals appropriate to the degree of risk, but not less than once per year, and shall have authority to observe or have a third party observe the consent process and the research.

§56.110 Expedited review procedures for certain kinds of research involving no more than minimal risk, and for minor changes in approved research.

(a) The Food and Drug Administration has established, and published in the FEDERAL REGISTER, a list of categories of research that may be reviewed by the IRB through an expedited review procedure. The list will be amended, as appropriate, through periodic publication in the FEDERAL REGISTER.

(b) An IRB may use the expedited review procedure to review either or both of the following: (1) Some or all of the research appearing on the list and found by reviewer(s) to involve no more than minimal risk. (2) Minor changes in previously approved research during the period (of 1 year or less) for which approval is authorized. Under an expedited review procedure, the review may be carried out by the IRB chairperson or by one or more experienced reviewers designated by the IRB chairperson from among the members of the IRB. In reviewing the research, the reviewers may exercise all of the authorities of the IRB except that reviewers may not disapprove the research. A research activity may be disapproved only after review in accordance with the nonexpedited review procedure set forth in §56.108(c).

(c) Each IRB which uses an expedited review procedure shall adopt a method for keeping all members advised of research proposals which have been approved under this procedure.

(d) The Food and Drug Administration may restrict, suspend, or terminate an institution's or IRB's use of the expedited review process when necessary to protect the rights or welfare of subjects.

[46 FR 8975, Jan. 27, 1981, as amended at 56 FR 28028, June 18, 1991]

§56.111 Criteria for IRB approval of research.

(a) In order to approve research covered by these regulations the IRB shall determine that all of the following requirements are satisfied:

(1) Risks to subjects are minimized: (i) By using procedures which are consistent with sound research design and which do not unnecessarily exposed subjects to risk, and (ii) whenever appropriate, by using procedures already being performed on the subjects for diagnostic or treatment purposes.

(2) Risks to subjects are reasonable in relation to anticipated benefits, if any, to subjects, and the importance of the knowledge that may be expected to result. In evaluating risks and benefits, the IRB should consider only those risks and benefits that may result from the research (as distinguished from risks and benefits of therapies that subjects would receive even if not participating in the research). The IRB should not

consider possible long-term effects of applying knowledge gained in the research (for example, the possible effects of the research on public policy) as among those research risks that fall within the purview of its responsibility.

(3) Selection of subjects is equitable. In making this assessment the IRB should take into account the purposes of the research and the setting in which the research will be conducted and should be particularly cognizant of the special problems of research involving vulnerable populations, such as children, prisoners, pregnant women, handicapped or mentally disabled persons, or economically or educationally disadvantaged persons.

(4) Informed consent will be sought from each prospective subject, or the subject's legally authorized representative, in accordance with and to the extent required by part 50.

(5) Informed consent will be appropriately documented, in accordance with and in the extent required by §50.27.

(6) Where appropriate, the research plan makes adequate provision for monitoring the data collected to ensure the safety of the subjects.

(7) Where appropriate, there are adequate provisions to protect the privacy of subjects and to maintain the confidentiality of data.

(b) When some or all of the subjects, such as children, prisoners, pregnant women, handicapped or mentally disabled persons, or economically or educationally disadvantaged persons, are likely to be vulnerable to coercion or undue influence additional safeguards have been included in the study to protect the rights and welfare of these subjects.

[46 FR 8975, Jan. 27, 1981, as amended at 56 FR 28028, June 18, 1991]

§56.112 Review by institution.

Research covered by these regulations that has been approved by an IRB may be subject to further appropriate review and approval or disapproval by officials of the institution. However, these officials may not approve the research if it has not been approved by an IRB.

§56.113 Suspension or termination of IRB approval of research.

An IRB shall have the authority to suspend or terminate approval of research that is not being conducted in accordance with the IRB's requirements or that has been associated with unexpected serious harm to subjects. Any suspension or termination of approval shall include a statement of the reasons for the IRB's action and shall be promptly reported to the investigator, appropriate institutional officials, and the Food and Drug Administration.

§56.114 Cooperative research.

In complying with these regulation, institutions involved in multi-institutional studies may use joint review, reliance upon the review of another qualified IRB, or similar arrangements aimed at avoidance of duplication of effort.

Subpart D - Records and Reports

§56.115 IRB records.

(a) An institution, or where appropriate, an IRB, shall prepare and maintain adequate documentation of IRB activities, including the following:

(1) Copies of all research proposals reviewed, scientific evaluations, if any, that accompany the proposal, approved sample consent documents, progress reports submitted by investigators, and reports of injuries to subjects.

(2) Minutes of IRB meetings which shall be in sufficient detail to show attendance at the meetings: actions taken by the IRB; the vote on these actions including the number of members voting for, against and abstaining; the basis requiring changes in or disapproving research; and a written summary of the discussion of controverted issues and their resolution.

(3) Records of continuing review activities.

(4) Copies of all correspondence between the IRB and the investigators.

(5) A list of IRB members identified by name; earned degrees; representative capacity; indications of experience such as board certifications, licenses, etc., sufficient to describe each member's chief anticipated contributions to IRB deliberations: and any employment or other relationship between each member and the institution; for example, full-time employee, part-time employee, a member of governing panel or board, stockholder, paid or unpaid consultant.

(6) Written procedures for the IRB as required by §56.108 (a) and (b).

(7) Statements of significant new findings provided to subjects, as required by §50.25.

(b) The records required by this regulation shall be

maintained at least 3 years after completion of the research, and the records shall be accessible for inspection and copying by authorized representatives of the Food and Drug Administration at reasonable times and in a reasonable manner.

(c) The Food and Drug Administration may refuse to consider a clinical investigation in support of an application for research or marketing permit if the institution or IRB that reviewed the investigation refuses to allow inspection under this section.

(Information collection requirements in this section were approved by the Office of Management and Budget (OMB) and assigned OMB control number 0910-0130)

[46 FR 8975, Jan. 27, 1981, as amended at 56 FR 28028, June 18, 1991]

Subpart E - Administrative Actions for Noncompliance

§56.120 Lesser administrative actions.

(a) If apparent noncompliance of these regulations in the operation of an IRB is observed by the FDA investigator during an inspection, the inspector will present an oral or written summary of the observations to an appropriate representative of the IRB. The Food and Drug Administration may subsequently send a letter describing the noncompliance to the IRB and to the parent institution. The agency will require that the IRB or parent institution respond to this letter within a time period specified by FDA and describe the corrective actions that will be taken by the IRB, the institution, or both to achieve compliance with these regulations.

(b) On the basis of the IRB's or the institution's response, FDA may schedule a re-inspection to confirm the adequacy of corrective actions. In addition, until the IRB or the parent institution takes appropriate corrective action, the agency may:

(1) Withhold approval of new studies subject to the requirements of this part that are conducted at the institution or reviewed by the IRB;

(2) Direct that no new studies be added to ongoing studies subject to this part;

(3) Terminate ongoing studies subject to this part when doing so would not endanger the subjects; or

(4) When the apparent noncompliance creates a significant threat to the rights and welfare of human

subjects, notify relevant State and Federal regulatory agencies and other parties with a direct interest in the agency's action of deficiencies in the operation of the IRB.

(c) The parent institution is presumed to be responsible for the operation of an IRB, and the Food and Drug Administration will ordinarily direct any administrative action under this subpart against the institution. However, depending on the evidence of responsibilities for deficiencies, determined during the investigation, the Food and Drug Administration may restrict its administrative actions to the IRB or to a component of the parent institution determined to be responsible for formal designation of the IRB.

§56.121 Disqualification of an IRB or an institution.

(a) Whenever the IRB or the institution has failed to take adequate steps to correct the noncompliance stated in the letter sent by the agency under §56.120(a), and the Commissioner of Food and Drugs determines that this noncompliance may justify the disqualification of the IRB or of the institution, the Commissioner will institute proceedings in accordance with the requirements for a regulatory hearing set forth in part 16.

(b) The Commissioner may disqualify an IRB or the parent institution if the Commissioner determines that:

(1) The IRB has refused or repeatedly failed to comply with any of the regulations set forth in this part,.and

(2) The noncompliance adversely affects the rights or welfare of the human subjects in a clinical investigation.

(c) If the Commissioner determines that disqualification is appropriate, the Commissioner will issue an order that explains the basis for the determination and that prescribes any actions to be taken with regard to ongoing clinical research conducted under the review of the IRB. The Food and Drug Administration will send notice of the disqualification to the IRB and the parent institution. Other parties with a direct interest, such as sponsors and clinical investigators, may also be sent a notice of disqualification. In addition, the agency may elect to publish a notice of its action in the FEDERAL REGISTER.

(d) The Food and Drug Administration will not approve an application for a research permit for a clinical investigation that is to be under the review of a disqualified IRB or that is conducted at a disqualified institution, and it may refuse to consider in support of a marketing permit the data from a clinical investigation that was reviewed by a disqualified IRB as conducted at a disqualified institution, unless the IRB or parent institution is reinstated as provided in §56.123.

§56.122 Public disclosure of information regarding revocation.

A determination that the Food and Drug Administration has disqualified an institution and the administrative record regarding that determination are disclosable to the public under part 20.

§56.123 Reinstatement of an IRB or an institution.

An IRB or an institution may be reinstated if the Commissioner determines, upon an evaluation of a written submission from the IRB or institution that explains the corrective action that the institution or IRB plans to take, that the IRB or institution has provided adequate assurance that it will operate in compliance the standards set forth in this part. Notification of reinstatement shall be provided to all persons notified under §56.121(c).

§56.124 Actions alternative or additional to disqualification.

Disqualification of an IRB or of an institution is independent of, and neither in lieu of nor a precondition to, other proceedings or actions authorized by the act. The Food and Drug Administration may, at any time, through the Department of Justice institute any appropriate judicial proceedings (civil or criminal) and any other appropriate regulatory action, in addition to or in lieu of, and before, at the time of, or after, disqualification. The agency may also refer pertinent matters to another Federal, State, or local government agency for any action that that agency determines to be appropriate.

Subpart B-Informed Consent of Human Subjects

SOURCE: 46 FR 8951, Jan. 27, 1981, unless otherwise noted.

§50.20 General requirements for informed consent.

Except as provided in §50.23, no investigator may involve a human being as a subject in research covered by these regulations unless the investigator has obtained the legally effective informed consent of the subject or the subject's legally authorized representative. An investigator shall seek such consent only under circumstances that provide the prospective subject or the representative sufficient opportunity to consider whether or not to participate and that minimize the possibility of coercion or undue influence. The information that is given to the subject or the representative shall be in language understandable to the subject or the representative. No informed consent, whether oral or written, may include any exculpatory language through which the subject or the representative is made to waive or appear to waive any of the subject's legal rights, or releases or appears to release the investigator, the sponsor, the institution, or its agents from liability from negligence.

§50.21 Effective date.

The requirements for informed consent set out in this part apply to all human subjects entering a clinical investigation that commences on or after July 27, 1981.

§50.23 Exemption from general requirements.

(a) The obtaining of informed consent shall be deemed feasible unless, before use of the test article (except as provided in paragraph (b) of this section), both the investigator and a physician who is not otherwise participating in the clinical investigation certify in writing all of the following:

(1) The human subject is confronted by a life-threatening situation necessitating the use of the test article.

(2) Informed consent cannot be obtained from the subject because of an inability to communicate with, or obtain legally effective consent from, the subject.

(3) Time is not sufficient to obtain consent from the subject's legal representative.

(4) There is available no alternative method of approved or generally recognized therapy that provides an equal or greater likelihood of saving the life of the subject.

(b) If immediate use of the test article is, in the investigator's opinion, required to preserve the life of the subject, and time is not sufficient to obtain the independent determination required in paragraph (a) of this section in advance of using the test article, the determinations of the clinical investigator shall be made and, within 5 working days after the use of the article, be reviewed and evaluated in writing by a physician who is not participating in the clinical investigation.

(c) The documentation required in paragraph (a) or (b) of this section shall be submitted to the IRB within 5 working days after the use of the test article.

(d)(1) The Commissioner may also determine that obtaining informed consent is not feasible when the Assistant Secretary of Defense (Health Affairs) requests such a determination in connection with the use of an investigational drug (including an antibiotic or biological product) in a specific protocol under an investigational new drug application (IND) sponsored by the Depart of Defense (DOD). DOD's request for a determination that obtaining informed consent form military personnel is not feasible must be limited to a specific military operation involving combat or the immediate threat of combat. The request must also include a written justification supporting the conclusions of the physician(s) responsible for the medical care of the military personnel involved and the investigator(s) identified in the IND that a military combat exigency exists because of special military combat (actual or threatened) circumstances in which, in order to facilitate the accomplishment of the military mission, preservation of the health of the individual and the safety of other personnel require that a particular treatment be provided to a specified group of military personnel, without regard to what might be any individual's personal preference for no treatment or for some alternative treatment. The written request must also include a statement that a duly constituted institutional review board has reviewed and approved the use of the investigational drug without informed consent. The Commissioner may find that informed consent is not feasible only when withholding treatment would be contrary to the best interests of military personnel and there is no available satisfactory alternative therapy.

(2) In reaching a determination under paragraph (d)(1) of this section that obtaining informed consent is not feasible and withholding treatment would be contrary to the best interests of military personnel, the Commissioner will review the request submitted under paragraph (d)(1) of this section and take into account all pertinent factors, including, but not limited to:

(i) The extent and strength of the evidence of the safety and effectiveness of the investigational drug for the intended use;

(ii) The context in which the drug will be administered, e.g., whether it is intended for use in a battlefield or hospital setting or whether it will be self-administered or will be administered by a health professional;

(iii) The nature of the disease or condition for which the preventive or therapeutic treatment is intended; and

(iv) The nature of the information to be provided to the recipients of the drug concerning the potential benefits and risks of taking or not taking the drug.

(3) The Commissioner may request a recommendation from appropriate experts before reaching a determination on a request submitted under paragraph (d)(1) of this section.

(4) A determination by the Commissioner that obtaining informed consent is not feasible and withholding treatment would be contrary to the best interests of military personnel will expire at the end of 1 year, unless renewed at DOD's request, or when DOD informs the Commissioner that the specific military operation creating the need for the use of the investigational drug has ended, whichever is earlier. The Commissioner may also revoke this determination based on changed circumstances.

[46 FR 8951, Jan. 27, 1981, as amended at 55 FR 52817, Dec. 21, 1990]

§50.25 Elements of informed consent.

(a) *Basic elements of informed consent.* In seeking informed consent, the following information shall be provided to each subject:

(1) A statement that the study involves research, an explanation of the purposes of the research and the expected duration of the subject's participation, a description of the procedures to be followed, and identification of any procedures which are experimental.

(2) A brief description of any reasonably foreseeable risks or discomforts to the subject.

(3) A description of any benefits to the subject or to others which may reasonably be expected from the research.

(4) A disclosure of appropriate alternative procedures or courses of treatment, if any, that might be advantageous to the subject.

(5) A statement describing the extent, if any, to which confidentiality of records identifying the subject will be maintained and that notes the possibility that the Food and Drug Administration may inspect the records.

(6) For research involving more than minimal risk, an explanation as to whether any compensation and an explanation as to whether any medical treatments are available if injury occurs and, if so, what they consist of, or where further information may be obtained

(7) An explanation of whom to contact for answers to pertinent questions about the research and research subject's rights, and whom to contact in the event of a research-related injury to the subject.

(8) A statement that participation is voluntary, that refusal to participate will involve no penalty or loss of benefits to which the subject is otherwise entitled, and that the subject may discontinue participation at any time without penalty or

loss of benefits to which the subject is otherwise entitled.

(b) *Additional elements of informed consent.* When appropriate, one or more of the following elements of information shall also be provided to each subject:

(1) A statement that the particular treatment or procedure may involve risks to the subject (or to the embryo or fetus, if the subject is or may become pregnant) which are currently unforeseeable.

(2) Anticipated circumstances under which the subject's participation may be terminated by the investigator without regard to the subject's consent.

(3) Any additional costs to the subject that may result from participation in the research.

(4) The consequences of a subject's decision to withdraw from the research and procedures for orderly termination of participation by the subject.

(5) A statement that significant new findings developed during the course of the research which may relate to the subject's willingness to continue participation will be provided to the subject.

(6) The approximate number of subjects involved in the study.

(c) The informed consent requirements in these regulations are not intended to preempt any applicable Federal, State, or local laws which require additional information to be disclosed for informed consent to be legally effective

(d) Nothing in these regulations is intended to limit the authority of a physician to provide emergency medical care to the extent the physician is permitted to do under applicable Federal, State, and local law.

§50.27 Documentation of informed consent.

(a) Except as provided in §56.109(c), informed consent shall be documented by the use of a written consent form approved by the IRB and signed by the subject or the subject's legally authorized representative. A copy shall be given to the person signing the form.

(b) Except[t as provided in §56.109(c), the consent form may be either of the following:

(1) A written consent document that embodies the elements of informed consent required by §50.25. This form may be read to the subject or the subject's legally authorized representative, but, in any event, the investigator shall give either the subject or the representative adequate opportunity to read it before it is signed.

(2) A *short form* written consent document stating that the elements of informed consent required by §50.25 have been presented orally to the subject or the subject's legally authorized representative. When this method is used, there shall be a witness to the oral presentation. Also, the IRB shall approve a written summary of what is to be said to the subject or the representative. Only the short form itself is to be signed by the subject or the representative. However, the witness shall sign both the short form and a copy of the summary, and the person actually obtaining the consent shall sign a copy of the summary. A copy of the summary shall be given to the subject or the representative in addition to a copy of the short form.

APPENDIX V

Declaration of Helsinki

Recommendations guiding physicians in biomedical research involving human subjects.

Adopted by the 18th World Medical Assembly, Helsinki, Finland, June 1964 and amended by the 29th World Medical Assembly, Tokyo, Japan October 1975, 35th World Medical Assembly, Venice, Italy, October 1983 and the 41st World Medical Assembly Hong Kong, September 1989.

Introduction

It is the mission of the physician to safeguard the health of the people. His or her knowledge and conscience are dedicated to the fulfillment of this mission.

The Declaration of Geneva of the Third Word Medical Association binds the physician with the words, "The health of my patient will be my first consideration," and the International Code of Medical Ethics declares that, "A physician shall act only in the patient's interest when providing medical care which might have the effect of weakening the physical and mental condition of the patient."

The purpose of biomedical research involving human subjects must be to improve diagnostic, therapeutic and prophylactic procedures and the understanding of the aetiology and pathogenesis of disease.

In current medical practice, most diagnostic, therapeutic or prophylactic procedures involves hazards. This applies especially to biomedical research.

Medical progress is based on research which ultimately must rest in part on experimentation involving human subjects.

In the field of biomedical research, a fundamental distinction must be recognized between medical research in which the aim is essentially diagnostic or therapeutic for a patient, and medical research, the essential object of which is purely scientific and without implying direct diagnostic or therapeutic value to the person subjected to the research.

Special caution must be exercised in the conduct of research which may affect the environment, and the welfare of animals used for research must be respected.

Because it is essential that the results of laboratory experiments be applied to human beings to further scientific knowledge and to help suffering humanity, the World Medical Association has prepared the following recommendations as a guide to every physician in biomedical research involving human subjects. They should be kept under review in the future. It must be stressed that the standards as drafted are only a guide to physicians all over the world. Physicians are not relieved from criminal, civil and ethical responsibilities under the laws of their own countries.

I. Basic principles

1. Biomedical research involving human subjects must conform to generally accepted scientific principles and should be based on adequately performed laboratory and animal experimentation and on a thorough knowledge of the scientific literature.

2. The design and performance of each experimental procedure involving human subjects should be clearly formulated in an experimental protocol which should be transmitted for consideration, comment and guidance to a specially appointed committee independent of the investigator and the sponsor provided that this independent committee is in conformity with the laws and regulations of the country in which the research experiment is performed.

3. Biomedical research involving human subjects should be conducted only by scientifically qualified persons and under the supervision of a clinically competent medical person. The responsibility for the human subject must always rest with a medically qualified person and never rest on the subject of the research, even though the subject has given his or her consent.

4. Biomedical research involving human subjects cannot legitimately be carried out unless the importance of the objective is in proportion to the inherent risk to the subject.

5. Every biomedical research project involving human

subjects should be preceded by careful assessment of predictable risks in comparison with foreseeable benefits to the subject or others. Concern for the interests of the subject must always prevail over the interests of science and society.

6. The right of the research subject to safeguard his or her integrity must always be respected. Every precaution should be taken to respect the privacy of the subject and to minimize the impact of the study on the subject's physical and mental integrity and on the personality of the subject.

7. Physicians should abstain from engaging in research projects involving human subjects unless they are satisfied that the hazards involved are believed to be predictable. Physicians should cease any investigation if the hazards are found to outweigh the potential benefits.

8. In publication of the results of his or her research, the physician is obliged to preserve the accuracy of the results. Reports of experimentation not in accordance with the principles laid down in this Declaration should not be accepted for publication.

9. In any research on human beings, each potential subject must be adequately informed of the aims, methods, anticipated benefits and potential hazards of the study and the discomfort it may entail. He or she

should be informed that he or she is at liberty to abstain from participation in the study and that he or she is free to withdraw his or her consent to participation at any time. The physician should then obtain the subject's freely-given informed consent, preferably in writing.

10. When obtaining informed consent for the research project, the physician should be particularly cautious if the subject is in a dependent relationship to him or her or may consent under duress. In that case, the informed consent should be obtained by a physician who is not engaged in the investigation and who is completely independent of this official relationship.

11. In the case of legal incompetence, informed consent should be obtained from the legal guardian in accordance with national legislation. Where physical or mental incapacity makes it impossible to obtain informed consent, or when the subject is a minor, permission from the responsible relative replaces that of the subject in accordance with national legislation.

Whenever the minor child is in fact able to give a consent, the minor's consent must be obtained in addition to the consent of the minor's legal guardian.

12. The research protocol should always contain a statement of the ethical considerations involved and should indicate that the principles enunciated in the present Declaration are complied with.

II. Medical research combined with professional care (clinical research)

1. In the treatment of the sick person, the physician must be free to use a new diagnostic and therapeutic measure, if in his or her judgement it offers hope of saving life, reestablishing health or alleviating suffering.

2. The potential benefits, hazards and discomfort of a new method should be weighed against the advantages of the best current diagnostic and therapeutic methods.

3. In any medical study, every patient - including those of a control group, if any - should be assured of the best proven diagnostic and therapeutic method.

4. The refusal of the patient to participate in a study must never interfere with physician-patient relationship.

5. If the physician considers it essential not to obtain informed consent, the specific reasons for this proposal should be stated in the experimental protocol for transmission to the independent committee. (§I-2)

6. The physician can combine medical research with professional care, the objective being the acquisition of new medical knowledge, only to the extent that medical research is justified by its potential diagnostic or therapeutic value for the patient.

III. Non-therapeutic biomedical research involving human subjects (Non-clinical biomedical research)

1. In purely scientific application of medical research carried out on a human being, it is the duty of the physician to remain the protector of the life and health of that person on whom biomedical research is being carried out.

2. The subjects should be volunteers - either healthy persons or patients for whom the experimental design is not related to the patient's illness.

3. The investigator or the investigating team should discontinue the research if in his/her or their judgement it may, if continued, be harmful to the individual.

4. In research on man, the interest of science and society should never take precedence over considerations related to the well-being of the subject.

REFERENCES

1. M. Montagne, The Role of Clinical Research in the Drug Development Process, *Clinical Research in Pharmaceutical Development* (B. Bleidt and M. Montagne, eds.), Marcel Dekker, New York, 1996.
2. B. Bleidt, Planning, Coordinating and Monitoring Clinical Trials, *Clinical Research in Pharmaceutical Development* (B. Bleidt and M. Montagne, eds.), Marcel Dekker, New York, 1996.
3. A. E. Cato and L. Cook, The Protocol and Case Report Form, *The Clinical Research Process in the Pharmaceutical Industry* (G. Matoren, ed.), Marcel Dekker, New York, 1984.
4. R. H. Fletcher and S. W. Fletcher, Clinical research in general medical journals, *N. Engl. J. Med. 301*: 180 (1979).
5. 21 CFR, Part 56, Appendix I.
6. Declaration of Helsinki, "Recommendations guiding physicians in biomedical research involving human subjects," Adopted by the World Medical Assembly in Helsinki, Finland, June 1964.

10

Patient Outcomes and Drug Usefulness

Barry Bleidt

Health Resources Consulting
South Charleston, West Virginia

Two of the most significant advancements made in the drug development process over the past decade have been the method by which clinical trials are now managed and the application of different types of research methodologies in order to obtain data on patient outcomes and drug usefulness. Both of these changes have been spearheaded by the efficiency efforts driven by the current economic climate. The project management techniques utilized in initial human studies are detailed in Chapter 8, "Planning, Coordinating, and Monitoring Clinical Trials" [1].

The health care industry is undergoing an enormous transformation similar to that experienced by other businesses. It is becoming much more customer focused, as other service industries have had to do. Now, medical care is being evaluated by consumers, instead of just being accepted by them. Patients are becoming increasingly aware of their treatment options and have a greater interest in receiving more information on the therapies prescribed for them or given to their families [2]. For example, one silver lining in the insidious AIDS epidemic has been that it has helped to demonstrate that when medical and public health information is disseminated to and understood by the right people, these data can help prevent the spread of disease and delay the onset of symptoms. One of the sources of this important type of data is outcomes research. Along with the changing consumer-oriented focal point in medical care, the drug development process has, likewise, had to respond to market pressures. Initial research efforts now must also focus on producing data that demonstrate how useful a new product will be on its own and in comparison with other therapies.

The next two chapters will discuss the types of information that are now mandated by the marketplace in order to gain acceptance of a new product and the methodologies that are utilized to generate such data. In Chapter 11, "Pharmacoeconomics and Quality of Life: Evaluating the Economic and Social Impact of Pharmaceuticals," Dr. McGhan discusses specific elements of pharmacoeconomic and quality-of-life research methodologies relating to new pharmaceutical development. The subjects of this chapter are the reasons behind the increased attention to patient outcomes data and how to design an outcomes research protocol.

I. INTRODUCTION

Medical care services now consume greater than 15% of our gross national product. This translates into the fact that more than $1 out of every $7 spent in this country goes toward paying for health care services. This figure is more than 30% higher than the corresponding percentages for other industrialized nations, such as Germany, Canada, and France [3]. The cost of medical care has increased by a larger percentage than that for general consumer goods every year since 1966, when the Medicaid and Medicare amendments to the Social Security Act were passed. In Table 1, data are presented that compare the average consumer price index (CPI) for all items to the mean CPI for prescription drugs and medical care services over the past 15 years. As can be seen, the increase in health care costs during the 1980s is significantly greater than that for general consumer goods and services. Between 1980 and 1994, the cost of health care and pharmaceuticals rose at twice the rate of inflation.

By the time this book is published, the United States will be spending over $1 trillion a year on health care. In 1974, only 7.4% of the gross national product (GNP) was spent on medical care services. What has happened over the past two decades to cause these rising costs? There are multiple contributing factors for these escalating expenditures. Some of the identifiable reasons are [3–6]:

An aging population (the number of people living into their seventies, eighties, and beyond are growing rapidly, thereby, causing a greater utilization of health resources)
A growing population (more people to serve)
Introduction of new diseases (AIDS, drug-addicted babies, etc.) that require the use of tremendous medical resource
Smoking (the generation that "popularized" cigarettes is now dying from their effects)
Old, untreatable conditions now can be managed (e.g., certain cancers, TB, pneumonia)
Higher expectations from the health care system
Expensive new technologies (e.g., organ transplants, imaging techniques)
Costly new therapeutic agents (some costing thousands of dollars per dose)

Table 1 Consumer Price Index (CPI) Mean Annual Changes

CPI	1980–85	1985–89	1989–90	1990–91	1991–92	1992–93
Rx Drugs	10.6	8.3	10.0	9.9	7.5	≈3.0
Overall	5.5	3.6	5.5	4.2	3.0	2.7
Medical care	8.6	7.1	9.3	8.9	7.6	5.4

Source: Bureau of Labor Statistics.

Overutilization of medical care (sometimes unnecessary procedures are ordered)
Overselling by the pharmaceutical, medical supply and device industries to the prescribers
Overconsumption of unhealthy items (fatty foods, dangerous drugs, caffeine, etc.)
Overdemand (we tend to think that more care is better)
Oversupply of physicians, hospitals beds, high-technology tools
General consumer goods inflation rate
Larger number of people who live in sub-poverty conditions
The practicing of defensive medicine (extra precautions taken as a prophylaxis against lawsuits)

The three most prominent factors are the increasing number of older Americans, the greater use of sophisticated medical technology, and poor personal health habits (overweight, smoking, lack of exercise, etc.).

The health care system has been under close scrutiny as a result of these financial pressures. Part of this surveillance includes seeking knowledge about how the medical care processes affect the patient and his or her well-being or health status. In order for our health care system to advance, we must come to understand outcomes—the result(s) of any given technology, product, or procedure on the entire system and the patient. This progress can be accomplished by recognizing and measuring the resources consumed to produce a result and in identifying and valuating the consequences of that particular outcome.

A depiction of the interrelationship among the various components of outcomes research, relating to the development of new drug products, is presented in Fig. 1. These elements are pharmacoeconomic research, clinical trials, and patient satisfaction and quality-of-life (QOL) measures [7]. Outcomes research seeks to answer several basic questions about a new drug product:

Is the patient benefiting from it?
Of all the various options for therapy, which one works best in the individual patient?
What are all of the costs associated with it?
Is there an improvement in the condition being treated?
What other consequences are experienced by the patient?
Does the patient feel better?
Are there any undesired effects?

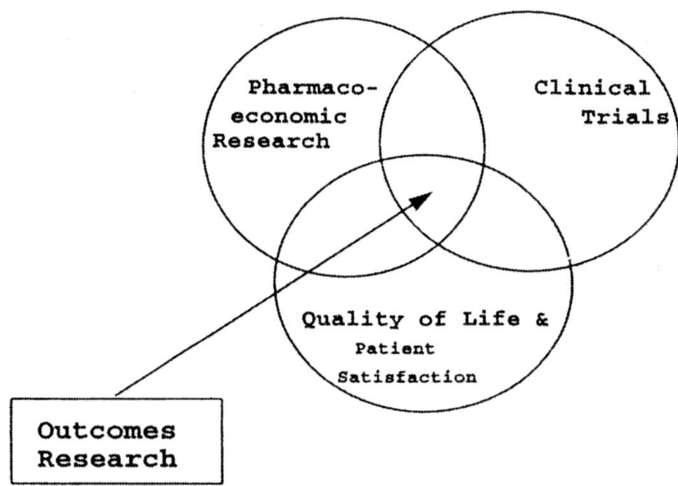

Fig. 1 Relationship of outcomes research elements.

How does the new treatment compare to the current "best value for the money spent"?

A synopsis of the differences between clinical and outcomes research is presented in Table 2. Generally, outcomes research focuses on the patient as a whole and his or her overall response to the treatment (improvement, adverse effects, costs, positive consequences, etc.) rather than on the drug itself. This focal point is different from that seen with traditional clinical research, where attention is primarily paid to the product. The data gathered from clinical trials plus that which is obtained from outcomes studies equals information about drug usefulness.

II. IMPLICATIONS

Health outcomes research can trace its roots back to the mid-1970s. At this time, health care researchers began their effort to understand the relationship between rapidly rising health care costs and whether or not there was a corresponding improvement in the patient's quality of life or an increase in his or her life expectancy.

Although spending on pharmaceuticals is less than 10% of the total medical bill, drugs are being closely watched because their costs have

Table 2 Comparison of Clinical Research and Outcomes Research

	Clinical research	Outcomes research
Objective	Safety, efficacy	Usefulness, efficiency
Study environment	Best if conducted under tightly controlled conditions	Best if performed in actual patient settings
Measures	Kinetic parameters, clinical end points	Costs, benefits, consequences, QOL
Focus	Determine indications, side effect profile	Total health impact, pt. health status, resource utilization

increased faster than those for other health care expenditures. The continually rising medical care bills and the growing complexity of the health care system will continue to drive a growing interest in outcomes research. The intricacy and dimensions of the health care financing system also will contribute to the increased emphasis on generating more outcomes data.

The largest financier of medical care, the federal government, has a vested interest in outcomes research. The Agency for Health Care Policy and Research (AHCPR) was formed by Congress in 1989 as a branch of the Department of Health and Human Services. It was created to sponsor outcomes research, formulate practice guidelines, and develop standards for assessing the effectiveness and efficiency of health care and ensuring its quality. By 1995, 10 practice guidelines had been brought forth for different treatments or were in the process of being developed.

In addition, many providers of medical care are reviewing and seeking information from the growing body of knowledge being generated from outcomes research. For example, the Department of Defense (DOD) established a Pharmacoeconomic Center in January 1993 in an attempt to control their expenditures on medicines. This group was charted to develop and implement a Tri-Service Formulary, "a list of those drug therapies, determined to be the most cost effective, that would be available at all DOD medical treatment facilities" [8]. Treatment guidelines for eight conditions (hypertension, peptic-acid disease, acute respiratory tract infections, depression, hyperlipidemia, asthma, osteoarthritis, and migraine headaches) have been completed or are near completion, using pharmacoeconomic and health outcomes data as the basis for these reports.

Other large providers and payers are going through similar processes in order to reduce their health care expenditures. Pharmacy benefit management companies have, traditionally, manipulated their costs downward through promoting generic substitution, negotiating deals for large purchases, decreasing the number of visits to a pharmacy (through larger number of doses dispensed), and reducing overutilization. Many of these plans are now using data generated from outcomes research in their decision-making processes and integrating this information into outcomes-driven initiatives [9].

The data generated from outcomes research can be utilized by institutions, providers, and payers in developing and managing their drug formulary, for establishing useful treatment guidelines, and as a basis for drug usage evaluation efforts. The emphasis on this research and the data derived from it are increasing and will continue to do so. The more outcomes-related information that can be gathered from early clinical trials, the quicker a new drug will be accepted and utilized. This assumes, of course, that the results show that the product has a more positive impact on overall outcomes than competing therapies.

III. OUTCOMES RESEARCH

The purpose of research, in general, is to obtain information that meets certain objectives that were determined before the study was initiated. Traditionally, in the case of a new drug, the findings are supposed to ascertain whether or not the product is safe and efficacious to use for its indications. Now, it is critical to gather a sufficient amount of data concerning the drug's impact upon patient outcomes and its comparability to other treatments in order to justify the product's use in practice.

The findings obtained from a study are only as credible as the research design. In a previous chapter, it was pointed out that planning a clinical research project and preparing for contingencies is one of the most critical steps in producing sound results [1]. This fact is also applicable for outcome studies.

A description of the components that a well-designed outcomes research study should contain is presented in the following sections.

A. Perspective

The first key question that needs to be answered before initiating the research planning process is: From whose perspective will the study be designed to address? Generally, outcomes studies address only one point of view. This outlook can be that of the first party, the patients—those who receive care; the second party, the physicians or other health care providers—those who deliver the care; the third party, the payers—those who finance the care; or society as a whole. In Table 3, a listing of the payers and providers is presented. As can be seen from this table, they are sometimes the same entities.

The various parties have differing, sometimes conflicting, points of view about new therapies. Even within the same group, there can be significant variations in perspective. For example, government-sponsored programs like Medicare are more concerned with overall, aggregate costs incurred over a lifetime. Therefore, it is in this payer's best interests to encourage

Table 3 A List of the Payers and Providers

PAYERS
Patients (out-of-pocket expenses)
Insurance companies (indemnity policies)
Sellers of managed-care or managed-cost plans
Small corporate benefit plans
Large corporate benefit plans
Self-insured benefit plans
State government (Medicare, Medicaid, state programs)
Federal government (Medicare, Medicaid, VA system)
Hospitals
Long-term care facilities
Managed-care organizations (HMOs, PPOs)
PROVIDERS
Physicians
Dentists
Pharmacists
Nurses
Allied health professionals
Hospitals
Long-term care facilities
Intermediate-term care facilities
Home health care agencies
Hospices
Some HMOs
State governments
Federal government
Local governments

therapies that keep down total medical expenses over time related to the condition. On the other hand, a for-profit, managed-care group has more current concerns. It is competing in the marketplace where the average customer only stays in the plan 4 to 5 years [6]. From this viewpoint, short-term, positive therapeutic options are more attractive than long-term, reduce-overall-medical-cost measures. In this way, the institution can stay within its set budget and turn a profit for its investors. Hospitals have yet another point of view. They are primarily affected by the costs and consequences that occur during the patient's stay. Benefits or costs that accrue after the patient leaves have traditionally not been their principal concern.

The differing perspectives are reflective of the group's values. Their viewpoints represent a composite of what they can afford or are willing to pay, what they are willing to accept in the way of consequences, and what their needs are.

It may be prudent to choose the perspective of the party (to whom to address the study's design) that best fits the preliminary profile of the new product or that best matches the needs of the sponsor. As methodologies evolve, it may become possible to design a protocol that will enable researchers to take into account more than one outlook. Until recently, the providers have been the most dominant force in medical care and there was a tendency to favor products that showed positive results from their point of view. However, the financial trends of very recent years have led to a change in the preponderant perspective; now power rests primarily with the purse strings, the payers. However, before designing a long-term protocol solely from one viewpoint, it is prudent to remember that this scenario of who is in control has changed recently and could do so again.

B. Questions

Once the perspective the investigation will be designed to address has been determined, the research protocol can then be developed. An outcomes study should be designed so that the following questions are answered:

Which analytical methodology is the best to utilize for the situation? Will it be used?

Which treatment alternatives will be compared? Are they the best choices?

Which variables or monitoring parameters are to be followed and quantified? Are they readily defined?

Which instruments best measure patient preferences, health status, or quality of life? Will they be used? Have they been validated?

What are the clinical end points? Do they make sense? Are they measurable?
What are the identifiable costs and consequences? Are the assigned values for each reasonable?
What is the appropriate discount rate?
What will be the sources of the data? Are they reliable:
How will the data be evaluated?
What will be limitations and assumptions of the study? Are they appropriate? Are they too limiting?

In addition, the final report and all manuscripts written from the data generated by the research should clearly answer these questions:

What are the results? Are they related to the original research objectives?
Was the discount rate chosen apropos to the perspective taken in the study?
Was a sensitivity analysis performed?
What generalizations are made in the study? Are they appropriate?
Are the results clinically, economically, or statistically significantly?
Do the conclusions match the questions asked in the research statement?

C. Study Methodology

Once the study protocol has been laid out using the above questions as a guide, the appropriate research methodology can be chosen. This process is also key to obtaining sound results. Using the wrong assumptions or analysis could invalidate the information gathered. It is important to select the analytical method before the study is initiated.

In order to determine which analysis is best to use, choose from among the following four scenarios as to which is most applicable to the product under development. Then, the proper study methodology can be utilized in analyzing the data.

1. If the proposed product is projected to produce identical outcomes with existing therapies, then perform a cost-minimization analysis (CMA).
2. If the proposed product is projected to produce a positive differential health benefit as compared to alternative therapies, then perform a cost-effectiveness analysis (CEA).
3. If the proposed product is projected to produce dissimilar results and effects on dollar amounts as opposed to other therapies, then perform a cost-benefit analysis (CBA).

4. If the proposed product is projected to produce an impact on the duration of life and/or preference for a certain state of health when compared to alternative therapies, then perform a cost-utility analysis (CUA) [10].

A more detailed presentation on each of the above analytical methodologies can be found in Chapter 11. Hypothetical drug development examples for each method are also provided.

D. Identifying Alternative Treatments

In a well-designed outcomes study, all suitable alternative therapies should be utilized in the comparative research and analysis. There are many possible options that can be considered for inclusion as a comparison in a study, including nonpharmacological interventions (such as surgery), alternative health care therapies (acupuncture, chiropractic procedures, etc.), homeopathic remedies, folk medicine practices—wherever they are applicable and have some demonstrable benefit. Choosing which of these possibilities to use is one of the keys to a successful research design.

It would be a waste of resources, for example, to contrast a proposed drug to therapeutic option X if this therapy is no longer considered to be the "treatment of choice" or deemed to be a valid alternative. The appeal of a new product can be enhanced to both providers and payers by using the current "gold standard" therapy and/or the market leader in the comparative studies. This, of course, assumes that the findings for the new drug are favorable in comparison to these treatments.

E. Tracking Relevant Variables

In order to produce sound results from an outcomes study, it is important to track relevant variables. The first step in this process is to select the appropriate clinical end points that are to be followed and measured. Some conditions, such as infectious diseases, have easily defined clinical end points. Other disease states, such as hypertension, have more ambiguous or harder-to-measure outcomes. For example, the true end point for controlling high blood pressure is a decrease in the incidence of stroke, myocardial infarctions, and other cardiac events. However, these end points are difficult and time consuming to measure and document. These complications are why a substitute outcome or surrogate end point is usually used to assess progress in this condition—a reduction in blood pressure. Similar measures are used in patients with diabetes, asthma, or arthritis.

F. Valuation of Costs and Discount Rate

A well-designed study must also identify and measure all costs and consequences that are relevant to the perspective taken by the study, including direct, indirect, and intangible ones. These costs should be stated in monetary terms. The quality and usefulness of the information gathered can be greatly impaired if applicable costs are not suitably specified and assembled.

Each of the four different types of studies measures outcomes differently. In cost-effectiveness analysis, the outcomes are measured in natural units applicable to the compared treatments. In cost-benefit analysis, the outcomes are measured in dollars. In cost-utility analysis, the outcomes are measured in patient preferences for various health states. In cost-minimization analysis, the outcomes are not measured or compared—they are assumed to be equal [10].

In most instances, the benefits are accrued or the costs are incurred over an extended time frame. In this case, the value attached to these future dollar amounts must be discounted back to a present value. This procedure is done because under normal circumstances, money is worth less in the future than it is today (due to inflation). Therefore, an appropriate discount rate must be applied to these analyses. It is important to establish this parameter before beginning the research.

Improper discounting can cast doubt on the conclusions drawn from the study. It is proper, however, to report more than one discount rate, if this is done constantly and consistently throughout the study. For example, convey a percentage representing the corporate viewpoint (opportunity lost dollars) and a different one for governmental interests (investment opportunity dollars). For projects or scenarios where all of the costs and consequences occur within one year, their values may not need to be discounted.

Further details on selecting the correct discount rate, identifying costs and attaching a value to them, and collecting cost data are presented in the next chapter.

G. Measuring Instruments and Data Sources

It is best to use standardized instruments, those that have already gained widespread acceptance among other researchers, especially for quality-of-life studies. By using established tools, the validity of the survey, technique, or methodology has already been demonstrated. In the case where a new instrument must be developed, it must undergo a validation process before it can be used. This validity testing is essential because of the fact that untested questionnaires are subject to uncertainties about whether or not they actually measure the items they are designed to assess. The more valid an instrument is proved to be, the more useful and acceptable the results obtained from it will be.

Another important consideration is determining and reporting the sources of the data. In the case of clinical research on new drugs, the information comes directly from the initial trials. Because outcomes studies are so expensive to perform, they have not traditionally been conducted during the early phases of clinical research. This scenario, however, is changing. It is becoming more economically feasible to gather this critical information sooner in the development process. Time equals money; the first company to market a new class of drugs or other therapeutic breakthrough usually reaps huge dividends.

Health economic studies draw much of their data from medical charts, hospital bills, computer files, and cross-referenced cost databases. This information is obtained from the records that have been maintained by third-party administrators, clinicians, and medical institutions. It is cross-checked with similar data from other sources to determine if the treatment circumstances and cost valuations match the study's design and those of similar research efforts. It is also key to note that the source of the data should match the interests of the group from whose perspective the study is designed. If the patient characteristics or cost considerations in the study are qualitatively or quantitatively different from those experienced by the users of the information, they may reject the results on this rationale alone.

In the next chapter, Dr. William McGhan delineates some of the more widely accepted survey instruments and patient preference questionnaires and discusses their applications.

H. Study Assumptions and Limitations

All the assumptions and limitations of a proposed project should be identified and delineated during the planning process, as well as presented clearly in the final reports. Reviewers and other interested parties will evaluate the findings based on these limitations and assumptions. They also will examine the report for any unstated, assumed inputs and how these were handled.

Some assumptions must be made in an outcomes study, and there will be limitations to extrapolating the project's results to other situations not directly measured by the research protocol. As long as these items have been clearly pointed out, there will be less misinterpretation of the data and fewer criticisms of the findings.

IV. PRACTICAL SUGGESTIONS

Several things can be done to enhance a new product's appeal to potential purchasers, besides conducting a well-designed clinical trial or outcomes study. Some of these items need to be developed and tested along with these clinical and outcomes research efforts. Presented below are some suggestions that can be utilized during the drug development process that will prove to be most beneficial in marketing a product once it is approved.

The first suggestion is to identify several outside experts, who are objective (i.e., have no ties with the sponsor) and who are known either in the field of outcomes research or in the therapeutic class of the new drug. The purpose of this panel is to review the protocol before implementing it for clarity, completeness, the capacity to accomplish its objectives, and whether or not it can measure those outcomes it is intended to assess. This group should also be asked to provide an endorsement of the findings, once they have been obtained.

Following this suggestion will significantly augment the believability of the results and the credibility of the overall research effort [11]. The vast majority of all outcomes research is sponsored by commercial interests with commercial interests in mind. Not surprisingly, in a study of pharmaceutical industry–sponsored research published in peer-reviewed medical literature, the vast majority of the articles reported results favorable to the interests of the funding company.

Another suggestion is to have drug use protocols and practice guidelines, if applicable, developed and tested during the early clinical trials. Most purchasers of pharmaceutical products find these tools useful for their facilities. These helpful guides assist in increasing proper drug usage and in decreasing overutilization and waste. Protocols provide an outline of what the institution considers appropriate indications for using the product, thereby creating a schematic for clinical interventions by pharmacists in their effort to manage proper drug usage.

Another good tool to formulate during the drug development process is Therapeutic Drug Monitoring (TDM) Guidelines. Implementing a TDM system is the next logical step to take after the development of a drug use protocol or treatment algorithm. These guidelines, when properly developed, establish objective criteria to assess efficacy and monitor safety of a particular therapeutic regimen. They help ensure compliance with the established institutional protocols by providing a practical guide for health professionals to follow in initiating and maintaining drug therapy with a new or established product. TDM guidelines should be able to answer the questions below from a checklist-like format of what parameters to observe and follow [12].

How well is the patient responding to treatment? How do you make this determination?
When is a dosing change in order?
When do you switch to another treatment?
What are the manifestations of adverse drug reactions?
When do you stop treatment?

Development of these therapeutic indicators has *not* been implemented by the pharmaceutical industry, yet. The first company to take the initiative of creating these standards for their products, both new and old, will direct the way for others and become a leader in a soon-to-be important field. This author predicts that TDM guidelines will be required for all products within the next decade, just as patient information has become a standard. These guides are particularly useful in managed-care settings, where restrictions are usually placed on new or expensive therapies. When prepared properly, TDM guidelines are convenient for use by nurses, physicians, pharmacists, and others and effective in managing patient therapy.

The final suggestion is to have a set format prepared for the final report and for *all* published findings. This concept, once implemented, will make it much more simple for reviewers and other interested parties to glean the answers from these articles or reports to the questions posed earlier in this chapter (Section III.B). This idea has not been proposed to limit content or to censor the results and discussions of the researchers and authors. The layout concept is suggested, however, in order to correct a key mistake of many outcomes studies (i.e., published articles whose findings are not easily discernible or readily understood by the readers).

V. DRUG USEFULNESS

According to the Congressional Office of Technology Assessment, only 10% to 20% of the medical procedures we currently utilize have ever been proved effective in controlled, randomized trials. In this era of declining resources, the available funds for health care delivery must be spent more wisely. It is for these reasons that outcomes research has become such an important part of the drug development process and a useful tool for the procurers of these products.

There is a cost and a consequence to all choices. One of the major consequences of rising medical-care costs is that there are fewer funds left to spend for other services and commodities. As a society, we must come to grips with the costs, consequences, and value concepts of health care. Outcomes research helps to answer certain questions by indicating the value and usefulness of certain procedures and therapies.

One of the new concepts that has evolved from outcomes research is outcomes management, which "involves the systemic use of outcomes data to improve results" [6]. Most providers and financiers of health care have already implemented such programs. The rest will follow in order to remain competitive. This trend again underscores the importance of gathering outcomes data early in the drug development process.

Outcomes research findings can also be a powerful marketing tool. Many pharmaceutical companies have already trained their sales forces in techniques of using outcomes data for selling their products. The drug industry is trying to evolve away from its image as "purveyors of pills" toward a new, seemingly softer approach, selling health. The professional representatives of the companies are armed with skills for determining the needs of their customers and prepared for supplying them with drug use algorithms, educational programs, outcomes data, or whatever may be needed in order to increase the use of their products.

Drug usefulness is characterized by a product that is safe and efficacious to use, and that in addition has a positive impact on the outcomes of the patient and/or medical facility. The usefulness of a new drug must be established during the early clinical trial phases using outcomes research technologies. The benefits of using these products must be weighed against their costs. In balancing these factors, costs usually include applicable humanistic, acquisition, administration, handling, economic, and clinical costs as well as the impact of the therapy on the patient as a whole. In today's health care environment, an additional, key question needs to be answered during the drug development process, besides the two traditional ones (Is the drug safe to use? Is the product efficacious?). This question is:

> Does the new product "contribute to more favorable outcomes in terms of total health resource utilization, total cost, and health-related quality of life than alternative treatment regimens"? [13]

REFERENCES

1. B. Bleidt, Planning, coordinating and monitoring clinical trials, *Clinical Research in Pharmaceutical Development* (B. Bleidt and M. Montagne, eds.), Marcel Dekker, New York, 1996 (pp. 125–150).

2. *CBS Consumer Survey on Prescription Drug Information.* CBS, New York, 1983.
3. G. J. Schieber and J. P. Poullier, Overview of international comparisons of health care expenditure, *Health Care Fin. Rev. Annual Suppl*:1–8 (1989).
4. U.S. Congress, Office of Technology Assessment, *Pharmaceutical R & D: Costs, Risks and Rewards*, OTA-H-522, U.S. Government Printing Office, Washington, DC, 1993.
5. E. H. Clouse, B. Bleidt, and A. McClocklin, Stress management, smoking cessation and weight control as pharmacists roles, *NARD J.* February (1989).
6. R. C. McDonald, *An Introduction to Health Economics*, Eli Lilly, Indianapolis, 1993.
7. N. U. Kaminsky, Conference focuses on importance of outcomes research, *Am. Pharm. NS35*:1:56–59 (1995).
8. K. L. Brier et al., Practical methodology for a pharmacoeconomic analysis, *Pharm. Managed Care 3*:3:4–6 (1995).
9. C. Anderson, Integrating outcomes data into pharmaceutical benefit management, *Pharm. Managed Care 2*:23:4–6 (1994).
10. W. F. McGhan, Pharmacoeconomics and quality of life: evaluating the economic and social impact of pharmaceuticals, *Clinical Research in Pharmaceutical Development* (B. Bleidt and M. Montagne, eds.), Marcel Dekker, New York, 1996 (pp. 213–231).
11. Zitter Group, *The 1992 Insurance Company Outcomes Study.* Zitter Group, San Francisco, 1993.
12. B. Bleidt, Unpublished correspondence with Taketa-Abbott Pharmaceuticals, February 1995.
13. C. E. Redder, Overview of Pharmacoeconomics and Pharmaceutical Outcomes Evaluations, *Am. J. Health Syst. Pharm. 52*:Suppl 4 (1995).

11

Pharmacoeconomics and Quality of Life: Evaluating the Economic and Social Impact of Pharmaceuticals

William F. McGhan

Philadelphia College of Pharmacy and Science
Philadelphia, Pennsylvania

I. PHARMACOECONOMICS

Clinical researchers and practitioners are becoming more involved in the economic questions being asked about pharmaceutical products. Cost-containment and health care reform is causing policy makers and decision makers in pharmaceutical research to examine closely the costs and benefits of both proposed and existing medicines. It is increasingly evident that organized purchasers and public agencies are demanding that health products and services be evaluated in terms of clinical and social outcomes related to costs incurred. Many pharmaceutical research groups are being asked to provide economic justification earlier in the investigational drug process in order to initiate, modify, or expand research efforts on "promising" chemical entities. Cost-benefit analyses, along with other pharmacoeconomic approaches, are a way to analyze the potential value of the product to the public as a supplement to the traditional marketplace value, measured by the prices that the patient or patron have been "willing to pay." As third parties are paying for a higher percentage of prescriptions, pharmaceutical companies are beginning to realize that their pharmaceuticals are requiring sound cost-justification in order to survive in the marketplace [1–5].

There is increasing competition among health interventions for the limited dollars and resources available in society. Within private and public arenas, pharmaceutical alternatives will have to compete increasingly for adequate reimbursement and payment [6,7]. Pharmaceutical firms will have to document the cost-benefits and quality-of-life impact of their new products.

The purpose of this chapter is to present the general concepts related to cost-benefit and cost-effectiveness analysis, and to suggest how these concepts can be applied in justifying and evaluating pharmaceutical products in development.

II. OVERVIEW OF COST-BENEFIT AND OTHER ECONOMIC METHODS

The intent of this section is to acquaint the reader with some of the methodological issues regarding cost-benefit analysis (CBA) and cost-effectiveness analysis (CEA). Table 1 provides a basic comparison of these two methods, as well as comparing operations analysis, cost-minimization, and cost-utility analysis. One can differentiate between the various approaches according to the units used to measure the inputs and outcomes, as shown in Table 1. For example, in operations research, the inputs may be measured in "staff

Table 1 Comparison of Evaluation Techniques Regarding Inputs and Outputs

Technique	Inputs	Outputs
Classical Operations Analysis	Units	Units
Cost-Effectiveness Analysis	Dollars	Natural Units
Cost-Benefit Analysis	Dollars	Dollars
Cost-Utility Analysis	Dollars	Utiles/Preferences
Cost-Minimization Analysis	Dollars	Assumed Equal

hours" and the output in "production" units such as "number of patients cured." In general, the outputs in CEA are various outcome measures, such as lives saved, life-years added, disability-days prevented, and so on. CBA is differentiated from CEA through the use of dollars to measure the output of the respective program. Further discussion and examples of these techniques have been presented elsewhere [1–3,8–16]. The evaluation mechanisms delineated may be helpful in demonstrating both the cost-effectiveness and cost-benefit of pharmaceuticals and may, thereby, grant new products greater acceptance by other health care providers, administrators, and the public.

A. Cost-Benefit Analysis

The use of CBA is not a new concept in evaluating health interventions. CBA is a basic quantitative tool that can be utilized to improve the decision-making process in the allocation of funds to health versus other social programs [10,17–26]. While the overall concept of CBA is simple, many of the methodological considerations require a certain degree of technical expertise in order to apply CBA appropriately.

CBA evolved from the need to ascertain estimates of the costs and benefits of public investment projects. Expenditures for health care should produce net social benefits for the public. CBA techniques can be applied to make such resource allocation decisions in the health care field. Economists have indicated that medical care is both an investment good and a consumption good. When considered as an investment good, medical care is an investment in human capital [25–27]. As Pigou has pointed out, "the most important investment of all is the investment in health, intelligence, and character of the people" [28]. In economic terms, the present value of a person's lifetime productivity is often considered an appropriate measure of the benefit from investment in human capital [27–30].

A major function of any pharmaceutical planning process is the formulation of alternative ways to achieve desired objectives and then choosing between those alternatives. Many times, decisions are made on the basis of intuition and personal judgment. Cost-benefit analysis—by requiring one to state precise definitions and objectives; to identify criteria for judging results; and to quantify the results of each alternative, formal evaluation of alternatives and examination of the effects of assumptions and uncertainties—provides a more solid basis for decision making.

Although it may not be easy to conduct a full economic evaluation, an important advantage of cost-benefit analysis is that it forces those responsible to quantify input (costs) and outputs (benefits) as thoroughly as possible rather than use vague qualitative judgments or personal hunches [29, 30].

Cost-benefit analysis consists of identifying all the societal benefits that will accrue from a pharmaceutical product of interest and converting them into equivalent dollars in the year in which they will occur. This stream of benefit-dollars is then discounted to its equivalent present value at the selected interest rate. On the other side of the equation, all costs of the program are identified and allocated to a specific year and, again, the costs are discounted to their present value at the same interest rate. Then, other things being equal, the program with the largest present value of benefits minus costs is the "best" in terms of its economic value.

Ideally, all benefits and costs caused by the intervention should be included. This presents considerable difficulty, especially on the benefits side of the equation, because many of the benefits are either difficult to measure, difficult to convert to dollars, or both. For example, benefits such as improved patient comfort, improved patient satisfaction with the health care system, improved working conditions for the physician, and so on are not only difficult to measure but are extremely difficult to convert into dollars [29–36].

Another problem in cost-benefit analysis is how one determines the proper interest rate for discounting future benefits and costs. Prest and Turvey recommend that the selection of a rate be based on similar projects, followed by sensitivity analysis of the problem to determine the effect of a range of discount rates as the final solution [29]. The problem of selecting an appropriate discount rate and other methodological considerations will be discussed in further detail later in this chapter.

B. Measuring Costs and Benefits

The economic benefits of a new or existing drug are defined as the reduction in costs realized because of the utilization of that product. The conventional classification of these benefits is threefold: direct, indirect, and intangible. As you study these terms, please also realize that programs have parallel terms on the cost side of the equation, with direct, indirect, and intangible costs [1,2].

1. Direct

Direct benefits are defined as "that portion of averted costs currently borne that are associated with spending for health services; they represent potential savings in the use of health resources." In other words, direct benefits are estimations of savings on direct costs. Direct costs include those costs incurred prior to diagnosis and hospitalization, during hospitalization, during convalescent care, and during continued medical surveillance. Rice suggested that these costs include "expenditures for prevention, detection, treatment, rehabilitation, research, training, and capital investments in medical facilities as well as professional services, drugs, medical supplies, and non-personal health services" [37,38]. Most often, direct benefits may be calculated with relatively little difficulty.

2. Indirect

Indirect benefits represent the potential savings on indirect costs. Despite extensive treatment in the literature, indirect benefits are difficult to measure. They are the result of the avoidance of earnings and productivity losses that would have been borne without the new drug or health program in question. Rice [38] provides a systematic method of measuring indirect benefits. Her estimates include wage and productivity losses resulting from illness, disability, and death based on age and sex for major causal categories of morbidity and mortality.

3. Intangible

Intangible costs of ill health are difficult, if not impossible, to measure. These costs may be described as the psychic costs of disease, such as those incurred from pain, suffering, and grief [38–40]. Although these are difficult to measure, we are constantly reminded of their potentially high economic impact in legal cases. In a clinical research trial, these intangible effects are measured through quality-of-life or utility assessment and sometimes "willingness-to-pay" type questions.

In summary, the measurement of such intangible benefits poses an almost insuperable task. However, Mishan [41] emphasizes that an attempt should be made to account for the extremely valuable "spillover" effects of programs, if at all possible. This might mean trying to examine the impact of a new drug on the patient's significant others as well.

C. Discount Rates

All benefits and costs that occur at different times must be adjusted to reflect comparable values. This is accomplished by converting dollar amounts into present values through the use of an interest rate referred to as the discount rate. Although most economists agree that discounting must be calculated, there is much discussion as to the appropriate rate for a given situation. The consequences of choosing a high or a low discount rate are as follows: clear: a low discount rate favors projects with benefits accruing in the distant future, whereas a high rate favors projects with costs in the distant future [41–45]. One commonly used rate is the current yield rate on long-term government bonds. This seems practical because it represents a low-risk, long-term alternative use of funds by a tax-free institution and, therefore, appears valid for use by hospitals in evaluating long-term investment proposals [2,43]. Theoretical support can be found in the literature for practically any figure between the pure time-reference (low risk) rate, as low as 4%, and the corporate return on capital, approximately 20% [44–48].

Cost-benefit methodology is based on certain assumptions; it is important to have these assumptions clearly in mind before proceeding [26]. The basic assumptions of CBA are these:

1. It is possible to separate one service from another service in a sensible way.
2. There is a possibility of choice between the interventions.
3. It is possible to estimate the outcomes associated with each service.
4. It is possible to value these outcomes.
5. It is possible to estimate the cost of providing each service.
6. These costs and benefits can be weighed against each other.
7. We should provide only those services/treatments in which the benefits outweigh the costs.

Using these assumptions, there are several mathematical methods for developing a benefit:cost ratio. All have the same objective, but they differ in the way in which they handle the data mathematically [50]. The most common method is the following calculation [50]:

$$\text{Cost Benefit Ratio} = \frac{\Sigma^n_{t=1}[B_t/(1+r)^t]}{\Sigma^n_{t=1}[C_t/(1+r)^t]}$$

where: B_t = total benefits for time period t
C_t = total costs for time period t
r = discount rate
n = number of time periods

The decision criterion is as follows:

If $B/C > 1$, then benefits exceed costs and program is socially valuable.
If $B/C < 1$, then benefits are less than costs; therefore, program is not socially beneficial.

A major problem with selecting this method is in choosing "r," the discount rate that was discussed earlier.

An equation that is viewed as more robust and useful than the ratio above relates to the logical concept of net present value (NPV) represented in the equation below [50].

$$\text{Benefit-Costs} = \text{NPV} = \Sigma^n_{t=1}[(B_t - C_t)/(1+r)^t]$$

All these cost-benefit equations can be misleading, depending on the potential differences in the magnitude of dollars and time involved when comparing the costs and benefits of competing programs. In Table 2, simplified versions of three different cost-benefit approaches have been presented to illustrate how the decision factors can vary. This third approach presented in the table includes calculation of a "rate of return" on the investment, which is a rearrangement of the above equations to allow calculation of an "interest rate" from an initial program investment over a potential stream of benefits over time. From these various calculation options, the formula

Table 2 Sample Comparison Using Three Different Cost-Benefit Equations

Program	Costs	Benefits	1 Cost Benefit Ratio	2 Net Present Value	3 Internal Rate of Return
	(@ t1)	(@ t1)	(B/C)	(B–C)	$\frac{(B-C)}{C}$
A	$ 10,000	$ 15,000	1.5:1	$ 5,000	50%
B	$100,000	$180,000	1.8:1	$80,000	80%

most appropriate to one's product or company must be selected; perhaps the calculated answers from all three CBA equations should be presented in the report. Many economics recommend the net present value (NPV) approach.

In the example provided in Table 2, Program A might represent a research proposal for an oral agent taken three times a day; Program B might represent a larger investment for development of a transdermal, sustained-release patch for drug delivery. Although Program B has a higher cost-benefit ratio and rate of return, it is an expensive approach and the pharmaceutical firm may not want to commit such a substantial amount of funds. Numerous other examples could be considered here that change the results from the various formulas and make it more difficult to select between programs.

It should be emphasized that for the limited investment streams presented in this example, the calculations have been greatly simplified. The calculations and comparisons become more complex as benefits are accrued at different increments of time and as costs and benefits are properly discounted with the more complete formulas presented earlier.

If a new project involves start-up costs, such as several laminar flow hoods for an I.V. product, calculations from the above formulas can be considered. If there are extra benefits accrued by a successful product on the market, the amount of money that must be saved as benefits each year becomes similar to amortizing a start-up load (SL) over time (t) with interest rate (r) and with extra yearly benefits (BX). Therefore:

$$BX = SL[r/1 - (1+r)^{-t}]$$

III. COST-EFFECTIVENESS ANALYSIS

Requirements for cost-effectiveness analysis [50–54] are that:

1. The optimal alternative (not necessary the least costly) for accomplishing an objective should be possible.
2. At least two alternative interventions should be possible.
3. It need not be cost-reduction analysis but rather an optimizing process.

In CEA, costs are calculated in dollars but alternative ways are then compared for achieving a specific set of results such as blood pressure or life expectancy changes. The objective is not just how to use funds most wisely; CEA also includes the preference that similar output measurements should be achieved in order to compare interventions [26]. Thus, CEA is applied to medical treatments in situations where the program's inputs can be readily measured in dollars, but the program's outputs are more appropriately stated in terms of the health improvement created (e.g., life-years extended). Weinstein and Stason provided an excellent explanation of the use of CEA for the practicing physician as well as for the physician-administrator [53]. This article is recommended for those interested in a more detailed discussion. Table 3 provides additional comparison points between the CBA and CEA.

Basic mathematical examples of the various economic analyses are presented for the following methodologies: cost-benefit (in Table 4); cost-effectiveness (in Table 5); cost-utility (in Table 6); and cost-minimization (in Table 7).

The cost-benefit example in Table 4 is a hypothetical comparison of two proposed drugs to be used for pain in terminal cancer. Drug A has a lower acquisition cost, but requires extra administrative cost, because it requires extra paperwork as a narcotic drug, whereas Drug B is a non-narcotic agent. Drug A has associated monitoring costs for kidney function; it also has more adverse effects that may have to be treated. So the overall costs of Drug A exceed those of Drug B, even though the acquisition cost of Drug B is higher.

On the hypothetical benefits side, both drugs get the patient out of the hospital sooner than comparative therapy, but the patient is able to go back to work for more months on Drug B. The simplified cost-benefit analysis shows that Drug B is the drug of choice under this scenario because it has a higher cost-benefit ratio. This ratio of 10 to 1 says that for every dollar spent on Drug B, Society (and the patients) would get back 10 dollars.

Table 3 Comparison of Cost-Benefit Analysis with Cost-Effectiveness Analysis

Cost-Benefit Analysis	Cost-Effectiveness Analysis
Usually uses dollar values for output measurement	Usually does *not* use dollar values output measurement
Determines maximum benefit or investment	Determines least-cost combination
Assumes limited resources	Assumes adequate resources
Expedites comparisons among several programs	Generally refers to different ways of reaching the same objective
Less flexible	More flexible
Micro-oriented tool of analysis	Micro-oriented tool of analysis
Maximizes output—not equity or distribution	Maximizes output—not equity or distribution

Table 4 Cost-Benefit Analysis: An Example Applied to a Proposed Drug Therapy

	Therapy	
	Drug A	Drug B
Costs ($):		
Acquisition cost	300	400
Administration	50	0
Monitoring	50	0
Adverse effects	100	0
Subtotal	500	400
Benefits ($):		
Days at work	1000	1000
Extra months of life	2000	3000
Subtotal	3000	4000
Benefit-to-cost ratio:	3000/500 = 6:1	4000/400 = 10:1

The cost-effectiveness example in Table 5 is a hypothetical comparison of two proposed drugs; let us say two antiviral agents for serious viral infections. Drug A has a lower acquisition cost but requires extra administration cost because it requires daily injections; Drug B is an oral agent. Drug A has associated monitoring costs to make sure it does not negatively affect

Table 5 Cost-Effectiveness Analysis: An Example Applied to a Proposed Drug Therapy

	Therapy		
	Drug A	Drug B	
Costs ($):			
Acquisition cost	300	400	
Administration	50	0	
Monitoring	50	0	
Adverse effects	100	0	
Subtotal	500	400	
Outputs:			
Extra years of life	1.5	1.6	
Cost-effectiveness ratio	500/1.5 = $333	400/1.6 = $250	per extra year of life

Table 6 Cost-Utility Analysis: An Example Applied to a Proposed Drug Therapy

	Therapy		
	Drug A	Drug B	
Costs ($):			
Acquisition cost	300	400	
Administration	50	0	
Monitoring	50	0	
Adverse effects	100	0	
Subtotal	500	400	
Utilities			
Extra years of life	1.5	1.6	
Quality of life (QOL) index	.33	.25	
QALYs*	0.50	0.40	
Cost-to-utility ratio:	500/0.5	400/0.4	
	= $1000	= $1000	per extra QALY*-year

*QALYs = Quality-adjusted life years.

liver function, and it also has more adverse effects that may have to be treated. So the overall costs of Drug A exceed those of Drug B, even though the acquisition cost of Drug A is lower.

On the hypothetical effectiveness side, Drug A keeps the patient alive for a longer period of time (1.5 years versus 1.6 years for Drug B). The simplified cost-effectiveness analysis shows that Drug B is the drug of choice

Table 7 Cost-Minimization Analysis: An Example Applied to a Proposed Drug Therapy

	Therapy	
	Drug A	Drug B
Costs ($):		
Acquisition cost	250	350
Administration	75	0
Monitoring	75	25
Adverse effects	100	25
Subtotal	500	400
Outcomes		
Antihypertension effectiveness	90%	90%
Result	Cost of Drug A > Cost of Drug B	

under this scenario because it has a better cost-effectiveness ratio. Thus, it would cost $333 per year-of-life gained using Drug A, but it would cost only $250 per extra life-years gained using Drug B.

The cost-utility example in Table 6 is a hypothetical comparison of two proposed antifungal medicines for serious, systemic fungal infections. Again, Drug A has a lower acquisition cost, but requires extra administration cost because it requires daily injections, whereas Drug B is an oral agent. Drug A has associated monitoring costs for liver function and has more adverse effects that may have to be treated. So, again, the overall costs of Drug A exceed those of Drug B, even though the acquisition cost of Drug A is lower.

On the hypothetical utilities side of the equation, Drug A keeps the patient alive for a longer period of time—1.5 years versus 1.6 years for Drug B—but through a quality-of-life questionnaire, we find that patients report a lower quality-of-life adjustment index for Drug A, 0.33 versus a 0.25 index for Drug B. The simplified cost-utility analysis shows that Drug A is equivalent to Drug B under this scenario, because they have equal cost-utility ratios. Thus it would cost $1000 per year-of-life gained with Drug A, and it would cost the same per year-of-life gained with Drug B.

In the cost-minimization example in Table 7, we have presented a hypothetical comparison of two proposed drugs: two antihypertensive agents. Drug A requires at least one clinic visit each year to measure intraocular pressure. Both drugs have associated blood chemistry monitoring costs to make sure that they do not negatively affect kidney function, but Drug A actually has more adverse effects that may have to be treated. So the overall costs of Drug A exceed those of Drug B, even though the acquisition cost of Drug A is lower.

On the hypothetical effectiveness side, cost-minimization analysis requires the assumption that both drugs are equally effective in controlling blood pressure. The simplified cost-minimization analysis shows that Drug B is the drug of choice under this scenario, because it has a lower overall cost. Thus it would cost $500 per year to treat patients with Drug A, but it would cost only $400 per year with Drug B. Therefore, both drugs are equally effective and the cost-minimization question is answered by stating that Drug B costs $100 less per year than Drug A.

IV. ECONOMIC PERSPECTIVES

An important consideration in understanding CBA and CEA is that a pharmaceutical product providing a positive benefit to cost ratio in terms of value to society as a whole may not be valued in the same way by separate market segments of society. For example, a drug therapy that reduces the number of patient-days in an acute care institution is positive from society's point of view but not necessarily from that of the institution's administrator, who may operate under a fixed level of revenue and who depends on a fixed number of patient-days to meet expenses. In other words, what is viewed as cost-beneficial to society may be viewed differently by third-party payers, administrators, health providers, governmental agencies, or even individual patients. One must determine whose interests are to be measured when identifying outcome criteria for evaluation. From a cost-benefit perspective, one must always consider who pays the costs and who receives the benefits. A proposal justifying a pharmaceutical product to a hospital administrator would obviously want to demonstrate that the product's benefits to the institution outweigh its costs.

V. QUALITY-OF-LIFE OUTCOMES AND PATIENT DECISIONS

Equally significant and misunderstood in pharmacoeconomics and patient outcomes management is the issue of quality of life [55,56]. Although we recognize that there are physical, mental, and social impairments associated with disease, we have not agreed on how to measure these factors. Consequently, the concept of satisfaction with care is often overlooked in cost-effectiveness studies and even in the approval process by the Food and Drug Administration. But pharmacoeconomics and outcomes research considers quality of life an important predictor in creating a full model of survival and improvement [54–56]. Quality of life is related to clinical outcomes as much as drugs, practitioners, settings, and types of disease. The question is how to select and utilize effective instruments (as listed in Table 8) for measuring quality of life and satisfaction with care in a meaningful way.

If adjustments are not made for preexisting comorbidities, the resulting health profile may be skewed. For example, untreated hypertension may escape a quality-of-life measurement because it does not overtly affect daily life, but a myocardial infarction resulting from the high blood pressure can definitely lessen quality of life. The FDA has been leery of approving drugs that make patients feel better while their life expectancy is reduced. Nevertheless, we must be able to present to patients the different probabilities between perfect health and death and the compromises associated with different treatments, and then administer care accordingly.

Table 8 Outcomes and Quality of Life Measurement Approaches

- I. Basic Outcomes List
  - A. Death
  - B. Disease
  - C. Disability
  - D. Discomfort
  - E. Dissatisfaction
- II. Major Quality of Life Domains
  - A. Physical status and functional abilities
  - B. Psychological status and well-being
  - C. Social interactions
  - D. Economic status and factors
- III. Expanded Outcomes List
  - A. Clinical End Points
    1. Symptoms and Signs
    2. Laboratory Values
    3. Death
  - B. Functional Parameters
    1. Physical (activities)
    2. Mental (depression)
    3. Social (friends)
    4. Role (work)
  - C. General Well-Being
    1. Pain
    2. Energy/Fatigue
    3. Health perceptions
    4. Opportunity (future)
    5. Life satisfaction
  - D. Satisfaction with Care
    1. Access
    2. Convenience
    3. Financial coverage
    4. Quality
    5. General
- IV. Sample of Instruments for Outcomes Measurement
  - A. Generic Instruments—Nottingham, MOS Short Form 36
  - B. Specific Instruments—Pain, Arthritis, Epilepsy, Cancer

In order to present these probabilities, though, we must monitor what happens to patients during clinical treatments over time and collect data on their utilities. This means that we should ask patients how they feel about their therapeutic options, which therapies they prefer, and how their quantity and quality of life are affected. Many pharmaceutical companies have sponsored work that examines probabilities, utilities, and cost-effectiveness and then charts the results over time. Using decision-analysis concepts, researchers can construct a decision tree of what actually happens to the patient from diagnosis to cure. As a result of utilizing such analytic approaches, we can clearly see not only costs, but also the probability of entering one health state over another.

From all these types of computer modeling we can develop treatment protocols for the best ways to treat patients even before the drug is approved for the market. Each of the branches of the decision tree designates specific treatments for patients at specific health states. In a simplified form, this tree doubles as an educational tool for presenting available therapeutic options and probable consequences to the patient [57,58].

Wennberg [58] has been exploring ways to involve patients in this type of decision-making process. His recent work is a computer-interactive program on prostate surgery. This program explains to patients the probability of success, what pain might be involved at each step, and what the procedure actually entails. After viewing this program with visual, graphic depiction of the surgery, many patients changed their decisions about wanting surgery over watchful waiting. This reduction in a major procedure resulted from a greater focus on quality of life and patient satisfaction. With further evaluation and perhaps modification of the computer program, it should also produce more cost-effective care. Wennberg's work is really just an application of outcomes research that helped to consider costs, utilities, and quality of life for the patient. This example shows how a concern for the patient's preferences can be balanced with health care cost considerations.

VI. CONCLUSION

Pharmaceutical research needs to give continuing attention to the greatest benefit we can generate for society as a whole which is to target and take more responsibility toward decreasing mortality, not just morbidity. Giving extra years of life to a patient population can be converted to dollars for society, which can greatly enhance the benefit-to-cost ratio of a product. Substantial research remains to be done on the potential impact of various medical interventions on mortality rate. It is expected that future reimbursement plans will include provider incentives to decrease patient mortality rates. In pursuing these mortality statistics, we must also realize that long-term clinical trials can be extremely expensive to conduct.

Pharmaceutical researchers and managers must consider cost-benefit and cost-effectiveness based on the outcomes of the services that a pharmaceutical product can provide for patients. There are a number of ways that a drug can produce positive outcomes on hospital services. For example, the product can:

Decrease morbidity in patient populations
Increase the percentage of patients in therapeutic control
Reduce the costs of the treatment by utilizing more efficient delivery systems
Reduce the number of physician visits
Reduce the rate of hospitalization attributable to or affected by the improper use of drugs
Decrease the incidence and intensity of iatrogenic disease, such as adverse drug reactions

In this chapter, a general explanation of cost-benefit and cost-effectiveness analysis has been provided with the intent that this will help the reader appreciate the impact of cost-justification efforts on the development of new pharmaceuticals. There is an ever-increasing body of literature demonstrating that pharmaceuticals have cost-beneficial effects for society. Still, it must be realized that even though this research is positive, there is a need to continue to develop medicines that *maximize* the net benefit to society and to institutions. Even though a pharmaceutical product can demonstrate a positive ratio of benefit to cost, society or the institutions will ultimately invest their resources in needed programs that have the higher benefit-to-cost ratio or highest net present value. Similarly, the health system must be convinced that these beneficial drugs are worth using with protocol modification or even deletion of other, less effective, interventions, if necessary. Pharmaceutical researchers and managers must fully understand evaluation tools such as pharmacoeconomics and quality-of-life assessment if their products are to thrive in the future [59].

REFERENCES

1. W. F. McGhan, Pharmacoeconomics and the evaluation of drugs and services, *Hosp. Form.* *28*:365–378 (1993).

2. W. McGhan, C. Rowland, and J. L. Bootman, Cost-benefit and cost-effectiveness: Methodology for evaluating clinical pharmacy service, *Am. J. Hosp. Pharm. 35*:133–140 (1978).
3. M. Ray, Administration direction for clinical practice, *Am. J. Hosp. Pharm. 36*: 308 (1979).
4. J. L. Bootman, W. F. McGhan, and S. W. Schondelmeyer, Application of cost-benefit and cost-effectiveness analysis to clinical practice, *Drug Intell. Clin. Pharm. 16*:235–243 (1982).
5. W. F. McGhan and N. J. Lewis, Guidelines for pharmacoeconomic studies, *Clin. Ther. 3*:486–494 (1992).
6. S. M. Enright, Changes in health-care financing resulting from the 1984 federal budget, *Am. J. Hosp. Pharm. 40*:835–838 (1983).
7. F. R. Curtiss, Current concepts in hospital reimbursement, *Am. J. Hosp. Pharm. 40*:586–591 (1983).
8. M. C. Weinstein and B. Stason, Foundations and cost-effectiveness analysis for health and medical practitioners, *N. Engl. J. Med. 296*:716–721 (1977).
9. D. S. Shepard and M. S. Thompson, First principles of cost-effectiveness analysis in health, *Public Health Rep. 94*:535–544 (1979).
10. R. Crystal and A. Brewster, Cost-benefit and cost-effectiveness analysis in the health field: an introduction, *Inquiry 3*:3–13 (1966).
11. J. Acton, Measuring the monetary value of life-saving programs, *Law Contemp. Prob. 40*:46–72 (1976).
12. H. E. Emlet, Jr., Use of cost-benefit analysis in solutions to national health problems, Presented at the 1968 Joint National Meeting of the Operations Research Society of America, San Francisco, California, May 1–3, 1968.
13. D. D. Gellman, Cost-benefit in health care: we need to know more, *Canc. Med. Assoc. J. 4*:998–999 (1974).
14. P. G. Goldschmidt, A cost-effectiveness model for evaluating health care programs: application to drug abuse treatment, *Inquiry 13*:29–47 (1976).
15. J. L. Bootman et al., Individualizing gentamicin dosage regimens on burn patients with gram-negative septicemia: a cost-benefit analysis, *J. Pharm. Sci. 68*:267–272 (1979).
16. J. L. Bootman et al., Individualization of aminoglycoside dosage regimens: a cost analysis, *Am. J. Hosp. Pharm. 36*:368 (1979).
17. P. V. Strange and A. T. Sumner, Predicting treatment costs and life expectancy for end-stage renal disease, *N. Engl. J. Med. 298*:372–378 (1978).
18. S. Cretin, Cost-benefit analysis of treatment and prevention of myocardial infarction, *Health Serv. Res. 12*:174–189 (1977).
19. W. Mattsson et al., Cancer chemotherapy in advanced malignant disease: a cost-benefit analysis, *Acta Radiol. Oncol. 18*:509–520 (1979).
20. W. Stason and M. Weinstein, Allocation of resources to manage hypertension, *N. Engl. J. Med. 296*:732 (1977).

21. R. J. Estershan, Jr., et al., Cost analysis of leukemia treatment: a problem-oriented approach, *Cancer 37*:646–52 (1976).
22. F. Bryers and V. M. Hawthorne, Screening for mild hypertension: costs and benefits, *J. Epidemiol. Commun. Health 32*:171–174 (1978).
23. W. L. Kissick, Cost-benefit studies in health planning in the U.S.A., *Health Econ. 42*:39–44 (1969).
24. H. Klarman, Application of cost-benefit analysis to health services and the special case of technological innovation, *Int. J. Health Serv. Res. 4*:325–352 (1974).
25. H. Klarman, Present status of cost-benefit analysis in the health field, *Am. J. Public Health 57*:1948–1958 (1967).
26. W. Smith, Cost-effectiveness and cost-benefit for public health programs, *Public Health Rep. 83*:899–906 (1968).
27. S. Mushkin and F. D'Accolings, Economic cost of disease and injury, *Public Health Rep. 74*:338–345 (1959).
28. A. C. Pigou, *Socialism Versus Capitalism, 129*, Macmillan Press, London, 1947.
29. A. R. Prest and R. Turvey, Cost-benefits analysis: a survey, *Economist J. 75*: 683–735 (1965).
30. G. H. Peters, *Cost/Benefit Analysis and Public Expenditures, Paper 8*. Institute of Economic Affairs, London, 1968.
31. J. Osteryoung, *Capital Budgeting: Long-Term Asset Selection*, Grid Inc., Columbus, OH, 1974.
32. J. B. Silvers and C. K. Praholed, *Financial Management of Health Institutions*, Spectrum Publications, New York, 1974.
33. J. C. Van Horne, *Financial Management and Policy*, Prentice-Hall, Englewood Cliffs, NJ, 1974.
34. G. Torrance, A generalized cost-effectiveness model for evaluation of health programs, Ph.D. Dissertation, State University of New York at Buffalo, 1971.
35. H. Klarman, Application of cost-benefit analysis to health services technology, *J. Occup. Med. 18*:172–186 (1974).
36. H. C. Schulbert, C. A. Sheldon, and F. Baker, *Program Evaluation in the Health Field*, Behavioral Publications, New York, 1969.
37. D. P. Rice, Measurement and application of illness costs, *Public Health Rep. 84*: 91–101 (1969).
38. D. P. Rice, Estimating the cost of illness, Health Economics Series No. 6, U.S. Government Printing Office, Washington, DC, 1966.
39. K. Rinehard, F. Felsman, and L. Moody, Time loss and indirect economic cost caused by disease among Indian and Alaskan natives, *Public Health Rep. 85*: 402 (1970).
40. R. G. Ridker, *Economic Cost of Air Pollution*, Praeger, New York, 1967.
41. E. J. Mishan, Evaluation of life and limb: an theoretical approach, *Benefit/Cost Analysis* (A. Harberger et al., eds.), Aldine-Atherton, Chicago, 1971, pp. 103–123.

42. A. H. Packer, Applying cost-effectiveness concepts to the community health system, *Oper. Res. 16*:227–253 (1968).
43. H. Klarman, *Economics of Health*, Columbia University Press, New York, 1965.
44. S. A. Marglin, The social rate of discount at the optimal rate of investment, *J. Econ. 77*:95–111 (1963).
45. W. J. Baumol, On the discount rate for public projects, *Public Expenditures and Policy Analysis* (R. Haveman and J. Margolia, eds.), Markham, Chicago, 1970, pp. 273–290.
46. J. Amadio, J. Mueller, and R. Grey, Benefit/cost ratio, *Public Health Report*, Illinois Department of Public Health, Southern Illinois University, Carbondale and Jackson County Health Department, 1976.
47. M. Joehnk, G. R. McGrail, and N. J. Degal, Application of a benefit/cost model to family practice Nes Denz, Prepared by the Department of Health, Education and Welfare. National Technical Information Service No. HRP-0007312, U.S. Government Printing Office, Washington, DC, 1975.
48. E. Cohn, *Public Expenditures Analysis*, DC Heath, Lexington, MA, 1972.
49. Ruchlin and Rogers, *Economics and Health Care*, Charles C. Thomas, Springfield, IL, 1973.
50. E. J. Mishan, *Cost-Benefit Analysis*, Hold, Rinehart and Winston, New York, 1976.
51. E. S. Quade, Introduction and overview, *Cost-Effectiveness Analysis* (T. A. Goldin, ed.), Praeger, New York, 1967.
52. W. A. Niskanen, Measurement of effectiveness, *Cost-Effectiveness Analysis* (T. A. Goldman, ed.), Praeger, New York, 1967.
53. M. C. Weinstein and B. Stason, Foundations and cost-effectiveness analysis for health and medical practitioners, *N. Engl. J. Med. 296*:716–721 (1977).
54. J. L. Bottman, R. B. Townsend, and W. F. McGhan, *Principles of Pharmacoeconomics*, Harvey Whitney Books, Chicago, 1991.
55. P. M. Ellwood, Outcomes management: a technology of patient experience, *N. Engl. J. Med. 18*:1549–1556 (1988).
56. L. D. MacKeigan and D. S. Pathak, Overview of health-related quality-of-life measures, *Am. J. Hosp. Pharm. 49*:2236–45, 1992.
57. T. R. Einarson, W. F. McGhan, and J. L. Bootman, Decision analysis applied to pharmacy practice, *Am. J. Hosp. Pharm. 42*:364–371 (1985).
58. J. E. Wennberg, The paradox of appropriate care, *JAMA 258*:2568–2569 (1987).
59. W. F. McGhan and M. D. Smith, Improving the cost-benefits of pharmaceutical services: pharmacoeconomics 101, *Pharm. Business*, Spring:6–10 (1993).

12

Pharmaceutical Marketing

Mickey C. Smith

The University of Mississippi
University, Mississippi

Lisa Ruby Basara

Rhône-Poulenc Rorer
Collegeville, Pennsylvania

I. INTRODUCTION

The thread of marketing is woven throughout the fabric of the pharmaceutical industry. It binds many aspects of the complex pharmaceutical industry and underlies the business operations of all successful companies. Whenever there is serious talk of strict government regulation of health care, policy makers and the public must recognize that marketing by the pharmaceutical and other health industries is integral to our evolving system.

There is probably no other industry that has been criticized so often, so inaccurately, and so unfairly for its "marketing" activities as the pharmaceutical industry. The term "marketing" has been used so imprecisely and in such a pejorative sense that a basic lesson in the subject is needed. A complete understanding of pharmaceutical marketing is required to recognize that not only is it a useful business function, marketing is *vital* to the nation's health.

Prescription medications are, in many ways, unlike any other goods. The most important distinction is the federal law that prohibits the purchases of prescription products without the authorization (prescription) of certain licensed health professionals. Other differences that render prescription drugs different, if not unique, from consumer products include:

Although consumers increasingly express their therapy preferences, especially since the advent of direct-to-consumer advertising, ultimately it is the prescriber who chooses the drug.

Generally speaking, consumers do not *want* prescription drugs. Compared with the many other products that offer gratification from their possession or consumption, prescription medications are no fun to own or consume.

The development and marketing activities for prescription drugs are the most highly regulated of any consumer product category. In no other industry are the results of the research and development (R&D) process so closely tied to marketing activities. A drug manufacturer is literally bound by what has been proved (to the satisfaction of the Food and Drug Administration [FDA]) in the research process when marketing the product.

One would expect that these characteristics would result in a close relationship between those involved in pharmaceutical R&D and those involved in marketing. Such is not always the case. The reasons vary, but must certainly include differences in the underlying approaches to the development and marketing of medications as well as some free-floating tension in the relationships.

With increasing global competition, changing drug development techniques (i.e., immunology, genetics), and enhanced knowledge and price-sensitivity of patients and payers, marketing and R&D activities must be coordinated and efficient to ensure that pharmaceutical companies prosper. As such, the goal of this chapter is to explain what marketing is and does, and how it must be a part of drug development from the beginning of each new project.

II. WHAT IS MARKETING?

Marketing is the process of planning and carrying out the creation, pricing, promotion, and distribution of ideas, products, and services that satisfy the needs and wants of consumers and organizations [1]. Marketing adds value to any product or service by making it more convenient, useful, and accessible.

It is important to remember that for prescription drugs, the real product from the patient's perspective is the *outcome*. Someone has said that no one wants a drill, they want *holes*. The same is true with pharmaceuticals. The drug products themselves have little appeal to most people It is the *effect* they have on a patient's life that counts.

There is obvious added value in having prescription medicines available in convenient dosage forms, palatable flavors, and efficient packaging. However, marketing adds many other, more profound values to pharmaceutical products. One of the basic principles of marketing involves its role in the overall economic system. That role is to provide economic utility to the patient—value is provided through the satisfaction of patients' needs. There are four types of utility: form, time, place, and possession:

Form utility is the value that comes from having medications in convenient dosage forms, palatable flavors, efficient packaging—all the things that can lead to appropriate prescription medication use and improved health outcomes.

Time utility is the value associated with the convenience of access and availability. It can be dramatically illustrated by the ability of emergency room staff to issue "stat" orders for medications with virtual assurance that the order will be filled as well as "open-all-night" pharmacies.

Place utility is explained by the fact that *any* prescription medicine can be obtained in *any* community in the United States through the thousands of retail and hospital pharmacies, which are themselves part of the pharmaceutical industry. Many pharmacies even deliver medicines to patients' homes.

Possession utility results from all the often hidden marketing activities, such as dealing with third-party payers, providing goods on credit, and handling paperwork, that ensure that patients (or their agents) can receive needed medicines.

A classic marketing text describes the concept of *macro-marketing* as "a social process that directs an economy's flow of goods and services from producers to consumers in a way that effectively matches supply and demand and accomplishes the objectives of society." Of special interest in health care is the realization that macro-marketing systems can vary in how effectively the society uses its scarce resources and how fairly it allocates its output of goods and services [2]. At a time when there is serious consideration at the national level of rationing health care goods and services, it is essential to recognize that marketing is and *must be* a vital part of the economic system that evolves.

A. The "Four P's" of Marketing

The American Marketing Association definition of marketing is consistent with the concept of the four P's of marketing that is described in traditional marketing texts and is still valuable today. The four P's and their interaction are called the *marketing mix* and constitute a company's basic marketing strategy. Understanding how pharmaceutical manufacturers manipulate the four P's will aid in understanding the positive contributions made by marketing. The four P's—product, price, promotion, and place—are described in turn.

1. Product: Marketing's Role in the Development of Pharmaceuticals

Pharmaceutical companies use market research to identify commercial opportunities—unmet medical needs. Although it does not take sophisticated research to know that there is a need for more and better cancer therapy, it does take work (and money) to determine gaps in therapy, troublesome side effects, and compliance problems that warrant correction. Marketing typically identifies such potential in the marketplace and supplies this information to R&D for action.

Product development is a cycle that starts with the patient, is guided by the patient, and ends with the patient. Marketing transmits information at each stage of the process. Marketing sequentially (a) guides the creation of medicines, on the basis of an assessment of patient needs, (b) communicates to physicians the availability and attributes of medicines, and (c) encourages patients in the medication's proper use. Marketing moves potential product users (i.e., the market) from a general condition of unmet needs to a stage where many of those needs are fulfilled by new therapies. The cycle begins again as marketing reveals product shortcomings.

Marketing does not force products on the medical profession—rather, it provides physicians with an informed choice of carefully crafted medications that fit specific needs of individual patients. Patients' medication needs vary widely on the basis of their disease and symptoms, concurrent diseases, concurrent medicines, tolerance to specific adverse effects, age, gender, ethnic background, previous experience with medicines, allergies, and many other factors. A broad choice of available agents enables physicians to precisely tailor medication therapy. Thus, marketing enables health care professionals to make informed choices by educating them about drug product attributes.

Marketing must take the lead from patients and physicians. Products designed to meet nonexistent needs will fail, despite the vigor of the sales force. Market failures are expensive, and, ultimately, these costs are passed along to consumers. Marketing helps hold costs down by weeding out those product candidates destined to fail commercially [3].

a. The Value of Marketing Research Research plays an important part in the marketing function as well as in drug development. Although the terms are often used interchangeably and definitions vary, we will offer two working definitions:

Market research is the assessment of the quantitative and qualitative characters of the people in a "market."

Marketing research is the assessment of the effectiveness and efficiency of manipulation of the components and subcomponents of the marketing mix. (Product research—clinical research—could be included as a kind of marketing research under this definition.)

In colloquial terms, *market* research can be thought as answering the question: "How much of my drug and my competitors' drugs is being or might be used?" *Marketing* research addresses the question: "how can we get patients to use more of my drug?" These questions might seem crassly commercial but, properly and ethically executed, such research ultimately results in enhanced products, better treatment, and greater provider and patient satisfaction.

There is no time in the life of a product when there is not some need for information that could be obtained from market or marketing research. The outline in Table 1, which is used by IMS America, provides examples of the

Table 1 Outline of Marketing Research Questions Asked During Drug Development

Stage I: Opportunity Analysis

Time period from 10 to 3 years pre-launch. At this point, the product has passed toxicological testing and is in Phase 1 human testing.

What Is the Opportunity?

Is the market defined:

- By Diagnosis?
  Our drug is used to treat these diagnoses. What other drugs are used as well?
- By drug?
  Our drug is like Product X. How is Product X being used?
- By prescriptions and length of therapy?
  What are the major population/disease trends in a diagnosis area?

What is the Opportunity?

How big is the market today

- By units?
- By dollars?
- By chemical weight?

How is the market growing? Which physicians prescribe these drugs most?

Who Is the Competition?

Which are the competitive products?

What are their key features and benefits:

- By form, strength, dosage, package pricing? How are they doing?
- By form, strength, dosage, package, delivery system?

Who are the companies involved? What are their corporate commitments?

What has been the cost of launching in this market to date?

What new products are in development?

Where is the new technology?

Stage II: Strategy Development

From 3 years to 6 months pre-launch, the product is in Phase 3 testing. The new drug application has been filed with the FDA and the product is a reality.

Positioning

Which are the competitive products for benchmarketing?

Which physicians use them?

What promotional messages do physicians receive? How do physicians respond?

- Do they use drugs as manufacturers intend?
- For what desired effects?
- With which patients?
- Under what therapeutic conditions? (diagnoses)
- In what therapeutic positions (first line, add-on, concomitant?)
- Where do new starts come from?

What promotion has been effective and/or efficient?

- Examine message effectiveness
- Examine media efficiency
- Examine spending efficiency

kinds of questions that might be asked of and by the market research divisions through the development of a product.

2. Price: Marketing's Role in Pharmaceutical Pricing

It takes a degree of temerity in today's environment to suggest that marketing has a negative effect on prescription medication prices. The most obvious way in which marketing employs prices to the benefit of the public is through price competition. For example, the entire generic pharmaceutical industry is based on price competition.

A recent investigation by Kolassa studied pricing behavior for "breakthrough" products and compared them with competing products that followed them to the market [4]. The findings are summarized in Fig. 1. It can be seen that successive products have been launched at *lower* prices, resulting in a continuing stream of lower-priced products for prescribing physicians to choose. It should be noted that the often-used epithet of a "me-too" product can, in fact, have been applied to medications offering equivalent therapy at lower prices.

3. Place: Role of Marketing in Distribution

Medications are useless to patients if they are not available where and when they are needed. A vital function of pharmaceutical marketing is the develop-

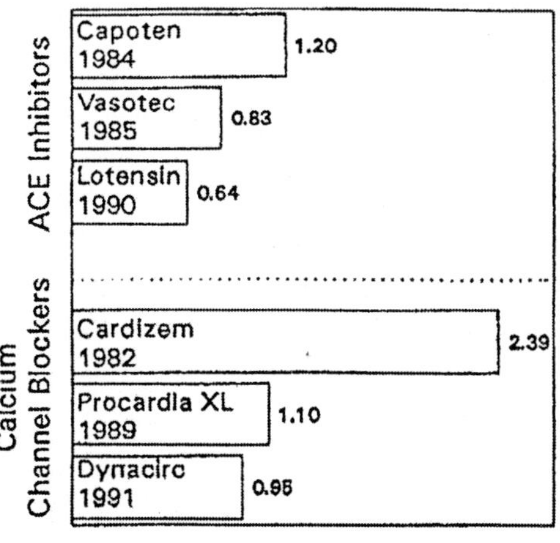

Fig. 1 Price competition among ACE inhibitors and calcium channel blockers.

ment and maintenance of a system for the physical distribution of medications.

Pharmaceutical products do not automatically find their way to pharmacy shelves. The pharmaceutical industry (i.e., manufacturing, wholesaling, and retailing segments) has facilitated the establishment of the United States drug distribution system—one of the most efficient and cost-effective in the world. One has only to realize that it is possible to obtain virtually any prescription medication in any town in the United States to appreciate the success of this effort. This system permits rapid distribution of new lifesaving medicines immediately after they are approved by the FDA. The availability of an important new medicine can be communicated immediately to all practicing physicians in the United States and the medication shipped to every pharmacy in the United States within 48 hours.

The medication distribution system also enables a rapid, corrective response to bad news by informing physicians and pharmacists about important newly discovered adverse effects. If quality control or tampering problems are discovered, batch destinations can be quickly traced to locate and recall products from individual pharmacies.

4. Promotion: Role of Marketing in Promotion

Promotion is what many people mean when they talk about "marketing." Promotion is also frequently used as a synonym for advertising. Actually, promotion is only a part of marketing, and advertising is only a part of promotion. Along with price, promotion is a frequent target of criticism in the pharmaceutical industry. Some of that criticism is made on the basis of an incomplete understanding of the positive contributions made by promotional activities toward patient care.

a. Providing Information About the Other Three P's Even though marketing succeeds in its basic task of providing the right product, place, price, it is still theoretically possible for the product to fail as a marketable item. The potential area of failure could be described broadly as communications. The part of the marketing communications process that might be most familiar is advertising. It is the most visible and perhaps most exciting form of communication. However, if marketing is performed efficiently, communication will be a two-way process.

The minimum amount of information that must be communicated by the manufacturer is the availability of a product. Obviously one does not purchase (or prescribe) a product that one does not know exists. The physician is engaged in what has been called a "vicarious search" (i.e., with a knowledge of the needs of the patient, the physician searches the characteristics of available medications for the patient—who is not equipped to judge—for the one that most closely meets a patient's needs). Even though physicians are engaged in this relatively active and educated search process, there is a strong possibility that they will not become aware of a given product unless someone—usually the manufacturer—has made a formal effort to communicate the drug's availability.

Promotion informs but, by definition, also attempts to persuade. While this latter aspect of promotion receives much of the criticism, some of it is, we believe, misplaced. Nowhere in the official approach to promotion is there any recognition of the real and potential contributions of efficient and effective promotion to optimal medication therapy. As a consequence, there is no hint of public policy to reward or encourage efficiency and effectiveness in the promotion of drugs of choice. Surely sometimes, perhaps *most* times, effective promotion results in optimal therapy.

b. The Industry's Role in Physician Education Successful pharmaceutical promotion relies on physician understanding of the condition being treated and the mechanism of action of the medication being promoted. Certainly, one of the tasks of those companies introducing the first beta blocker or the first H_2 antagonist was to review the physiologic principles underlying the drugs' actions. No one can deny that considerable educational value accrues from this activity.

Sometimes traditional product detailing activities, which lead to physician prescribing, must be preceded by efforts to assist physicians in disease awareness and diagnoses. An example is the condition of depression. Research showed that physicians, especially those involved in primary care, were slow to reach an accurate diagnosis, resulting in inordinate delays in selecting effective therapy, sometimes with tragic results. Promotional efforts by manufacturers of leading antidepressant medications were targeted at improved diagnosis. Certainly, these marketing activities enhanced sales, but the educational effects also led to improved patient care, an effect that cannot be ignored.

III. CORPORATE PERSPECTIVES ON R&D/MARKETING INTERACTION

In all industries, more attention than ever is being given to the development of the total corporation through managed creativity in every business function. In addition to new and improved products and processes, corporations seek growth and efficiency through new distribution channels and customers, new financial and administrative practices, and new marketing strategies. Close interaction and collaboration between R&D and marketing is necessary to support various corporate development plans and objectives.

Unquestionably, investing in long-range R&D requires an act of faith by industry managers. In spite of the elaborate models available for identifying market opportunities, establishing research priorities, and forecasting return on investment (ROI), research investment still requires the judgment of top-level management. There is no effective measurement system that can prove that an investment will be paid back.

There is little doubt, however, that the success of a major new drug product can have a profound impact on a firm's sales and profits, and it is this possibility that often encourages continued investments in R&D in many firms. The introduction of Tagamet, a new drug for the treatment of ulcer disease, contributed significantly to a doubling in sales and profit for the SmithKline Corporation for the nine months ending September 1978, as compared with the same period a year earlier.

IV. MARKETING AND R&D PERSPECTIVES

There are obvious conceptual differences between R&D and marketing groups, the most apparent of which is the constant conflict between the long- and short-term demands for the firm's resources. Marketing wants "bottom line" performance and output *today*, whereas the goals of research are often focused on the future. Moreover, in many firms, at least in the past, R&D has traditionally been treated with unusual deference by management. Left to pursue its own ways, the research function sometimes acquires its own mystique, which serves as a protective cloak over its inner workings and prevents management from providing adequate direction and monitoring. Furthermore, research philosophy frequently adheres to the spirit of the freedom of scientific inquiry and independence.

The conceptual differences between R&D and marketing sometimes contribute to an antagonistic and mutually suspicious relationship in which they compete in fixing the blame for lack of new products or new product successes. Increasingly, new organizational approaches and communication channels are being developed within companies to improve rapport between marketing and R&D operations. The penalties for lack of coordination can be severe in terms of costly, unproductive, or scattered research and commercialization efforts.

V. MARKETING AND R&D INTERACTION—A TIMELINE

The balance of this chapter is devoted to describing the valuable role that marketing personnel play in each phase of drug discovery, development, and marketing. The goals of marketing and R&D interaction during each phase of a compound's life cycle are characterized, and the value of these interactions in terms of product success is clarified.

A. Exploratory Drug Discovery Research

The decision to explore therapeutic areas from which new leads might emerge is essentially made by research management, although it is influenced by broad marketing considerations. Some factors that influence these research decisions within a firm include the following:

Use of the existing bank of skills and resources within the firm
"Breakthrough" or emerging research areas
"Visceral" knowledge and experience of research managers and scientists
Persistence of the project "champion"
Need for "critical mass" of expertise internally
New animal pharmacologic screens developed to provide novel leads
Competitive research activity and strengths
External consultants providing expert opinions, guidance, and ideas
Influence of university research, a source of ideas and cooperative ventures
Medical need and market potential
Serendipity and its unexpected role in the discovery process
Development projects that may generate new basic knowledge/leads
Project and research synergies—one research area influencing another

The impact of marketing on the R&D process varies with the stage of the process. As we move from the exploratory end of the R&D spectrum to the point at which leads are identified and a decision is made to pursue an investigational new drug (IND) and a new drug application (NDA), project goals become better defined and the role of marketing increases. At any point, either inadequate marketing inputs or attempts to exert excessive control over the research process can create major problems. Difficulties can also arise when research programs are too unstructured and are not in tune with marketing strategies and the near-term concern for increased revenues and profits.

When projects are formalized, marketing needs to monitor progress and to provide important insights concerning: (a) the nature of the clinical studies to be undertaken and the desired claim structure for the product, (b) dosage forms to be developed and their characteristics, and (c) the timing of the NDA submission.

Marketing should also exert considerable influence on research activities in support of existing products, including broadened claims, new dosage forms, and overall defensive efforts. Because of the decline in the evolution of new chemical entities over the past two decades, there has been more emphasis on "defensive" projects, those aimed at prolonging the life cycle of currently marketed products. Even in the large research-based firms, as much as 20% to 25% of the R&D budget can be directed to such defensive activities.

B. Project Selection

Project selection decisions are often influenced by a number of important considerations in addition to the size of the research budget. Not all the factors in Table 2 are of concern in every decision influencing project selection and priorities, but the compilation represents a checklist of areas often considered before decisions are finalized (Table 3).

From Table 2 it can be noted that many research, manufacturing, and marketing concerns must be considered that influence project selection decisions. Consider, for example, the following factors for a firm wishing to develop a market position in antibiotics—essentially a new area for the firm that has a couple of exciting research leads:

1. Do we have specific objectives in the antibiotic field with regard to market position and target date? Can we obtain resources (i.e., people, funds, facilities) to obtain these objectives? Should our emphasis be near term (2 to 3 years) or long term (5 to 10 years)?
2. What are the risks and uncertainties associated with the effort? What are the financial implications of these uncertainties?
3. What is the nature of the competition in terms of marketed products and current development efforts? What are their strengths, weaknesses, and abilities?
4. What other known antibiotics are actively being developed? What are their potential market advantages and disadvantages?
5. What are the competitive advantages of the products we are considering to develop? What is the expected market life cycle? Are there possible follow-on products?
6. What are the pricing structure and profit trend with antibiotics?

Table 2 Factors Influencing Project Selection

Scientific factors	Marketing considerations	Organizational and other elements
Interrelationship with other research activities—synergistic advantages or competition with other programs	Projected sales and profits from effort	Relationship to activities at other research center or units within the company
Probability of achieving project objectives	Relationship to need as reflected by current state of consumer satisfaction	Timing of project with respect to other activities in marketing, research, etc.
Time required to achieve project objectives	Status and efficacy of current competitive products or means of meeting consumer need	Manufacturing capabilities and needs
Impact on balance of short- and long-term programs within research	Compatibility with current marketing capabilities and strengths	Prestige and image value to the company
Estimated cost of the project in the coming year and to completion	Influence of new competitive products under development	Effect on organizational esprit de corps and attitudes
Use of existing research talent and resources		Impact of governmental and public opinion and other environmental pressures
Value as a means of generating experience and technical expertise in a field—a foundation for future research activities		Alternative uses of scientific personnel and facilities if project dropped after a few years
Need for critical mass of expertise and activity to ensure progress		Moral compulsion to develop drugs meeting medical need but having little profit potential
Elasticity of resource input and probable output relationships		
Patentability or exclusivity of discoveries from project		
Competitive research effort in the area (i.e., academic and government research centers		

Source: R. E. Faust in M. C. Smith, *Principles of Pharmaceutical Monitoring*, 3rd ed., Lea and Febiger, Philadelphia, 1983.

Table 3 Marketing Checklist for Assessing New Product Ideas

Characteristic	Range of criteria
Third-year sales estimate	Dollar sales
Market potential	Number of patients
Patentability/exclusivity	Availability of use and process patents Number of years of patent life remaining
Overall market trend	Growing or declining market
Promotional effort required	Primary or secondary demand stimulation needed
Breadth of utility	Range of practitioner types who might use the products
New or existing market	New product concept or entry into crowded market
Nature of competition	Number and trends of competitors
Effect on other products in company portfolio	Good fit for potential "cannibals"
Sales force expertise	Need for major training
Price structure	Very competitive to stable
Regulatory climate	Current FDA positions

Source: D. J. Mazzoni, Rx for the Pharmaceutical Marketer: Preventive Marketing, *Med. Marketing Media* 7(2):19 (1972).

7. Who are the customers (i.e., physicians, third-party payers, government) and what "value" is each looking for? How will value differences affect our market positioning and opportunities?
8. Can we market antibiotics more successfully with a dedicated sales group or through our existing field force? Are special promotional efforts needed?
9. How will the drug be produced? If agents are manufactured by us, where? How much investment is needed? Do we have adequate in-house technical expertise to manufacture? What are the new material requirements? Do we need specialized facilities?
10. What is the patent position for each of our potential market entities? Are areas of litigation a concern?
11. What is the R&D cost to support our strategy? Do we have the internal technical and scientific expertise to support the needed research effort? How will a move to antibiotic research influence other research efforts?

12. If we accomplish our objectives, what is the most likely response of competitors? How will we respond to them and what will be the impact on our market share and profitability?

C. Marketing and Drug Discovery

Although it might be difficult to picture "bench scientists" and marketers working together to create a molecule with therapeutic value, this scenario is occurring, at least in a figurative sense, frequently in the pharmaceutical industry. The need for an integrated approach to drug development is critical as the activities of pharmaceutical companies, including new product decisions, are scrutinized by government agencies, competitors, health care professionals, and consumers. By working together to optimize drug discovery and development, pharmaceutical researchers and marketers can enhance compound selection, ensure efficient resource use, and minimize the time needed to bring the new product to market.

While many pharmaceutical companies use different approaches, the *best* time for marketing to become involved in product development decisions is as soon as possible. The ability of R&D and marketing to work together is mandatory in today's health care environment. Their primary goal is to ensure the appropriation of financial and manpower resources to viable market candidates. However, to many researchers, the involvement of marketers ("non-scientists") has the potential to suppress creativity and inhibit breakthrough discoveries.

As we all know, innovation cannot be *planned* like budgets and advertising expenditures. At the same time, however, innovation *can* be expedited through knowledge of the market, including patient needs and competitor's activities, as well as efficient resource allocation. Thus, it is important to balance the role of R&D and marketing in the drug discovery process.

1. Market Potential for New Compounds

In many pharmaceutical companies, pharmacologists, toxicologists, and chemists involved in drug discovery request the assistance of marketing for several tasks. Often, scientists are interested in the size of the patient population that might benefit from a compound with particular activities. For example, on the basis of animal studies, a scientist might hypothesize that a new family of compounds has activity related to dopamine receptors in the brain, and might benefit patients with Parkinson's disease. Before continuing research, the scientist is likely to contact marketing—usually informally—for an estimate of the number of patients with Parkinson's disease, the number and character of current competitors in this therapeutic area, and the compound's "fit" with the company's existing products. In an equally informal way, marketing is likely to respond with the desired information and a recommendation regarding the commercial value of such a compound. After obtaining this information, scientists can assess the emphasis, time, and resources that are needed for evaluation of the compounds.

2. *Minimum and Ideal Product Profiles*

Pharmacologists value minimum and ideal product profiles for new compounds early in drug discovery and development (i.e., before an IND application has been submitted to the FDA). The minimum product profile provides a list of characteristics that a compound must exhibit for development to continue. For example, most new products must not be teratogenic, should have no severe (life-threatening) adverse effects, and should be as efficacious as competing marketed products. The minimum product profile either explicitly or implicitly implies benchmarks or "go–no go" decision points. If a compound does not exhibit particular attributes during preclinical testing, Phase 1 testing, and so on, research in the particular therapeutic area is discontinued. Many times, a compound or family of compounds will have several minimum profiles, depending on the number of potential uses of the compound.

The ideal product profile lists attributes that a compound should ideally demonstrate (i.e., relatively high efficacy level, low dosing frequency, high safety level, improvement in patients' quality of life) [5]. The list of ideal product characteristics will differ among compounds on the basis of their chemical activity, the diseases for which they are likely to have value, and the nature of the markets for the therapeutic category.

The product profiles are dynamic sets of criteria that should be updated periodically on the basis of both preclinical and clinical research outcomes and market knowledge. As such, it is relatively easy to see that marketing becomes important in the development and updating of the minimum and ideal product profiles. For example, disease characteristics, competition, market potential, and patient needs can be determined using secondary data sources, such as prescription audit data, and primary market research, including interviews and surveys of thought leaders, health care professionals, and patients. This information is highly relevant as the product is developed and optimized for the marketplace.

3. Project Termination Decisions

In the early stages of drug discovery and development, the minimum product profile is not formalized to the extent that it is in later stages of product development. However, the development of a set of explicit criteria that preclinical researchers can use to determine whether to continue or terminate research in a particular therapeutic area is valuable to scientists, marketers, and, ultimately, the company. One reason is the need for organized decision making regarding research project termination.

Project termination is a key concern for many multinational pharmaceutical companies. In many companies, R&D can be hesitant to request project termination, making marketing input and justification extremely valuable. Consequently, well-defined decision points should be developed as early as possible and internationally to conserve resources and encourage true innovation.

While many pharmacologists and preclinical researchers prefer rather unstructured responsibilities, there is a desire for fewer, better-defined, potentially successful projects. The continuation of several projects with questionable value can be both frustrating and wasteful. Without a formal mechanism by which to eliminate unproductive activities, scientists can feel as if they are "spinning their wheels" rather than contributing meaningfully to the success of the company. To answer this need, one pharmaceutical firm has designated each member of senior management as a champion for a high-priority project. As a result, decisions are expedited and resource barriers are overcome, resulting in demonstrable time compression in product development and marketing [6].

Much has been made over the years about the number of so-called "me-too" prescription drug products. The fact is that there would certainly be many more if the decision to continue a drug in development was made on the basis of whether it is safe and effective. The "marketability" of a drug is also a key consideration in whether to proceed at various decision points in the development process. Market failures are expensive and are ultimately costly to the patient and the health care system.

4. Increased Research Involvement in Product Crafting

Like many "inventors," preclinical researchers, chemists, and pharmacologists invest much time, effort, and emotion in the discovery and development of a new compound. As such, they have a desire to follow through with their discoveries. Marketing involvement in drug development can help scientists in this regard. For example, many researchers express interest in conducting studies to answer questions regarding additional product indications. Currently, such studies are deemed valuable only prior to IND submission. However, such studies can add value to a marketed product later in its life and represent opportunities for the researcher and the company to advance knowledge in the therapeutic area.

Another way for researchers to maintain longer-term involvement with new compounds is by identifying structure-activity relationships, optimal dosage forms, kinetic parameters, dosing intervals, and the effects of food on the compound's bioavailability. Medical and marketing departments require this information as early as possible throughout the compound's travel along the development pipeline to facilitate the crafting of a product that will meet the market's needs.

The bottom line throughout marketing and R&D interactions in both drug discovery and development activities is *internal agreement*. It is imperative that marketing and R&D agree on what accomplishments are preferred for each compound, and then work toward those goals. As mentioned earlier, the process is a dynamic one that requires open communication and a mutual respect for each other's contributions.

D. Marketing and Drug Development

The goal of marketing and R&D interaction is to build competitive advantages and innovation into new pharmaceutical products as early as possible. While "me-too" products are valuable to patients and payers in many ways, there is a need on the part of pharmaceutical companies to discover blockbuster products. It is these products that translate into long-term profits and company longevity.

1. Building Innovation into New Products

To facilitate the development of unique pharmaceuticals with maximum commercial value, some companies have formalized a concept revolving around what is called a "proposal of innovation." This proposal is prepared jointly by medical and marketing for each new product after its Phase 1 trials have been completed. The proposal's purpose is to document the new compound's value and differentiating characteristics, and to elucidate points during development when researchers must clearly demonstrate that the desired characteristics do indeed exist. If the product exhibits the desired attributes, increased financial commitment is provided. If not, the project is terminated, and other alternatives are considered (i.e., licensing, test for different indication, etc.).

The ultimate value of the proposal of innovation is to force all members of the project team to consider the product objectively and document its perceived value early in the development process. If the project team cannot document how the new product can improve therapy compared with existing agents, the project is terminated and resource waste is minimized. Ultimately, following the "survival of the fittest" theory, only the best products are moved forward.

2. Clinical Development Plans

After it has been determined that a new product warrants continued testing (i.e., when Phase 2 and Phase 3 are completed), medical and marketing develop a detailed clinical development plan. The purpose of this document is to outline the specific activities that will be undertaken as the product is developed. Marketing plays a valuable role in the design of clinical trials, especially comparative trials in Phase 3. Using the guidelines provided in the proposal of innovation, marketing determines which products and in which patient types a new product should be tested. The characteristics that are theorized to differentiate the new product must be clearly demonstrated through clinical trials so that related claims can appear in the product's labeling and advertising.

According to Jim Ueberroth, director of operations at Boehringer, in a 1991 interview, drug development must ultimately focus on the market needs of various nations, practitioners, and patients. The direction provided by marketing is crucial to designing trials that will position a drug with the right indications, formulation, delivery system, and price [7]. More companies are learning (many times by making mistakes) that proactive identification and acquisition of particular indications and claims is extremely valuable in optimizing a product's performance. The history of digoxin (Lanoxin, Burroughs Wellcome Co.) effectively illustrates the value of proactive clinical trial conduct and publication. One of the most commonly used agents in the first-line treatment of congestive heart failure, digoxin is derived from a plant, commonly known as foxglove, that has been known for centuries to possess medicinal properties. At least 6 years prior to the manufacturer's introduction of Lanoxin, comparative long-term product efficacy studies had been requested. For budgetary and other reasons (i.e., the product had no specific competition with which to contend), it was deemed that such trials were unnecessary. Although it has been an extremely successful product, one wonders what Lanoxin's market potential could have been if the Randomized Assessment of the Effect of Digoxin on Inhibitors of the Angiotensin Converting Enzyme (RADIANCE) study, which was published in July 1993, had appeared earlier in the product's life. (This study demonstrated the value of digoxin by showing that its discontinuation in patients with chronic stable heart failure who are using ACE inhibitors carries substantial disease risk [8].) Additional indications for digoxin might have multiplied its annual sales if medical and marketing had established all of the product's potential uses earlier in its life cycle.

Another product that served as a lesson for Burroughs Wellcome Co. was acyclovir (Zovirax). Acyclovir was developed and introduced in the early 1980s as an ophthalmic ointment for herpes eye infections. Later, topical and oral formulations were developed for cold sores and genital herpes, respectively. Subsequent indications were researched and added in a linear fashion. Today, for a compound like acyclovir, the company would review all potential indications and choose the largest in terms of size and market value. Other indications would be added soon after product launch. Throughout this synchronized process, Phase 2 and 3 trial designs would include marketing considerations that were identified using comprehensive marketing research and competitor evaluation. Thus, desired efficacy, safety, and other marketing claims could be documented and disseminated to the marketplace.

When considering the value of additional indications and clinical trials as a compound's patent life shortens, it is necessary to consider the potential risks and benefits. The expenses associated with the conduct, reporting, and publication of trial data, as well as the marketing costs associated with educating the marketplace about a product's new application, grow as time passes. Thus, while somewhat more risky, testing a new compound for use in various indications early in its development can translate to cost-effectiveness of research activities: larger market applicability and enhanced market performance soon after launch rather than years later. Such improvements in product performance are even more valuable in light of today's short product patent lives and the ability of generic products to erode market share quickly after loss of brand-name patent protection.

3. *Crafting Product Attributes*

In addition to facilitating the design of effective and valuable clinical trials, marketing is involved in dosing regimen, dosage form, and packaging decisions, as well as the identification of the product's brand and generic names. In many cases, a new product's dosing regimen and forms are predetermined. Depending on the compound's characteristics and the diseases for which it has value, researchers might be able to produce a limited number of dosage forms. For example, an oral medication is not feasible for the acute treatment of heart attacks. For a compound with low solubility, a liquid formulation might not be possible. Thus, preclinical and Phase 1 studies provide a basis for marketing's regimen and dosage form requests.

In situations in which several dosage forms and administration regimen options are feasible, it is the responsibility of marketing to determine which options will be most successful in the marketplace. The availability of more than one strength of a medication, for example, can indicate "dosing flexibility" to physicians. Additionally, several dosage forms can enhance both acceptability and patient compliance, which can translate into increased efficacy and a higher likelihood of patient/ prescriber satisfaction and repeat use. However, if research demonstrates that a new product's dosage regimen alternatives are either twice a day or three times a day, and the therapeutic product market is dominated by once-daily products, the new product should probably be discontinued. Clearly, the expertise of marketing research is valuable in making these decisions.

4. *Refining Product Profiles*

As described earlier, minimum and ideal product profiles are used to define product characteristics as early as possible and identify decision points for project continuation or termination. As a compound moves through Phase 2 and Phase 3 clinical testing, marketing input is valuable in refining the product profile so that it describes the *target* product characteristics. While the minimum and ideal product profiles are somewhat speculative, a new product's target profile is determined on the basis of chemistry, toxicology, and other preclinical data, as well as knowledge garnered through clinical trials and marketing research.

5. *Evaluating a Product's Commercial Value*

Sales forecasting is one of the most difficult and least scientific aspects of drug development activities. By comparing the clinical characteristics of the new product with those of existing competitors, the new product marketing department can estimate the adoption rate of the new product. Other information, such as market size, prescriber characteristics, reimbursement policies, and company financial needs, are then considered to estimate a price and calculate sales forecasts. Some companies have developed or use marketing research agency's computer software to facilitate this process. Sales forecasts are often refined throughout the product's development and pre-launch to provide the most accurate estimate of performance and product success.

E. Marketing and Pre-Launch

If all marketing activities associated with new product development are conducted effectively, pre-launch marketing activities are well defined. Because promotional messages and target markets have already been identified, the primary goal during pre-launch is to increase health care professionals' and the FDA's awareness of the new product with the ultimate objective of positively influencing the product's performance after marketing. This goal is accomplished through presentation of clinical information at scientific meetings, using posters and other exhibits, and the publication of articles in scientific journals.

The value of pre-launch activities is substantial. With the presentation of sound medical data, a product's manufacturer develops a reputation as an innovative company that provides "good science." This image can generate interest in the product among clinical investigators and medical opinion leaders. These individuals, who are highly influential among their peers, become external product champions and, later, can influence the rate at which a new product is adopted by physicians and other health care professionals. Obviously, the quality and utility of scientific information provided at meetings and through publications must be high enough to convincingly demonstrate meaningful differences between the new product and older products (e.g., patient convenience, cost-effectiveness) [9]. Clinical trial design becomes critical in this regard, because the trial results must meet not only FDA requirements, but the market's need for meaningful information.

In the later phases of pre-launch marketing activities, determining market size, the product's sales forecast, competitive activities, relevant disease issues, and the education level of both prescribers and patients is important. Marketing research is often conducted to refine target audience messages that generate awareness of the differentiating characteristics of the new product. Pricing options for the new product are also tested during this time. Finally, companies will send press releases for inclusion in newspapers and broadcasts, as well as advertise in health care professional journals using reminder messages ("coming soon" advertisements). All of these activities are designed to allow a smooth and successful launch once FDA marketing approval has been granted.

F. Marketing and Launch

Prior to the launch of a new product, the goals of R&D and marketing are to (a) develop an effective launch plan, (b) ensure realistic expectations on the part of the company, including the product managers to whom the new product is delivered, and (c) reduce uncertainty about the particular market and the product's performance. Both groups are involved in these activities because of the valuable information that each can convey to the company's business directors and administrators. For example, medical and R&D personnel are most knowledgeable regarding the product's clinical benefits and the nature of the competition. At the same time, marketing personnel can provide a more complete picture of the political, social, economic, and health care issues that affect product use decisions, as well as the attitudes of decision makers regarding the new product.

Primary marketing activities also include development and assessment of launch campaigns, detailing messages, direct mail activities, symposia and publication strategies, and other promotional tactics that target health care professionals, managed care and hospital administrators, and other decision makers. Evaluation of marketing activities is conducted by the marketing research department in cooperation with product management. Continuous research, reevaluation of marketing plan, and shifts in strategy on the basis of market response occur in response to changing market and company needs.

Continued research and development is valuable during the post-launch phase of the product's life. Evaluating and testing new indications for the product can take advantage of patient needs, as well as the product's patent status. Table 4 provides a list of selected prescription medications that have profited from the addition of new indications in 1992.

Table 4 New Indications for Marketed Pharmaceuticals, 1992

Pharmaceutical product	New indication
Cardizem CD	Angina
Cefizox	Pelvic inflammatory disease
Ceftin	Gonorrhea
Estrace	Osteoporosis prophylaxis
Intron A	Hepatitis B
Narcan	Hypotension
Synarel	Precocious puberty
Zantac	Erosive esophagitis
Zovirax	Chicken pox

Source: Adapted from *Med. Ad. News*, February 1993:57.

Product line extensions (i.e., extended-release products, various dosage forms) or switching the product from prescription status to over-the-counter are long-term strategies that are considered after the product's performance has been determined. It is during this period that one sees developments such as:

Lower-dose products for use by elderly patients or children
Long-acting delivery systems to reduce dose frequency
Improved flavors, tablet sizes, etc.
Convenient packages
Further definition and quantification of adverse reactions

VI. CONCLUSION

Clearly, the interaction between marketing and R&D is complex and dynamic. Changing corporate and departmental needs throughout the drug development process influence the nature and frequency of marketing and R&D communications. Table 5 provides a summary of marketing's role in the drug development process.

The relationship of the two divisions is synergistic—high quality and continuous communication results in a more efficient and profitable pharmaceutical development process. This alliance will only grow in importance as the United States health care system undergoes alteration. It is highly probable

Table 5 Summary of Marketing Involvement in New Product Development

- Determine ideal therapeutic areas for concentration by researchers.
- Determine unmet needs of patients, prescribers, and payers, including therapeutic, social, economic, and emotional needs.
- Determine which of several new products should be developed further or terminated (portfolio evaluation).
- Identify the characteristics of the market for a particular new product (i.e., size, distribution, drug use patterns, competition, promotion needs and responsiveness).
- Identify characteristics of the new product that can be best used to market the product to decision makers.
- Select a selling price that is appropriate for a new drug in a particular market.
- Identify opportunities for product extensions, such as new indications and dosage forms

that the pharmaceutical industry will continue to be asked to streamline drug development activities, while still maintaining sufficient profitability to ensure future advances in pharmaceutical discovery.

For those researchers and marketers in traditional pharmaceutical firms, the growing need for interaction might initially generate tension. However, for those companies that have embraced the idea of a marketing/R&D partnership, the rewards are clear: faster speed to the international market; improved patient satisfaction and health; and revenue to continue the drug discovery, development, and marketing cycle.

REFERENCES

1. American Marketing Association, Official Statement, 1985.
2. E. J. McCarthy and W. D. Perrault, *Basic Marketing*, 8th ed., Irwin, Homewood, IL, 1984.
3. J. A. W. Ansell, Across the great divide: R&D and marketing cooperation, *Pharm. Exec.* December *12*:30,33–35 (1987).
4. E. M. Kolassa, Reductions in pharmaceutical price growth: an assessment of list price changes in the U.S. pharmaceutical market, 1989 to 1992, Research Institute of Pharmaceutical Sciences, The University of Mississippi, February 1993.
5. B. W. Spilker, *Multinational Drug Companies: Issues in Drug Discovery and Development*, Raven Press, New York, 1989, p. 436.
6. E. Rule, Squeeze time for speedier drug approvals, *Pharm. Exec. 7*:72–76 (1993).
7. W. Koberstein, Executive profile: Jim Ueberroth, *Pharm. Exec. 2*:26–30, 32, 34, 36, 40 (1991).
8. M. Packer, M. Gheorghiade, J. B. Young, et al., Withdrawal of digoxin from patients with chronic heart failure treated with angiotensin-converting-enzyme inhibitors, *N. Engl. J. Med. 329(1)*:1–7 (1993).
9. D. K. Crossen, Where selling meets research, *Pharm. Exec. 1*:59–60 (1987).

13

Ethics in Clinical Drug Research

Robert L. McCarthy

Massachusetts College of Pharmacy and Allied Health Sciences
Boston, Massachusetts

I. INTRODUCTION

The use of clinical trials to test new drugs is considered the standard scientific approach for determining whether or not new chemical entities can safely and effectively treat medical conditions and diseases. Evaluations of drugs that do not include testing in humans are unable to gain approval for marketing by the Food and Drug Administration (FDA) in the United States. Hundreds of drugs are tested on thousands of volunteers every year. The breadth of this research requires us to consider our ethical and moral responsibility to those individuals who agree to participate in such programs.

Clinical drug research is not without its risks. Toxicities may develop, diseases or medical conditions may not be effectively treated, and healthy subjects may be exposed to risks they would not have otherwise encountered. How then can we rationalize our use of human subjects in drug research? As Mappes and Zembaty [1] note, two common justifications are used for clinical drug research: "1. Human experimentation enhances the discovery of new diagnostic and therapeutic techniques; and 2. Controlled experimentation is necessary for sound medical practice. Possible iatrogenic illnesses will be prevented only if clinical research provides necessary knowledge about human reactions to specific therapies." Despite these justifications, however, ethical questions remain.

This chapter will, through the use of ethical principles and moral rules, attempt to provide an ethical framework for clinical drug studies. Further, it will explore several important ethical questions relating to research in special populations (e.g., children, women) and healthy volunteers, and the parameters for abandoning clinical drug trials. Also discussed will be ethical dilemmas surrounding the use of placebos and the nature of drug trial funding.

Unlike most areas in medicine, ethical analyses do not always provide clear answers to questions raised. Nor does such examination ensure that the decisions arrived at will produce moral action. What ethical evaluation does do, however, is provide some rigor to responding ethically to moral questions. It is this framework for analysis that is found throughout clinical medicine, but that is all too often missing when ethical dilemmas present themselves.

II. ETHICAL PRINCIPLES

A. Autonomy

Autonomy states that an individual's liberty of choice, action, and thought is not to be interfered with. As Beauchamp and Childress have noted, "Autonomy has . . . been used to refer to a set of diverse notions including self-governance, liberty rights, privacy, individual choice, liberty to follow one's will, causing one's own behavior, and being one's own person" [2]. In medicine, we think of autonomy as the right of individuals to make decisions about what will happen to their bodies (e.g., whether or not to have surgery), what choice will be made among competing options (e.g., surgery vs. medical management) and what they choose to take, or not take, into their bodies (e.g., compliance vs. noncompliance with prescribed medications). We also allude to questions of autonomy when we refer to choice among health care providers (e.g., physicians, hospitals, pharmacies) and the choice to refuse medical treatment (e.g., right to die, physician-assisted suicide).

Autonomy also has important application to the area of clinical research. Whether or not a patient chooses to participate in a clinical research trial is a decision that a patient, as an autonomous individual, has a right to make freely, without coercion either overt or subtle. Any attempt to subvert this principle would be considered unethical unless there is ethically justifiable reasons for doing so. There are two generally accepted, ethically justifiable exceptions to the principle of autonomy. The first of these is referred to as the "harm principle." Under this exception, one is justified in overriding another's autonomy if in the exercise of that autonomy, harm may come to others. The second exception is that of "weak paternalism." Weak paternalism allows an individual's autonomy to be violated if that individual is not or does not appear to be autonomous. Of these two exceptions, weak paternalism may have the greatest applicability to clinical research. It might allow, for example, parents or legal guardians to make decisions for children about their children's participation in a clinical drug trial.

The principle of autonomy is also a vital component of informed consent. When one provides informed consent to an individual contemplating participation in a clinical research trial, one respects that individual's right to make an autonomous decision. Informed consent and its elements will be discussed in more detail later in the chapter.

B. Beneficence/Nonmaleficence

Beneficence and nonmaleficence are ethical principles which, in a sense, are complementary to one another. To act in a beneficent manner indicates that one will act to "do good" for another. Nonmaleficence refers to "avoiding harm" or "taking due care." Beauchamp and Childress [2] compare these related principles by noting, "The word nonmaleficence is sometimes used more broadly to include the prevention of harm and the removal of harmful conditions. However, because prevention and removal require positive acts to assist others, we include them under beneficence along with the provision of benefit. Nonmaleficence is restricted . . . to the noninfliction of harm."

These principles have direct application to clinical research. Nonmaleficence directs researchers to avoid harm to their clinical subjects. What is problematic about such a simple directive is, what is meant by "avoid harm"? Does this simply refer to ensuring that no "serious" harm, including death, occurs, or does it suggest that any harm, such as minor drug adverse reactions, is to be eliminated?

A similar lack of clarity exists with reference to the principle of beneficence. To what extent does the obligation of the researcher to "do good" extend? Is he or she simply doing good by attempting to determine the safety and efficacy of a new therapeutic agent, or must he or she show direct benefit to the individual subject-patient? Beneficence is also an important consideration in the use of placebos. Placebos have no direct benefit to a subject in a clinical trial (unless the placebo is being used for its psychological effect); therefore, is their use unethical? An even more difficult question is the use of placebos in early clinical trials involving healthy volunteers. In these instances, there is no direct benefit to the patient even if the drug being tested demonstrates therapeutic efficacy. An argument can be made that although placebos may not have a direct benefit for a given subject-patient, their use in clinical trials may result in benefit to the population affected by a given disease or condition. These questions will be explored further later in this chapter.

C. Fidelity

The rule of fidelity is the obligation to be "loyal" or to "keep promises made." We often refer to fidelity in health care with respect to the obligation of health care providers to care loyally for their patients. In clinical research, fidelity has implications in terms of the responsibility of investigators to their patient-subjects. This responsibility includes allowing the study participant to decide whether or not to enter a clinical trial and whether or not to withdraw (autonomy), providing full disclosure of pertinent information about the research (informed consent), and ensuring as many safeguards in the research as possible to protect the patient.

As Beauchamp and Childress suggest, a conflict of fidelity often exists between the obligations of the physician as the clinician and the physician as the researcher. They contend, "The dual role of research scientist and clinical practitioner may conflict and present a range of problems. . . . As an investigator, the physician acts to generate scientific knowledge that ultimately benefits individual patients. As a clinical practitioner, he or she may have specific contracts and responsibilities for care and in general must act in the patient's best interests" [2].

D. Informed Consent

Informed consent is an essential component of all clinical research. It instructs that patients must be fully "informed" about their potential participation in a clinical trial and must follow this disclosure with their autonomous consent. Informed consent is always obtained in clinical research, for both legal and ethical reasons, formally in an informed consent form. These documents are usually drafted by the investigator or pharmaceutical manufacturer and subsequently approved by the Institutional Review Board (IRB) where the research will take place. The role of the IRB will be discussed in the next section. Informed consent is composed of five elements: disclosure, understanding, voluntariness, competence, and consent.

Disclosure requires that all the pertinent information necessary for an informed decision be made available to the patient-subject. What constitutes "pertinent" information and how much information is adequate is a point of contention. Several standards of disclosure have been suggested, both legally and ethically. The professional practice standard states that a patient-subject should receive all the information that a "reasonably prudent" professional would disclose; that is, a researcher should disclose what the "average" researcher in similar circumstances would disclose. The reasonable person standard states that a researcher should disclose to a patient-subject what a "reasonable person" or "average person" would need to know in order to make an informed decision. Both the professional practice standard and reasonable person standard have inherent problems. What constitutes the disclosure provided by a "reasonably prudent" researcher? What does an "average person" need to know in order to make an informed decision? In response to these problems, a third standard of disclosure has been suggested. The subjective standard directs that a researcher should disclose to a patient-subject what that "individual patient" needs to know in order to make an informed decision. This standard seems to deal with the problems of "average" disclosure presented by the first two standards. Unfortunately, it also presents a new problem. A researcher is required to determine what an individual patient-subject needs to know in order to make an informed decision. If the patient-subject is not well known to the researcher, as is usually the case, biased perceptions by the investigator of what an individual patient-subject may need to know can result in inappropriate disclosure. It should be apparent from this brief discussion of disclosure that determining what should make up the information provided to a patient either informally or formally in an informed consent form is a difficult task.

The second element of informed consent is understanding. Understanding can often be a barrier in obtaining a patient-subject's informed consent. Language problems is one of the most frequently cited factors in causing this barrier to occur. Such difficulties can take several forms. The most obvious of these is the barriers which result from trying to transmit information to a patient-subject who is non-English speaking. This barrier may be overcome in a number of ways. Information can be transmitted either verbally or in writing in the patient-subject's native language. A family member, friend, or professional translator may be used to interpret the information. A second, and perhaps less apparent, barrier to understanding may occur when medical terminology or complex language is used either verbally or in an informed consent form. It is the ethical responsibility of both the researcher and the IRB to ensure that this type of language barrier does not occur. Information given to study participants must be in simple, easy-to-understand lay language, not always an uncomplicated task when dealing with complex medical procedures, disease states and therapeutic entities.

The third element of informed consent is voluntariness. Study participants must choose to enroll in a research endeavor free from coercion. Such coercion includes not only that which is overt, but also any subtle pressure that may be applied to sway an individual toward study participation. Subtle coercion of this type occurs more frequently than one might expect. For example, a physician-researcher may present several therapeutic measures that might be chosen to treat a medical malady. One of these alternatives could be participation in a clinical trial examining the therapeutic effectiveness of a new drug. An ethical question could be posed as to whether or not the physician has utilized the physician-patient relationship to subtly coerce the patient-subject to choose the study drug alternative. Another type of coercion, somewhat less subtle, is the practice of financially remunerating research study participants. This question will be explored later in this chapter.

The fourth element of informed consent is competence. This component of informed consent requires that patient-subjects functionally have the ability to make decisions for themselves. Obvious examples of individuals whose competence is in question include children, the mentally ill, and individuals suffering from neurological conditions such as Alzheimer's disease. Questions of competency that are especially difficult to answer are those that lie at the fringes. At what age is an individual competent? Does the legal age for competency parallel the moral age? At what point in their illness (mental, neurological) do individuals lose their ability to make independent choices? The question of determining competence is further complicated by the fact that an individual who may be deemed incompetent at a given point in time may not always be designated as such. For example, an individual who has undergone an emotional trauma (e.g., the loss of a loved one) may not be able to make competent decisions for a given period, but this does not mean that she will be perpetually unable to do so. Likewise, an individual who is deemed to be mentally incompetent at one point in his life may not always fit that characterization.

The fifth element of informed consent can be achieved only after the previous four have been met. Consent is the final legal and moral criterion that must be met in order to ensure that informed consent has been obtained. It provides the patient-subject with a point of decision with regard to his or her potential participation in a clinical research study. This consent is always designated with the patient-subject's signature on an informed consent form. For legal purposes, and for those who are illiterate and affix an "X" to the document, this written consent is verified with the signature of one or more witnesses.

It should be apparent at this point that obtaining true informed consent is not a simple process. It requires diligence and genuine commitment to acting ethically by all those involved in the clinical research project. However, the ultimate ethical responsibility for ensuring informed consent lies with the IRB that is overseeing the study.

E. Distributive Justice

Distributive justice refers to how the benefits and burdens of society are distributed among its members. It concerns itself with questions of fairness and equality. Distributive justice has important applicability in clinical research because it instructs us to pause and examine the construct of such investigations as to their treatment of study participants. For example, as discussed earlier in this chapter, the use of placebos in clinical research has become an integral part of what we consider to be sound scientific inquiry. However, the use of placebos also brings into question the issue of distributive justice. Are investigators who employ placebos acting ethically toward the patient-subjects who will receive them, even if such individuals are informed of the likelihood of their receiving such entities? An even more far-reaching question may be whether the accepted framework for clinical research ensures fairness and equality to all. Are some (e.g., poor college students, the indigent, the mentally ill, prisoners) being "sacrificed" to advance medical knowledge in order to benefit society at large?

III. ETHICAL CODES

Ethical principles and rules that apply to medical practice and research, such as autonomy, beneficence, and justice, have long served as the basis for a system or code of ethical conduct. Western medical ethics is primarily based on the Hippocratic code established by the Greek philosopher Hippocrates in the fifth century B.C. Medicine (American Medical Association) and Pharmacy (Philadelphia College of Pharmacy) developed codes of conduct for their respective practitioners in 1848. As Montagne [3] notes, "The guiding principles of these codes were a respect for human life and service to humanity."

The Holocaust during the Second World War, and the subsequent Nuremberg trials, prompted the first major development of a code dealing specifically with experimentation on human subjects. The Code of Nuremberg identified three primary ethical obligations on the part of clinical researchers: "obligations to the individual subject involved in the research experiment must be placed above obligations to the state (governments); the distinction between therapeutic and non-therapeutic research is taken to have moral implications; and informed consent from the subject is morally essential" [3]. These guidelines, based on ethical principles, remain the cornerstone of contemporary research ethics. By placing the obligations to the individual above those to the state, the patient-subject's autonomy is respected. Likewise, the clear distinction between therapeutic and nontherapeutic interventions invokes the complementary principles of beneficence and nonmaleficence. Perhaps most important is the vital role assigned to informed consent in the clinical research process.

Subsequent to Nuremberg, several other codes of medical ethics were established. In 1949, the World Medical Association drafted the Geneva Convention Code of Medical Ethics, a contemporary version of the Hippocratic oath. In the 1960s, the same organization established an ethical code on clinical research. In 1964, and revised in 1975, the Declaration of Helsinki was adopted based on the Nuremberg principles [3]. The Helsinki Code deals with several issues that the Nuremberg Code does not: "1. The Helsinki Code distinguishes between clinical (therapeutic) and nonclinical (nontherapeutic) biomedical research and sets forth specific criteria of ethical acceptability for each, as well as other basic principles common to both. 2. The Nuremberg Code is silent regarding the informed consent requirement in the case of the legally incompetent. The Helsinki Code addresses itself to such cases, asserting the ethical acceptability of what is sometimes called 'proxy consent' " [1]. In 1977, the Declaration of Hawaii provided ethical guidelines for clinical research in psychiatry [3].

In the United States, several ethical guidelines governing the use of human subjects in research have been codified into law or regulation. In 1966, the Office of the U.S. Surgeon General directed that research that was funded by the federal government must be subject to "committee review," a reference to the concept of an IRB. Likewise, in 1974, the then U.S. Department of Health, Education and Welfare required that departmental-funded projects be reviewed by a "local committee," and "that those committees have the expertise to review the legal and community relations aspect as well as the scientific and medical aspects of research" [4]. Effective July, 1981, FDA and the U.S. Department of Health and Human Services regulations required, among other things, "Institutional Review Board (IRB) Review for most federally funded research, specifying composition and procedures for IRBs [and] directions about the elements of informed consent which must be provided to any research subject . . ." [4].

Taken together, these codes provided practitioner-researchers in the United States and across the world with principles to guide clinical investigations involving human subjects. However, ethical principles and codes cannot hope to provide practitioner-researchers with answers to every moral question that may arise in the course of their investigation. Ethical questions in medicine, whether in clinical research or clinical medicine, involve decision-making that is usually situation-specific. The purpose of such principles and codes is not to provide practitioner-researchers with right and wrong answers, but to offer them a framework to use when faced with ethical questions. As Montagne [3] points out, "The formulation of an oath or ethical code does not remove the moral choices and the need to carefully consider each individual situation and the alternative actions or decisions that can be made."

IV. THE INSTITUTIONAL REVIEW BOARD (IRB)

The Institutional Review Board (IRB) is that body responsible for overseeing all clinical research that is conducted within a given institution. Traditionally, most clinical drug research was conducted in hospital settings; however, with the shift in the locus of health care delivery from the in-patient to the ambulatory setting, IRBs are now found in managed care organizations and other ambulatory facilities.

The IRB has two primary responsibilities. The first is to ensure the integrity and scientific rigor of the proposed research study. The risk versus benefit to study participants is evaluated. Should risks outweigh benefits, the IRB would likely reject such research. The board acts as somewhat of a "subject advocate" to ensure that the patient-subject's rights and welfare are protected [5]. The IRBs second major responsibility is to evaluate and approve informed consent forms used in conjunction with the research. Such forms should be drafted consistent with the elements of informed consent discussed previously. IRBs vary in their size and representation. Their membership may include physicians, nurses, other allied health professionals (including pharmacists), institutional administrators, attorneys, clergy, medical ethicists, and community members.

The FDA regulations that outline the responsibilities of IRBs are consistent with the ethical obligations of such bodies. They include minimizing risks to subjects, a reasonable benefit-to-risk ratio, the equitable selection of subjects, the necessity of obtaining informed consent from each subject, the documentation that informed consent was obtained, the existence of adequate subject monitoring, and respecting subject confidentiality [6].

V. ETHICAL RESEARCH QUESTIONS

A. The Nature of Drug Trial Funding

An important ethical consideration for clinical investigators to consider is the source of funding for their research. Several ethical questions relating to funding arise. First, is it ethical for a pharmaceutical company to recruit practitioner-researchers to conduct clinical drug trials? Second, is it ethically acceptable for such practitioner-researchers to receive direct or indirect financial remuneration from the pharmaceutical manufacturer? Third, should patient-subjects be informed of the practitioner-researchers' financial or other "stake" in the project?

Because clinical drug research is conducted primarily at teaching institutions, the participation of practitioner-researchers, primarily physicians, is essential. However, the dual role of these individuals may be in conflict. Their responsibilities as practitioners require them to choose a mode of treatment that best meets the needs of their patients. Generally, this fidelity obligation means choosing a treatment that is a well-accepted, proven intervention. Such a commitment would, at times, appear to be in direct conflict with their responsibility to the research, which, by definition, is of an experimental nature. Logically, then, it would seem to be inherently unethical, or at least in conflict with their Hippocratic obligations, for such practitioner-researchers to engage in clinical research. Such a characterization would be, however, an oversimplification. Clinical drug research, by definition, involves the testing of new therapeutic entities in humans. Pharmaceutical manufacturers must rely on academic centers, which have a dual mission of patient care and research, to conduct such investigations. Without the involvement of these teaching institutions, clinical research would be virtually impossible. Medical practice could not be assured that new drugs or new uses for existing drugs were therapeutically beneficial. The fact that the partnership between the pharmaceutical industry and teaching centers is essential for conducting clinical research does not, however, absolve practitioner-researchers of their obligation to their patients. It is the role of the institution's IRB to ensure that practitioner-researchers are meeting their responsibility to patient-subjects. Patient-subjects, through the use of study design, must be protected from excessive harm (nonmaleficence). Further, through the use of informed consent forms, patients must be informed of all facets of their participation in the study, and have full autonomy to choose either not to participate or to withdraw from participation at any time without prejudice to future care.

The second question raised above involves the financial benefit, indirectly or directly, a practitioner-researcher may gain from a clinical study. As Finkel [7] notes, "In recent years there has been increasing concern that the large grant payments being awarded to clinical investigators by pharmaceutical companies to conduct trials of new drugs may further increase the persuasiveness of investigators in their recruiting efforts among patients." This poses the risk that patients may be hastily enrolled and their disease state may not be fully evaluated in terms of the experimental treatment. The patients' best interest may not be served by their enrollment in a study and "the patient might be better served by conventional treatment or no treatment at all" [8]. This is especially true of "per capita" grants, which provide funding to practitioner-researchers based on the number of patients enrolled in a study [9]. In these instances, investigators risk violating their obligation to patients to act in a beneficent manner—that is, in such a way as to do good or benefit their patient.

Shimm and Spece [8] have proposed that the source of funding of the trial, the amount, and how the researcher is being reimbursed be disclosed to patient-subjects. Further, Finkel [7] has suggested that this information should also be given to IRBs, who may decide that grants offered to the practitioner-researcher are excessive. Such safeguards, Shimm and Spece [8] suggest, may decrease the chance of "this money [posing] a temptation for the clinical investigator to enter a patient into an experimental study for a condition for which another treatment is known to be effective or even surmissed to be superior."

The financial involvement of practitioner-researchers in a clinical research project may, in some circumstances, be further complicated by their direct financial interest in a pharmaceutical manufacturer. As Healy and colleagues [9] point out, a conflict of interest may result when "researchers hold stock in or serve as paid consultants to a company whose products they are investigating." Even though trials are conducted as randomized and double-blinded, researchers are ultimately responsible for interpretations and final analysis of data [9]. The potential for conflict is obvious. Researchers might be tempted to draw conclusions that are of a positive nature by misinterpreting or misrepresenting data so that a new drug gets a favorable report.

Given the problems associated with such financial arrangements, it would seem to be necessary, as a component of the informed consent process, to ensure that patients are informed about the grant support for the project they are considering participation in. Somewhat surprisingly, however, Finkel [7] found that "providing information on the financial aspects of a trial is of little or no importance to patients." Rather, they seemed more concerned with the experimental treatment and whether or not they would benefit from it. Finkel [7] suggests that this lack of concern with finances may be due, in part, to patients' trust in their physician. This apparent apathy by patients does not lessen the ethical obligations of IRBs to ensure that patients are informed about such matters. IRBs have a responsibility to assess clinical trials for conflict-of-interest issues, and to approve or reject a trial based on unethical financial arrangements. Morally questionable grants, such as per capita payments, should, as the United Kingdom's Royal College of Physicians stated in their 1991 guidelines, be considered unacceptable [7].

B. The Use of Placebos

The use of placebos has long been an integral component of clinical drug research. Whether the drug being tested is a new drug compound or an existing drug under study for a new indication, placebos have served as a point of comparison for determining therapeutic efficacy. Although the use of placebos in some instances has been shown to provide therapeutic usefulness (e.g., pain control), placebos, by definition, are agents devoid of pharmacological activity. Patient-subjects who receive placebos as a component of their participation in a clinical drug study can generally not hope to derive any benefit (beneficence) from these substances. This raises the question of whether the use of placebos in drug research, despite the obvious scientific advantages, is ethical. This question is further complicated by the expectation that placebos will be employed in clinical research. An FDA regulator has stated that "it is desirable to include some placebo controlled studies unless it is considered unethical to do so" [10]. This suggests that the use of placebos is ethical in certain instances, but unethical in others.

Freedman [10] reports that the American College of Gastroenterology has established guidelines for its fellows on the ethical use of placebos in drug research. These guidelines recommend that it is appropriate to employ a placebo in (a) situations in which a standard therapy is for one reason or another unavailable, ineffective, inappropriate, or of unproven efficacy; (b) conditions in which the placebo is in and of itself relatively effective therapy; and (c) cases in which even the ongoing disease process has little if any adverse impact on the patient's overall health.

Although helpful, these guidelines are somewhat ambiguous. For example, consider the drug ondansetron (Zofran), which was tested for its efficacy in the treatment of nausea and vomiting associated with the administration of chemotherapy. In the clinical trials, ondansetron was compared with placebo because no "best" anti-emetic treatment for chemotherapy-induced nausea and vomiting had been defined. Despite the absence of a "best" treatment, several regimens had successfully been used. In fact, in the ondansetron trial, prochlorperazine was used as a rescue medication for patients who could not tolerate the chemotherapy-induced nausea and vomiting. However, because no treatment for this condition was "established," the use of a placebo was ethical under the American College of Gastroenterology guidelines [11]. Citron [11] cites the ondansetron study as evidence of why he believes that "eliminating a placebo arm will minimize the risk to patients in clinical trials." Freedman [10] adds his support to Citron's opposition to the use of placebos by noting that their use does not provide a comparison of new versus old treatment. Even if no treatment is considered to be the "best," some treatment or treatments are invariably employed to treat a given disease or condition. Unless a placebo is the current mode of therapy, its use precludes obtaining comparative evidence that a new drug is superior to current therapy. Unfortunately, if Citron and Freedman's advice is followed, the scientific validity and reliability of many clinical trials would come into question. A more realistic approach might be to evaluate each clinical drug trial independently against general parameters similar to those established by the American College of Gastroenterology. Investigators and IRBs must evaluate each project in terms of patient-subject benefit versus potential harm. This approach is valid for clinical trials in which the subjects are patient volunteers (Phase 2, etc.) as well as those that involve healthy volunteers (Phase 1).

C. Drug Testing in Healthy Volunteers

Phase 1 clinical drug trials, which evaluate clinical pharmacology and toxicology, utilize normal healthy volunteers. This component of the FDA drug approval process determines the drug's dosage range, route(s) of administration, absorption, target organ(s), and toxicity [12]. Because patients who participate in Phase 1 trials do not have the disease state or medical condition for which the drug is intended, they cannot hope to benefit medically (beneficence) even if the drug shows therapeutic promise. Consequently, ethical questions can be raised about whether such individuals should participate in drug research.

Because healthy volunteers will not derive any therapeutic benefit from the investigational drug being studied, why would they choose to participate? One reason might be their desire to contribute to "medical knowledge." Such a justification for participation would be laudable, and certainly some individuals do enroll in clinical studies for this reason. In reality, however, healthy volunteers are often recruited through advertisements that offer to financially reimburse individuals for their participation. This practice, whether used to enroll healthy volunteers or patients who actually have the disease state or medical condition (Phase 2, etc.), may violate one of the elements of informed consent, voluntariness, even in cases where formal informed consent has been obtained. The reason for this may lie in the types of individuals who respond to requests for healthy volunteers. They include college students, the indigent, and others who may be lured to participation purely out of financial need. The necessity to improve their financial situation may induce these individuals to participate in research and accept the accompanying risks when they might not otherwise choose to do so.

D. Drug Testing in Pediatrics

Children utilize more acute and chronic medications every year than perhaps any subgroup of the population other than the elderly. These drugs include both those that are available over-the-counter (OTC), as well as those that may be obtained only via a physician's prescription. A commonality shared by many drugs used therapeutically in pediatrics is the absence of clinical data about their proper use in children. As Dr. Paula Botstein, deputy director of FDA's Office of Drug Evaluation I noted in a 1991 interview, most drugs are approved for use in adults, but include a disclaimer that safety and effectiveness have not been established for use in children [13]. This information void requires physicians to rely on a combination of experience and pediatrics texts of questionable usefulness when determining drug dosing. Relying on adult-generated clinical data to determine pediatric dosing ignores the differences in absorption and metabolism between adults and children [13].

Many new therapeutic moieties that might be indicated to treat acute (e.g., infections) and chronic (e.g., seizure disorders) diseases in children must be tested in pediatrics. In response to this information void, the FDA has included a "pediatric page" in the review of new drug applications. This component of the NDA package focuses on "what is known about the drug from the perspective of pediatrics: whether it has been tested in children, what uses are promising and the like" [13].

From an ethical perspective, the first consideration that needs to be established is the level of risk children should be subjected to. Freedman and colleagues [14] pose the questions, "Is it ever ethical to expose children to risks associated with research? If it is, what are the ethical limits to such risk?" They respond by discussing the concept of "minimal risk." "Minimal risk is the concept used in American regulation to serve as an anchoring measurement of allowable risk in clinical research" [14]. Minimal risk is defined as "the risk of daily life or that encountered in routine physical or psychological exams" [14]. Presently, the "critical threshold for allowable research risk in children is not minimal risk itself, but rather a minor increment over minimal risk" [14]. This definition of minimal risk is somewhat lacking, however, because individuals in different situations live their lives differently and therefore encounter different risks. Therefore, as Freedman suggests, a more precise characterization of minimal risk "may refer to all the risks any person may encounter or to those that all of us encounter" [14].

Because of these difficulties in defining minimal risk, it may be necessary to establish what is meant by minimal risk with reference to a specific research project. Even if this is done, however, there will still remain different interpretations by researchers of what minimal risk is and what level of risk in a given project is ethically acceptable.

Another way of characterizing minimal risk is to think of it as a standard of comparison between new experiences and the experiences of everyday life [14]. Because the child involved in research will be placed in a new situation, one which is not encountered in everyday life, a researcher must compare the risk of the research to the risks of everyday life. "Almost by definition, exciting and important research ventures into the unknown. A prohibition of such research involvement would be to the long term detriment of children, just as a prohibition on new experiences is harmful to children over the long term" [14]. Ultimately, it falls upon the IRB to assess the "risk to knowledge ratio, [that the ratio] is reasonable and that the scientific importance of the undertaking [of any research protocol] is proportional to the risks subjects will be undergoing" [14]. The IRB must evaluate research requests using the "minor increase over minimal risk" standard. This responsibility of IRBs is of even greater importance in situations in which parents may be incapable of considering the ethical implications of their decision to give legal consent for their children to participate in a clinical study. As Levine [15] suggests, "It is possible for a 'poor' parent [to] feel alienated from their child's care by health care workers who fail to include them in discussions and to inform them fully about options. Their consent may be legally valid, but less than fully informed." In such instances, it is the IRB, acting paternally, who must ensure that children enrolled in the research will not be subjected to greater than a "minor increase over minimal risk."

A further complication of obtaining informed consent in pediatric drug research is the question of who decides whether a child will participate when the natural parents are either deceased or unavailable. The use of investigational drugs to treat children with AIDS is a common example of this problem. As Levine [15] notes, "There are many children infected [with AIDS] coming from poor, uneducated families or foster families where the natural parent cannot be reached. . . . More than 331,000 children are currently in foster care . . . 785 were known to be HIV-infected and only 15 were enrolled in clinical trials." Levine also points out that reports indicate that because of the problem of determining who is responsible for providing informed consent, 181 eligible foster children were not enrolled into clinical trials.

New York City has established a process to deal with the problem of children who are unable to participate in potentially beneficial clinical drug trials because of the absence of a parent to provide informed consent. The procedure, established by the City's Human Resource Administration (HRA), evaluates research protocols and determines whether it is appropriate for foster children to participate. If HRA approves, an agreement is drawn up with the institution conducting the research. The responsibility then reverts to the foster agency to make a "diligent search" to contact the natural parents. If the agency is unable to do so, the decision regarding enrollment falls upon the physician-researcher, who then simply must contact the child welfare administration [15]. In theory, this process appears to be sound ethically. Unfortunately, a number of problems may still exist. For example, leaving the decision of enrolling a child in a clinical trial up to a physician-researcher, who may not be aware of the child's emotional status or how enrollment in the trial might affect the child, may not be in the child's best interest. As Levine [15] points out, "A determination that a protocol is the best option for foster children is not the same as a determination that a protocol is the best option for a particular foster child."

E. Drug Testing in Women

The involvement of women as subjects in clinical drug research largely parallels that of children. FDA regulations formalized in 1977 banned the participation of women in Phase 1 and Phase 2 clinical trials because of a fear that "women included in the trials might get pregnant and bear deformed children" [16]. However, the reasons for wanting to conduct investigational drug research in women are similar to those for pediatrics. Testing done solely in men fails to establish a drug's efficacy in women and differences in dosing parameters that may be required.

It seems clear that gender bias exists in drug testing. As Rehm [17] reports, there is a vital need for the inclusion of women in clinical drug trials. Dr. Margaret Jensvold, director of the Institute for Research on Women's Health, argues "women have more adverse reactions to drugs than men. We don't really know why. It hasn't been looked at nearly enough" [17]. The research director goes on to note that the hormonal differences in women that complicate drug evaluation are precisely the reason why such testing is needed. If women will eventually take these medications, it is in their best interest to know how the drugs may affect them.

In April, 1993, it was reported that the FDA will respond to the exclusion of fertile women by lifting the 1977 ban on drug testing in women and including them in early clinical trials [18]. The lifting of the ban on drug testing in premenopausal women does not, however, mean that pharmaceutical manufacturers will be eager to enroll women in clinical trials. Ethical and legal questions still exist. For example, what is the moral obligation to both the woman and the fetus should a female subject in a drug trial become pregnant during testing? Will pharmaceutical manufacturers be held liable for a test drug's teratogenic effects? Many pharmaceutical manufacturers may continue to avoid the enrollment of women in clinical trials because of a fear of litigation. Even the existence of a signed informed consent form may not be enough to prevent a successful lawsuit if the damages to the fetus are severe enough [16].

F. Drug Testing in Prisoners

The complexity of the ethics of drug testing involving prisoners is based largely on the direct benefit that may accrue to prisoners as a consequence of their participation in the clinical trial. The testing of a drug that may have therapeutic benefit for a specific prisoner with a disorder (e.g., epilepsy) or for a disease or medical condition that is endemic to a prison population (e.g., AIDS) may have an ethical basis. In such instances, justification for participation may be based on the principle of beneficence, which requires a practitioner-researcher to act in a way that will benefit the patient-subject. Even in clinical trials in which direct benefit might be obtained by the prisoners' participation, questions exist as to whether such participation still requires informed consent on the part of the prisoner. A strong argument can be made that even though patients may have lost their physical autonomy through imprisonment, they still retain their biological autonomy. As a result, the ethical standards that preclude the enrollment of subjects into clinical studies without their informed consent would apply equally to prisoners.

Much more problematic is the question of prisoners' participation in clinical drug trials where they cannot hope to benefit directly (Phase 1). Not only is informed consent as vital a component as when there is direct benefit to the prisoner, but a further question is raised as to whether their participation under any circumstances can be justified on ethical grounds. Some have argued that prisoner participation in Phase 1 trials should occur only when "The type of research fulfills an important social or scientific need, and the reasons for involving prisoners are compelling . . ." [4]. However, ethical questions that weigh the interest of society versus the interest of the individual are not simple to answer.

G. Drug Testing in the Mentally Ill

Drug testing in patients with some degree of mental impairment presents as many ethical questions as any specialty group about whom the morality of clinical research is discussed. The fundamental question about drug testing in this group of patients involves to what degree these individuals have a right to make an autonomous decision about their willingness to participate in clinical research. This query would be simplified somewhat if all individuals with mental illness demonstrated the same level of impairment. Unfortunately, this is not the case. As a result, the clinical investigator is left with the same problem that practitioners not involved in research face: Should individuals be given medications either without their assent or, more problematically, against their will?

The ethically justifiable exception to the principle of autonomy, weak paternalism, may be applicable in determining whether or not the mentally impaired should participate in clinical research. As discussed earlier in this chapter, weak paternalism enables one to override another's autonomy if that individual is not or does not appear to be autonomous. The enrollment of individuals into clinical drug trials may be ethically acceptable based on the weak paternalism exception. This would be the case whether patients were enrolled without their consent or against their wishes. However, even with the use of the weak paternalism exception, investigators are still confronted with the difficulty of determining the degree of mental impairment requisite for this exception to be invoked. In instances in which it is unclear as to the state of an individual's ability to make an autonomous decision, one must err on the side of the patient-subject, whatever that may mean. In a number of these instances this lack of clarity is helped by the involvement of a family member, if one is available and willing to become part of the decision-making process. Investigators also are guided by the IRB, who must evaluate not only the research design and informed consent form, but also the criteria by which enrollment will take place.

The principle of beneficence may also be of assistance in determining an investigator's obligation to this group of patient-subjects. In research studies in which patients may potentially benefit directly from their participation, their enrollment may be ethically justified based on beneficence, even in situations where the patient's autonomy is in question. In cases where patients are unlikely to benefit from their participation, beneficence is not useful as a justification for their enrollment. In fact, in projects where subjects may be placed at risk, beneficence and nonmaleficence would preclude their involvement.

Clinical drug research involving individuals who suffer from mental illness, especially those who are institutionalized, is sometimes justified by the benefit that may result to others. Patients are sometimes administered medications simply to prevent them from being disruptive to other patients or staff. As Levine and Holder [4] write, "Tranquilization may, at times, be done more in the interest of maintaining order in the institution than in the interests of fostering the patient's recovery. . . ." The use of medications, either new drug entities or existing medications with possible new indications, may be as a component of a clinical research project. In these instances the line between research done to benefit the patient and that which is done to benefit others within the institution may be blurred. Such action may be rationalized ethically by the application of the harm principle exception to autonomy. Potential or actual risk of harm to others within the institution may justify the administration of medications to patients without their consent.

H. Abandoning Clinical Drug Trials

Clinical drug trials may be abandoned for one of two primary reasons: the drug demonstrates an unacceptable level of toxicity or lack of therapeutic activity, or the trial has produced results that are so dramatically positive that continuation of the trial would prevent significant benefit for patients at large.

Clinical drug research projects that reach Phase 1 trials have demonstrated at least some promise as a therapeutic entity. Nevertheless, only a tiny fraction of all such drugs ultimately make it to market. One-half to three-quarters of trials that reach this point are abandoned because of unacceptable toxicity or lack of efficacy. Similar losses occur at Phases 2 and 3 [12]. Because of such high attrition rates, investigators are often faced with the question of at what point in the trial the research should be terminated.

The ethical principles of beneficence, nonmaleficence, and fidelity provide some guidance. Drug research is conducted for the purpose of finding new therapeutic entities (or new uses for existing products) that may be beneficial to patients. Despite the fact that both healthy volunteers and subjects receiving placebos will not gain direct personal benefit from their participation in a clinical trial, their involvement is intended to benefit others.

As is discussed elsewhere in this chapter, the participation of these individuals, even under the best of circumstances, raises ethical questions. Therefore, when it is clear that unacceptable levels of toxicity are present, nonmaleficence directs that their participation be terminated. Even in the case of subjects who are receiving a study drug from which it was hoped they might benefit, their continued involvement in the face of undesirable levels of toxicity is unacceptable.

Similarly, fidelity obligations of investigators toward subjects of any type (healthy volunteers, placebo recipients, study drug recipients) requires that projects that demonstrate either high levels of toxicity or clear lack of therapeutic viability should be abandoned. The covenant established between the investigator and subject is based on the clinical testing of the drug within parameters outlined by the informed consent form and approved by the IRB. When the research results in toxicity or therapeutic inefficacy, the investigator's fidelity obligation requires at least the consideration of project termination.

The second reason for clinical trial abandonment, dramatic positive results, produces a similar conflict for the investigator. When a drug has demonstrated dramatic results of a positive nature when compared with either placebo or the currently accepted therapy, investigators face the question of whether to terminate the research—which may have a potentially negative impact on their results—or continue the trial, thereby preventing patients from receiving a drug with proven therapeutic benefit. Again, the principles of beneficence, nonmaleficence, and fidelity appear to provide a clear course of action. Beneficence directs that such trials be terminated so that not only might subjects participating in the trial who have not been receiving the study drug be able to receive it, but also so that non-study patients might initiate treatment. Similarly, nonmaleficence instructs that all patients who might benefit from the new treatment, whether study participants or not, should have the drug available to them if it has the potential to avoid harm. The fidelity obligation of practitioner-researchers toward both study participants and other patients further reinforces the ethical direction established by the two previous principles.

REFERENCES

1. T. A. Mappes and J. S. Zembaty, *Biomedical Ethics*, 3rd ed., McGraw-Hill, New York, 1991, pp. 206, 211.
2. T. L. Beauchamp and J. F. Childress, *Principles of Biomedical Ethics*, 3rd ed., Oxford University Press, New York, 1989, pp. 67, 68, 114, 349.

3. M. Montagne, Ethics of drug making, *Encyclopedia of Pharmaceutical Technology*, Vol. 5 (J. Swarbrick and J. C. Boylan, eds.), Marcel Dekker, New York, 1992, pp. 303, 304.
4. R. J. Levine and A. R. Holder, Legal and ethical problems in clinical research, *The Clinical Research Process in the Pharmaceutical Industry* (G. M. Matoren, ed.), Marcel Dekker, New York, 1984, pp. 68, 82, 84.
5. J. F. Gallelli, P. K. Hiranaka, and G. J. Grimes, Jr., Investigational drugs in the hospital, *Handbook of Institutional Pharmacy Practice*, 2nd ed. (T. R. Brown and M. C. Smith, eds.), Williams and Wilkins, Baltimore, 1986, p. 487.
6. J. J. Donahue, Research quality assurance, *The Clinical Research Process in the Pharmaceutical Industry* (G. M. Matoren, ed.), Marcel Dekker, New York, 1984, p. 364.
7. M. J. Finkel, Should informed consent include information on how research is funded? *IRB 13*:1–3 (1991).
8. D. S. Shimm and R. G. Spece, Industry reimbursement for entering patients into clinical trials: legal and ethical issues, *Ann. Intern. Med. 115*:148–151 (1991).
9. B. Healy et al., Conflict-of-interest guidelines for a multicenter clinical trial of treatment after coronary-artery bypass-graft surgery, *N. Engl. J. Med. 320*:949–951 (1989).
10. B. Freedman, Placebo-controlled trials and the logic of clinical purpose, *IRB 12*:1–6 (1990).
11. M. L. Citron, Placebos and principles: a trial of ondansetron, *Ann. Intern. Med. 118*:470–471 (1993).
12. L. R. Basara and M. Montagne, *Searching for Magic Bullets: Orphan Drugs, Consumer Activism and Pharmaceutical Development*, Haworth, New York, 1994, p. 83.
13. L. Bachorik, Why FDA is encouraging drug testing in children, *FDA Consumer 25*:14–17 (1991).
14. B. Freedman, A. Fuks, and C. Weijer, In loco parentis: Minimal risk as an ethical threshold for research upon children, *Hastings Center Report 23*:13–19 (1993).
15. C. Levine, Children in HIV/AIDS clinical trials: still vulnerable after all these years, *Law, Medicine and Health Care 19*:231–237 (1991).
16. T. Watson, FDA wants to invite women into drug trials earlier, *Nature 360*:289 (1992).
17. D. Rehm, Is there gender bias in drug testing? *FDA Consumer 25*:8–13 (1991).
18. P. Cotton, FDA lifts ban on women in early drug tests, will require companies to look for gender differences, *JAMA 269*:2067 (1993).

14

Legal Aspects of Prescription Drug Development in the United States

Horace D. Nalle

Merck & Co., Inc.
Rahway, New Jersey

I. INTRODUCTION

This chapter provides a survey of legal aspects of single-source drug development in the United States. Intended primarily for nonlawyers, it focuses selectively on those points in the process that commonly raise issues that require advice of counsel: from patents through clinical trials, from the new drug application process through marketed use. The whole process is, of course, pervasively regulated by the U.S. Food and Drug Administration (FDA).

II. THE LEGAL RIGHT TO THE COMPOUND

At the beginning of any single-source drug development plan, before the in vitro, animal, and clinical studies, before government approval, before the manufacturing and marketing, it is necessary to obtain the legal right to the compound. There are generally two ways to do so: (a) obtain a *patent* on the drug, either form the Patent Office or the patentee, or (b) obtain a *license* from the patentee.

A. Patents

1. Obtaining a Patent

The United States Constitution empowers Congress "To promote the Progress of Science and useful Arts, by securing for limited Times to Authors and Inventors the exclusive Right to their respective Writings and Discoveries" [1]. Congress first enacted a patent statute in 1790. The current statute is the Patent Act of 1952 [2].

A U.S. patent is the United States Patent and Trademark Office's recognition of the exclusive right of an inventor to prevent all others from making, using, or selling the patented invention in the United States [3]. (As a rule, a drug developer must obtain a separate patent in every country in which market exclusivity is desired.) Because the patentee can exclude competition, it theoretically enjoys monopoly power over the invention while the patent lasts.

There are two ways to obtain a patent. One way is to purchase it (typically referred to as "taking an assignment" of it). The other way, available only to the inventor, is to convince the Patent and Trademark Office (PTO) that the invention is (a) a product or a process (it can be a process either of manufacture or of use) and (b) novel, not obvious, and useful [4].

In drug development, disputes usually center on who owns the patent, or whose patent is valid. Some cases turn on whether the invention was truly nonobvious or novel, rather than generically claimed under a previously granted patent. A recent example of such a case was the dispute between Xoma and Centocor on the subject of Centoxin, then a promising compound for sepsis. Although the PTO granted Centocor a patent on Centoxin, Xoma persuaded a jury that Centoxin infringed a Xoma patent [5]. (The case later settled under an agreement that Centocor would pay Xoma a royalty [6].) In other cases, the question is who the inventor was, or at what point the invention occurred. For example, in a 1993 court decision, the generic manufacturer Barr Laboratories challenged Burroughs Wellcome's patent to azidothymidine (AZT), a treatment for AIDS. Barr contended that the scientists Burroughs Wellcome listed as inventors never reached a true "conception" of the use of AZT, because no such conception was possible until other researchers at the National Institute of Health had tested

AZT against viruses. (The Court rejected this challenge [7].) Given complex dilemmas involving the proper identification of patentable compounds and the timing of the patent application, handling patent law questions is arguably the most important role for counsel to play in the entire drug development process.

In the United States, patents last 20 years [8]. That presents a problem for drug developers, because testing and regulatory review consume years of a patent's life without generating any income. Partially in response to this phenomenon, in 1984 Congress passed the Drug Price Competition and Patent Term Extension Act; it offered qualifying drug patentees the opportunity to extend patent exclusivity beyond the date when the patent otherwise would have expired. The length of the extension is the subject of a complicated formula. It cannot last longer than 5 years or (when added to the original patent period) longer than 14 years after the date of approval of the drug by the FDA [9].

2. *Remedies for Infringement*

In cases of alleged patent infringement, litigants' remedies include injunctions, declaratory judgments, and damages.

There are two kinds of injunction. The first, a preliminary injunction, is a court order granted early in the litigation that directs the defendant to stop infringing, pending the outcome of the case. This remedy requires the plaintiff to establish at the outset that he or she is likely to win at the end—a burden that is particularly difficult to carry in a technologically complex case. Such injunctions are therefore very rare. The second kind of injunction is a permanent injunction. Granted at the end of the case, a permanent injunction is final and bars the defendant from further infringement.

A declaratory judgment, unlike an injunction, does not direct either party to do anything. Instead, it simply declares whether a patent is valid. Such a remedy is often desirable to the party who *lacks* the patent and therefore wishes judicial assurance that the patent is *in*valid.

The final category of remedy is damages. While it is often difficult to quantify precisely the amount owed, courts will often award damages anyway, on the theory that it is not fair to punish the innocent patentee for uncertainties caused by the wrongdoing of the infringer. In addition to damages, the Patent Act provides for exemplary ("punitive") damages of up to three times the regular damages award [10]. There is also a provision for the award of attorneys' fees [11], but they are awarded only in exceptional cases.

3. Limitations on Patents

Patents have limitations. To begin with, they are an acknowledgment of exclusivity by the PTO, but not by competitors. One scholar notes: "While perhaps it is only the more marginal patents that are regularly judicially scrutinized, the failure rate of litigated patents has been above 75 percent over an arguably representative period spanning 15 years or so" [12]. A good example of a court overturning a patent granted by the PTO, discussed above, is Centocor's patent on Centoxin. On the day that a jury found that Centoxin infringed Xoma's patent, the market equity of Centocor dropped by about 9%.

Another disadvantage of patents is the disclosure of a trade secret. A valid patent is an exchange: the government grants the patentee a right to exclude others from using the invention, but in return, the patentee has to publish the secret. Accordingly, inventors face a choice between two ways of preventing others from using the invention: seek a patent and trust the courts to enforce it, or keep the invention secret. The latter course is not practical in the case of drug compounds, because the FDA requires certain disclosures in the New Drug Application and in labeling [13]. It remains an option, however, for certain manufacturing processes.

A third limitation on the value of patents is the rise of "me-too" drugs and therapeutic advances, both outside the scope of the patent, that successfully compete with the product long before the patent itself expires [14]. Technological advances have enabled competitors quickly to design molecules that are just different enough from the patented compound not to infringe the patent—but still similar enough to produce a comparable therapeutic effect. These "me-too" drugs are typically rushed to market at a discount within a few years after the innovator drug. Cost-conscious buyers insist on the "me-too," and the innovator's patent is powerless to prevent the erosion of market share. Worse still for the patentee (but, happily, better for patients) is the development of a whole new class of *better* agents—not a rare occurrence, given the breathtaking record of drug discovery in the past 20 years.

B. Licenses

Unlike a patentee (or his or her assignee, who effectively owns the patent), a licensee owns only a contractual privilege to use a patent without fear of suit by the licensor for infringement. Ordinarily the licensee purchases this right from the patentee in exchange for a royalty.

Licensing is a matter of negotiation between free parties, ordinarily limited only by their imagination and bargaining power in deciding what to license, how, and to whom. (Antitrust law can provide an exception to this freedom, invalidating licenses that result in restraints of trade or "excessive" market power.) In the absence of some other legal constraint, parties may license, among other things:

1. U.S. patent rights
2. Foreign patent rights
3. U.S. patent applications
4. Foreign patent applications
5. Inchoate (i.e., not yet legally established) U.S. patent rights to existing inventions
6. Inchoate foreign patent rights to existing inventions
7. Existing trade secrets (proprietary know-how)
8. Existing nonproprietary know-how
9. U.S. patent rights to future inventions made or acquired by the licensor
10. Foreign patent rights to future inventions made or acquired by the licensor
11. U.S. patent rights acquired by the licensor from third parties after execution of the license agreement
12. Foreign patent rights acquired by the licensor from third parties after execution of the license agreement
13. U.S. trademark rights
14. Foreign trademark registrations and rights
15. U.S. trade name rights
16. Foreign trade name rights and registrations [15]

A license may be exclusive, conferring on the licensee the right to sue anyone else for infringement. Or it can be nonexclusive, so that various competing licensees can exploit the patent without fear of infringment action by the patentee or each other. Some patentees grant licenses that are exclusive but only within limited territories.

The license may be coextensive with the patent or may pick and choose various rights, granting, for example, the right to manufacture but not to market a compound. Or it can grant a right that expires before the patent does, reserving to the licensor the right to exploit that right after the license expires.

Under appropriate circumstances, the licensor can negotiate a "grant back," in which the licensee pledges to give the licensor access to any improvements the licensee makes.

III. CLINICAL TRIALS

Once the drug developer has established the legal right to the compound, he or she will turn to registering the drug for marketing in the United States. The process begins with in vitro and animal testing, subjects that, although heavily regulated, can generally be handled with relatively little assistance from lawyers. It is when the drug enters testing in humans that counsel plays a greater role. A newly developed prescription drug can lawfully be used in human subjects in the United States only under an Investigational New Drug Application (IND)—which must be filed before testing in humans begins—or a New Drug Application (NDA)—which must be approved before marketed use begins. Under both regulatory schemes, an overriding goal is the protection of human subjects. To promote that end, the regulations require informed consent and establish institutional review boards.

A. Informed Consent

1. *Historical Sources of Law*

The history of modern informed consent law originates with the Nuremberg Code, handed down in the famous trials of 23 German physicians for "crimes against humanity" committed in medical experiments on prisoners of war and civilians during World War II. The Nuremberg Code (1948) was followed by the Declaration of Helsinki (1964), which raised the requirement of "the patient's freely given consent after . . . full explanation" to a matter of international treaty law [16].

The main source of the current U.S. federal law of informed consent is the FDA's regulations on the subject [17]. There are also state statutes, however [18]. Federal law concerning devices [19] expressly preempts (that is to say, supersedes) such state laws [20], but there is no analogous express federal preemption concerning plasma [21], vaccines [22], or drugs [23]. In fact, the informed consent requirements in the FDA regulations "are not intended to preempt any applicable federal, State, or local laws which require additional information to be disclosed for informed consent to be legally effective" [24].

2. *FDA Regulations*

For human clinical trials, the fundamental rule is: "No human research can take place without the legally effective informed consent of the subject or his representative" [25]. Consent shall be obtained only under circumstances that provide the subject adequate opportunity to decide whether to participate.

There can be no coercion or undue influence, and the information must be provided in plain language. The consent cannot contain a waiver or a release of legal rights that the patient may have in case of negligence or other legal fault on the part of anyone involved in the study [26].

The informed consent *must* include:

1. A statement that the study involves research, an explanation of the purposes of the research and the expected duration of the subject's participation, a description of the procedures to be followed, and identification of any procedures that are experimental [26]
2. Reasonably foreseeable risks or discomforts
3. Any benefits reasonably to be expected
4. Appropriate alternative procedures that might be advantageous to the patient
5. A description of the confidentiality of records, including the possibility that the FDA and the sponsor will inspect them
6. Information on whether compensation will be provided, and on where the patient can get further information
7. Information about whom to contact for answers to questions about research, patient rights, and injury
8. A statement that the subject's participation is voluntary; that refusal to participate will cause no penalty or loss of benefits; and that the subject may discontinue at any time without penalty [27]

In addition, informed consent *may* include:

1. A statement that the treatment may involve risks that are now unforseeable
2. Anticipated circumstances under which the subject's participation may be terminated by the investigator without regard to the subject's consent
3. Additional costs to the subject that may result from participation
4. Consequences of the subject's early withdrawal from the study, together with procedures for orderly termination
5. A statement that significant new findings developed during the research that may relate to the subject's willingness to continue will be provided to the subject
6. The approximate number of participants in the study [28]

The consent should be in writing, signed by the subject or his or her legal representative, and the investigator must give a copy to the signatory [29]. While there is a provision for oral consent, it ordinarily provides no legal advantages and should be used only if it is deemed necessary to enroll illiterate patients. Investigators wishing to use oral consent must obtain from the Institutional Review Board (IRB) a written summary of what is to be said. There must be a witness to the oral presentation, and the witness must sign both the short form and the summary [30].

3. Exceptions to the Informed Consent Requirement

The law generally recognizes five exceptions to the informed consent requirement: emergency [31], incompetency [32], waiver [33], "therapeutic privilege" (the physician's right to withhold information whose disclosure would be harmful) [34], and certain studies conducted by the Department of Defense on military personnel [35]. The exceptions are fraught with legal peril, however, and plaintiffs' lawyers will be eager to construe them narrowly. Investigators should never dispense with informed consent in clinical trials without prior consultation with counsel. Clinical trials conducted on prisoners require special consideration, including additional safeguards to protect study subjects [36].

B. The Institutional Review Board

Federal regulations require that an Institutional Review Board of at least five members [37] approve the initiation of, and periodically review, all biomedical research involving human subjects [38]. The primary purpose of such review is to assure the protection of the rights and welfare of the human subjects [38]. In keeping with this mission, the regulations require that the IRB be qualified not only through experience and expertise, but also through "diversity, including consideration of race, gender, cultural backgrounds, and sensitivity to community attitudes, to promote respect for its advice and counsel in safeguarding the rights and welfare of human subjects" [39].

The IRB approves or disapproves the research plan [40]. Criteria for approval include that risks to subjects are minimized [41], that they are reasonable in relation to anticipated benefits and the importance of the knowledge that are expected to result [42], that the selection of subjects is equitable, particularly considering vulnerable populations [43], that there is adequate informed consent [44], and that data are monitored adequately and kept confidential [45]. Once the protocol is approved, the IRB enforces compliance with the informed consent regulations [46]. The Board must keep adequate records [47] and may be sanctioned for noncompliance [48]. The FDA has published a compliance guide concerning IRBs [64].

C. The Agreement Between the Sponsor and the Clinical Investigator

Lawyers sometimes play a role in the negotiation of agreements between sponsors and clinical investigators. Subject to the parties' duties as fixed by the regulations, this agreement is, essentially, a matter of freedom of contract. It is typical for the parties to agree on the scope of the work (usually by reference to the protocol); the projected completion date; the amount and payment of funds; confidentiality of trade secrets, proprietary data, and patient information; study termination; ownership of any inventions; publication rights; and the use of each other's names. Since passage of the Generic Drug Enforcement Act of 1992, some manufacturers require a certification that the investigator has not been debarred from practice before the FDA (see "Debarment" below). Some clinical investigators demand that the manufacturer indemnify them, especially against product liability claims, and manufacturers often agree to do so. This agreement is ordinarily conditioned, however, on the investigator's committing no negligent or wrongful act; complying with all laws and with the protocol; maintaining appropriate records concerning drug supplies; reporting promptly any significant or alarming developments, including claims; and allowing the sponsor to conduct the defense and to settle any suits at its discretion. Such agreements also typically feature purely legal issues, such as provisions for amendment; prohibitions on assignment; termination procedures; and a choice of which jurisdiction's law shall govern the contract. The FDA has published compliance guides concerning contract research organizations [65] and clinical investigators [147].

D. Debarment

The Generic Drug Enforcement Act of 1992 [49] arose out of the generic drug scandal. While its main thrust aims at the generic industry, the act also reaches individuals and, to a lesser extent, companies in the research-based industry. It empowers the Secretary of Health to "debar" *firms* "from submitting, or assisting in the submission of" certain new drug applications. The grounds for debarment are a variety of state and federal crimes, most of which have to do with corruption in the drug development or approval process. The Secretary may also debar *individuals* "from providing services in any capacity to a person that has an approved or pending drug product application" for similar crimes. There is also a provision for debarment of certain "high managerial agents" who fail to report such misconduct [50].

In addition, the government may impose civil penalties, for each violation, of up to $250,000 for an individual and $1 million for a firm [51].

Applicants must certify in NDAs that they have not used the services of any debarred person [52]. Because FDA interprets "any person" as broadly as the law allows, it is reasonable for sponsors to oblige any vendor or supplier, including investigators, to certify that they do not employ any debarred individual [53].

E. Conflict of Interest

In the past several years, there has been increased attention to conflict of interest on the part of clinical investigators. General principles are as follows:

The outcome of the research should have no relation to the investigator's compensation.

The investigator should have no interest in the product (such as a patent or a significant equity stake in the sponsor).

If the investigator thinks he or she is not qualified to run a study center, he or she should decline to participate.

If the investigator thinks the protocol is not scientifically legitimate, he or she should decline to participate.

Government employees face other conflict-of-interest guidelines. These include prohibitions on outside employment "not compatible with the full and proper discharge of the duties and responsibilities of . . . Government employment" [54] and a ban on the receipt of certain honoraria [55]. Most government departments have their own internal guidelines on conflicts of interest. Investigators who are government employees should consult their departmental ethics officers before conducting clinical trials sponsored by outside manufacturers.

F. "Seeding Studies"

For present purposes, a "seeding study" is one that is designed not to answer a real scientific question, but rather to induce physicians to prescribe the study drug for commercial reasons. Hallmarks of these studies are the absence of controls, a very large number of investigators (especially in relation to the number of subjects), scientifically slipshod protocols (or none at all), payments based on the number of new patients prescribed the study drug, and the requirement that subjects be switched from a competing drug. (The presence or absence of one or more of these characteristics does not necessarily mean the study is or is not a seeding study. Such studies should be evaluated on a case-by-case basis.)

The Office of the Inspector General of the U.S. Department of Health and Human Services has called attention [56] to the possibility that seeding studies might violate the Medicare and Medicaid anti-kickback law [57]. The anti-kickback law makes it a federal felony to knowingly give or receive anything of value to induce the purchase of a drug for which Medicare or Medicaid might pay. The penalty is a fine of $25,000 per infraction, imprisonment for 5 years per infraction, or both. Investigators or sponsors who are concerned that a protocol might be deemed a seeding study should consult with counsel.

G. Payment to Patients

The informed consent regulations contemplate that patients can be compensated for participating in clinical trials [58]. The amount of the compensation should be consistent with common sense and good judgment. In no event should there be any possibility of a connection between compensation and study results.

On the other hand, it is permissible to induce patients to continue in a legitimate study (absent some medical or ethical reason to discontinue) by setting up a schedule of periodic payments, and making receipt contingent on the patient's continuation. Under such an arrangement, it is wise to give pro rata payments if the patient terminates.

H. Patient Populations

Commentators have recently paid much attention to the question whether women, African-Americans, and Hispanic-Americans have been underrepresented in clinical trials [59]. There is reason to believe that underrepresentation can produce gaps in scientific knowledge of the efficacy and safety of study therapies, because some therapies appear to work differently in different patient groups [60]. Accordingly, in designing clinical trials, sponsors and investigators should consider diversity in the patient population. FDA takes the view that "drugs should be studied in all age groups, including the geriatric, for which they will have significant utility" [61]. Although there remain valid pregnancy-related reasons to exercise special care in studies involving women, similar principles should be considered in connection with gender [62] and race. This is not to say that manufacturers have absolute duties to study drug candidates in every foreseeable population; such a requirement would be unworkable and would deter the development of useful therapies.

IV. PRE-APPROVAL PUBLICITY

If a drug is a promising candidate for marketing, the sponsor will face temptations—and perhaps duties—to inform the public about it. Public disclosures about unapproved drugs (or unapproved claims) are the subject of strict regulation and considerable FDA sensitivity.

A. The Regulations

The IND regulations generally prohibit pre-approval promotion:

> A sponsor or investigator, or any person acting on behalf of a sponsor or investigator, shall not represent in a promotional context that an investigational new drug is safe or effective for the purposes for which it is under investigation or otherwise promote the drug [65].

That does not end the analysis, however. In fact, the sponsor or investigator can make at least four kinds of statements before a drug is approved: scientific exchange, securities disclosures, "institutional" advertising, and "reminder" advertising.

B. Scientific Exchange

The same regulation that generally prohibits pre-approval promotion goes on to distinguish promotion from scientific exchange:

> This provision is not intended to restrict the full exchange of scientific information concerning the drug, including dissemination of scientific findings in scientific or lay media. Rather, its intent is to restrict promotional claims of safety or effectiveness of the drug for a use for which it is under investigation and to preclude commercialization of the drug before it is approved for commercial distribution [65].

Under this regulation, "scientific exchanges" are legitimate, but "promotional claims of safety or effectiveness" are not. In that fine line between "scientific exchange" and "promotional claims" lies much controversy about the FDA's legal authority to regulate "public relations."

To date, the FDA has apparently never objected to the publication, in scholarly journals, of the data upon which an NDA depends. Even if it is the sponsor or investigator who authors the paper, and even though the paper describes a use the FDA has not approved, the agency tolerates such disclosures as legitimate scientific exchange. The same agency tolerance would apply to a paper presented orally in accordance with customary academic procedures. (This is not to say, however, that the same paper may be used promotionally.)

C. Securities Disclosures

The second exception to the ban on publicity discussing unapproved drugs involves securities disclosures. At least for sponsors whose securities are publicly traded, the federal securities laws [66] require the public disclosure of certain information that is "material" to investors—regardless of whether that information is consistent with the approved labeling of an approved prescription drug. Suppose, for example, that a publicly traded biotechnology company with a product in Phase 2 trials discovers some attribute that gives the product such great commercial potential as to multiply the value of the company's stock. Under the securities laws, the "insiders" who have such information have a duty to disclose it to the market, so that ordinary investors enjoy an equal opportunity to benefit from an upward correction in the stock price.

To date, the FDA has apparently not taken the position that a press release regarding the results of key studies of investigational products or indications is a violation of the regulation generally prohibiting pre-approved promotion—provided that five requirements are met. First, the communication should be a sober disclosure rather than a publicity blitz [67]. Second, the sponsor must not pay for the publication [68]. Third, the sponsor should "label investigational uses and unapproved claims as such" [68]. Fourth, the release must be "representative of what is known or should reasonably be known to the sponsor about the product discussed" [68]. Fifth, if the subject is an unapproved claim for a marketed drug, the sponsor should provide a copy of the approved package insert [68].

While agency policy appears to be in some state of flux, it appears that manufacturers should submit to the FDA, under the NDA reporting regulation that applies to advertising and promotional labeling [69], all "public relations materials that promote drug products and that are issued by or on behalf of those who market the drugs" [70]. The agency has also opined that any such materials that are part of a launch campaign for a new drug should be voluntarily submitted to the FDA for pre-review prior to use.

D. "Institutional" Advertising

After scientific exchange and securities disclosures, the third type of permitted communication about an unapproved drug is the "institutional" advertisement. Such promotion "generally conveys the message that 'Brand Name' drug company is doing research in cardiovascular medicine (for example) to develop new and important drugs" [71], but does not mention the name of the drug candidate.

E. "Reminder" Advertising

Finally, the FDA permits "advertisements which merely announce the name of a new product which will be available soon," without making any statement (including a graphic statement, such as a picture of a heart) about safety or efficacy [71]. (This format is not available for a drug expected to carry a boxed warning in its labeling [71].) Once a sponsor chooses an institutional or reminder format, "it may not switch simultaneously or subsequently to the other format at any time during the preapproval period" [71].

V. SCIENTIFIC OR REGULATORY MISCONDUCT

Scientific misconduct during drug research can carry significant criminal and civil liabilities. The Public Health Service Act obliges the recipients of government support to follow certain procedures and make certain disclosures when misconduct arises [72]. Federal prosecutors have recently charged criminal violations [73] in cases involving the sale of adulterated medical devices [74], warehouse sanitation violations [75], the sale of misbranded veterinary drugs [76], the theft of proprietary trade secrets [77], providing cash gratuities to government regulatory officials [78], marketing a new drug without submitting a new drug application to the FDA [79], and submitting fraudulent abbreviated new drug applications (ANDAs) [80].

When an institution discovers that one of its agents has fabricated data—or retaliated against anyone who has reported such misconduct—two quite different roles for counsel emerge: "doing the right thing" and ensuring due process for the alleged wrongdoer.

As for the "right thing," counsel for the sponsor may help scientific and regulatory personnel fulfill their duties of corrective disclosure to the FDA or any other appropriate regulatory or funding body [81]. Often, the sponsor must reanalyze study results after excluding the tainted data. Any application that is based solely on the falsified data should ordinarily be suspended or withdrawn. This is not only good ethics; it is also good business, in that juries in tort cases could easily be influenced in favor of a plaintiff injured by a product whose approval was based on fabricated data.

Turning to due process, internal review procedures should ensure prompt but fair justice for the accused. This means, ordinarily, "notice and an opportunity to be heard." Notice means advance disclosure (to the accused) of the charges, the procedures to be followed, some description of the evidence, and the identities of the witnesses. A fair opportunity to be heard means the right to respond to the charges, present testimony or documentary evidence, and cross-examine hostile witnesses, all before a neutral decision-maker. The misconduct review committee is well advised to rely on legal counsel to design procedures that will allow fairness to the accused [82]. Whether to allow the accused an attorney is a question properly left to the discretion of the institution investigating the misconduct [83].

VI. GOVERNMENT INSPECTIONS

Various agencies assert the right to inspect pharmaceutical research ventures, including the FDA [84], the Environmental Protection Agency, the Nuclear Regulatory Commission, the Occupational Safety and Health Administration, the Drug Enforcement Agency, the U.S. Department of Agriculture, state environmental and health agencies, and nongovernmental accreditation agencies, such as the American Association for Accreditation of Laboratory Animal Care. Clinical investigators are subject to three kinds of FDA inspections alone: surveillance inspections, "for cause" inspections, and bioequivalence study inspections [85].

It is an important part of drug development planning to establish procedures to deal with inspections. Because lawyers are trained in procedures that ensure fair access without permitting disorder or "fishing expeditions," they play a useful role in developing such procedures. Good procedures typically include a list of files that will routinely be available to inspectors; procedures as to how those files will be made available (preferably in a conference room rather than in file storage areas); standards for the protection of confidential information; and designation, competence, and training of a "point person" within the institution to accompany the inspectors and otherwise coordinate the inspection [86].

Once the procedures are in place, there is divided opinion on whether layers should actually supervise the investigation. On the one hand, lawyers generally do not know the documents, the facilities, or the issues as well as their clients. Moreover, many lawyers have a tendency to be excessively adversarial, a trait that is often unhelpful when an institution depends on the goodwill of regulators to fulfill its mission. On the other hand, lawyers can be useful if the inspectors seek information to which they have no legal right.

VII. ADVERSE EXPERIENCES

The identification and communication of adverse experiences associated with a drug candidate are two of the most important tasks in drug development. For sponsor's legal counsel, it is a task of paramount importance to ensure that the sponsor adequately communicates information about hazards to prescribers. For investigator's counsel, it is critical that prescribers receive and give adequate warnings to patients. Full disclosure is necessary not only on medical grounds; it also reduces civil liability exposure.

A. Reporting Adverse Experiences to FDA

In separate sets of regulations, the FDA requires all sponsors to disclose to the agency adverse effects associated with any drug that is the subject of an IND or an NDA. The regulations are detailed, and there is space here only for a summary [87]. The consequences of failure to report can be severe: at least two major U.S. pharmaceutical companies have pleaded guilty to criminal charges, and several individuals have pleaded "no contest" [88].

For IND purposes, "associated with the use of the drug" "means that there is a reasonable *possibility* that the experience *may* have been caused by the drug" [89]. The IND regulations [90] require a report within 10 working days if the adverse experience is serious (i.e., is fatal or life-threatening, permanently disabling, requiring inpatient hospitalization, a congenital anomaly, a cancer, or an overdose) [91] and unexpected (not identified in nature, severity, or frequency in the current investigator brochure [91]). In addition, the regulations require the sponsor to make a telephone report within 3 days after any fatal or life-threatening adverse experience. "Life-threatening" means there was "immediate" risk of death. An experience that could, but did not, immediately threaten death is not life-threatening [92]. Filing a report is not an admission "that the drug caused or contributed to an adverse experience" [93]. These IND reporting requirements continue for all IND studies, including those conducted after the NDA is filed or even approved.

The holder of an NDA must report any serious, unexpected adverse experience within 15 working days of receipt of the information [94]. (For NDA purposes, an adverse drug experience is "any adverse event associated with the use of a drug in humans, *whether or not considered drug related*" [95]. The applicant must report serious, expected adverse experiences "periodically" (quarterly for the first 3 years after approval and annually thereafter), and must report an increased frequency in such reports within 15 days after detecting it [96]. Most other adverse experiences must be reported "periodically" [97].

An adverse experience is not exempt from reporting merely because it happened abroad. The holder of an IND must report within 10 days any foreign adverse experiences that are serious, unexpected (i.e., not identified in the *U.S.* investigator's brochure), and possibly causally related to the drug. Likewise, the holder of an NDA must report within 15 days a foreign event if it is serious and unexpected. The key is that reportability is judged by FDA standards, even if the regulatory standards are more lenient in the jurisdiction where the adverse event occurred. Nor is a foreign experience exempt if the drug is slightly different from that registered in the United States [98].

B. Disclosing Adverse Experiences in Labeling

It is in the labeling that sponsors inform prescribers and dispensers about adverse experiences. Such information is critical for the safe and effective use of prescription drugs—and also for limiting civil liability.

The NDA must contain "specimens of the labeling proposed to be used for [the] drug" [99]. As used in U.S. drug law, "labeling" does not simply mean the sticker on the bottle (the *label*) [100]. Rather, "labeling" means "all labels and other written, printed, or graphic matter (1) upon any article or any of its containers or wrappers, or (2) accompanying such article" [101]. This includes the *prescribing information*, the primary opportunity for the manufacturer to discharge its duty of communicating drug information to the learned intermediary, as will be discussed below ("Civil Liability").

The regulations provide detailed requirements of what the prescribing information must contain, including contraindications, warnings, precautions, and adverse reactions [102]. A key point is that the labeling must alert physicians to a serious hazard whenever "reasonable evidence" indicates an "association" with the drug. *A causal relationship need not have been proved* [103]. From a medical point of view, compliance with the U.S. regulations' requirement that hazards be disclosed even in the absence of a demonstrated causal relationship is conservative, putting patient safety first. From a product liability point of view, compliance also provides a key defense in court. Most product liability actions hinge on a charge that the manufacturer failed to disclose a hazard. The more hazards the prescribing information discloses, the fewer hazards plaintiffs can accuse manufacturers of failing to disclose.

The sponsor has a duty to keep the prescribing information up-to-date as it learns of additional hazards after the NDA is approved:

> [T]he act and FDA regulations require a warning in drug labeling as soon as a hazard is associated with the use of a drug. In the case of a drug subject to an approved NDA, [a regulation[104]] permits the addition to the drug's labeling or advertising of information about a hazard without advance approval of the supplemental application by FDA. In considering these regulations in a product liability case, at least one court has held that an NDA holder may have a duty to add a warning before FDA approval of a supplemental application. *See McEwen v. Ortho Pharmaceutical Corp.*, 528 P.2d 522 (Ore. 1974) [105].

This rule needs, however, to be viewed in context. From time to time, the FDA instructs manufacturers *not* to disclose certain adverse experiences—even those the manufacturer had added "without advance approval"—ordinarily because the agency believes there is no causal relationship. Under such circumstances, jurors (who are usually not bound by FDA determinations on causation)have been permitted to hold a manufacturer liable for failing to disclose side effects that it actually *tried* to disclose, only to be prohibited by the FDA.

Drug developers must beware the natural instinct—even scientists have it—to turn a blind eye on the shortcomings of the products they work so hard to bring to market. It is not only unethical but foolish from a business point of view to hide real risks. They will be found out sooner or later in marketed use, and nothing can damage a compound more than the allegation of a cover-up. The history of U.S. drug development is replete with examples of drugs that succeeded both medically and commercially despite excruciatingly full disclosure of serious hazards.

Because it falls to counsel to handle the legal consequences of undisclosed risks, counsel has institutional incentives to promote full disclosure at all times. Accordingly, counsel should play a key role in ensuring that the prescribing information is up-to-date and discloses all appropriate hazards.

VIII. CIVIL LIABILITY

A. The Risk

Anyone who develops or markets a drug for use in the United States must budget for product liability expenses that are greater than those seen in other countries. There are more lawsuits in the United States, and the cost of resolving a lawsuit is greater than the international norm. The significance of this cost on drug development should not be underestimated. According to a RAND Institute for Civil Justice study focusing specifically on drug development,

> numerical simulations suggest that liability can substantially decrease incentives to innovate in product areas for which large liability costs seem plausible or financial disaster from liability is believed to be even a slight possibility.

Liability costs can in principle threaten even large companies with financial disaster. Both the possibility of mass torts and the unlimited nature of punitive damages appear to play important roles in this regard [106].

According to the American Medical Association, U.S. tort rules "are having a profound negative impact on the development and utilization of potentially life-saving medical technologies" [107]. Civil liability costs have driven U.S. developers from the markets for certain vaccines [108], contraceptives [109], and medications for use during pregnancy [110].

Product liability and malpractice costs are not limited to marketed use, but are also incurred during drug development. Moreover, the awarding of *nine*-figure damages in postmarketing cases gives any rational drug developer pause: it takes only one such case to make most drug development programs unprofitable.

B. Uncertainty and the Role of Summary Judgment

1. Uncertainty

To the drug developer, a prominent feature of the American civil liability system is its uncertainty. Although courts enunciate fairly clear rules, and some of the rules seem favorable to drug developers, the judicial process that enforces those rules is unreliable. Most cases that are not settled are ultimately decided by a jury of six to 12 ordinary citizens who are not learned in law or medicine. Forced to choose between a suffering plaintiff and corporate defendants—who are presumed (often wrongly) to be backed up by insurance companies with deep pockets—many juries will predictably order defendants to pay.

The award of compensation to suffering plaintiffs makes considerable good sense. In the U.S. civil liability world, however, juries have and use the power to give such awards (a) with little or no attention to abstruse rules of law and (b) without evidence of fault or defect on the part of the defendants. The paradoxical effect is that sometimes the sponsors and investigators whom courts order to pay are blameless under the law.

The unreliability of the jury-dominated U.S. courts in enforcing certain legal rules favorable to drug developers is compounded by the unpredictability of the *amount* of damages awarded. There have been individual awards of over $100 million in U.S. product liability cases in which the victim survived. By comparison, the estates of victims who died have received less than one percent of that amount.

This is not to say that defendants never win civil liability cases. The problem is that it is impossible for the defendants comfortably to predict which cases they will win—and how much they will pay if they lose.

Ironically, this uncertainty has deprived many drug developers of the product liability insurance that jurors commonly assume they have. Faced with insurers' refusal to cover such an unpredictable risk, many drug developers will find it necessary to reserve substantial sums of their own funds against product liability losses.

2. Summary Judgment

American courts provide certain opportunities for judges to take cases away from the jurors. The main such procedure is the *motion for summary judgment*. In the U.S. legal system, it is typically the jury's province to determine the facts, and the judge's to apply the law to those facts. If there is no dispute about the facts, then there is nothing for the jury to do. Thus, in a defense motion for summary judgment, the sponsor or investigator asks the judge to consider only those facts that are not in dispute. On that record, the defendant urges, the judge should rule that the defendant is entitled to a judgment as a matter of law.

Typically, the plaintiff responds by claiming that the facts *are* in dispute, or that he or she has not had enough time to discover the facts, and the judge often agrees. Regardless of how certain the judge may be personally that the defendant should not be held liable, he or she must order the case for jury trial if there is a "material" fact in dispute. When the jury returns its verdict, the judge must defer to it, so long as it is not irrational (or the result of an error the judge has made).

C. Kinds of Claims

Plaintiffs who claim to have been injured by a prescription drug ordinarily base their claims on one or more of four footings: strict liability, intentional tort, malpractice (negligence), and contract. The main thrust against manufacturers is usually strict liability; the main thrust against physicians is usually malpractice (negligence).

1. Strict Liability

In the United States, manufacturers are generally held "strictly" liable for injuries caused by "defective" products. Strict liability means, in essence, liability regardless of fault. The plaintiff need not prove the manufacturer was negligent to win—and may recover even if he or she was negligent. All the claimant needs to prove is that the product was defective, and that the defect caused an injury [111].

A product can be "defective" if the manufacturer fails to deliver an adequate warning about how to use it. There is an exception, however, for "unavoidably unsafe products":

> There are some products which, in the present state of human knowledge, are quite incapable of being made safe for their intended and ordinary use. These are especially common in the field of drugs. . . . It is also true in particular of many new or experimental drugs as to which, because of lack of time and opportunity for sufficient medical experience, there can be no assurance of safety, or perhaps even of purity of ingredients, but such experience as there is justifies the marketing and use of the drug notwithstanding a medically recognizable risk. The seller of such products, again with the qualification that they are properly prepared and marketed, and proper warning is given, where the situation calls for it, is not to be held to strict liability for unfortunate consequences attending their use, merely because he has undertaken to supply the public with an apparently useful and desirable product, attended with a known but apparently reasonable risk [112].

Courts that have squarely addressed the issue have usually found marketed prescription drugs "unavoidably unsafe" [113], and therefore not subject to strict liability, although in some states, the conclusion is not automatic, but is made on a case-by-case basis [114]. Given the exception's express reference to "experimental drugs," it seems inevitable that an investigational drug is "unavoidably unsafe" and therefore not defective [115].

Plaintiffs in strict liability drug cases have not had good success charging defects other than failure to warn. Manufacturing defects, although actionable, are rare. With exceptions [116], judges have generally declined to "review the adequacy of prescription drug designs" [117].

2. Negligence (Including Malpractice)

In order to win a negligence case, a civil plaintiff must show:

1. A duty, or obligation, recognized by the law, requiring the person to conform to a certain standard of conduct, for the protection of others against unreasonable risks.
2. A failure on the person's part to conform to the standard required: a breach of the duty.
3. A reasonably close causal connection between the conduct and the resulting injury. This is what is commonly known as "legal cause" or "proximate cause" and which includes the notion of cause in fact.
4. Actual loss or damage [118].

There are the classic elements of a nonintentional "tort."

In a typical malpractice case, the patient asserts (a) that the physician had a duty to provide medical care that conformed to community medical standards, (b) that the physician breached the duty, and (c) that the breach caused his or her injury. As to the manufacturer, the plaintiff would typically claim negligence in the manufacture of or research into the drug. Claims of negligent research are difficult for plaintiffs to win; generally a drug that withstands FDA review is researched according to the prevailing standards of care.

3. Intentional Tort

In many jurisdictions, an unauthorized medical procedure is treated as a "battery" [119]. In the law, a battery is an intentional "harmful or offensive contact" [120]. Generally, however, the greater number of decisions now regard the failure to disclose a mere risk of treatment as involving a collateral matter, and negligence rather than intent, and so have treated the question as one of negligent malpractice only, which brings into question standards of professional conduct [120].

4. Contract

Many sponsors choose to entitle study subjects to compensation in the event of an adverse experience. (FDA regulations allow but do not require such an entitlement [121].) In the event of an adverse experience, the informed consent operates like a contract, obliging the sponsor to provide the promised compensation if the contractual requirements are met.

One typical provision entitles the subject to reimbursement for the cost of treatment for an adverse experience resulting directly from the study drug, provided that the cost is not paid for by any other third party (for example, the subject's insurer) and provided that the treatment and its cost are reasonable.

D. Selected Defenses

1. The Critical Importance of the Warning

Regardless whether the plaintiff asserts strict liability, negligence, or intentional tort, he or she will typically accuse the sponsor or investigator of *failure to warn.* (In a strict liability case, a failure to warn is a "defect" in the product; in a negligence case, failure to warn itself may constitute malpractice; in an intentional tort case, a failure to warn defeats defendants' argument that plaintiff consented.) For that reason, an adequate warning is the bulwark of the defense of any claim of personal injury due to a prescription drug, regardless of plaintiff's theoretical cause of action.

From the sponsor's perspective, however, it is not always enough to give an adequate warning in the prescribing information. Despite such a warning, the sponsor may be liable if its sales force "overpromotes" the drug—that is, if their sales presentations are inconsistent with the prescribing information [122]. For this reason (among others), counsel can play a critical role in reviewing promotion. See "Planning for Promotion," below.

2. The Learned Intermediary Rule

As a rule, it is the sponsor's duty to warn the prescribing physician, and the physician's duty to warn the patient. As a corollary, a sponsor that is a pharmaceutical company ordinarily has no duty to warn the patient. At least 25 states, the District of Columbia, and Puerto Rico follow the "learned intermediary" rule, which requires that the manufacturer need warn only the physician [123]. The learned intermediary rule also applies in clinical trials of investigational drugs, even if the physician is paid to participate [124]. Certain courts have suggested, however, that the learned intermediary rule should not apply in circumstances where the prescription does not occur on an individualized basis. Examples include (a) vaccines administered in mass vaccination programs and (b) oral contraceptives [125].

3. Consent

Just as the sponsor discharges its duty by alerting the prescriber, the prescriber discharges his or her duty by alerting the patient. In the eyes of the law, a fully informed, competent patient may *consent* to the risks of therapy, and cannot later sue for injuries to which he or she has consented. Some courts refer to the consent defense as "assumption of the risk." Legal theorists have spent considerable time mapping the boundaries and overlap between the two defenses ("it is now generally recognized that the basis of the [assumption of the risk] defense is not contract but consent" [126]), and a detailed description is beyond the scope of this chapter. For present purposes, the physician can and should fully inform the subject about the risks of therapy, allowing him or her to make an informed decision about whether to run those risks.

The consent defense should not be confused with an argument that a study subject "waived" his or her claim in signing an informed consent before entering into a clinical trial. As noted earlier, it is unlawful to obtain a plaintiff's release or waiver of liability for negligence or other legal fault as a condition for his or her participation in a clinical trial [127]. That prohibition does nothing, however, to impair the defenses of assumption of the risk and consent. Although the informed consent form cannot contain a release, it can and should be drafted to provide a complete defense to any negligence or product liability claim arising out of an investigational use.

4. How Informed Must Consent Be?

Neither the physician nor the sponsor can tell the patient about a risk that is not known [128]. A patient can assume *unknown* risks—can "consent to take his chances as to unknown conditions" [129]. The physician must, however, tell the subject all known information that is "material" to the patient's decision to consent [130]. Most states require the physician to give information according to the standards of physicians in the medical community [131]. A growing minority, by contrast, require the physician to give as much information as a reasonable patient would want to know [132].

In the typical case, where the plaintiff charges that he or she was not warned, the defense will ask whether the patient would have declined the compound if he or she *had* been warned. In many states, it is not enough for the plaintiff simply to testify that he or she would have declined. The question is, instead, "whether the reasonable patient in the plaintiff's position would have withheld consent . . . had the material risks been disclosed" [133]. In other states, however, the plaintiff's own subjective view will be dispositive [134]. Additional defenses to lawsuits charging lack of informed consent are as follows:

> [T]he physician is not required to disclose risks that are unexpected or immaterial, by whatever standard, nor even material risks where disclosure is precluded by an emergency situation, by the patient's incapacity, by the patient's waiver of his right to receive the information, or where disclosure would be harmful to the patient, which gives the doctor a "therapeutic privilege" to withhold the information [134].

E. Bedside Manner

Many plaintiffs claim that their doctors are cold, aloof technocrats, especially when things go wrong. Sometimes—not always—physicians can reduce litigation by managing patients wisely during and after an adverse experience. This goes beyond the obvious: that the patient should receive adequate medical care for the adverse experience. If the adverse experience occurs during a clinical trial, the investigator should work with the sponsor to ensure prompt payment of any compensation to which the subject is entitled under the consent form. The patient and his or her family should be given only such assurances as are appropriate about his or her prognosis. The physician should empathize with the patient's experience. Possessed of common sense, and having signed the informed consent, study subjects should not need to be reminded that clinical research involves risk. For the physician, being available to the patient, relating to him or her as a human being, and caring about his or her welfare can reduce the frequency of suit.

IX. PLANNING FOR PROMOTION

A. The Need for Adequate Studies

Although prescription drug promotion generally is beyond the scope of this chapter, any systematic approach to drug development in the United States requires an understanding of the FDA's advertising rules. A core requirement of the regulations is that drug is "misbranded" if its advertising

> represents that a drug is better, more effective, useful in a broader range of conditions, safer, has fewer, or less incidence of or less serious side effects or contraindications *than has been demonstrated by substantial evidence* or substantial clinical experience [135].

In effect, this regulation requires most claims in promotion to be supported by "substantial evidence." Accordingly, the development of U.S. advertising depends on the development of adequate and well-controlled clinical trials. If the drug developer intends to market its own brand as superior in efficacy to its competitor's, it will need "adequate and well-controlled studies" [136] to show superiority.

To be sure, the pivotal trials necessary to obtain initial FDA marketing approval will provide much clinical support for eventual advertising claims. Many drug developers, however, conduct postmarketing trials, often for the main purpose of generating scientific data to support advertising for the drug. Legal counsel can be useful at the protocol stage of such studies to ensure that the study design is consistent with labeling.

According to the regulations, most clinical investigations of prescription drugs should be carried out under an Investigational New Drug Application [137]. A study is exempt only if it is not intended to support any significant change in the labeling or advertising for the product [138]. Unfortunately, to date, there has been very little indication from the FDA as to what constitutes "a significant change in the advertising for the product." It is clear, however, the FDA ordinarily considers comparative claims versus another drug "significant."

Comparative promotional claims require particular attention at the planning stage. The advertising regulations provide that a drug is misbranded if it "presents the drug as better or safer than another drug (comparative claim) without adequate substantial evidence or clinical experience" [139]. Generally, two or more adequate and well-controlled studies are required to support comparative promotional claims [140]. A single study may be an acceptable basis for a comparative claim if there is "clearly no doubt as to the significance of a study because of size, particular design and/or difference between treatments," and if the study is "fully detailed in the promotional materials" [140].

The advertising regulations also impose other requirements. Generally, the promotion must (a) be consistent with the prescribing information, once the drug is approved [141]; (b) not be false or misleading [142]; (c) be balanced [143]; and (d) not omit important information [144]. It is wise to have legal counsel review all promotion to ensure compliance.

B. Penalties for Advertising Violations

The consequences of violations of the advertising rules can be severe. "Any person" who commits a "prohibited act" "shall be imprisoned for not more than one year or fined not more than $1,000, or both" [145]. For repeat offenders, or offenders in bad faith, the penalty escalates: 3 years in jail or a fine of not more than $10,000. Criminal penalties are not the only risk. "Any . . . drug . . . that is . . . misbranded" may be seized [146]. Thus, theoretically, the government has the power to jail any "person" who causes a prescription drug advertisement to be "false or misleading in any particular," and to seize all stocks of the drug in question. There are lesser sanctions, as well. Despite legal questions about its authority to do so, the FDA has required corrective advertising, "Dear Doctor letters," pre-clearance of advertising, and even the recall of misbranded products. The most common type of FDA action is compliance correspondence. This usually takes the form of a letter contending that promotion is false and misleading. The company usually is given an opportunity to respond, and, often, the matter is resolved through negotiation. Less common and more serious is a Warning Letter. Addressed to the chief executive officer of the company, a warning letter amounts to a threat to begin a legal action unless immediate action is taken to correct the advertising.

Because of the potential severity of sanctions for violative advertising—and because of product liability implications—it is critical that every piece of promotion be reviewed by counsel.

X. CONCLUSION

For reasons having to do with patents, regulations, and liability, drug development in the United States is a law-intensive process. Nothing is more important than securing, via patent or license, the legal right to the product under development. As for the regulations, they are pervasive and detailed, and while medical and scientific personnel are well qualified to interpret many of them, questions requiring the advice of legal counsel arise often. Finally, given the U.S. product liability climate, it is useful to involve lawyers throughout drug development, because liability is an area in which an ounce of prevention is truly worth a pound of cure.

ACKNOWLEDGMENT

The author is grateful to Ronald S. Henshall, R. Brent Olson, and Joseph DiPrima for comments on the manuscript, and to Marcia Nass and Judith Goldberg for assistance in gathering source materials. All opinions are exclusively those of the author, and cannot be attributed to Merck, or any other person.

REFERENCES

1. U.S. Constitution, Article 1, Section 8.
2. 35 U.S.C. § § 100–293.
3. Roger Milgrim, *Milgrim on Trade Secrets*, Matthew Bender, New York, 1993, pp. 9–18.
4. 35 U.S.C. § 101.
5. *F-D-C Reports Inc. (The Pink Sheet) 53(44)*, Trade & Government Memos 1, November 4, 1991.
6. *F-D-C Reports Inc. (The Pink Sheet) 54(31)*, Trade & Government Memos 1, August 3, 1992.
7. *Burroughs Wellcome Co. v. Barr Labs., Inc.*, 828 F. Suppl. 1208 (E.D. N.C. 1993).
8. 35 U.S.C. § 154.
9. 35 U.S.C. § 156.
10. 35 U.S.C. § 284.
11. 35 U.S.C. § 285.
12. Roger Milgrim, *Milgrim on Trade Secrets*, Matthew Bender, New York, 1993, pp. 9–73.
13. 21 U.S.C. § 355(b).
14. *See generally* M. M. Eisman, W. M. Wardell: The decline in effective patent life of new drugs. *Research Management 21*:18–21 (1981); W. M. Wardell, L. E. Sheck: Is pharmaceutical innovation declining? Interpreting measures of pharmaceutical innovation and regulatory impact in the USA, 1950–1980, *Anne Ryde Symposium on Pharmaceutical Economics* (B. Lindgren, ed.), Swedish Institute for Health Economics, Stockholm, 1984, pp. 177–189.
15. Steven Z. Szczepanski, Eckstrom, *Licensing in Foreign and Domestic Operations*, Clark Boardman Callaghan, Deerfield, Ill., 1991, 1-28-29.
16. For the text of the Nuremberg Code and the Declaration of Helsinki, see George J. Annas, Leonard H. Glantz, and Barbara F. Katz, *Informed Consent to Human Experimentation: The Subject's Dilemma*, Ballinger, Cambridge, Ma., 1977, at Appendices A and B.
17. 21 Code of Federal Regulations (CFR) part 50.
18. George J. Annas, Leonard H. Glantz, and Barbara F. Katz, *Informed Consent to Human Experimentation: The Subject's Dilemma*, Ballinger, Cambridge, Ma., 1977, p. 38 n. 45 (citing statutes in 18 states).
19. 21 U.S.C. § 360k(a).
20. *Mitchell v. Iolab Corp.*, 700 F. Suppl. 877 (E.D. La. 1988).
21. *Hillsborough County v. Automated Medical Labs.*, 471 U.S. 707 (1985).
22. *Hurley v. Lederle Labs.*, 851 F.2d 1536 (5th Cir. 1988).
23. *MacDonald v. Ortho Pharmaceutical Corp.*, 394 Mass. 131, 475 N.E.2d 65, cert. denied, 474 U.S. 920 (1985). See Comment, *Federal Preemption and the FDA: What does Congress want?* 58 U. Cin. La. Rev. 263 (1989).
24. 21 CRF 50.25(c).
25. 21 CFR 50.20.

26. Note that disclosure that a therapy is experimental is indispensable not only under the regulations, but also under product liability law. *Gaston v. Hunter*, 121 Ariz. 33, 47, 588 P.2d 326, 340 (Ariz.App. 1978).
27. 21 CFR 50.25(a).
28. 21 CFR 50.25(b).
29. 21 CFR 50.27(a).
30. 21 CFR 50.27(b)(2).
31. 21 U.S.C. § 355(i) (1964) (informed consent required except where not feasible); 21 CFR 50.23(a)(1); see also Meisel, The "exceptions" to the informed consent doctrine: striking a balance between competing values in medical decision making, *1979 Wisc. L. Rev. 413*, 434.
32. 21 U.S.C. § 355(i) (1964) (informed consent required except where not feasible); 21 CFR 50.23(a)(2); see also Philip M. Bein, Surrogate Consent and the Incompetent Experimental Subject, 46 *Food Drug Cosmetic Law Journal* 739–71 (1991), Keeton, *Prosser and Keeton on Torts*, § 18 at 114–17 (5th ed., 1984); Meisel, The "exceptions" to the informed consent doctrine: striking a balance between competing values in medical decision making, *1979 Wisc. L. Rev. 413*, 439.
33. Meisel, The "exceptions" to the informed consent doctrine: striking a balance between competing values in medical decision making, *1979 Wisc. L. Rev. 413*, 453.
34. 21 U.S.C. § 355(i) (1964) (informed consent required except where, in the investigator's professional judgment, it is "contrary to the best interests" of the subjects"). See also Meisel, The "exceptions" to the informed consent doctrine: striking a balance between competing values in medical decision making, *1979 Wisc. L. Rev. 413*, 460.
35. 21 CFR 50.23(d).
36. 21 CFR 50.40–50.46.
37. 21 CFR 56.107(a).
38. 21 CFR 56.102(g).
39. 21 CFR 56.107(a).
40. 21 CFR 56.109(a), (d).
41. 21 CFR 56.111(a)(1).
42. 21 CFR 56.111(a)(2).
43. 21 CFR 56.111(a)(3).
44. 21 CFR 56.111(a)(4)–(5).
45. 21 CFR 56.111(a)(6)–(7).
46. 21 CFR 56.109(b)–(c).
47. 21 CFR 56.115.
48. 21 CFR 56.120–121.
49. 21 CFR 335a, b.
50. 21 CFR 335a(b)(2)(B)(iv).
51. 21 CFR 335b.
52. 21 CFR 335a(k)(1).

53. *U.S. Regulatory Reporter*, May 1993, p. 5.
54. 5 CFR 735.203.
55. 5 U.S.C. § § 501 *et seq.* For other federal conflict of interest rules, *see* 18 U.S.C. § § 201 *et seq.*, 5 C.F.R. Part 735.
56. Office of Inspector General, Dept. of Health and Human Services, *Promotion of Prescription Drugs through Payment and Gifts* (August 1991).
57. 42 U.S.C. § 1320a-7b.
58. 21 CFR 50.25(a)(6).
59. Rebecca Dresser, Wanted: Single white male for medical research, Hastings Center Report, January–February, 1992 at 24; E. L. Kinney, et al., Underrepresentation of women in new drug trials,*Ann. Intern. Med. 95*:495–99 (1981); Paul Cotton, Is there still too much extrapolation from data on middle-aged white men? *JAMA 263*:1049 (February 23, 1990); J. H. Gurwitz et al., The exclusion of the elderly and women from clinical trials in acute myocardial infarction, *JAMA 268*:1417 (September 16, 1992); General Accounting Office, *Women's Health: FDA needs to ensure more study of gender differences in prescription drug testing*, U.S. Government Printing Office, Washington, D.C., 1992; El-Sadr, The challenge of minority recruitment in clinical trials for AIDS, *JAMA 267*: 954 (February 19, 1992).
60. For example, there are reports of evidence that Asians metabolize ß blockers more rapidly than do Caucasians, and require less of a dose; that low birth weight in African-American infants may be compounded by an increased neuroendocrine response to stress; that the lithium-sodium countertransport mechanism in blacks is not as efficient as in whites; that Asian Indians have much lower bone density than Caucasians. Paul Cotton, Examples abound of gaps in medical knowledge because of groups excluded from scientific study, *JAMA 263*:1051 (February 23, 1990); *see also* L. Elizabeth Bowles, The disfranchisement of fertile women in clinical trials: the legal ramifications of and solutions for rectifying the knowledge gap, *45 Vand. L. Rev.* 877, 880 n. 13, 1992.
61. United States Food and Drug Administration, *General Considerations for the Clinical Evaluation of Drugs*, Washington, D.C., U.S. Government Printing Office, 1977, p. 4; *see also* United States Food and Drug Administration, *Guidelines for the Study of Drugs Likely to be Used in the Elserly*, Washington, D.C., U.S. Government Printing Office, 1989, p. 6.
62. United States Food and Drug Administration, *Guidelines for the Study and Evaluation of Gender Differences in the Clinical Evaluation of Drugs, 58 Fed. Reg.* 39,406 (July 22, 1993).
63. But see *Taylor v. Wyeth Labs.*, 139 Mich. App. 389, 362 N.W.2d 293 (Mich. App. 1984) (jury entitled to hear evidence that manufacturer should have tested relationship between blood clotting and the drug in women with blood type A, who have a greater propensity than other women to have pulmonary embolisms).
64. Food and Drug Administration Compliance Program Guidance Manual, program 7348.809 (June 1989).

65. Food and Drug Administration Compliance Program Guidance Manual, program 7348.810 (June 1989).
66. *See, e.g.*, 15 U.S.C. § 78j.
67. Letter from Kenneth P. Feather, Branch Chief, Drug Advertising Regulation Branch, Div. of Drug Advertising and Labeling, Office of Drug Standards, dated May 25, 1984, to Monroe I. Klein, Ph.D., Director, Anti-Infective Group, Regulatory Affairs, Smith Kline & French Laboratories, 1500 Spring Garden Street, P.O. Box 7929, Philadelphia, PA 19101.
68. Letter from William V. Purivs, Assistant to the Director, Div. of Drug Advertising, Bureau of Drugs, United States Food and Drug Administration, dated January 3, 1978 to George P. Nicholas, Lobsenz-Stevens, Inc., 645 Madison Avenue, new York, NY 10022.
69. 21 C.F.R. § 314.8(b)(3).
70. Letter from Carl C. Peck, M.D. to "Dear Sir or Madam," faxed on or about August 1, 1991.
71. United States Food and Drug Administration, Reissuance of Pre-Approval Promotion Guidance (August 1986).
72. 42 C.F.R. Part 50, Subpart A.
73. References in this sentence are taken from B. L. Willcox, The changed landscape of criminal enforcement actions in food and drug cases, speech delivered at the Food Drug Law Institute, February 10–11, 1992.
74. *United States v. Pagones*, no. 88–0581–CR (S.D. Fla. 1988).
75. *United States v. Maroun Warehouse*, No. 90–10027T (D. Mass. 1990).
76. *United States v. Dall*, No. CR–88–3009 (D. Iowa 1988).
77. *United States v. Botzolakis*, Crim. No. HAR–91–0328 (D. Md. 1991).
78. *United States v. Par Pharmaceutical, Inc.*, Crim. No. HAR–89–xxxx (D. Md. 1989).
79. *United States v. Hiland*, 909 F.2d 1114 (8th Cir. 1990).
80. *United States v. Bolar Pharmaceutical Co.*, Crim. No. HAR–91–0063 (D. Md. 1991).
81. See 42 CFR Part 50, Subpart A.
82. Association of American Medical Colleges, *Beyond the "Framework": Institutional Considerations in Managing Allegations of Misconduct in Research* at 19 (1992).
83. Association of American Medical Colleges, *Beyond the "Framework": Institutional Considerations in Managing Allegations of Misconduct in Research* at 31, 41 (1992).
84. See United States Food and Drug Administration, *Compliance Program Guidance Manual*, Chapter 48—"Bioresearch Monitoring—Human Drugs" (Program 7348.810); United States Food and Drug Administration, *Compliance Policy Guides*, Chapter 51—"Inspectional" (Guide 7151.02).
85. *See generally* United States Food and Drug Administration, *Compliance Program Guidance Manual*, Chapter 48—"Bioresearch Monitoring—Human Drugs" (Program 7348.811); FDA Inspections of Clinical Investigators, United States Food and Drug Administration, May 1989.

86. *See* F. H. Branding, Anticipating unannounced inspections, *The Corporate Counselor*, December, 1990, p. 3.
87. For an excellent analysis, see E. J. Flannery, Reporting foreign ADRs and ADRS in phase IV studies, and the significance of the causality assessment, *Food Drug Cosmetic Law Journal*, Vol. 46, p. 43, 1991. See also Department of Health and Human Services, Food and Drug Administration, Center for Drug Evaluation and Research, "Guideline for postmarketing reporting of adverse drug experiences," March 1992.
88. "Smithkline peads guilty on drug tied to deaths," *New York Times*, December 14, 1984; P. Shenon, "Report says Eli Lilly failed to tell of 28 deaths," *New York Times*, August 27, 1985.
89. 21 CFR 312.32(a) (emphasis added).
90. 21 CFR 312.32(c)(1)(i).
91. 21 CFR 312.32(a).
92. 21 CFR 312.32(b)(1)(ii).
93. 21 CFR 312.12(e).
94. 21 CFR 314.80(c)(1)(i).
95. 21 CFR 314.80(a) (emphasis added).
96. 21 CFR 314.80(c)(1)(ii).
97. 21 CFR 314.80(c)(2)(i).
98. Department of Health and Human Services, Food and Drug Administration, Center for Drug Evaluation and Research, "Guidelines for postmarketing reporting of adverse drug experiences," March 1992 at p. 12.
99. 21 U.S.C. § 355(b)(1)(F).
100. 21 U.S.C. § 321(k).
101. 21 U.S.C. § 321(m).
102. 21 CFR 201.56–57.
103. 44 Fed. Reg. no. 124 at 37436 (June 26, 1979) (preamble to 21 CFR 201.56).
104. 21 CFR 314.70(c)(2).
105. 44 Fed. Reg. no. 124 at 37447 (June 26, 1979).
106. Steven Garber, *Products Liability and the Economics of Pharmaceuticals and Medical Devices*, RAND, Santa Monica, Calif., 1993 at pp. xxix, xxxi.
107. American Medical Association Board of Trustees, *Impact of Product Liability on the Development of New Medical Technologies* 1 (June 1988); *see also* Lasagne, The chilling effect of product liability on new drug development, *The Liability Maze: The Impact of Liability Law on Safety and Innovation* (P. Huber and R. Litan, eds.), pp. 334, 336, 1991. Material covered in this and the next three footnotes and accompanying text is adapted from Comments of the Pharmaceutical Manufacturers Association on the *Restatement (Third) of the Law of Torts: Products Liability*, Preliminary Draft No. 1 (April 20, 1993) at 22.
108. *See Brown v. Superior Court*, 44 Cal.3d 1049, 751 P.2d 470, 479–81 (Cal. 1988); Lasagne, The chilling effect of product liability on new drug development, *The*

Liability Maze: The Impact of Liability Law on Safety and Innovation (P. Huber and R. Litan, eds.), 1991, pp. 334, 336, 341–44; *Institute of Medicine, Vaccine Supply and Innovation* (1985), pp. 10–11; Is liability slowing AIDS vaccines? *Science 256*:168 (1992).

109. L. Mastroianni, P. Donaldson, and T. Kane, *Developing New Contraceptives: Obstacles and Opportunities*, 1990, p. 141.
110. *See, e.g., Brock v. Merrell Dow Pharmaceuticals, Inc.*, 874 F.2d 307, 309 (5th Cir.), *modified* 884 F.2d 166 (5th Cir. 1989), *cert. denied*, 110 S. Ct. 1511 (1990).
111. Restatement (Second) of Torts, section 402A.
112. Restatement (Second) of Torts, section 402A, comment k.
113. *Brown v. Superior Court*, 44 Cal.3d 1049, 245 Cal. R. 412, 751 P.2d 470 (1988); *Grundberg v. Upjohn Co.*, 813 P.2d 89 (Utah 1991). Other courts have reached similar holdings but without relying on *Brown. Krasnopolsky v. Warner-Lambert Co.*, 799 F. Supp. 1342 (E.D. N.Y. 1992), citing *Wolfgruber v. Upjohn Co.*, 72 App. Div.2d 59, 61, 423 N.Y.S.2d 95, 97 (1979); aff'd, 52 N.Y.2d 678, 436 N.Y.S.2d 614 (1980); *In re Eli Lilly & Co., Prozac Products Liability Litigation*, 789 F. Supp. 1448, 1452 (S.D. Ind. 1992); *Hahn v. Richter*, Pa. Super., A.2d, 1992 Pa. Super, LEXIS 275 (February 13, 1992).
114. *See, e.g., West v. Searle & Co.*, 305 Ark. 33, 806 S.W.2d 608 (1991); *Adams v. G.D. Searle & Co.*, 576 So.2d 728 (Fla. App.), *review denied*, 589 So.2d 290 (Fla. 1990); *Savina v. Sterling Drug, Inc.*, 247 Kan. 105, 795 P.2d 915 (1990); *Pollard v. Ashby*, 793 S.W.2d 394 (Mo. App. 1990); *White v. Wyeth Labs., Inc.*, 40 Ohio St.3d 390, 533 N.E.2d 748 (1988); *Kociemba v. G.D. Searle & Co.*, 695 F. Supp. 432 (D. Minn. 1988); *Castrignano v. E.R. Squibb & Sons, Inc.*, 546 A.2d 775 (R.I. 1988). Other courts have reached this result without citing *Brown. Rohrbough v. Wyeth Labs, Inc.*, 719 F. Supp. 470, 476 (N.D. W. Va. 1989), *aff'd*, 916 F.2d 970 (4th Cir. 1990).
115. *Gaston v. Hunter*, 121 Ariz. 33, 46–47, 588 P.2d 326, 339-40 (Ariz. App. 1978).
116. *E.G., Brochu v. Ortho Pharmaceutical Corp.*, 642 F.2d 652 (1st Cir. 1981).
117. Henderson and Twerski, A proposed revision of Section 402A of the Restatement (Second) of Torts, *77 Corn. L. Rev.* 1512, 1536 (1992).
118. Keeton, *Prosser and Keeton on Torts*, § 30 at 164–65 (5th ed. 1984); see also *Restatement of the Law, Torts*, 2d, § 281.
119. Keeton, *Prosser and Keeton on Torts*, § 18 at 120 (5th ed. 1984); see also *Gaston v. Hunter*, 121 Ariz. 33, 58, 588 P.2d 326, 351 (Ariz. App. 1978); *Whitlock v. Duke University*, 637 F. Supp. 1463, 67 (M.D.N.C. 1986), *aff'd*, 829 F.2d 1340 (4th Cir. 1987) (North Carolina law).
120. Keeton, *Prosser and Keeton on Torts*, § 9 at 39 (5th ed. 1984).
121. 21 CFR 50.25(a)(6).
122. *Love v. Wolf*, 226 Ca. App. 2d 378, 38 Cal. R. 183 (1964); *Holley v. Burroughs Wellcome Co.*, 318 N.C. 352, 348 S.E.2d 772 (1986); *Incollingo v. Ewing*, 444 Pa. 263, 282 A.2d 206 (1971); *Baldino v. Castagna*, 505 Pa. 239, 478 A.2d 807 (1984).

123. Annotation, Liability of Manufacturer or Seller for Injury or Death Allegedly Caused By Failure to Warn Regarding Danger in Use of Vaccine or Prescription Drug, 94 A.L.R. 3d 748 (1979 & Supp. Aug. 1990) (citing cases).
124. *Tracy v. Merrell Dow Pharmaceuticals*, 58 Ohio St.3d 147, 569 N.E.2d 875, 879 (Ohio 1991).
125. *See Garside v. Osco Drug, Inc.*, 764 F. Supp. 208 (D. Mass. 1991), rev'd, 976 F.2d 77 (1st Cir. 1992).
126. Keeton, *Prosser and Keeton on Torts*, § 68 at 484 (5th ed. 1984).
127. 21 CFR 50.20.
128. *Leibowitz v. Ortho Pharmaceuticals*, 224 Pa. Super. 418, 433–34, 307 A.2d 449, 458–59 (1973).
129. Keeton, *Prosser and Keeton on Torts*, § 68 at 489 (5th ed. 1984).
130. Keeton, *Prosser and Keeton on Torts*, § 32 at 191 (5th ed. 1984).
131. Gerald F. Tietz, Informed consent in the prescription drug context: the special case, *Wash. L. Rev. 61*:367, 368 no. 8 (1986), *citing Watkins v. United States*, 482 F. Supp. 1006 (M.D. Tenn. 1980); *Finley v. United States*, 314 F. Supp. 905 (N.D. Ohio 1970); *Carmichael v. Reitz*, 17 Cal. App. 3d 958, 95 Cal. R. 381 (1971); *Calabrese v. Trenton State College*, 162 N.J. Super. 145, 392 A.2d 600 (1978), *aff'd*, 82 N.J. 321, 413 A.2d 315 (1980); *Koury v. Follo*, 276 N.C. 366, 158 S.E.2d 548 (1968); *Boyer v. Smith*, 345 Pa. Super. 66, 497 A.2d 646 (1985); *Malloy v. Shanahan*, 280 Pa. Super. 440, 4212 A.2d 803 (1980). See also Keeton, *Prosser and Keeton on Torts*, § 32 at 191 (5th ed. 1984).
132. Gerald F. Tietz, Informed consent in the prescription drug context: the special case, *Wash. L. Rev. 61*:367, 368 n. 8 (1986), *citing Canterbury v. Spence*, 464 F.2d 772 (D.C. Cir. 1972), *cert. denied*, 409 U.S. 1064 (1972); *Cobbs v. Grant*, 8 Cal. 3d 229, 104 Cal. Rep. 505, 502 P.2d 1 (1972); *Hamilton v. Hardy*, 37 Colo. App. 375, 549 P.2d 1099 (1976); *Harnish v. Children's Hosp. Medical Center*, 387 Mass. 152, 439 N.E.2d 240 (1982); *Cooper v. Roberts*, 220 Pa. Super. 260, 286 A.2d 647 (1971); *Holt v. Nelson*, 11 Wash. App. 230, 523 P.2d 211 (1974). See also Keeton, *Prosser and Keeton on Torts*, § 32 at 191 (5th ed. 1984).
133. Keeton, *Prosser and Keeton on Torts*, § 32 at 191 (5th ed. 1984).
134. Keeton, *Prosser and Keeton on Torts*, § 32 at 192 (5th ed. 1984).
135. 21 C.F.R. § 202.1(e)(6)(ii).
136. 21 C.F.R. § 314.126.
137. 21 C.F.R. § 312.2(a).
138. 21 C.F.R. § 312.2(b)(1)–(2).
139. 21 C.F.R. § 202.1(e)(6)(ii). See also Comments of David Banks, Assistant to the Director, United States Food and Drug Administration, Division of Drug Advertising and Labeling, RAPS Annual Meeting, September 27, 1988, Alexandria, Virginia.
140. United States Food and Drug Administration, Compliance policy guidance regarding comparative promotional claims (undated).
141. 21 C.F.R. § 201.100(d)(1).

142. 21 U.S.C. § 352(a).
143. 21 C.F.R. § 202.1(e)(5)(ii).
144. 21 C.F.R. § 202.1(e)(5)(iii).
145. 21 U.S.C. § 333(a)(1).
146. 21 U.S.C. § 334(a).
147. Food and Drug Administration Compliance Program Guidance Manual, program 7348.811 (June 1989).

15

Social Aspects of Pharmaceutical Development

Michael Montagne

Massachusetts College of Pharmacy and Allied Health Sciences
Boston, Massachusetts

Corporate strategies in the pharmaceutical world now view drug development as a series of regulatory hurdles, not as a research endeavor, let alone in its broader social context [1]. In many instances, social (and also behavioral, cultural, and historical) factors can have a major influence on the drug discovery and development process. The primary way in which nonpharmaceutical factors affect drug development is through the beliefs and perceptions of those who use drugs. Future innovations in drug development will find it necessary to attend to the important impact social factors have on the development, approval, regulation, prescribing, and use of pharmaceutical agents.

I. SOCIAL PERSPECTIVES ON DRUGS, DRUG USE, AND DRUG DEVELOPMENT

Beliefs and perceptions about drugs and drug use evolve as social knowledge within a given culture. Social knowledge refers to the collective knowing of something, based mostly on available information and past experiences. This knowledge consequently influences behaviors and the nature of experiences. What an individual or group of drug takers knows about drugs—from reading information, listening to the media and promotional campaigns, receiving descriptions of others' experiences, and recalling their own previous experiences—affects their actual use of drugs [2–4].

Social knowledge also has a symbolic component. The nature and meaning of drug taking often is described, remembered, and transmitted through a society in symbolic form, as images, portrayals, or metaphors [5]. The spread of ideas, information, attitudes, behaviors, and even actual drug products occurs within the various social networks that exist in that cultural context. With regard to drug taking, this concept was first defined and studied in research on physician prescribing behaviors and the adoption of new drug products.

Culture can impose specific values on knowledge and behavior. For instance, there are different models of madness (e.g., medical, moral, social, psychoanalytic, and psychedelic), each with its own etiology of illness, methods of diagnosis, and approaches to treatment. There are different values that direct drug use [6]. There is, for example, a therapeutic ethic in Western societies: a goal-oriented approach to achieving a state of harmony or equilibrium. Tranquilizer use, from the perspective of this ethic, attempts to produce happiness, contentment, accommodation, or adjustment. Other values would oppose the use of tranquilizers, however, but for different reasons.

Corporate culture has been defined as "a system of shared meanings whose key characteristics are beliefs and values, and emergent norms generated and supported by them" [7]. Corporate culture in the pharmaceutical industry has been found to be an important determinant of organizational image and functioning. Strong, well-defined corporate cultures seem to be indicative of highly effective organizations, and even entrenched cultures can be modified. The most successful organizations have corporate cultures that are conceptualized, managed, and changed relevant to the needs and demands for their products and services.

As Svarstad [8] has noted, pharmaceutical scientists define or classify drugs based on a physical, chemical, or physiological characteristic (e.g., structure, solubility, stability, potency) of the object; social scientists classify drugs based on social meanings and functions. Pharmaceutical scientists are interested in how drugs are isolated, synthesized, absorbed, distributed, metabolized, and excreted, whereas social scientists are interested in issues regarding the promotion, dispensing, control, and use of drugs.

Pharmaceutical and medical scientists argue that drug action and drug effect are equatable because pharmacological activity is the foundation for all changes that occur during a drug experience. Some scientists agree that nonpharmacologic factors can influence some people's experiences, primarily in the occurrence of side effects. A sociological viewpoint, however, holds that drug effects are nothing more than applied labels drawn from the drug user's social knowledge, certainly not the result of the drug's pharmacological activity. This component of knowledge is socially constructed from the user's past knowledge of and experiences with drugs, through interaction with other people concerning their drug taking experiences, and through additional interaction within the social environment of drug taking.

The pharmacological theory of drug effects has reached paradigmatic proportions, and it controls most thinking about and use of drugs called medicines [9]. This theory states that drug action results from the interaction, through a physicochemical bond, of a drug molecule with a cell or constituent part of a cell in the human body. This notion evolved into the receptor concept, providing the basis for relating structural similarities in drug molecules with similarities in biological activity. The concepts of biochemical specificity, involving cellular receptors, and dose-response relationships have become the central tenets of the pharmacological theory of drug effects. These tenets have affected the ways in which drug effects are studied and measured, new drugs are developed and tested, clinical pharmacology is understood and taught, and drug therapy is prescribed and monitored.

This theory's major tenets have proved to be very relevant in explaining how many drugs act in the body to produce effects, such as antibiotics and chemotherapeutic agents, opiates and synthetic narcotics, and certain cardiovascular agents. But it does not explain or predict all aspects of a drug-taking experience. This can be noted in the changes of major indications for a drug over time, the inability of this theory to explain many drug experiences (e.g., placebo phenomena, anesthesia, most psychoactive drug effects, differences in main versus side effects, and descriptions of effects by drug user compared to those of an observer, such as a researcher or clinician), and the occurrence of effects not seen in research studies or expected based on pharmacological information. For instance, recent research from this perspective has attempted to explain the placebo phenomenon as resulting solely from the activity of endogenous neurotransmitters such as endorphins.

Sociological theories of drug effects are radically different in conception and description. From this perspective, drug effects are basically social in origin. The use of literary and other popular accounts of drug-taking experiences by drug users in constructing an ideology and social reality of drug taking has led some social scientists to redefine the nature of drug effects into social terms, often in direct opposition to what has been called the chemicalistic fallacy [10]. This fallacy involves the view that a specific drug causes specific effects that are a function of the biochemical properties of the drug. Sociological theories assume that drug effects are not a direct function of the pharmacological activity of the drug, but are primarily a function of the user's beliefs and perceptions and social expectations and definitions for that drug.

These theories have assisted in explaining better how effects occur for many types of drugs and in describing more tacit drug-taking experiences. These theories focus more on the following tenets: (a) the user must perceive changes in body state or mood, (b) the user actively interprets these changes and defines them based on available social knowledge, and (c) the defined effects must be attributed to the drug that was taken by the user in order for these effects to become a part of that user's social knowledge about drugs.

II. ASSESSING THE NATURE AND EXTENT OF DRUG-TAKING AND DRUG-USE PROBLEMS: PHARMACOEPIDEMIOLOGY AT THE SOCIAL LEVEL

The development of conceptual frameworks and methodological strategies to assess drug-taking behaviors has increased in recent years with a resurgence of interest in drug epidemiology, or as it is now called, pharmacoepidemiology [11]. Although the term is relatively new, actual research has been taking place for at least four decades in epidemiology and public health. Epidemiology provides a theoretical basis for examining the source of supply and flow of drugs throughout a population. Pharmacoepidemiology assesses the frequency and distribution of pharmaceutical care, or drug use, outcomes in a population. From this information, the nature and extent of specific types of drug use can be determined in a given population, and potential or real problems can be identified.

The focus of this type of research includes: (a) what is being used, an assessment of specific drugs used in certain situations; (b) how is it being used, an assessment of the patterns of use (including how much, where and when, and by whom); and (c) why is it being used, an assessment of the reasons for drug-taking behaviors and the functions that drugs serve in society. This latter focus on the reasons for use is included only rarely in most pharmacoepidemiologic studies.

The World Health Organization focuses pharmacoepidemiologic efforts at assuring the quality, safety, and efficacy of drugs and their use in specific populations [12]. Pharmacoepidemiologic studies are performed to (a) describe current patterns of drug use; (b) determine changes in use over time; (c) measure the impact of information, education, promotional activities, media accounts, and price on drug use; (d) detect inappropriate drug use and associated problems; (e) estimate drug needs in terms of disease patterns and outbreaks; and (f) plan the selection, supply, and distribution of drugs.

There are many different sources of data and information on drug-taking behaviors (see Table 1). Each source of data on drug use has its own unique

Table 1 Sources of Data on Drug Use

Sources
Experimental Data
Clinical trial results
Institutional Record Systems and Databases
Hospital-based medical audits (in-patient)
Systemwide Databases
Institutional-based reviews (outpatient)
Health insurance groups and third-party payers
Pharmaceutical organizations
Commercial vendors of marketing studies and sales data
National Databases
Government-sponsored studies
Essential drug lists and inventory data
Pharmacoepidemiologic surveillance systems
Local and Regional Studies
Private or public surveys
Industry-based (adverse drug reaction reporting)
Field Studies
Drug sellers/retailers/distributors
Drug-taking behaviors of individuals and groups

advantages and limitations. Many studies report only frequencies of use without any basis in the population from which they were derived. Epidemiologic measures are based on rates, with a numerator divided by a denominator, like a percentage. Reporting that 100 patients are using a new drug (the numerator), without giving a sense of whether this is occurring in a population of 1000 or 100,000, provides only marginally useful information. This is even more important in studying trends in drug use. Denominator data are very important, because without them, comparisons are really impossible.

These classic epidemiologic approaches focus mostly on the "what" and "how" of drug use, but only recently, the need for assessing the "why" of drug use also has become important. Studies of nonmedical drug "epidemics," and attempts to explain significant differences in the rates of drug use among subgroups of a population (e.g., more women use psychotropic medications than men), pointed to the need to collect and analyze societal data on drug use perceptions. This additional piece of information, along with the quantitative assessment of the patterns of drug use, can provide a

Table 2 Preventing and Solving Drug-Use Problems with Pharmacoepidemiology

Medical Drug Use
Inappropriate prescribing behaviors
Patient noncompliance
Irrational self-medication practices
Poor outcomes and increased cost of pharmacotherapies
Nonmedical Drug Use
Social-recreational drug use problems
Acute incidents of drug toxicities
Chemical dependencies
Outbreaks of drug "epidemics"

much clearer and more detailed picture of what is occurring in the patient population. More importantly, it can provide ideas for bringing about changes in these patterns of use, especially to prevent or limit drug-use problems.

The future for pharmacoepidemiologic studies has unlimited potential. There is a need to broaden the focus to include societal data on people's perceptions about drugs and cultural factors important in structuring drug-taking behaviors. These approaches and techniques for assessing the nature and extent of drug-taking behaviors, and the reasons behind unsafe or irrational drug use, will allow us to develop strategies to prevent or limit drug-use problems (see Table 2). With these tools, the products of organized drug development efforts can be used more effectively, with minimal problems, for the benefit of both individual patients and society.

III. BELIEFS AND PERCEPTIONS ABOUT DRUGS AND DRUG USE

The original Greek term for drug, *pharmakon*, has three meanings: remedy, poison, and magical charm [5]. Chemical substances used in a medical context are thought of as remedies, but many such substances also can induce negative effects (i.e., side effects, adverse reactions) and toxic episodes. Thus, the drug as remedy is also thought of at times as the drug as poison. In earlier times, remedies and potions also were imbued with magical or charmed abilities. Even today, medicine and society still refer to some drugs, newer entities, in a magical context.

This phenomenon of labeling drugs, drug taking, and drug users has had an impact on the use of drugs in medical contexts. These portrayals are influential in the development of conceptions and attitudes toward drug entities and of meanings that are attributed to drugs and drug effects [3,13, 14]. These meanings, structured and expressed as symbols or metaphors, assist drug users, health professionals, and general society in perceiving and describing drug-taking experiences, and in actually directing drug-taking behaviors.

Drug takers employ a variety of metaphors to understand and describe their reasons for use and the effects they experience (see Table 3) [5,15,16]. These meanings also are reflected in social drug policy, societal discourse (especially media accounts and promotional campaigns), program planning, and drug laws and regulations. The meanings therefore are very important in constructing social realities of drug use, either personally or at the societal level. Drug development also has its metaphors, in which drug discovery and development have been viewed and thought of as a pipeline, horse race, poker game, orchestra, hurdles race, ocean liner, connect-the-dots game, maze, and high jump [7].

Table 3 Symbols and Metaphors of Drugs and Drug Use

Drug As [Is]	Drug Use As [Is]
magic bullet/placebo	vacation/trip/break/escape
solution/answer/panacea	safe place
death/poison	disease/plague
tool/vehicle/computer program	artificial paradise
passport/ticket	mental or moral weakness
pacifier/consoler/comforter	normal daily event (afternoon tea)
helper/missing mate/friend	military mobilization
enslaver/straitjacket	Turkish bath/relaxing setting
crutch/prop/support/Band-aid	social image/lifestyle
lock/vice/prison	social control
lifeline/life enhancer	fog/barrier/imprisonment
standby/security	evil necessity/plague/scourge
resource/barter/money	denial of other behavior
life/food	zombification
fuel/tonic	
hero/army/police	
enemy/killer	
other drugs (aspirin/penicillin/laxatives)	

There are some dominant pharmacomythologies—cultural conceptions about drugs—that are illusory, yet they have achieved the status of and exist as fundamental principles [18]. Many people believe that a drug produces only one effect, or a primary effect that is referred to as its "main" effect, with a positive connotation. If other effects are experienced, they are considered "side" effects, with a negative connotation. Drugs in fact produce a whole array of physiological and psychological changes.

There also is a belief that a drug produces the same main effect every time it is taken and in each person who takes it. In essence, these drug effects are *caused* by the chemical compounds that are ingested, and by extension, "drug effects" are a property of and reside in chemical compounds and are not a function of some change in living organisms. Yet, as Albert Hofmann and many pharmacologists have noted, "we can say of many drugs that we know *how* they act and in what way, but we are still quite unable to say *why* they act as they do" [19].

In reality, there still are no known laws defining the relationship between chemical constitution and pharmacological activity. Our knowledge of associations between specific chemical structures and measured pharmacological activity, let alone experienced drug effects, is ultimately based solely on empirical data. Most of our knowledge about the pharmacology of drugs is based on a tautological notion that chemical responses, usually observed and measured in a laboratory setting often involving parts (cells and organ systems) of animals, are presumed to be chemical causes. Again, Albert Hofmann has stated rightly, and many pharmacologists and clinicians concur, that "it is impossible to predict the biological activity of a substance in man from the pattern of activity demonstrated in laboratory animals" [19].

As a result, there is, unfortunately, a general belief that most prescription drugs and many nonprescription drugs cure, but the vast majority do not; they only ameliorate symptoms, prevent exacerbation of acute conditions, or limit the extent of damage of chronic conditions, usually only over a restricted period of time. Most of these drug effects occur only as long as the drug is present physically in the organism, and drugs that are external chemical replacements rarely are as effective as endogenous substances. Drugs as chemical substances affect only biological systems, and the belief in Western scientific cultures that illness has only a biological basis leads to the notion that drugs are the primary, or only, form of medical treatment.

What impact do these pharmacomythologies have in everyday life? Drug makers focus on the main effect, attempt to optimize the biochemical activity of the molecule, increase specificity, and look to increase effectiveness through enhancement of that one effect and to reduce or limit all other effects. This mind-set is very similar to that of health professionals, who are interactive with drug makers at least through industry-generated drug information, and who focus on treating their patients with a drug with one main effect. Many of them realize that there is individuality in response to drugs among their patients, so they search for the most active compound that works with the highest degree of specificity, often at the lowest dosage, thus equating activity with potency and with the fewest side effects. Drug consumers, however, focus on a variety of changes that occur after they ingest a drug, and great confusion can ensue because they are experiencing and focusing on more than just that one main effect.

IV. PATIENT BELIEFS, COMPLIANCE, AND DRUG-USE PROBLEMS

These various beliefs and perceptions that drug users hold, whether in the role of research subject or treatment patient, are instrumental in understanding how and why these individuals actually use pharmaceutical agents. In drug development, these drug beliefs are especially important in compliance during clinical trials and in the occurrence of problems resulting from drug use.

A. Patient Compliance in Clinical Drug Research

The failure of patients to take drugs as prescribed, called noncompliance, has been documented and its implications for patient care are well known to health professionals [20]. The impact noncompliance can have on the drug development process, from clinical trials to marketing, has not been appreciated much by pharmaceutical manufacturers and regulators [21]. Noncompliance occurs for a variety of reasons, and many determinants have been identified through research. Some patients may even exhibit "intelligent noncompliance," either because they are experiencing side effects or no therapeutic effects, and so decide to discontinue treatment, or because they take their medications only for symptomatic reasons.

Noncompliance by participants in clinical trials affects the evaluation and approval of new pharmaceutical agents at two stages [22]. First, during the pre-approval drug development phases, noncompliance may alter results of clinical investigations that determine optimum dose and package insert labeling. After the drug has been approved and is marketed, noncompliance, especially if widespread, may lead to the emergence of unanticipated problems such as irregular dosing, overprescribing, failures to achieve patient care outcomes, and toxicities.

Some drug approval delays can be attributed to noncompliance and the failure of clinical investigators to recognize it. There may be difficulty in demonstrating a drug's effectiveness in "intent-to-treat" analyses, which assumes that patients follow the regimens to which they were assigned. Noncompliance also can interfere with determination of therapeutic dosage ranges. Most trials that now report the safety and efficacy of a drug do not reflect the individual patient's response to a prescribed dosage. They truly reflect a composite of the responses of patients who fail to comply, those who partially comply, and those who fully comply with the therapeutic regimen.

Adjustments for noncompliance in analysis of clinical trial data would be opposed to the "intent-to-treat" approach. It is necessary to take into account the impact of known compliance (or noncompliance) on estimates of a drug's safety and efficacy. Giving equal weight to compliant patients who took the drug and to patients who never took the drug, took the wrong drug, or took inadequate amounts increases the probability of overestimating the therapeutic dose range. Adverse reactions then could occur when patients take the recommended dose in practice. It becomes obvious, then, that noncompliance affects the cost of drug development. Additional trials may be necessary for approval, and the problem resides with patient noncompliance, not the drug product's dose or formulation.

There are a number of indicators of possible noncompliance in a clinical trial. Precise diaries on drug use and exact pill counts that are provided by a patient who is more casual about other aspects and details of the protocol can be a warning sign. When the therapeutic response varies from excellent to poor from visit to visit, or there is inconsistent reporting of drug-taking behavior upon interview, then the investigator should suspect noncompliance. Factors that lead to noncompliance include a complex regimen of long duration, psychiatric diagnosis, side effects, a degree of behavioral change, lack of understanding, lack of perceived effectiveness or usefulness, social isolation, health beliefs, and lack of incentive to adhere to treatment.

Patient compliance is measured in a number of ways, each varying in degree of ease, invasiveness, and validity, from patient self-reports to pill counts to drug testing of tissue samples (see Table 4). In short-term protocols, such as bioavailability studies, actual observation of ingestion and swallowing is used. In long-term studies, less direct methods are employed. Measurement of patient compliance should be an integral part of any clinical trial and postmarketing surveillance study, as well as a topic in general discussions of the drug approval process [23]. Strategies for improving patient compliance in clinical trials have been developed and tested (see Table 5).

Table 4 Methods for Measuring Patient Drug Use Compliance in Clinical Trials

Observed ingestion with mouth inspection
Pill count
Device that notes times when pill container is opened
Diary of times of ingestion
Measurement of blood, urine, or other tissues samples for principal agent or inert marker
Measurement of predictable pharmacodynamic response
Patient/subject self-report

They range in complexity, cost, degree of compliance enhancement, and ease of administration. Compliance monitoring can be performed now using computer systems [24].

Clinical trial research, particularly on chronic diseases, is finding the need to develop new end points [25]. Priority needs to be given to subjective in addition to objective end points, which imply a focus on risk factors and symptomatic treatments over cures. Such research needs to emphasize the psychosocial component as important or more so than the biological com-

Table 5 Strategies for Improving Patient Compliance

Dosage form design.
Improved packaging, careful labeling and directions.
Special pill packaging and reminder devices.
Checklist form or diary.
Follow-up procedures.
Written and verbal drug education.
Written contracts and agreements (form of behavioral modification).
Connect medication taking to a key event in patient's daily life.
Monetary or material rewards.
Relationship with study staff; length of time spent with staff.
Treat subjects with promptness (appointments, response to concerns).
All contacts with subjects should be friendly, informed, and in a professional manner that reflects the importance and uniqueness of the patient.
Research protocol should clearly state those unique outcomes the patient might expect in return for their participation.

ponent. These areas of study are exploring the emergent quality-of-life concepts and new ethical priorities in health care.

Compliance and subject retention can be enhanced by a careful recruitment and screening process, especially with detailed descriptions of what is involved in being a participant in a clinical trial [26]. Clinical trial planning should emphasize patient education activities and follow-up reminders to increase compliance [27,28]. Monetary or material rewards also have been used by investigators to improve appointment-keeping, diary maintenance, and return of pill containers. Developing checklist forms or a diary facilitates compliance better than providing the patient with a lot of printed material or no information at all. In general, the principal investigator and staff should get to know the patients well enough to understand what motivates and satisfies them in terms of their participation in the research process.

B. Drug-Taking Behaviors and Drug-Use Problems

Drug giving and drug taking are complex, dynamic phenomena. No single individual or group is solely to blame for inappropriate drug-taking behaviors and associated problems. Most drug-use problems result from an intricate interplay of social knowledge and beliefs, value foundations and reasons for drug use, the nature and meaning of actual effects experienced by drug users, the availability of or accessibility to drug products, and the ability of control mechanisms to regulate drug taking and to prevent or limit drug-use problems.

Medicalization is the process of redefining or relabeling a personal or social "life" problem as a medical condition, thus necessitating involvement in and control by the health care delivery system. More broadly, it can be seen as the imposition or substitution of medical care, and the biomedical model of health and illness, for care or activities that before were nonmedical in nature. Medicalization may occur conceptually, institutionally, or interpersonally [29]. Many aspects of life are influenced or dominated by biomedicine, to the point that some have argued we are seeing the medicalization of everything in life over the latter half of the twentieth century. There is no consensus, however, as to whether the medicalization process, and its outcomes, are positive or negative.

The issue of promoting medications for personal or social problems involves a difficult balance between medical definitions of what constitutes a disease and consumers' perceptions of what they want or need in the way of optimal health and well-being [30]. There are certain symptom states and conditions that are poorly defined in terms of the biomedical model of disease. Other conditions, such as child abuse, ordinary stress and tension ("pressures of life"), small breasts, thinning hair, mental fatigue, and certain personal and social problems of life are often considered diseases by some (e.g., afflicted consumers, health product manufacturers and promoters), but not by others (e.g., health professionals, health insurance companies).

Unique and innovative drugs restructure our thoughts and actions regarding states of health and illness. Patients often view new drugs as magical (e.g., magic bullets) with mystical abilities not only to ameliorate symptoms but also to cure. This is evident in the case of oral contraceptives to prevent (control) pregnancy [31], and more recently with the use of human growth hormone in children who are just slightly short of the "average" height [32]. In part, these problems reflect the passing of new medications through stages of acceptance [33]. Upon introduction, a new drug entity may be overvalued and thus overused as long-term problems are not yet apparent. As problems arise with greater use, the drug may become condemned and undervalued. In the end, as the benefits and dangers of using the drug become clear, its use is one hopes, more appropriate.

V. IMPACT OF PUBLIC PERCEPTIONS ON DRUG DEVELOPMENT

The context of drug development now has three major components: (a) availability of financing and resources; (b) organizational structure and a corporate culture; and (c) public opinion of the value of the research [34]. Public perceptions regarding specific drug products and their use are reflected in society's mass media, and the media can be instrumental in affecting many aspects of drug development and drug use.

A. Public Attitudes and Media Representations of Drugs

In a study of the media and its accounts of prescription drug use, 34% of the media stories reported on the effects, good but mostly bad, of prescription drugs, and 24% reported about new drugs and uses [35]. Concerns about pricing and the economics of prescription drug development account for 20% of the stories. About one-quarter of these were "media events," such as press conferences held to describe a new drug discovery. Great discoveries and major breakthroughs, though, are very rare events.

The benzodiazepine tranquilizers represent an excellent example of the development of drug images and their influence on attitudes and use. Negative reputations for this class of drugs were generated through an interplay of public attitudes and perceptions, the media's involvement, and personal accounts of drug-use problems by the users themselves. Most of the objections to the use of these tranquilizers have been based on moral judgments and seem to have little basis in sound scientific or clinical research [36]. The result has been a conflict between medical metaphors, which support the use of these drugs by viewing mental illnesses with the classic disease model, and societal metaphors, which view the use of these drugs as a sign of moral weakness or a lack of self-control [36–38].

The cultural beliefs, value systems, and symbolic images regarding tranquilizers and their use have greatly influenced decision making on the part of both physician and patient [15]. In the biomedical researcher's and clinician's minds, there is this view of anxiety in which the sympathetic nervous system is pulsating with neurochemicals. And of course, the best route to treatment is to suppress the physiological activity of these endogenous substances. A good deal of tranquilizer prescribing is done by general practitioners, or others without specific training in pharmacotherapeutics; thus, they do not have a well-developed "culture" of what constitutes optimal prescribing behavior. They do not have a strong cultural mind-set to direct them. Those physicians with specialty training, on the other hand, may have been acculturated into the biological model of the brain. For instance, one prominent professional metaphor for tranquilizers views them as tools to fine-tune the body-machine, or as a computer program to correct an error in the computer's (i.e., brain's) functioning.

There is also the issue of tranquilizer prescribing and use as a form of medicalization [37]. Because of the dominance of biological reductionism in medicine, wherein problematic human behavior is described solely or ultimately in biological or biochemical terms, personal or social problems become medical conditions. In most Western societies, health is a supreme value, and the physician is the universal healer. Yet the disease, anxiety, that is being treated is ill-defined, and this may lead to uncertainty and frustration on the part of the physician. The prescribing of tranquilizers represents a solution to the problem of not being able to clearly define and diagnose the disease, in biological terms, and thus knowing the corresponding treatment, and the problem of feeling uncertain about how to portray expertise to the patient. The lack of quality information about the drugs can further confuse the process of adequately diagnosing and treating the problem [39].

B. Premature Drug Product Removal

The premature removal of drug products from the marketplace is a very complex, interactive phenomenon, with a number of social and regulatory factors playing important roles in the process [40]. Previous cases indicate that the focal point of most premature removal situations is the drug's effects, usually viewed negatively, or the drug's image in mass media and society [41].

This is a time when societal forces and collective consumer consciousness, in any form, can influence, change, or impede the drug development process. These forces can be marshalled by mass media, consumer advocacy groups, regulatory and other governmental agencies, and even individual patients. The process through which a drug product is removed prematurely from the marketplace has been identified and described [40].

Knowledge about drug effects has a profound impact on the perception, understanding, and satisfaction of those consumers who are using the specific drug product. These effects, whether viewed as positive or negative, might be new indications for use, side effects and adverse reactions, societal notions about effects (real or not), and effects from unintended uses. Antecedent factors may be important in generating, structuring, or enhancing individual and societal beliefs about drug effects. Such factors include specific patterns of consumer use, the drug manufacturer's promotional activities, media accounts of drug use problems, postmarketing surveillance results, and even surreptitious phenomena.

As a result of this new or recurring knowledge about a drug's effects, and in a broader sense, the drug's image, a response can occur on the part of an individual or group of consumers. The nature and extent of this response can be modified by a number of factors, many of which are interrelated and recursive. Modification can involve media overhype of the situation, consumer overreaction with changes in attitudes about drugs and drug manufacturers, and government regulation. This process seems to result in either forced or voluntary removal of the drug product, positive modifications (e.g., indications, packaging, promotion) as indicated (and forced or voluntary compliance with these changes), or in some cases, a change or significant result does not occur. The outcome for the product can be a change in use and sales; for the pharmaceutical manufacturer, outcomes can consist of positive or negative changes in its image, financial situation, its other drug products, or overall health of the company.

C. Patients Evading Traditional Drug Development Systems

A renewed interest by many people in taking charge of their own health care has emerged recently due to the pervasive "consumerism" movement in American society. This movement, which has been growing in the United States since the 1960s, is an expression of consumer consciousness that is evolving through three stages:

Stage I: The producer of a good or the provider of a service controls all aspects of the interaction or exchange with a consumer.
Stage II: The consumer (patient) begins to question the way things are done and asks for more information.
Stage III: The consumer has equal input into the interaction or decision making, and often even control over it.

This expanding consumer consciousness, and the desire to know more about what is going on and to have a say in it, is very evident in health care. Patients want more information about their state of health and their diseases. They want personal control over managing their health and in making health care decisions. They want to be "in charge" of staying healthy or getting better if they become ill.

A major part of this trend is the development of a consumer self-care movement. For a variety of reasons, more people want to engage in self-diagnosis when they experience symptoms or think that they are sick. They also want to direct their choice and use of treatment. Consumers now are using a number of nontraditional approaches, including herbal remedies, that exist outside of organized health care systems. While self-care and self-medication are beneficial in many situations, most patients will make such decisions and act without the assistance or supervision of a pharmacist, physician, or other health professional.

There are many reasons why patients and consumers attempt to circumvent the traditional system for obtaining drugs [42]. These people get their ideas and information from some source, including their family, friends, and coworkers, mass media, and other consumer information resources. Books, pamphlets, newsletters, organized patient support groups, and consumer advocates often promote unproved or unapproved therapies for patients. They suggest that patients can buy drugs from overseas supply houses, show them how to find orphan drugs, and they even will provide or include sample forms required by U.S. Customs, lists of suppliers, and catalogues from those suppliers with drug costs and shipping charges.

Patients, especially those with seriously debilitating or life-threatening diseases, have focused their concern and anger primarily at two groups, the U.S. Food and Drug Administration and the pharmaceutical companies [43]. The FDA is viewed by many people as an agency whose major function has been to slow progress in the development of new treatments. Concerns for public safety have turned obsessive and counterproductive. Some consumers feel that the FDA has become overly protective of society as a whole at the great expense of individual patients who are dying. In addition, like most government agencies, the FDA is too large and bureaucratic to change in significant ways anytime soon. AIDS activists, however, have changed the drug approval process [43,44]. Many AIDS patients have not wanted to wait to be enrolled in a clinical trial, especially if it means they become part of the placebo group, and they have gone underground for drug supplies and to participate in unapproved clinical trials. Consumers' desires to use wonder drugs often result in a consumer movement that can greatly influence the FDA and the pharmaceutical manufacturer [45].

VI. CONCLUSIONS

In the real world of medication use, humans often are not rational when making decisions to use pharmacologically active substances. Health professionals, who are dominated by the scientific, technological approach to medicine, are not aware, nor do they make their patients aware, of alternative healing models and other types of treatment, most often meaning non-drug therapies. Consumers, especially those involved in self-care and self-treatment practices, are not aware of all possible treatment options in arriving at a therapeutic plan. A recent survey found that most patients do not think of themselves as consumers [46]. Many patients lack motivation to practice consumer behaviors such as seeking information, exercising independent judgment, and applying cost sensitivity.

Social factors have been found to have an impact on the development and use of drugs. Although greatly unappreciated in the planning and administration of clinical research, specific social factors nonetheless may influence the outcomes of clinical trials, the focus and impact of promotional activities, the results of postmarketing surveillance of marketed drugs, and even the image of the drug product and its maker.

The future of drug discovery and development has seen the end of the chemical era and the beginning of the biotechnology era. But even the focus on biotechnology and genetic approaches to drug development have their limitations. Major innovations in the drug development and approval process soon will need to broaden their perspective and consider the social and cultural context of drug discovery and use.

REFERENCES

1. D. M. Cocchetto and R. V. Nardi, *Managing the Clinical Drug Development Process*, Marcel Dekker, New York, 1992.
2. P. Conrad, *Soc. Sci. Med. 20*:29–37 (1985).
3. M. Montagne, *J. Drug Issues 14*:491–507 (1984).
4. M. Montagne, *J. Drug Issues 18*:139–48 (1988).
5. M. Montagne, *Soc. Sci. Med. 26*:417–24 (1988).
6. R. M. Veatch, *J. Drug Issues 7*:253–62 (1977).
7. L. Narine and T. R. Einarson, *J. Pharm. Marketing Management 6*:33–42 (1991).
8. B. L. Svarstad, Sociology of drugs in health care, *Pharmacy Practice: Social and Behavioral Aspects* (A. I. Wertheimer and M. C. Smith, eds.), 3rd ed., Williams & Wilkins, Baltimore, MD, 1989.
9. M. Montagne, *Int. J. Addictions 32*, in press.
10. R. Dubos, On the present limitations of drug research, *Drugs In Our Society* (P. Talalay, ed.), Johns Hopkins University Press, Baltimore, MD, 1964.
11. A. G. Hartzema, M. S. Porta, H. H. Tilson, *Pharmacoepidemiology: An Introduction*, 2nd ed., Harvey Whitney Books, Cincinnati, OH, 1991.
12. World Health Organization, *The Rational Use of Drugs*, WHO, Geneva, 1987.
13. A. Arluke, *Human Organization 39*:84 (1980).
14. L. A. Rhodes, *Culture Medicine Psychiatry 8*:49–70 (1984).
15. M. Montagne, The culture of long-term tranquilliser users, *Understanding Tranquilliser Use: The Role of the Social Sciences* (J. Gabe, ed.), Tavistock/Routledge, London, 1991.
16. C. G. Helman, *Soc. Sci. Med. 15B*:521–33 (1981).
17. B. Spilker, *Multinational Drug Companies: Issues in Drug Discovery and Development*, Raven Press, New York, 1989.
18. M. Montagne, The Pharmakon phenomenon: Cultural conceptions of drugs and drug use, *Contested Ground: Public Purpose and Private Interest in the Regulation of Pharmaceuticals* (P. Davis, ed.), Oxford University Press, New York, 1996.
19. A. Hofmann, Planned research and chance discovery in pharmaceutical development, *Clinical Research in Pharmaceutical Development* (B. A. Bleidt and M. Montagne, eds.), Marcel Dekker, New York, 1996.
20. D. A. Hussar, Patient compliance, *Remington: The Science and Practice of Pharmacy* (A. R. Gennaro, ed.), 19th ed., Mack, Easton, PA, 1995.
21. B. A. Kehr, *Pharm. Times 58*:76, 78, 80–81, 86 (April 1992).
22. L. Lasagna, *Drug Topics 136*:33–35 (Suppl. 3, 1992).
23. G. W. Pledger, *J. Clin. Res. Pharmacoepi. 6*:77–81 (1992).
24. S. A. Heen and J. Ceppaglia, *Am. J. Hosp. Pharm. 49*:2746–48 (1992).

25. T. J. M. Cleophas, *Clin. Res. Reg. Affairs 12*:273–82 (1995).
26. F. L. Iber, W. A. Riley, and P. J. Murray, *Conducting Clinical Trials*, Plenum, New York, 1987.
27. A. E. Cato, ed., *Clinical Drug Trials and Tribulations*, Marcel Dekker, New York, 1988.
28. B. Spilker, *Guide to Planning and Managing Multiple Clinical Studies*, Raven Press, New York, 1987.
29. P. Conrad and J. W. Schneider, *Deviance and Medicalization: From Badness to Sickness*, Mosby, St. Louis, MO, 1980.
30. M. Montagne, *J. Drug Issues 22*:389–405 (1992).
31. H. B. Holmes, B. B. Hoskins, and M. Gross, eds., *Birth Control and Controlling Birth: Women-Centered Perspectives*, Humana Press, Clifton, NJ, 1980.
32. M. Benjamin, J. Muyskens, and P. Saenger, *Hastings Center Report 14*:5–9 (1984).
33. S. Cohen, *J. Psychoactive Drugs 15*:109–13 (1983).
34. Y. C. Martin, E. Kutter, and V. Austel, eds., *Modern Drug Research: Paths to Better and Safer Drugs*, Marcel Dekker, New York, 1989.
35. C. Winick, Reporting drug truth in the media, *Society and Medications: Conflicting Signals for Prescribers and Patients* (J. P. Morgan and D. V. Kagan, eds.), Lexington Books, Lexington, MA, 1983.
36. J. P. Morgan, *J. Psychoactive Drugs 15*:115–20 (1983).
37. R. Cooperstock and H. L. Lennard, *Sociology Health Illness 1*:331–47 (1979).
38. M. C. Smith, *Small Comfort: A History of the Minor Tranquilizers*, Praeger, New York, 1985.
39. H. L. Lennard, *Mystification and Drug Misuse*, Jossey-Bass, San Francisco, 1971.
40. M. Montagne and B. A. Bleidt, *Clin. Res. Prac. Drug Reg. Affairs 5*:83–127 (1987).
41. H. A. Smith, *Clin. Res. Prac. Drug Reg. Affairs 5*:129–46 (1987).
42. L. R. Basara and M. Montagne, *Searching for Magic Bullets: Orphan Drugs, Consumer Activism, and Pharmaceutical Development*, Haworth Press, Binghamton, NY, 1994.
43. J. Kwitny, *Acceptable Risks*, Poseidon Press, New York, 1992.
44. D. J. Rothman and H. Edgar, *Hosp. Prac.*, pp. 135–42 (July 15, 1991).
45. P. W. Davis, *Social Problems 32*:197–212 (1984).
46. D. Lupton, C. Donaldson, and P. Lloyd, *Soc. Sci. Med. 33*:559–68 (1991).

Nomenclature

ACE	angiotensin-converting enzyme
ACP	Associates of Clinical Pharmacology
ADR	adverse drug reaction
AHCPR	Agency for Health Care Policy and Research
AIDS	acquired immuno-deficiency syndrome
ANDA	abbreviated new drug application
AWP	Average Wholesale Price
AZT	zidovudine (Retrovir®)
BX	extra yearly benefits
CBA	cost-benefit analysis
CBER	Center for Biologics Evaluation and Research
CCRA	Certified Clinical Research Associate
CCRC	Certified Clinical Research Coordinator
CDER	Center for Drug Evaluation and Research
CEA	cost-effectiveness analysis
CFR	Code of Federal Regulations
CL	clearance

CL_{cr}	creatinine clearance
CL_h	hepatic clearance
CL_o	other clearance
CL_r	renal clearance
CMA	cost-minimization analysis
CPI	Consumer Price Index
CRF	case report form
CRO	contract research organization
CSDS	core safety data sheet
CUA	cost-utility analysis
CV	curriculum vitae
DBP	diastolic blood pressure
DC	District of Columbia
DHHS	Department of Health and Human Services
DO	Doctor of Osteopathy
DOD	Department of Defense
EC	European Community
EIR	establishment inspection report
EKG	electro-cardiogram
"F"	bioavailability
FDA	Food and Drug Administration
FOI	Freedom of Information Act
FTC	Federal Trade Commission
GCP	good clinical practices
GFR	glomerular filtration rate
GI	gastrointestinal
GNP	gross national product
HIV	human immunodeficiency virus
HMO	Health Maintenance Organization
HOT	Hypertension Optimal Therapy (study)
HR	heart rate
HRA	Human Resource Administration (of New York City)
ICH	International Conference on Harmonization
IND	investigational new drug

IRB	institutional review board
K_E	elimination rate constant
kg	kilogram
LSD	lysergic acid diethylamide
MD	Doctor of Medicine (allopathy)
MI	myocardial infarction
MOS	Medical Outcomes Study
NDA	new drug application
NME	new molecular entity
NPR	net present value
OTC	over the counter
pH	minus the log of the hydrogen ion concentration (measure of relative acidity or basicity)
Pharm.D.	Doctor of Pharmacy
Ph.D.	Doctor of Philosophy
PI	principal investigator
PLA	product license application
PMA	Pharmaceutical Manufacturers Association
PPO	preferred provider organization
PTO	Patent and Trademark Office
PV	present value
QA	quality assurance
QALY	quality-adjusted life years
QOL	quality of life
QWB	quality of well-being (scale)
R&D	research and development
RADIANCE	Randomized Assessment of the effect of Digoxin on Inhibitors of the Angiotensin Converting Enzyme (study)
RN	registered nurse
ROI	return on investment
RPh	registered pharmacist

SAR	structure-activity relationship
SBP	systolic blood pressure
SL	start-up load (in cost benefit analysis)
SOP	standard operating procedure(s)
$t_{1/2}$	drug half-life
TB	tuberculosis
TDM	therapeutic drug monitoring
U.S.	United States
V_d	volume of distribution

Glossary

Abbreviated New Drug Application (ANDA) A new drug application for a product already approved for marketing in the United States by another manufacturer. The drug's sponsor must demonstrate that their product is equivalent to the pioneer (or first marketed) drug, as well as affirm adherence to current good manufacturing practices. In this case, safety and efficacy studies are not necessary as these parameters have already been proved through the studies sponsored by the first manufacturer.

Accelerated New Drug Application A new drug application for a product that has the potential to cure or treat a serious or life-threatening illness. In this case, the time required for the regulatory review process for drugs that receive this classification is shortened in order to give patients the opportunity to use the drug as quickly as possible. This is accomplished through enrolling larger numbers of patients in the Phase 2 trials than are normally permitted for products not meeting this criterion.

Adverse Drug Reaction (ADR) A response to a drug which is noxious and unintended, and which occurs at doses normally used or tested in humans for prophylaxis, diagnosis, or therapy of disease, or for the modification of physiological function.

Adverse Event (or experience) Any untoward medical occurrence in a patient treated with a pharmaceutical product, but which does not necessarily have a causal relationship with this treatment.

Allopathy The system of medical practice based on the theory that in order to combat disease, remedies are used that produce effects different from those produced by the special disease treated.

Approvable Letter A correspondence from the FDA to a product's sponsor indicating that the regulatory review process is near completion. In most cases, the sponsor must respond within ten days to the issues raised in the letter.

Biologics Any virus, therapeutic serum, toxin, antitoxin, vaccine, blood, blood component or derivative, allergenic product, or similar product applicable to the prevention, treatment, or cure of diseases or injuries in humans.

Biotechnology A collection of disciplines and processes used to discover and produce pharmaceutical products using biological processes. These techniques include gene splicing, immunology, hybridoma technology, and protein engineering.

Code of Federal Regulations (CFR) The name given to the collection of regulations promulgated by federal regulatory agencies under the authority of laws passed by the United States Congress. They are arranged by different titles, for example, Title 21 is reserved for most of the regulations affecting the discovery, development, approval and marketing of drugs.

Controlled Clinical Trial A clinical trial in which some patients are placed in a control group receiving either a placebo (no treatment) or a traditional therapy and other patients, the treatment group, receive the drug under study. The use of a control group is designed to provide a meaningful yardstick against which to measure the value of a new product.

Cross-Licensing The marketing and distribution of a product by two or more different manufacturers. In some cases one holds the patent and the other(s) pay royalties on the use of the licenses; in other circumstances it is used as a remedy for disputes over marketing exclusivity rights granted by patents or orphan drug status designation.

Decision Tree The fundamental analytic tool for decision analysis, it is a way of displaying the temporal and logical sequence of a clinical decision problem. Its form highlights three structural components: the alternative actions that are available to the decision maker; the probabilistic events that follow from and affect these actions, such as clinical information obtained or the clinical consequences revealed; and the outcomes for the patient that are associated with each possible scenario of actions and consequences.

Direct Costs Costs that are wholly attributable to the service or project in question; for example, the services of professional and paraprofessional personnel, laboratory and other research equipment, and materials.

Discounting A process for computing how much a good, such as a dollar, payable or gained one or more years from now, is worth today.

Drug A natural or synthetic substance that is effective in the prevention, treatment, or cure of disease or the mitigation of symptoms.

Drug Development The purposeful pursuit of scientific data, characterizing and quantifying a new drug, in order to gain FDA approval to market the product through documenting its safety, efficacy, and usefulness.

Drug Usefulness Characterized by a product that is safe and efficacious to use and, in addition, has a positive impact on the outcomes of the patient and/or medical facility. It is the summation of data gathered from clinical trials plus that which is obtained from outcomes studies.

Efficacy The ability of a product to treat effectively or reduce the symptoms of a disease or condition.

Empirical Approach The treatment of disease or maintenance of wellness using first-hand observations and experimentation in individual patients, as opposed to the scientific method which uses research methodologies and statistical techniques proved to show benefits and differences.

Federal Register A weekly disclosure published by the federal government that prints proposed regulations so that affected parties can comment on them and have input into their promulgation as well as the exact wording of the final regulations with effective dates and penalties for noncompliance.

Form Utility The value that comes from having medications in convenient dosage forms, palatable flavors, or efficient packaging, that is, all of the things that can lead to appropriate prescription medication use and improved health outcomes.

Gold Standard A therapy that is used as the current treatment of choice for a particular condition.

Hybridoma Technology A process by which products are manufactured using living organisms to replicate and produce the molecules, such as monoclonal antibodies and interferon.

Incremental Benefit The incremental benefit of the Nth unit of output is the total benefit of N units of output minus the total benefit of N – 1 units of output. It is also called the marginal benefit.

Incremental Cost The incremental cost of the Nth unit of output is the total of N units of output minus the total cost of N – 1 units of output. It is also called the marginal cost.

Indication The specific disease(s) or condition(s) for which a drug product has been approved by the FDA based on data from a sponsor accompanying a new drug application submittal.

Indirect Costs Costs that are shared by many services or projects concurrently; for example, maintenance, electricity, and administrative expenses. Also known as overhead costs.

Informed Consent The permission granted by a patient participating in a clinical trial after being notified and understanding the risks and benefits of the experimental therapy; the consequences of not following more established therapies; and the purpose, design, duration, confidentiality procedures, and voluntary nature of participating in the study. Written informed consent must be granted before a subject can be enrolled in a clinical trial.

Investigational New Drug (IND) A new chemical entity for which human safety and efficacy have not yet been proved, but has evidence of such based on the results of animal studies. The sponsor of the product has completed sufficient preclinical experiments to apply for and receive an exemption to the human use regulations so that clinical trials can be conducted on the product. There are strict regulations governing the distribution and use of these products.

Labeling All information that accompanies or is affixed to an approved drug product's container. It includes the package inserts, box holding the dosage forms, and all promotional materials bearing the drug product's name or its likeness.

License A contractual privilege to use a patent without fear of a lawsuit by the licenser for infringement. This right is normally purchased from the patentee for a royalty.

Macro-marketing A social process that directs the flow of goods and services from producers to consumers in a way that effectively matches supply and demand and accomplishes the objectives of society.

Market Research The assessment of the quantitative and qualitative characteristics of the people in the "market."

Marketing The process of planning and carrying out the creation, pricing, promotion, and distribution of ideas, products, and services that satisfy the needs and wants of consumers and organizations.

Marketing Mix Constitutes the interaction of the four "P's" of marketing: Product, Price, Promotion, and Place. In some texts, it is the six "P's", adding Pride and People to the other four.

Marketing Research The assessment of the effectiveness and efficiency of manipulation of the components and subcomponents of the marketing mix.

Marginal Benefit (*see* Incremental Benefit)

Marginal Cost (*see* Incremental Cost)

Medicalization The process of redefining or relabeling a personal or social "life" problem as a medical condition, thus necessitating involvement in and control by the health care delivery system.

Nanotechnology Discipline or technology capable of grasping, maneuvering, and altering a single molecule.

Net Present Value Takes a future revenue stream and converts it by using a discount rate into today's dollars for comparison purposes, as in between two therapies or two programs.

New Combination The product contains two or more compounds that have not previously been marketed together in a drug product in the United States by any manufacturer.

New Drug Application (NDA) A comprehensive set of documents filed by a product's sponsor with the FDA upon completion of safety and efficacy testing in humans. This application is filed in anticipation of receiving approval to market the drug in the United States.

New Formulation The compound is marketed in the United States by the same or another manufacturer, but the particular dosage form or formulation is not.

New Indication A currently marketed product in the United States adds a new indication.

New Molecular Entity (NME) A chemical compound the active portion or moiety of which has not been marketed (as a parent compound, salt, ester, or derivative) in the United States for use as a single or combination drug product.

New Salt A chemical compound the active moiety of which is marketed in the United States by the same or another manufacturer, but the particular salt, ester, or derivative is not yet marketed in the United States either as a single or combination product.

Orphan Drug A drug product classified for use in a rare disease. (*see also* Rare Disease)

Osteopathy The system of medical practice based on the theory that diseases are due chiefly to mechanical derangement (especially displacements of bones such as vertebrae), with resultant pressure on nerves and blood vessels and corresponding interference with innervation and circulation.

Overhead Costs (*see* Indirect Costs)

Patent A protection afforded by the laws of the United States that gives the inventor of a new and useful process exclusive rights to market the resultant product with substantial penalties imposed upon those who infringe upon this right. This contract is given in exchange for a full description of the invention.

Pharmacoeconomic Analysis The underlying premise of pharmacoeconomic analysis in health-related decisions is to compare the cost of pharmaceutical inputs against the patient outcomes and consequences. It is assumed that for any given level of resources available, the decision maker wishes to maximize the aggregate health benefits conferred to the population of concern. Alternatively, a given health benefit goal may be set, the objective being to minimize the cost of achieving it.

Pharmacoepidemiology The study of the frequency and distribution of pharmaceutical care and drug use outcomes in a population.

Pharmacokinetics The study of how drugs act within the body; it involves describing their absorption, distribution, metabolism, and excretion.

Pharmacomythologies Cultural conceptions about drugs, that are illusory, yet have achieved the status of and exist as fundamental principles in spite of their inaccuracies.

Pharmagenesis (*see* Pharmageny)

Pharmagenology The study of the process involved in the origin of new drug products.

Pharmageny The genesis of new drug products.

Phase 1 Clinical Trials The first in-human studies usually performed on healthy volunteers that are used to quantify pharmacokinetic parameters. Sometimes, these trials are used as early indication trials (in life-threatening conditions) and to explore medical outcomes methodologies.

Phase 2 Clinical Trials The first-in-patient studies usually performed on a small number of subjects (except in life-threatening conditions). They consist of placebo and gold-standard comparative trials, used to refine dosage parameters, and to provide data on efficacy and safety measures, early medical outcomes data, and comparative trials. The decision on whether or not to proceed to market (i.e., filing an NDA) is usually made here.

Phase 3 Clinical Trials Usually performed on a larger number of patients. They include expanded trials to prove efficacy, to demonstrate safety, and to show benefit on patient outcomes.

Phase 4 Clinical Trials Post-marketing studies. They are performed to look for rare side effects; unofficially, to look for new uses (which would require more Phase 3 studies to verify); and to continue to gather pharmacoeconomic data for marketing purposes.

Place Utility The value associated with the fact that any prescription medication can be obtained in any community in the United States or that the products are available in the areas where they are needed.

Possession Utility Results from all of the often hidden marketing activities (such as dealing with third-party payers, providing goods on credit, and handling paperwork) that ensure that patients (or their agents) can receive needed medications.

Postmarketing Surveillance (*see* Phase 4 Clinical Trials)

Preclinical Studies Animal experiments that provide the initial marketing potential assessment, safety evaluation, indication determination, and data for the investigational new drug application documents.

Present Value The present value (PV) or value today, of a future good is its worth calculated as a function of the number of years (N) until it is obtained and the annual rate of discount (D).

Probability The probability of an event can be thought of as the frequency with which the event occurs in a population, or the proportion in a population experiencing that event. A probability can also denote a degree of conviction in the truth or occurrence of an event. The probability of an event can range from zero (impossible: never occurs) to 1.0 (certain: always occurs).

Production Costs The total of all direct costs and indirect costs.

Prodrugs Products that are inactive in and of themselves, but are converted through a physiological function of the body into a pharmacologically-active drug.

Quality-Adjusted Life Years A unit of measurement used to quantify health outcomes resulting from some intervention. The number of quality-adjusted life years (QALYs) is the number of years at full health that would be valued equivalently to the number of years of life experienced in a less desirable health state. For example, if a year of life confined to bed is considered one-half as desirable as a year spent in full health, then ten years of survival confined to bed would be counted as five QALYs.

Rare Disease A disease in which less than 200,000 patients per year are affected or one in which more than 200,000 individuals are affected, but the major costs of drug development and marketing are unlikely to be recouped. (*see also* Orphan Drug)

Sensitivity Analysis Any test of the stability of the conclusions of an analysis over a range of structural assumptions, probability estimates, or value judgments.

Serious Adverse Event Any untoward medical occurrence that at any dose results in death, requires inpatient hospitalization, prolongation of existing hospitalization, results in persistent or significant disability/capacity, or is life threatening.

Signal Reported information on a possible causal relationship between an adverse event and a drug, the relationship being unknown or incompletely documented previously.

Supplemental New Drug Application (sNDA) A request submitted by the sponsor of a currently marketed product in the United States to add a new indication or provide different information in the labeling of the drug, or when manufacturing processes have changed.

Surrogate End Point An expedient process that utilizes short-term evidence of a drug's effectiveness in the treatment of a serious, life-threatening illness. These end points are used to justify approval of such drugs to be used and distributed to needy patients. Continual safety and efficacy studies are still necessary before full marketing approval is considered. (*see also* Treatment IND)

Therapeutic Drug Monitoring The process of following a drug's actions; it includes observing the patient for signs and symptoms of adverse drug reactions and interactions, overseeing physiological functions for drug efficacy, and monitoring the patient-as-a-whole to determine the entire range of effects elucidated by a pharmacological intervention.

Threshold Analysis A variant of sensitivity analysis. It tells us at what level of each of the probabilities or utilities, taken one at a time, the decision maker would consider the currently favored strategy no better than its nearest competitor.

Time Utility The value associated with the convenience of access and availability of a drug product when the need arises.

Treatment IND A compassionate use mechanism that permits the usage (in a shorter time frame than usual) of promising new drugs in a larger number of patients who are suffering from a terminal condition or who are seriously ill.

Unexpected Adverse Drug Reaction An adverse reaction, the nature or severity of which is not consistent with applicable product information or labeling.

Usefulness (*see* Drug Usefulness)

Utility A measure of the value of an outcome that reflects attitudes toward risk. Suppose that the best and worst outcomes in a decision problem have been identified, and that outcome X is valued equivalently to a gamble giving a change of p at the best and a chance of $1 - p$ at the worst. Then p is the utility of outcome X on a utility scale of 0 to 1. Utilities are averaged out to give the expected utility of a decision. (*see also* Form Utility, Time Utility, Place Utility, *and* Possession Utility)

Index